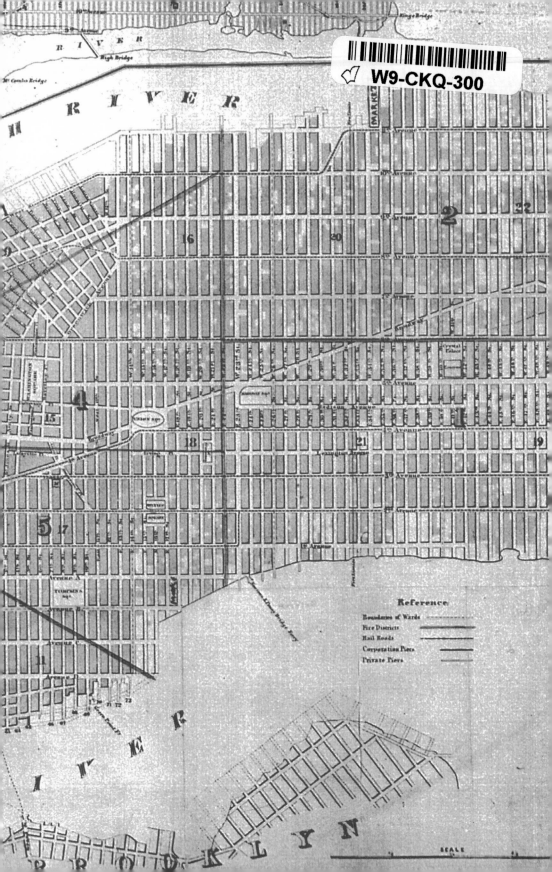

LOW

LIFE

LUC

SANTE

Lures and Snares

LOW

of

LIFE

Old New York

[· FARRAR · STRAUS · GIROUX ·]

NEW YORK

Copyright © 1991 by Luc Sante

All rights reserved

Printed in the United States of America

Published simultaneously in Canada

by HarperCollinsCanadaLtd

First edition, 1991

Designed by Barbara de Wilde

Library of Congress Cataloging-in-Publication Data

Sante, Luc.

Low life : lures and snares of old New York / Luc Sante.

Includes bibliographical references and index.

1. Manhattan (New York, N.Y.)—History.   2. Manhattan (New York,

N.Y.)—Social conditions.   3. New York (N.Y.)—History.

4. New York

(N.Y.)—Social conditions.

5. Marginality, Social—New York (N.Y.)

I. Title.

F128.47.S23   1991   974.7'1041—dc20   90-25790   CIP

Additional copyright data follow on page 413.

Drive your cart and your plow
over the bones of the dead.

—William Blake
Proverbs of Hell

ACKNOWLEDGMENTS

Three people who contributed in fundamental ways to the birth of this book are no longer alive to receive my thanks; it is with sadness and gratitude that I salute the memory of Jonathan Lieberson, Luis Sanjurjo, and Chris Cox. This project would never have gotten under way without the early enthusiasm and skills of John Herman and Mark Polizotti; my debt to them is enormous. My research was made possible with the patient and knowledgeable assistance of the staffs of the Mercantile Library and the Local History room at the New York Public Library, as well as of Meredith Collins at Brown Brothers, Gretchen Viehmann and Terry Ariano at the Museum of the City of New York, Patricia Paladines at the New-York Historical Society, Terry Geesken and Mary Corliss at the Museum of Modern Art Film Stills Archive, Eleanor J. Mish at the American Museum of the Moving Image, and the staff of the research library at the Municipal Archives. For allowing me to spin off some of my preoccupations into article form during the gestation period of this work I am obliged to Duncan Stalker (in his capacities at Manhattan, Inc., The Condé Nast Traveler, *and the ill-fated* New York Sunday Post) *and to Wendy Lesser at* The Threepenny Review. *For miscellaneous advice, suggestions, comfort, sympathy, and encouragement I give thanks to Elizabeth and Richard Devereaux, David Higginbotham and Elizabeth Sacre, Jim Jarmusch and Sara Driver, Paul Pavel, Simon Pettet, Darryl Pinckney, Irv Schenkler, David Shapiro, and Chuck Wachtel. For being an exemplary and kind landlady during a difficult time I hail Martha Fedorko. For their extraordinary industry, perseverance, fortitude, and, above all, belief, I am grateful to my agent, Joy Harris, and my editors, Jonathan Galassi and Rick Moody. I owe an inexpressible debt to April Bernard, who felt every bump along the road and suffered them and me with humor, gallantry, sagacity, and charity. And I wish to thank my parents, Lucien and Denise Sante. This first book is for them.*

· *Preface* ·

THIS IS A BOOK ABOUT NEW YORK. IT MAY BE BRIEFLY
DESCRIBED AS CONCERNING THE VICES AND LURES THAT
THE CITY PROFFERED TO THE LOWER CLASSES IN THE
NINETEENTH CENTURY, AND THE STREETS AND ALLEYS
that were their theater. Its time span covers the roughly eighty years
of the city's adolescence and early adulthood: from about 1840, when
New York began to be transformed by railroads, tenements, and other
accoutrements of the modern city, until 1919, which was not only the
year of the Volstead Act and the Red Scare but a portal into a new
technological era that would alter the city yet again. Geographically,
the story is confined to Manhattan, and mostly dwells on the realms
of attraction and concealment, the bazaars and the underworld: the
Bowery, Satan's Circus, Hell's Hundred Acres, Hell's Kitchen, the
slums, the waterfront. In spite of its being thus limited in temporal
and topographical scope, this is also, I believe, a book about New York
City today.

The firmament that is New York is greater than the sum of its
constituent parts. It is a city and it is also a creature, a mentality, a
disease, a threat, an electromagnet, a cheap stage set, an accident
corridor. It is an implausible character, a monstrous vortex of contra-
dictions, an attraction-repulsion mechanism so extreme no one could
have made it up. New York, which has been called the capital of the
twentieth century, as Paris was that of the nineteenth, would seem on
the face of it to be founded on progress, on change, on the bulldozing

of what has faded to make way for the next thing, the thing after that, the future. The lure of the new is built right into its name; it is the part of the name that actually registers, since the "York," a commemoration of a colonial lineage, carries no resonance and exists only as a vestige. New York is incarnated by Manhattan (the other boroughs, noble, useful, and significant though they may be, are merely adjuncts), and Manhattan is a finite space that cannot be expanded but only continually resurfaced and reconfigured. Manhattan is a wonderland of real estate speculation, a hot center whose temperature cannot but increase as population increases and desirability remains several paces ahead of capacity. The myth of Manhattan, therefore, is cast in the future tense. It does not hark back to a heroic past, lacks its Romulus and Remus (except in the image of that transaction between Peter Minuit and the Canarsies, which is simply the first clever deal, the primordial ground-floor entry). New York has no truck with the past. It expels its dead.

The dead, however, are a notoriously perverse and unmanageable lot. They tend not to remain safely buried, and in fact resist all efforts at obliterating their traces. Cultures that glorify and memorialize their dead have simply found a clever way to satisfy and therefore quiet them. When the dead are endlessly represented in monuments, images, memorials, and ceremonies, their vigor passes into these objects and events; it is safely defused, made anodyne. New York, which is founded on forward motion and is thus loath to acknowledge its dead, merely causes them to walk, endlessly unsatisfied and unburied, to invade the precincts of supposed progress, to lay chill hands on the heedless present, which does not know how to identify the forces that tug at its rationality.

The gestures that New York makes toward the past are perfunctory, symbolically evasive, mercantile. The immigrants who passed through the harbor, who were processed at Ellis Island, and who clocked a generational shift or two in the tenements are acknowledged for their part in the machinery of progress by being identified with the Bartholdi figure of Liberty on the former Bedloes Island (once a place of execution): a crowd of dark figures in hats and kerchiefs gathers reverently by the railing of a ship, collectively willing their transformation into a streamlined and bareheaded generation of go-getters. Those who did succeed are given witness by institutions—their names, suspended from context, attached to hospital wings, museum annexes, additions to faculties of metallurgy. The harbor through which they passed has itself been superseded by technology, and its tombstone is the South Street Seaport, which displays its bars and boutiques among the detritus of outmoded forms of commerce and industry. There and about town, once useful objects are presented as decorative artifacts, bereft of purpose except to evoke vague images of an era about which little need be known other than that it was a "simpler time."

The common word for this kind of distortion is "nostalgia." This word can be generally defined as a state of inarticulate contempt for the present and fear of the future, in concert with a yearning for order, constancy, safety, and community—qualities that were last enjoyed in childhood and are retroactively imagined as gracing the whole of the time before one's birth. Recently it has become a category of trade, under which are marketed the knickknacks and ephemera of past decades; in this function it encompasses connoisseurship, fetishism, fashion cycles, and social history, and makes them all equally base coin. Nostalgia also has another function, however.

In mercurial New York, tradition, dominant elsewhere and at other times, has always been slippery. Such tradition as once existed was cultivated within the precincts of now vanished milieux—neighborhoods that could boast a continuity of at least three generations, saloons that had stood for upwards of a quarter century without significant change in clientele. Tradition, in its old meaning, has fallen victim to flux and dispersal, and to the broadening, homogenizing, and scattering effects of the electronic media. On the other hand, these media have assisted in the perpetuation of another stream of tradition, one which is often lumped under the rubric of nostalgia. Past decades come into vogue at regular intervals, at the point at which people who experienced those decades as children and adolescents attain positions of power in the world. In their years of struggle they primarily looked to the future; having both achieved their goals and failed to realize their fondest wishes, they have the rue and the leisure, the complacency and dissatisfaction to look backward, and the means to broadcast an idealized version of the remembered past, from which, however, the grime of history cannot entirely be washed. Then the tales, the legends, the styles and prejudices and assumptions of those decades are transmitted to younger generations, and these pass along the lore in further fragmented form to their successors. The telephone-game relay of progressive distortion present in this transmission closely resembles the entropic tendency of oral tradition.

An example of this may be seen in the late 1920s and thirties, when the United States was just beginning to subject its culture to a truly national media network, when the influence of radio and the movies was beginning to erode regional characteristics in speech, music, customs, and mores. Leading writers, artists, and filmmakers who had been young in the 1890s looked back at that decade with fondness and disbelief across a gulf of technological change and population growth, and their stories appealed to a younger public who in the midst of Prohibition and economic depression could appreciate an era that seemed wide-open, freewheeling, and optimistic by contrast. The fruits of this nineties revival—Mae West's films, Herbert Asbury's books, John Held, Jr.'s satirical fake woodcuts, among a panoply of others—entered the popular mind, and the commonplaces of the turn of the century appeared as scenery on many stages, from "high" culture to "low," from H. L. Mencken's *American Mercury* to Max Fleischer's Popeye cartoons. These works, particularly those on film, were disseminated to subsequent generations, who retained images from them even if they were totally ignorant of their historical context. Such images stand as archetypes in the popular imagination even today: the bartender with his handlebar mustache and spit curls; the crook with his striped sweater, cloth cap, and domino mask; the soubrette with her petticoats and rouged cheeks; the bohemian with his beret and flowing necktie; the poker player with his sleeve garters and green eyeshade;

the cop with his twirling nightstick and Irish accent. They appear in cartoons, on menu covers, on the musical comedy stage, in the public domain of clip art—places where the shorthand of conventional imagery requires a jocular turn, as well as contexts in which imagery is least examined by viewers, and thus is most involuntarily absorbed.

In New York the absorption of such imagery into the city's unconscious takes on the contours of actual tradition because the images are accompanied by names and places, even if in semi-random fashion, so that the inhabitants of the city are the custodians of a history of which they are seldom consciously aware. How else explain, for example, that the Bowery retains in its name a faint odor of honky-tonk and barrelhouse that it has not deserved since roughly 1914? It is probably in some measure owing to the fact that Bowery Boys comedies were being made as late as 1958, and continue to be shown on television. These low-budget pictures featured a troop of amiably rowdy adolescents whose good hearts were sorely tested by the temptations of the boulevard. (They got their start as an ensemble in the 1935 Broadway production of Sidney Kingsley's *Dead End* and were at times also known as the Dead End Kids and the East Side Kids.) Although the movies were set in a generic slum, the Bowery part of their name was chosen presumably to reflect an image of the Bowery as both lurid and impoverished which had lately been refreshed by such things as Raoul Walsh's 1933 film *The Bowery*, itself a spirited if historically unreliable evocation of the 1890s. As it happens, the "Bowery Boys" was a name that had graced a succession of Manhattan gangs going back to the eighteenth century, a fact that may indeed not have been consciously known by anyone involved with the series. Meanwhile, the cinematic Boys' style, which featured such details as pronounced New York (originally Bowery) accents and a choice of headgear ranging from porkpie hats to baseball caps with the bills worn sideways, echoed the style of turn-of-the-century gangs and in turn exerted an influence on later punk mannerisms, coming full circle with the aesthetic that developed in the mid-1970s around CBGB's, the now venerable club actually located on the Bowery.

There are other places in Manhattan that are thick with recurrences, points that seem magnetized by a genius loci. In our time prostitutes walk where prostitutes walked a hundred years ago; the homeless are camped on the sites of nineteenth-century shantytowns; street peddlers pitch their wares in spots that once saw pushcart lineups or thieves' markets. Around Tompkins Square Park are flurries of anarchist factions, just as there were in 1887, when the police were engaged in making preemptive arrests in the wake of Chicago's Haymarket Riot. Itinerant banco swindlers still, amazingly, operate out of decoy storefronts in the former Hell's Hundred Acres, the present SoHo. Such echoes have many overlapping causes: coincidence, building stock, geographical disposition, the limitations that are endemic to Manhattan. For that matter, there are numerous parts of the city that have been so thoroughly refashioned in this century that their former identities have left no trace. But the most altered areas share a significant common trait: they are, with few exceptions, the most valuable properties (and on this island those tend to be the points farthest inland, the geographical center of the city as it slid over time from Bowling Green to Central Park South). The places that seem consigned to eternal repetition of poverty and low life and carnival traffic are made so by accrued prejudice, which is another tributary of the underground stream of tradition, involving as it does perpetuated responses to forgotten stimuli. Streets or neighborhoods that acquired a bad name by being associated with Federal-period garbage dumps or Dutch tanneries or stagnant ponds long since paved over continue to bear a stigma; no one at all remembers the tannery, but it was succeeded by a rookery, then by two generations of tenements, and then by a housing project, which has now gone to seed. The project's decay is in some measure a consequence of the odor of that tannery. Such is the work of the city's ghosts.

The ghosts of Manhattan are not the spirits of the propertied classes; these are entombed in their names, their works, their constructions. New York's ghosts are the unresting souls of the poor, the marginal,

Bowery Boys, from Frank Moss's *The American Metropolis*, 1897

The Bowery Boys, left to right: Bobby Jordan, Billy Halop, Huntz Hall, Gabriel Dell, Leo Gorcey, in a production still from *Dead End*, 1937

the dispossessed, the depraved, the defective, the recalcitrant. They are the guardian spirits of the urban wilderness in which they lived and died. Unrecognized by the history that is common knowledge, they push invisibly behind it to erect their memorials in the collective unconscious. The myth of the city insists on progress, bigger and better and more all the time; nostalgia of the usual sort is founded on regret for vanished coziness and civility. The city's unconscious is the repository of all that these two outlooks omit, the repressed history of vice and crime, misery and graft, panic and despair, chaos and saturnalia. While New York has adopted as its nickname the Big Apple, that hopeful tag given it by jazz musicians when their art was remuneratively in fashion, the city might more truthfully answer to the twin appellations by which it was known to tramps: the Big Smear and the Big Onion.

This book came about as a result of my having lived on the Lower East Side for more than a decade. I had gone there in pursuit of bohemia and youth culture, in addition to the fact that it was a cheap place to live. I slept and worked and caroused in tenements with sloping floors, crumbling plaster, corroded plumbing, erratic heating, looked out through barred windows at garbage-filled air shafts and decaying masonry, but I was securely cocooned in marginality. The steam-table food in Ukrainian coffee shops was cheap, and so were the old clothes in thrift shops; discarded furniture was free. My monthly rent was roughly equivalent to my weekly wage, which was minimal. Relative material deprivation was not much of a sacrifice, considering that the payoff was independence from the social and cultural mainstream. At the time, New York was on the verge of bankruptcy. It was a buyers' market: every other storefront in my neighborhood was abandoned, and most residential buildings that were not altogether derelict were only half occupied. The city seemed almost rustic in its quiet desolation, as conducive to meditation in its manner as the ruins of Greece and Rome. In the way that its isolation from the America of suburbs and shopping malls mirrored my own frame of mind, it also paradoxically seemed charged with possibilities.

In the early 1980s the economic mirage of the Reagan Administration changed everything, bringing in a pestilence of speculators, developers, profiteers of all sorts, as well as a whole new breed of go-getters whose like had not been seen in the area since the exurban migration after World War II. The empty apartments filled up seemingly overnight, and rents shot up correspondingly. Around the same time, I had had enough of youth culture and began asking myself what I was doing in my miserable neighborhood. Cosmetic improvements wrought by landlords and shopkeepers had only succeeded in making the place look even more like a slum. New wallboard only highlighted the basic structural defects of buildings; elaborate wooden moldings, cast-iron supports in the shape of Corinthian columns, mosaic-tile floors, and dazzlingly complex pressed-tin ceilings were gutted and replaced with featureless standard-issue fixtures; dim but warm incandescent lamps in entries and hallways were jettisoned in favor of harsh fluorescent lighting that illuminated every cockroach and mouse dropping. For that matter, none of the changes actually improved the lot of people who had been living in the neighborhood all along. Hard drugs, ever a local feature, became even more available, and their effects quantitatively more devastating. Landlord-tenant disputes and rent strikes became much more common and even more bitter than before. Taxis now cruised down Avenue A, something which was formerly unthinkable, but most old residents couldn't afford them anyway, and they did little but add to the congestion in the once rather quiet streets.

In the midst of all this upheaval, as I noticed one amenity or landmark after another being obliterated by what passed for progress, I began for the first time to wonder what had gone on before, who had lived in these tenements when they were first built. I wanted to get a complete picture of the area at the time from which those rococo cornices and high stoops and carved doorways dated (and the time frame of this book, circa 1840 to 1919, turns out to span exactly the era during which existing Lower East Side tenements were constructed, a conjunction which was unintentional but hardly accidental). I wanted to know how people got around the city, what noises they heard in the street, what the posters slapped on fences promised them, and, even more, what their fears and lures and temptations were, since I myself had been drawn to the city by those qualities. I was not all that interested in the honest and hardworking immigrants; their story had been well told already, and, anyway, I had come to the United States as an immigrant myself—although some years too late to be funneled through Ellis Island—and so the process of gradual orientation and assimilation did not seem so mysterious to me. I wanted to know about New York as circus and jungle, as the realm of danger and pleasure, the wilderness that it must have been then, as it is now.

I began to read and snoop around, look at pictures and flip through ephemera, guided by serendipity. There were times, when this project was new, when my research would get the better of me and I would almost lose track of what year it was outside. At least once, late at night, and under the influence of alcohol and architecture and old copies of the *Police Gazette*, I staggered around looking for a dive that had closed sixty or eighty years before, half expecting to find it in mid-brawl. This kind of hallucination is not difficult to sustain, even now, on certain empty streets where the buildings are the same ones that were once chockablock with blind tigers and stuss houses and bagnios. An extraordinary number of edifices survive that formerly housed the worst deadfalls in the city, from Kit Burns's Rat Pit to McGurk's Suicide Hall. I was instinctively drawn to such places, in fact and in imagination, just as I would have been had I been around in their heyday. Through the mediating factors of time and reading, however, I had the luxury to be at once the sucker, the sharper, and the sadder but wiser observer. Vice drew me, but I could also trace the ruinous course of its effects, and note the political and economic forces that sustained it, and know who profited from it.

This book is thus an expression of love and hate, as is appropriate for a work about New York, where loneliness is a threat and a shield, where poverty forces an imaginative response from those caught in it, so that it can seem more alluring than bland security, where the most colorful elements are often the most poisonous, where ecstasy is purchased at the cost of death, where the navel of the world and the frontier of civilization lie a few blocks apart. The city was like this a century ago, and it remains so in the present. There are, in fact, only two really significant differences between that world and ours: now there is a lot more technology, and everything is much more expensive, even proportionately.

The book is organized into four sections. The first, "Landscape," sets forth the lay of the land, the material conditions of housing and the look of the streets. The second, "Sporting Life," concerns temptation and escapism. The third, "The Arm," is a view of the forces of order, repression, and profit. The fourth, "The Invisible City," attempts to inventory transcendence, the ways in which some people tried to make their own, alternative city, by will or by default. Within those sections are chapters, arranged according to broad and relatively obvious categories. These categories pertain to the city's essential commonplaces, elements that are still factors of New York life even if their details have changed. "The Lights," for example, which refers to popular entertainments, shows that even if their locus has moved from the stage and the dime museum to the video-game arcade and the movie theater specializing in car-chase and slasher films, many of the enticements have remained constant: blood, fire, speed, and flesh. The categories can be seen as corresponding to the cards in a Tarot deck of New York City, or, to choose a metaphor more closely tied to the city's history, to the archetypal figures in a gambler's dream book. They are the constituents of New York's vocabulary of symbols, the objects and creatures in its zodiac: the island, the tenement, the sign, the show, the bar, the drug, the game, the whore, the crook, the cop, the politician, the sky pilot, the tourist, the orphan, the nomad, the beatnik, the riot, the night.

This is by no means a work of academic history. In researching it, I was guided more by chance and intuition than by method. I was more interested in legends than in statistics, in rumors than in official reports. I was purposely interested in the stories that circulated, rather than their correction or emendation, and while I brought all my skeptical and critical faculties to bear on whatever seemed discrepant or improbable, I did not set out to nail down any definitive accounts. This book can be seen as an attempt at a mythology of New York, a pool of tales and cautions and ornaments and shibboleths that potentially contains the source of current superstitions and tabloid fixations and apparently purposeless rituals. It is an attempt to extract some essence of New Yorkness not tied to commerce or public relations but resident in the accumulated mulch of the city itself, through generations of bent twigs grown into a twisted whole.

C O N T E N T S

Fex urbis, lex orbis.
(Dregs of the city, law of the world.)

—St. Jerome

A knife, a fork, a bottle and a cork:
That's the way we spell New York.

—Dillinger
"Cokane in My Brain"

PART 1.

[· *Landscape* ·]

1 · *The* BODY

LONG, NARROW MANHATTAN ISLAND
SITS IN THE BAY, AMONG OTHER IS-
LANDS, OUTCROPPINGS, FLATLANDS,
LIKE A SILHOUETTE OF A RIGHT
whale navigating a rocky passage; on the area
map, among blank-faced formations all like
itself colored yellow for density of population, it lies like a smelt in a pan. From the
air it looks prickled, spiny, a bed of nails, a
forest of peaks, a mesa of terraced, carved,
eroded formations run through with canyons.
On a street map it is crosshatched and shaded
as if to represent an organism unknown in
nature: flat, marked by rigidly rectilinear
striations in the center mass, given character
at the top by twisted, laborious lines and
gnarled spits of solid green and at the bottom
by converging, warring zones of intermittently regular incision.

The layout of Manhattan's streets gives away their history. They look as if they had been established at first haphazardly, in fits and starts, and then later, as settlement moved northward, realized in one grand plan, all except the very uppermost part, where order was finally sacrificed to the dictates of topography. This is, in fact, more or less what happened. The Dutch village of the seventeenth century is preserved in the close and knotted scale of the streets at the island's lower tip, the English merchants' port that succeeded it in the names given those streets: Gold, Pine, Beaver, and Ann, William, Hanover. The breakup of the big family estates in the late eighteenth and early nineteenth centuries has left both names—Rutgers, Delancey, Lispenard, Stuyvesant—and lumps of right-angled blocks that abruptly cut each other off at Division Street, at Grand, at Houston, recording the piecemeal pattern of development. The drill imposed by the grid plan, surveyed in 1807 by John Randel, Jr., and established in 1811 by a Board of Commissioners, begins at First Street on the East Side and moves gradually northwest until it goes island-wide at Fourteenth. Then it sweeps up the face, challenged only insignificantly, before it is finally hemmed in by the uptown cliffs, and numeration is defeated at the bottleneck of Fort George Hill, near 194th Street.

All cities begin as a point of activity, usually a harbor, and settlement concentrically grows around this point in increasingly wider rings. Manhattan is unique in its shape and circumstances and in its growth, which resembled (to add to an already crowded roster of metaphors) a thermometer. The speed of this growth—its rising temperature—is best conveyed by a well-known fact: when the present City Hall was built, between 1803 and 1812, its front and sides were made of marble, but its rear was thought to be so far north that no one would ever see it, so it was built of much cheaper red sandstone. Needless to say, this back face was already surrounded by buildings before it was finished. At some point in the early nineteenth century, popular conviction shifted, and the idea of the city passed from peaceable stasis to galloping development, so that by 1849, when the city barely existed above Fourteenth Street, Herman Melville could write satirically:

*. . . The New York guidebooks are now vaunting of the mag-
nitude of a town, where future inhabitants, multitudinous
as the pebbles on the beach, and girdled in with high walls
and towers, flanking endless avenues of opulence and taste,
will regard all our Broadways and Bowerys as but the paltry
nucleus to their Nineveh. From far up the Hudson, beyond
Harlem River, where the young saplings are now growing,
that will overarch their lordly mansions with broad boughs,
centuries old; they may send forth explorers to penetrate into
the obscure and smoky alleys of the Fifth Avenue and Four-
teenth-street; and going farther south, may exhume the present Doric Custom-house; and quote it as proof that their
high and mighty metropolis enjoyed a Hellenic antiquity.*[1]

The appearance of the city through much of its history has left little
mark or analogue today—not until about a century ago did the place
begin to take on some of the characteristics with which we familiarly
associate it. Manhattan's identity as a natural site is particularly irre-
trievable—the fact that it once contained two substantial ponds, was
crisscrossed by streams, possessed marshlands and flats, hills and val-
leys, was ringed by a coastline alternately rock-ribbed and swampish.
The great work of excavating, leveling, and reclaiming has left the
island in its southern portion almost flat, with only a few gentle rises
in the avenues to mark any sort of topographical ancestry. Manhattan's
largest body of water was the Collect Pond (a corruption of the Dutch
"Kalchhook," or Lime Shell Point), which lay approximately within
the bounds of the present-day streets Franklin, Worth, Lafayette, and
Baxter. Once abundantly stocked, it was nearly fished out by the mid-
eighteenth century, and began to fill with refuse. Drainage schemes
were much discussed, but nothing was done until 1808, when depressed economic conditions provoked general unrest, and local authorities authorized funds for a public works project to subdue the
population. A canal was built east and west (later to be filled in and

eventually known as Canal Street), and the drained pond was paved over, its site swiftly becoming the city's first slum.

Canal Street was the city's northern limit through the 1820s, but by that time village clusters had sprung up at Greenwich and Chelsea, while isolated farms sparsely dotted the landscape well up toward the northern end. Washington Square was converted from a potter's field to the centerpiece of a fashionable enclave circa 1835; Union and Madison Squares and Gramercy Park were cleared and opened for development within the following decade. The advance guard of progress generally marched about ten blocks ahead of the actual surge of settlement, so that there was in each case a lag between the leveling of natural features and archaic structures and the beginning of planned construction. Although the great Croton Reservoir was built at Fifth Avenue and Forty-second Street in 1842, and the short-lived Crystal Palace behind it in 1853, the surrounding area was far from settled even by the time of the Civil War. Maps of the period optimistically show the grid plan covering the island, even postulating Thirteenth and Fourteenth Avenues up in the future Fort Tryon and Inwood, and numbered streets up to 229, but the specks indicating buildings in the northern part of the city fail to respect the theoretical street lines in their scattered disposition.

Uptown, there were farms, some of them large and prosperous; small settlements at Bloomingdale, Yorkville, Manhattanville, Carmanville; and shantytowns. These were slap-up encampments (the Bohemia of the Poor, someone called them) inhabited by dirt-poor Irish squatters; for years the largest lay at Dutch Hill, at the far eastern end of Forty-second Street. Edgar Allan Poe described a typical dwelling in 1844:

> It is, perhaps, nine feet by six, with a pigsty applied exter-
> nally, by way both of portico and support. The whole fabric
> (which is of mud) has been erected in somewhat too obvious
> an imitation of the Tower of Pisa. A dozen rough planks,
> "pitched" together, form the roof. The door is a barrel on

*end. There is a garden, too, and this is encircled by a ditch
at one point, a large stone at another, a bramble at a
third.*²

The squatters were squeezed into the temporarily unused zone between
the urban blocks and farmland, which made their situation precarious
and their lives nomadic as the zone moved relentlessly northward.
"Usually they remain while the quarrymen who are opening streets
almost undermine their shanties, and then if the buildings are not
blown away, they pull them down and pack them away like tents to
another dwelling place," wrote the reformer Charles Loring Brace in
1872.³ It should be noted that in many cases the shanty dwellers and
the quarrymen were one and the same people, hired at pittance wages
to uproot themselves over and over again while they cleared the way
for progress. The shantytowns spread through the late nineteenth century to all those dormant spots around and within the unrealized
Central Park and well up into Harlem, the last of them not disappearing
until the beginning of the present century, when they melded into the
slums of Battle Row and San Juan Hill. Collectively, the uptown
squatting areas were called the Goats by outsiders, who knew them
mostly as eyesores and as a place of exile for insubordinate or merely
indiscreet police officers, who were sentenced to endure the lack of
perquisites and jollification in that wilderness.

Meanwhile, land prices were multiplying with astonishing speed. A
forty-acre farm in the vicinity of Seventy-second Street and Fifth Avenue, bought for about $40,000 from the City Corporation in the
1820s, was assessed at $9 million in 1875, when it was still innocent
of any building. Farsighted individuals were buying single or multiple
lots here and there and erecting houses like slices of cake, windowless
on the sides and covering the full width of the property, and usually
drawn up just short of the street, leaving no room for a front yard. An
1861 engraving of Second Avenue and Forty-second Street shows such
rowless row houses sprinkled along one side of the avenue, while across
the way ramshackle frame houses are perched on eroding hillocks, high

above the graded road. In an 1890 photograph of a block of West 133rd Street, clusters of three and four brownstones, complete with their own sidewalks, crop up at intervals along the frontage, leaving large blank spaces through which similarly irregular development can be glimpsed in the blocks beyond. After the mid-nineteenth century, the parts of Manhattan that lay ahead of the pick and shovel jumped directly from rural to urban without an intervening suburban stage, as the tempo of construction accelerated. By World War I there was virtually no farmland left, although the last farm, at Tenth Avenue and 214th Street, was not leveled until the 1940s, when it was replaced by subway yards.

Once streets had been laid in a section of the island, they often remained the only index of stability within the turmoil of change. Just as their names bore witness to the circumstances of their foundation, the streets themselves were the only common thread through a district's violent shifts of fortune, through building and rebuilding, prosperity and decline, reclamation and destruction. Cherry Street, for example, went from wealthy suburb to waterfront slum in less than thirty years. Fires were a common event, and some were cataclysmic, such as the Great Fire of the winter of 1835, which decimated a huge stretch of the commercial district around Wall Street. The constantly altering cityscape perforce encouraged a sense of foreshortened history. In 1836 an editor of the *American Magazine of Useful Knowledge*, probably the young Nathaniel Hawthorne, commented in a caption to a street view made before the Great Fire:

> *It is a singular truth that the mere shadowy image of a*
> *building . . . is likely to have a longer term of existence*
> *than the piled brick and mortar of a building. Take a print*
> *like this . . . and an edifice like the large one on the right*
> *hand corner, and the chances are that, a century hence, the*
> *print will be as good as ever, while the edifice . . . will*

The forest of signs: looking north from Brooklyn Bridge
toward Cherry Street, circa 1900. Photograph by Byron

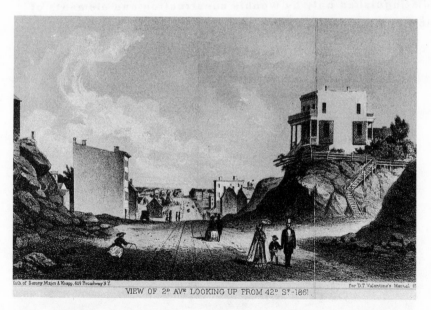

Lith of Sarony Major & Knapp. 449 Broadway N.Y.   VIEW OF 2ᴰ AVᴱ LOOKING UP FROM 42ᴰ Sᵀ-1861.   for D.T Valentine's Manual

The old New York, right, and the new, left: a city growing
into its clothes. From *Valentine's Manual*, 1861

THE FIVE POINTS IN 1859.
View taken from the Corner of Worth & Little Water St.

The Five Points, looking rustic and rather sedate, distinguished only by wobbly construction and elements of low comedy. From *Valentine's Manual* for 1860

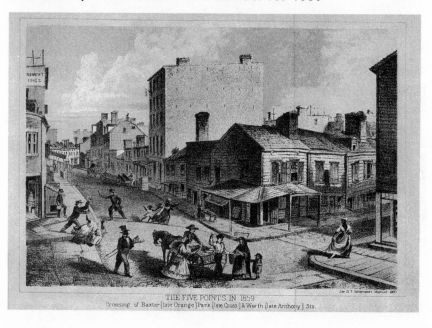

THE FIVE POINTS IN 1859
Crossing of Baxter (late Orange) Park (late Cross) & Worth (late Anthony) Sts.

*probably have been torn down to make room for modern im-
provements, or utterly destroyed by fire. Should posterity
know where the proud structure stood, it will be indebted for
its knowledge to the woodcut.*[4]

The early New Yorkers already knew that they were not building a
Rome and that the thoroughfares themselves would be their monument.

Of all streets, the oldest was Broadway. Originally an Indian trail,
subsequently known under the Dutch as De Heere Straat, or Main
Street, and then forming the lower leg of the Boston Post Road, Broadway has remained consistently the chief of streets throughout New
York's history. The chronicle of its paving roughly follows the progression of Manhattan's urbanization: up to Duane Street by 1818, to
Canal Street by 1830, to Astor Place by 1837, and gradually up to Fifty-
ninth by the time of the Civil War. Broadway leads in a straight line
from the Battery some three miles up to Tenth Street, where it swerves
left for reasons that remain obscure but are popularly attributed to the
intransigence of Jacob Brevoort, who in the eighteenth century owned
the property now occupied by Grace Church.[5] Uptown, the old Bloomingdale Road, which ran up the west side to King's Bridge on the
Harlem River, was gradually straightened and paved and in 1868 was
opened as the Boulevard, which constituted a northward expansion of
Broadway. By the early twentieth century it had been renamed Broadway, and so, too, had a chain of roads that led all the way to Yonkers,
making Broadway, by popular legend, the longest street in the world.

For most of its history Broadway contained the bulk of retail shops,
hotels, and theaters in the city, as well as a great number of major office
buildings. Paradoxically, its importance as an artery and as a business
district meant that it was never widened in proportion to the increasing
volume of the traffic it supported. This traffic was such by the Civil War
that police patrols were sent in to "unblock" the flow during business
hours, and crossing between the "shilling" (east) and "dollar" (west)[6]
sides was so hazardous that in 1867 a hatter who had a shop on the

corner of Fulton Street succeeded in persuading the Common Council to allocate funds for a pedestrian footbridge. Made of cast iron and known as Loew Bridge, it was pulled down less than a year later, after legal challenges by rival hatters nearby.

Broadway always was the first thoroughfare to benefit from innovations: the first sidewalk, built of brick, between Vesey and Murray Streets in the mid-1700s; the first numbered houses, starting in 1793; gas lighting in 1825; electric arc lights in 1882. As business activities increased, Broadway was the first avenue to divest itself of residences, bit by bit, eventually making itself wholly commercial up to Fifty-ninth Street. It did not, however, succeed in ridding itself of low life, which was substantial, though its dives, concert saloons, and gambling hells had a bit more tone than those on the side streets, and in spite of the periodic order to beat cops that they reroute open prostitution from its sidewalks. It was said in the 1880s that you could stand on the corner of Broadway and Houston Street and fire a shotgun in any direction without hitting an honest man. A story of the nineties had it that at Broadway and Forty-second someone yelled, "There's the man who stole my watch!" whereupon twelve men ran off.

Broadway's unorthodox diagonal thrust through midtown created open plazas otherwise unprovided for by the procrustean grid plan. Union Square resulted from its collision with Fourth Avenue, and then Madison Square came up at Fifth, Greeley and Herald Squares at Sixth, Times and Longacre Squares at Seventh, and Columbus Circle at Eighth. The squares downtown—Washington, Stuyvesant, and Gramercy in particular—were enclosed and protected in such a way that they became private parks for the tightly controlled residences that fronted on them, but Broadway's plazas were open and overrun, and naturally became places of amusement. The theatrical nexus—or one of them, at least—began inching along Broadway after the Revolution, had reached the area around Spring Street just before the Civil War, and thereafter clocked in at each of the squares, one after the other, at approximately ten-year intervals, halting at Times Square at about the same time that that square was so named, when the Times building was erected between 1902 and 1904. Although the appellation the Great White Way did not come until the twentieth century, it was noted much earlier that whatever stretch of Broadway happened to be hosting the greatest number of theaters was the most brilliantly lit area of the city.

Broadway had two shadow companions: starchy, upper-class Fifth Avenue on the one hand, and on the other the Bowery, the proverbial den of all vices. The dichotomy between Broadway and the Bowery began early, as their respective theatrical districts came to epitomize respectability in the case of the former and cheap flash in the latter, and as the years went on, these qualities expanded in the popular mind, so that the two avenues came, however inaccurately, to stand for moral poles. The scene is set, for example, in Charles Hoyt's hit song "The Bowery" (introduced quite irrelevantly into the 1891 musical play *A Trip to Chinatown*, set in San Francisco), giving the complaint of the rube:

> *Oh, the night that I struck New York,*
> *I went out for a quiet walk;*
> *Folks who are "on to" the city say,*
> *Better by far that I took Broadway;*
> *But I was out to enjoy the sights,*
> *There was the Bow'ry ablaze with lights;*
> *I had one of the devil's own nights!*
> *I'll never go there anymore.*
> Chorus:
> *The Bow'ry, the Bow'ry!*
> *They say such things and they do strange things on the*
>   *Bow'ry!*
> *The Bow'ry! I'll never go there anymore!*

The Bowery started life as De Bouwerie, or bower-path, the track that led from New Amsterdam proper to the outlying farms, going as far as Pieter Stuyvesant's property near what is now Astor Place. Like

Broadway, its course followed that of an Indian trail, one that abutted to the south near the present Chatham Square, and it was linked to the village by two connections, which eventually became Park Row and Pearl Street, respectively. Its term as a quiet country lane lasted about a century; its use as a highway by cattle drovers plying between the village downtown and the Bowery village that had grown near the Stuyvesant manor house soon engendered taverns, inns, and suchlike, and before long, taverns were what it was known for.

Many locations in downtown Manhattan acquired a reputation of somewhat disproportionate scale when New York was a small town; as the city grew, such places tended to grow into their legends. The Bowery was stamped early on with the brand of an idyllic spot gone to seed, and at some point this became an image of decline. From there it has continued to decline, down to the present day, although over the years the character of that fall has changed continuously, from country lane to turnpike to working-class resort to casbah to amusement park to gangland to skid row. In any case, until fairly recently, the Bowery always possessed the greatest number of groggeries, flophouses, clip joints, brothels, fire sales, rigged auctions, pawnbrokers, dime museums, shooting galleries, dime-a-dance establishments, fortune-telling salons, lottery agencies, thieves' markets, and tattoo parlors, as well as theaters of the second, third, fifth, and tenth rank. It is also a fact that the Bowery is the only major thoroughfare in New York never to have had a single church built on it.

Besides being the capital of dissipation, the Bowery was also the main street of the lower classes. It was a motley stew well before the great waves of immigration, as a chronicler of 1852 observed of Chatham Square:

> *Here you see Jew and Gentile, Priest and Levite, as well as all the other classes—the old and young of all the natives upon the earth, and all the conditions and hues of the* genus *homo . . . Chatham Street is a sort of museum or old curiosity shop, and I think Barnum would do well to buy the*

whole concern, men, women, and goods, and have it in his
world of curiosities on the corner of Ann and Broadway.[7]

The Bowery was the place not only where the poor came to divert themselves but where they met and joined together in organizations of varying size and stability. These social clubs may have begun idly enough, but nearly always acquired political significance. The gangs, often in the early days more fraternal than criminal in nature, threw their weight behind favored politicians and worked as enforcers and repeaters at the polls, as did the fire companies, which were basically gangs equipped with fire engines. Their politics were usually Democratic, running the gamut from the radicals of the 1820s to various species of Tammany Hall shoulder-hitters and ward heelers, although up until the later nineteenth century there was also enough of a native-born element to constitute a significant Nativist presence. Essentially, though, the mob was unpredictable and uncontrollable; when the district arose as an entity, its power could be fearsome. If New York never actually experienced a revolt of the underclass, it came perilously close a number of times: the anti-Abolitionist riots of 1834, the Astor Place Theater riot of 1849, the Draft Riots of 1863. That these uprisings represented mass opposition variously to aristocratic reformers, to English actors, and to enforced conscription in the Civil War is a partial and misleading truth. The Republic of the Bowery was a powder keg of pre-political class rage that required only a slim excuse to go off.

The Bowery was the forum of the slums, the strand where bodies spilling forth from the tightly packed blocks to the east and south could collect. It was to some degree an ethnically neutral zone; there were always large numbers of Germans, Irish, Jews, blacks, and the "narrowbacks" of Anglo-Saxon descent. Also present, according to an 1872 account, were "the piratical-looking Spaniard and Portuguese, the gypsy-like Italian, the chattering Frenchman with an irresistible smack of the Commune about him, the brutish-looking Mexican, the sad and silent 'Heathen Chinee.' "[8] The Bowery was a great clearinghouse for migrants; nearly anyone not of the gentry passing through New York would make his or her way there eventually. Naturally, some halted there and never left, falling into the mire of drinking or prostitution or getting themselves murdered for their boots or maimed for their good looks. Very early, the Bowery acquired a reputation as the last stop on the way down; a typical casualty was the songwriter Stephen Foster, who had achieved national fame before the age of thirty with classics like "My Old Kentucky Home" and "Jeannie with the Light Brown Hair" but who drifted East and drank his way to obscurity, finally dying in a flophouse hallway in 1864, when he was thirty-eight. Somehow, dipsomania and death are the only constituents of the Bowery legend to have remained current; nowadays, the temptations have gone elsewhere, but the consequences are still abundantly in evidence.

The Bowery's course is not long. It begins at traditionally brawling Chatham Square (with a tendril shot south that was once the New Bowery but was later respectably rechristened St. James Place) and bends its way a mere mile to Cooper Square, where at the institutional prow of Cooper Union it splits in twain, becoming Third and Fourth Avenues. About the latter, little can be added to O. Henry's turn-of-the-century description:

> *Fourth Avenue—born and bred in the Bowery—staggers northward full of good resolutions.*
>
> *Where it crosses Fourteenth Street it struts for a brief moment proudly in the glare of the museums and cheap theaters. It may yet become a fit mate for its high-born sister boulevard to the west, or its roaring, polyglot, broad-waisted cousin to the east. It passes Union Square; and here the hoofs of the dray-horses seem to thunder in unison, recalling the tread of marching hosts—Hooray! But now come the silent and terrible mountains—buildings square as forts, high as the clouds, shutting out the sky, where thousands of slaves bend over desks all day. On the ground floor are little fruit shops and laundries and bookshops . . . And next,—poor*

*Fourth Avenue!—the Street glides into medieval solitude. On
each side are the shops devoted to "Antiques."*
    *With a shriek and a crash Fourth Avenue dives headlong
into the tunnel at Thirty-fourth Street and is never seen
again.*[9]

Some minor details of mercantile disposition aside, neither Fourth
Avenue proper nor that part of it renamed Park Avenue South has
changed very much in the past ninety years. Third Avenue, however,
its "broad-waisted cousin to the east," has been altered so much as to
be unrecognizable. Its leading feature, the elevated railroad, was torn
down in 1955, and the raffish blocks of saloons and cigar stores have
been razed. For much of its history, Third Avenue was the avenue of
the respectable poor, the proletariat to the Bowery's lumpen. First and
Second Avenues were similar, and they, too, had an elevated road,
which ran along First below Twenty-third Street and along Second
above it; this was torn down in 1940. First Avenue was otherwise not
noted for much besides pushcart markets, but Second Avenue below
Fourteenth Street possessed the distinction of acting as main street to
a succession of ethnic enclaves, variously German, Austrian (Klein
Wien), Hungarian (Goulash Row), Polish, and Ukrainian. It is best
remembered for its half-century term as the Jewish Rialto, the home
of the Yiddish theater, which at its peak was staged in as many as two
dozen legitimate houses along the span.
    Among these avenues and east of them lay a patchwork quilt of
ethnic settlements that periodically shifted or expanded with barely
visible capillary motion. The German presence, which dominated the
Lower East Side above Houston Street for half a century after the
failure of the bourgeois revolution of 1848, was an exception to this
rule by virtue of having had a distinct end. In the late nineteenth
century, the Germans were probably the single most powerful minority
in the city, establishing a strong network of political clubs, fraternal
organizations, Männerchors, Turnvereins, and a substantial press, and
on Second Avenue, or Avenue A (Dutch Broadway), more people spoke

the Saxon tongue than the Anglo-Saxon. Then, on June 15, 1904, 1,020 people of the neighborhood, mostly women and children, died in the wreck of the *General Slocum*, an excursion steamer which caught fire on the East River and broke up near North Brother Island. The victims, members of the Lutheran congregation of St. Mark's, on Sixth Street,[10] had been bound for their annual picnic and cruise on Long Island Sound; their vessel was a disaster waiting to happen, with rotting life jackets, unusable lifeboats, and an incompetent crew. The toll was such that the funeral procession made use of every hearse in the city. The tragedy broke the spirit of the neighborhood, and although a mass migration of the victims' families ensued, with the bulk of them relocating to Yorkville, the German community was never the same again. A decade later, rabid anti-German sentiments arising from World War I administered the coup de grâce.

East and south of the German area lay the Hungarian, which snaked around the lower-numbered streets and the waterfront blocks as high as the Dry Dock section around Tenth Street, and this shaded into and was eventually overtaken by the Jewish territory, radiating outward from a center that could be putatively located at Rutgers (later Straus) Square, where Canal and Essex Streets and East Broadway come together. East and south of that point, the Jewish area faded into the Irish slums between Cherry Hill and Corlears Hook, some of them continuously inhabited by the poor since the Revolution. The Chinese turf, a little to the west, began with a few houses on Mott and Pell Streets in the 1870s and over the years spread in four directions, gradually absorbing the progressively abandoned ethnic settlements around it. A bit to its north was one of the larger of the city's three or four Little Italys, this one centered on the Old St. Patrick's Cathedral at Mott and Prince Streets.

On the west side, slums ran continuously up from the Battery well into the streets numbered in the sixties. Around Washington Market— the city's great produce market for nearly two centuries, until its business was relocated to Hunt's Point in the Bronx and its site leveled to

The Bowery circa 1905, near Grand Street: in the shade of
the El, a mile-long parade of invitations to pass the time.
Photograph by Brown Brothers

The Bowery as seen by
Milt Gross: decline
becomes self-parody.
From *He Done Her
Wrong*, 1930

An unidentified street of the Lower East Side, circa 1910, with pushcart traffic, sanitation men, and the passing parade. Photograph by Brown Brothers

make way for the World Trade Center—lay a motley collection of settlements, including a Syrian district. Between the former St. John's Park at Varick and Laight Streets and lower Greenwich Village lay an ancient slum inhabited by native-born Anglo-Saxons until the area was razed after a public outcry in the early twentieth century. The city's first distinct African-American neighborhood, known as Little Africa, ran from lower Thompson Street in what is now SoHo up to the streets near the old Minetta Water, one of the last streams on the island to be paved over. Greenwich Village itself was first settled by prosperous families fleeing the cholera epidemics of the early nineteenth century, but later became a heterogeneous slum, famously bohemianized and subsequently gentrified just before and after World War I.

Sixth Avenue northeast of the Village acquired a reputation not long after the Civil War as a competitor to the Bowery. Legend has it that the area was christened by the notoriously corrupt Police Captain Alexander "Clubber" Williams, when, upon being transferred in 1876 from the Oak Street Station in the drably commercial far downtown to West Thirtieth Street, he said, "I've been living on chuck steak for a long time, and now I'm going to get a little of the tenderloin."[11] The Tenderloin was a bonanza for the grafter, far more lucrative than the Bowery because its fleshpots were on a much larger scale and frequented by more prosperous patrons. Whereas the Bowery was a gantlet of temptations for, by, and of the poor, the Tenderloin explicitly appealed to slummers, straying husbands, visiting firemen, businessmen on a tear. Its heyday was relatively brief, most of its dance halls, brothels, and gambling hells having been shut down by reform movements before World War I, but during the nineties and oughts the Tenderloin set what was probably the city's all-time standard for vice in one district. Within a few blocks of each other could be found establishments purveying the whole range of gambling possibilities, from dollar stuss to six-figure baccarat; an equally wide field of sexual services, varying in specificity and price; saloons from the shabbiest blind tiger to the most exalted champagne bar; opium by the pipe in tenement cellars or in elegantly decorated town houses reserved exclusively for that pursuit; and, of course, every sort of swindle, blackmail, con job, racket, and just plain robbery.

Westward, and up and down along the waterfront of the North River (now more generally known as the Hudson, after its upstate continuation), lay slums that were, if anything, even worse than their East Side counterparts. The name generally applied to this district was Hell's Kitchen, first specifically the name of a tenement at Fifty-fourth Street and Tenth Avenue and said to derive from the designation of a London slum;[12] experts differ as to the precise boundaries of the area, but at various times Hell's Kitchen comprised the whole range west of Eighth Avenue, from Twenty-third to Fifty-ninth Streets. It was first inhabited by the Irish spilling over from Cherry Hill, and not long after, they were joined by blacks who had lost the battle—fought out with razors—over southern Greenwich Village to the Italians. The district grew up helter-skelter in a malodorous environment of slaughterhouses, soap and glue factories, and waterfront effluvia, in patches that bore names like Poverty Lane and Misery Row. Tenth Avenue was known as Death Avenue, mostly because the Hudson River Railroad ran straight down its middle, without benefit of elevation or even crossing barriers. "Cowboys" had the job of riding on horseback in front of the engine, announcing its presence as it plowed from Spuyten Duyvil down to Laight Street. The northern end was converted to a system of viaducts in the 1920s, and the southern portion was eventually run through a cutting below ground level, in time approximately for the railroad's elimination as a viable form of urban freight transport.

Tensions ran high among ethnic groups, mostly between Catholic and Protestant Irish, a struggle typified by the Orange Riot of 1875; and between the Irish and the blacks. Race riots began in the 1870s and culminated in the cataclysmic riots of 1901, when battles ranged throughout the blocks between Twenty-fifth and Thirty-seventh Streets west of Eighth Avenue, which contributed mightily to the black migration farther uptown a few years later. Similarly volatile was the area directly above Hell's Kitchen, known as San Juan Hill in commemoration of the Tenth (Negro) Cavalry, who, popular accounts notwithstanding, actually took the eponymous Puerto Rican elevation well in advance of Teddy Roosevelt's Rough Riders. The southern portion of the neighborhood was black, a turf which extended to the middle of Sixty-second Street, the north side of which was Irish. This made the street the site of myriad small skirmishes, which took place as far as the no-man's-land of the rail yards between Fifty-ninth and Sixty-third Streets along West End Avenue.

Blacks began to leave the middle West Side around the turn of the century, settling, in small groups at first, in Harlem. Harlem had begun as one of the city's smaller outlying villages, a place of summer homes for the rich. It developed at an alarming rate in the 1880s, following the construction of the four El lines. Real-estate trusts and reform elements enthusiastically joined in a project to leaven the overpopulation of the East Side slums by constructing large, solid, well-planned apartment buildings, where sizable flats could be let for rents lower than or comparable to those of the airless rooms in the downtown rookeries. The project was a success, at least insofar as Harlem was immediately peopled, although the rate of immigration kept the Lower East Side constantly refilled anyway. Soon Harlem resembled an orderly, assimilated version of downtown, more middle-class and less tribal, although it had its ethnic territories, including two Little Italys— one around East 114th Street, the other near 110th and Amsterdam— and a large Scandinavian district that included the commercial heart of 125th Street. By the 1890s, Harlem had become, in effect, an outer borough, comparable to recently annexed Brooklyn. Subways were built; the construction of churches mushroomed. Harlem possessed large branches of downtown department stores and a belt of legitimate and vaudeville theaters that for traveling shows and troupes constituted the stop immediately before or immediately after Broadway. Soon Harlem was acclaimed as a law-abiding, familial place, with a level of dullness of the highest suburban standard.

Around 1902 the white press first noticed an influx of blacks into the blocks between 133rd and 135th Streets, between Lenox and Seventh

Avenues, and it examined motives—not of the settlers, but of the white brokers who had let them their apartments. Treason was alleged; Southern-style white citizens' councils were formed. Eventually, however, money talked, particularly after the canny black real-estate firm of Nail and Parker began transacting in large lots of buildings. Their sale in 1911 of ten apartment houses on 135th Street to the trustees of St. Philip's Colored Presbyterian Episcopal Church began a trend that saw the prosperous black churches of the West Side arriving one after the other with their congregations. The district grew steadily through the 1920s, south toward the top of Central Park, west to Morningside and St. Nicholas Parks, east as far as Fifth Avenue, and north nearly to Washington Heights. By World War II, Black Harlem went almost river to river above 125th Street and up past the Polo Grounds. With relative ease, all things considered, the district had changed its face entirely in less than a quarter of a century, and African-Americans, traditionally the most vulnerable of New York's ethnic blocs, had found a berth.

Neighborhood stability has been something of a chimera in Manhattan's history. In many if not most cases, especially after the great waves of immigration, an ethnic group's hard-fought settlement of an area was immediately followed by its moving elsewhere. The only constants that obtained were: (1) improvements in status and income spurred people to leave their neighborhoods, rather than to ameliorate them; and (2) within Manhattan, the motion was always northward. Attempts to find any other sort of logic in the flux do not fare well in retrospect. A 1904 observer, for example, thought he had located a natural order of sorts:

> It is a curious fact that the poor French usually move into
> districts from which the negroes are just moving out. The ne-
> groes have usually frozen out the Irish . . . The Jews, as a

rule, follow the French or the Italians, and anti-Semitic
prejudices give them an undisputed possession.[13]

Not only have these assertions not been borne out by time, they were
only glancing half-truths even then. Movement was as fluid as it was
constant, with the pattern no more graspable than mercury.

The great machinery of movement in Manhattan has not yet stopped,
of course, nor is it likely to do so any time soon. At first the task lay
in pushing forward into the wilderness, in cutting down trees, evicting
animals, leveling rises, draining ponds, blocking streams, banking
marshes, blasting rock. The twenty-odd square miles of the island of
Manhattan appeared limitless at the start, and even as the engines of
what is called progress pressed on in fits that grew closer and closer
together until they became an uninterrupted threshing noise, even as
the island was blocked off, squared off, and demolished so as to be built
upon, this movement continued to be thought of as never-ending. The
conquest of Manhattan was a microcosm of that of the whole of America, with its spaces so vast it was assumed they could be squandered
and there would still be so much left over that errors could be over-
looked. In New York the natural wilderness was much more concisely
and thoroughly swept away, so that a human wilderness could take its
place.

The overcrowding of Manhattan's neighborhoods was due not to
any desire for spatial economy but only to the harshness of financial
economy. When a relative degree of prosperity was achieved by the
inhabitants of a quarter, they would throw that quarter away, and it
would be picked up and moved into by their successors on the lower
rung. This relay became ritualized early; for years the first of May was
the day all leases expired, and on that day mass migrations would take
place, with families lugging eiderdowns and ancestral portraits through
the streets, as if in a parody of the march of the wagon trains. The
greater the number of moves made by a family, the more American
they might become, both because each upward motion indicated a
relatively higher degree of worldly success and also because there was

an entropic principle factored in; the cohesion of the ethnic or cultural unit could not survive too many displacements. Gradually the migrants would mix in with other communities, and children of disparate heritage going to school together would develop more in common with each other than they had with their parents. It could be said, too, without being overly reductive, that while assimilation moved uptown, success moved inland, toward the fabled Fifth Avenue. Immigrants or their children who made good could map their progress by increments represented by successive addresses. This became part of the vocabulary of the success story; accounts of figures like Al Smith or Irving Berlin would invariably note their rise from Oliver Street or Monroe Street to prominent uptown precincts.

Meanwhile, the physical fabric of the original slums rotted away even as they continued to be overpopulated, and nobody cared very much, not even the inhabitants, as long as they thought they had a chance to move elsewhere. Surely it is not coincidental that the first serious attempts at improving slum conditions were not made until Manhattan was nearly used up. The prospect of Manhattan's being built over meant that the migratory flow had to be diverted outward, and this eventuality was one of the factors that led to the 1874 annexation of Kingsbridge, Morrisania, and West Farms in what became the Bronx, and the final consolidation of Greater New York in 1898. It was not until well into the twentieth century that the far reaches of Queens, southeast Brooklyn, the north Bronx, and Staten Island were fully urbanized, and at that point the cycle had to return to Manhattan. In this way, the heraldic emblem of the city has changed from the image of a thermometer to the image of the worm Ouroboros, its tail forever in its mouth.

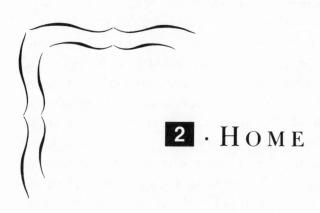

2 · HOME

THE TENEMENT IS THE BASIC FA-
ÇADE IN NEW YORK, THE FACE OF
THE SLUMS, A SLAB OF TOMBSTONE
PROPORTIONS, FOUR TO SIX STO-
ries, pocked by windows. Above is the towering tin cornice, a confection of scallops and
curlicues, with foliaceous brackets, often
topped by a semicircular peak, a disk en-
closing a rayèd sun. Below this, on the cornice, there may be a name, that of the
builder, the owner, a female relative, or an
allegorical quality: Hope, Columbia, Gertrude. The cornice exists in disdain of practical qualities; it possesses one, vaguely, in
adjusting the roof's pitch so that rainwater
will run off to the rear of the building, but
this function yielded to an aesthetic and then
to a nearly heraldic role. It is the most conspicuous item in the tenement's equipment
of fictitious grandeur. Below the cornice is

the façade proper, a mosaic composed mostly of red brick, but with lacings of white trim; with entablatures greater and lesser; false columns and caryatids; faces, urns, and emblems in bas-relief. The window frames may vary per floor, often the result of the architect's giving full rein to his eclecticism, so that the upper story might be severely classical and the others increase in ornamentation and exoticism as they near the street level. The oldest buildings are the plainest; as the years advance in the history of tenement-building, through the eighties, nineties, oughts, and teens up to the end of the boom just before World War I, each decade seems to bring a new twist to the frenzied denial of interior realities manifested by the exterior. There are tenements displaying parodies of portes-cochères, false lanterns, pseudo-portcullises, others that compose themselves vertically like wedding cakes, going beyond merely styling the window frames to pretending that each story is a separate edifice. The façade is all: it is the aspect of the tenement visible to idlers and passersby, to the gentry. If these must, of necessity, glimpse the unavoidable fire escapes, those grim reminders of fatality must be wrought and bowed and garlanded with iron vines so that their respectable beholders can believe them to be Spanish balconies or trellises of creeper roses. The façade is a mask, not the domino or half mask of the upper classes *en travesti* but a giant sunburst or devil's head from animist ritual: behind it is the frail and wretched thing of kitchens and urinals. But then this was a period of façades, in American architecture as in other aspects of society—and here we are talking about the extremes of the reform tenement, the very idea being itself a sort of mask. This was the time when frontier towns presented Main Streets of imposing two- and three-story fronts which were merely billboards; the actual edifices were single-story shacks. From such pretense to the false fronts of the Western movie set was no great leap.

The fiction of the tenement's face to the street might continue briefly within the door, or mouth, of the building—usually up to the second door. Between the doors lay a pocket vestibule which might at a later date hold mailboxes. It would have a floor of mosaic tiles, sawtooth moldings and possibly marble inlays on the walls. The doors might be carved, might have glass in them, might be curtained. Or not, depending on the expediency of the project; a single door might suffice, after all. Within, the ornamentation might not cease abruptly: the stairs might be balustraded, the hall floors tiled and their walls half covered with pressed-tin wainscoting; the walls of the rooms might boast complex moldings at waist level and just below the ceiling. But then the rooms themselves were stingily proportioned, contained the bare minimum of natural light, with walls and ceilings of hastily slopped plaster sensitive to dampness and cold, and floors of rough-hewn boards that separated, splintered, jutted out. Plumbing was a joke, heating only slightly less so. And in most of these cases such elements were the result of reforms, from a time when comforts were yet more minimal, when interior lighting, plumbing, heating, ventilation, for example, scarcely existed at all.

In its prime, the tenement was to Manhattan as the tree is to the forest, the basic and irreducible unit of measure. Between the Civil War and World War I, the tenement plantations spread up the whole of the East Side from just north of City Hall to the Harlem River and through the south and middle of the West Side, excepting only the patches of industrialization here and there and some old streets of Greenwich Village. Inland and on the upper west lay the more prosperous areas where the single-family brownstone and the French flat, or apartment house, prevailed. A photograph, from the period, of a random stretch of one of the avenues—First or Third or Sixth, say— is virtually impossible to situate precisely. The tenements grow like hedges, undifferentiated contiguous elements. Such a thing is difficult to imagine now that tenements are confined to stray clumps along the avenues, or gathered into certain unregenerate neighborhoods, slums fashionable or unfashionable, with gaps like missing teeth where arson and collapse have picked off buildings. Yet at the same time it is surprising that so many have survived.

The ones that have are, by and large, representative of that later, more elaborate, and more ostensibly humanitarian phase of tenement history. They are, in fact, the end point of such development, after which would come a succession of experiments in model housing culminating in the housing project, an engineering exercise in functionally adequate shelter that is in effect a sort of super-tenement. Before the late tenement phase lay decades' worth of unbelievable rookeries. What all sorts of tenements have in common is the principle of containing the greatest number of people in the least amount of space. The basic unit of calculation for the tenement is the 25-by-100-foot lot. If we assume four apartments per floor, six floors per building (the maximum that reform laws finally permitted to be constructed without an elevator), this gives us lodging for twenty-four families, perhaps a hundred people. Around the turn of the century, such an edifice could be built for $25,000, which made for a relatively long-term investment, but would scarcely encourage the endowment of amenities by the owner. The sum would take care of such reform requirements as air shafts down the center of both flanks, and hall toilets on each floor; these were not negotiable. Neither could the owner stretch his dollar by housing tenants in the cellar, or by extending his building in back to the full reach of the lot.

Only two decades before, he could have done all of it and more. Tenements in the seventies and eighties were boxes up to seven stories in height, and an additional two below ground, in which there were as many rooms as could be fit between the exterior walls. These buildings were not large by modern standards, but poverty and lack of scruple kept them filled with incredible numbers of people. The ancestors of the tenement served as their model: disused factories that became barracks for the poor. The most notorious of these was the Old Brewery, a five-story structure built in 1792 on the banks of the old Collect Pond and run as Coulter's Brewery until 1837, when it had become too rotted for industrial purposes. For fifteen years the Old Brewery had a second life as a human dump of almost mythic proportions. At various times, the unverifiable legends would have it, it housed in excess of a thousand people at once, in a warren of chambers in the cellar and in the former machinery rooms above. The largest

room, known as the Den of Thieves, lodged about seventy-five persons.
The Irish and black inhabitants existed without furniture or much of
anything else, and tended to stay put for weeks at a time, since if they
left, their possessions or even their floor space would be stolen. It can
only be conjectured how they ate. Natural functions were discharged
in the corners; bodies were buried in the dirt cellar floor. Contemporary
depictions of the place tended to be at once sensational and prim.
Much was made of the vice of murder, in that Victorian way of seeing
murder as a sybaritic pleasure indulged in by those sated with mere
sex.[1] At the same time, a print depicting "The Dying Mother—A Scene
in the Old Brewery" shows this parent expiring in a counterpaned if
rough-hewn bed, surrounded by weeping children in conventionally
full-draped garments, and by a brace of religious images on the walls
and shelves. Acknowledgment of dire poverty seems relegated to the
idea of death itself, and further symbolized by a nicked doorframe and
an overturned stool. It may be doubted whether shelves and stools,
let alone counterpanes, existed in the Old Brewery.

When in 1852 the Ladies' Home Missionary Society of the Methodist
Episcopal Church bought the building for $16,000, razed it,[2] and built
a mission on its site, the self-satisfaction of reform elements was great
and resulted in numerous verses and sermons. The action was little
more than symbolic, however. After all, the ladies were primarily
interested in bringing the gospel to the inhabitants, and had fired their
original missionary in the area, the Reverend Lewis Morris Pease, for
spending too much time dwelling on the material needs of his charges.
The putative thousand former inhabitants of the Old Brewery were
merely turned out to workhouses or to similar if smaller rookeries.
They might go to the Rag Pickers' Den, between Pitt and Willett Streets,
inhabited by Germans and ravaged by cholera; to Rotten Row, on
Laurens Street (now West Broadway), where, in the words of one
contemporary, "no drove of animals could pass by and keep its numbers
intact"[3]; to the squatters' colony at Dutch Hill; to the slums of Cherry
and Water Streets, Hammersley Street (now West Houston), West
Seventeenth Street. There was no shortage of slums.

Their nexus, however, continued to be the Lower East Side. The Old Brewery was the magnetic center of the area called the Five Points, the intersection of Orange (now Baxter), Cross (now Park), and Anthony (also known as Cat Hollow, now Worth) Streets, the immediate area also bounded by Ryndert (now Mulberry) and Little Water (also known as Dandy Lane and since built over). Prints of the period depict this slum as a jumble of gabled frame houses, drawn comically tilted and helter-skelter in an awkward attempt to picture decay, with their wooden sidewalks and the occasional awning, with a grocery on every corner—"grocery" being the contemporary euphemism for grog shop—and with, alternatively, placid smoking citizens and thin dogs standing around, or frantic policemen, thieves, and whores rushing through. The short street called Little Water ended in a cul-de-sac called Cow Bay, site of an actual tiny bay in the Collect Pond. Cow Bay was an alley around which tenements clustered, such notorious ones as Jacob's Ladder, the Gates of Hell, and Brickbat Mansion, frame houses linked by tunnels handy for evading the police.[4] The names testify to the ferocity with which the dwellers repulsed visitors, particularly of the official variety, so it is not surprising that little information survives as to how they were actually disposed and inhabited. Those witnesses who did make it in tended to be of the sort that, in the mode of the time, had confused notions about vice and poverty and their reciprocal relationship, as for example the anonymous author of *Hot Corn* (1854):

> *If you would see Cow Bay, saturate your handkerchief with camphor, so that you can endure the horrid stench, and en-ter. Grope your way through the long, narrow passage—turn to the right, up the dark and dangerous stairs; be careful where you place your foot around the lower step, or in the corners of the broad stairs, for it is more than shoe-mouth deep of steaming filth. Be careful, too, or you may meet someone, perhaps a man, perhaps a woman, who in their drunken frenzy may thrust you, for the very hatred of your*

better clothes, or the fear that you have come to rescue them
from their crazy loved dens of death, down, headlong down,
those filthy stairs. Up, up, winding up, five stories high,
now you are under the black smoky roof; turn to your left—
take care and not upset that seething pot of butcher's offal
soup that is cooking upon a little furnace at the head of the
stairs—open that door—go in, if you can get in. Look, here
is a Negro and his wife sitting upon the floor—where else
could they sit, for there is no chair—eating their supper off
the bottom of a pail. A broken brown earthen jug holds
water—perhaps not all water. Another Negro and his wife
occupy another corner; a third sits in the window monopo-
lizing all the air astir. In another corner, what do we see? A
Negro man and a stout, hearty, rather good-looking young
white woman. Not sleeping together? No, not exactly that—
there is no bed in the room—no chair—no table—no noth-
ing—but rags, and dirt, and vermin, and degraded, rum-
degraded human beings.[5]

Here we see miscegenation as equivalent to drinking, and drinking as equivalent to deprivation. The Cow Bay tenements were otherwise noted as places where animals lodged comparably or even in preference to humans—pigs in the main room, goats upstairs. The Five Points flourished—if that is the word—until 1868, when a crusade headed by Horace Greeley led to the removal of a house at the end of Anthony Street, which opened up the enclosure, although the major slum that dominated the imagination of the last quarter of the century was that of Mulberry Bend, a block or two away.

The first building put up deliberately as a tenement would seem to be the house built by James Allaire in 1833 at the eastern end of Water Street, hard by Corlears Hook. It had four floors, each housing a single family. If this sounds rather spacious, comparatively, it must be borne in mind that at the time the fiction of the single-family dwelling remained paramount. The notion of housing multiple families and heterogeneous individuals within a single unit was not acknowledged as an option, at least officially. Poverty was generally held to be a consequence or attribute of vice, and the sharing of dwellings a licentious indulgence, rather than the dictate of necessity; tenements were hardly unknown before 1833, but they were the result of accommodating structures built for other purposes. In any case, once the taboo had been broken, developers got to work. The first reliable survey of tenements, that of 1864, reveals the presence of more than 15,000 such houses in Manhattan. There were more than 18,000 in 1867; more than 20,000 by 1872.

The typical tenement of the mid-nineteenth century consisted of two buildings, front and rear, and was popularly known as the double-decker. The front structure measured 25 feet by 50, the rear was 25 feet square, and they were separated by a 25-square-foot court. The front rooms of the front building were the most desirable, since they were guaranteed natural light and air; the rooms in either building fronting on the court, slightly less so. The interior rooms of the front house got no light or air at all, and neither did the back rooms of the rear, since that structure generally abutted on its counterpart across the block. Below lay two subterranean levels, both fully inhabited: basements, thought to be comparable to the upper stories since they lay partly above the ground, and cellars, completely submerged, airless and lightless. In 1864 there were 15,224 such populated cellars.

Cellars were the lowest rung of habitation, but this did not prevent landlords from commanding princely sums for them, as much as $200 per month for a cellar apartment during the inflationary period after the Civil War. At the time, about 100,000 people lived in such confines, primarily as tenants of the subterranean hostelries known as bed houses. If cholera, tuberculosis, typhoid, and a passel of other diseases ravaged the tenements, especially in the enclosed interior spaces, their potential damage below the ground can only lead one to wonder that anybody survived at all. In 1869, out of some 12,000 inhabited cellars (statistics of the period fluctuate), precisely 211 were passed by the Board of Health.

Police station lodgers, photographed by Jacob Riis, late 1880s

East Side lodging house of a relatively high standard, to
judge by the separate, fully accoutered beds. Photographed
in the late 1880s by Richard Hoe Lawrence,
one of Riis's understudies

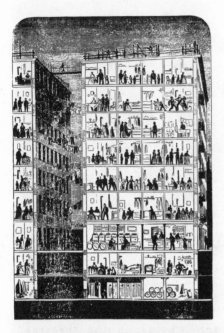

Tenement cutaway
from James McCabe's
*Lights and Shadows of
New York Life*, 1872.
Note cellars, saloon,
roof garden, catwalk,
as well as the rich
variety of domestic
dramas

Tenement interior circa 1905: making the best of a bad
situation. Photograph by Brown Brothers

A survey cited by Jacob Riis in the 1890s distinguished between the respective dangers of single tenements and double-deckers: the mortality rate for the First Ward, for example, was 29.08 per thousand in the former case and 61.97 per thousand in the latter.[6] Infant-mortality rates show an equally dramatic divergence: 109.58 for single dwellings, 204.54 for tenements containing rear buildings. (There are no similar surveys differentiating between levels above or below ground.) The sources of disease were hardly mysterious: containment, festering, layers upon layers of dirt. Within or adjacent to tenements, businesses engaged in a variety of unsanitary activities: slaughtering, bone-boiling, ragpicking. Add to this the accumulation of offal and manure from the omnipresent animals and their carcasses when they were not immediately recycled after death, as well as the effluvia from the toilets, which might be located in cellars, in excavated alleys, in wooden outhouses in the court or yard. Water supply was limited to one common tap per floor in the very best of circumstances, and baths were, unsurprisingly, rare. One late-nineteenth-century survey found an allocation of three tubs for 1,321 families, which is a fairly typical ratio.

And disease was only one of the hazards. There was fire, for instance. In 1867 a law was passed requiring buildings of four stories to possess staircases made of fireproof materials, but builders evidently found loopholes in the measure, so that in 1892 a similar law was passed requiring fireproof stairs in five-story buildings. Riis reported that the Superintendent of Buildings, questioned on the enforcement of this statute, averred that he was satisfied with hard wood, which "burns slowly." The rate of tenement-house fires was, in fact, wildly disproportionate to all conflagrations. Frame houses went up like tinderboxes, and the opportunities for them to do so were manifold, beyond the risk of simple carelessness. The standard means of heating and cooking were unreliable kerosene stoves, which were bad enough, but the use of tenements by industry, whether in ground-floor establishments or through piecework done by tenants in their own apartments, provided tremendous hazards from the storage and use of materials like gasoline,

naphtha, benzene, turpentine, the simultaneous generation of sparks
by machines—the scenario is not hard to imagine.

The buildings were hastily constructed and deteriorated rapidly.
They were so badly engineered, in many cases, that they were dangerous even when new. A tenement in the middle West Side collapsed
during construction in 1885; the builder, wishing to cut costs, had
used loam from the excavation of the cellar, instead of sand, in the
mortar. The foundation, poured in winter, buckled in the spring. In
a similar case from the 1840s, it was found that a just-completed
building's retaining walls consisted of a single layer of brick with a
wash of plaster on the interior—an overall density of about three inches.
Construction standards did exist on the books, but they were rarely
applied or enforced.

The density of population is difficult to imagine by present-day standards; nineteenth-century statistics do not sound terribly inflated until
one realizes that there were no residential structures more than seven
or eight stories high, and that the average was four stories, many of
these floors inhabited by single families. In 1872, for example, the
Seventeenth Ward, bounded by Fourteenth Street on the north, Avenue
B on the east, Rivington Street on the south, and the Bowery and
Fourth Avenue on the west, held one-fortieth of Manhattan's total area
but one-tenth of its population. It housed a population equal to that
of Richmond, greater than that of Cleveland. The Tenth Ward,
bounded by the Bowery, Rivington, Norfolk, and Division Streets, had
a population of 47,554 in 1880, the equivalent of 423.3 persons per
acre; in 1890, there were 57,596 (522 per acre); by 1895, there were
70,168 (643.08 per acre). In 1890, a block between Canal, Hester,
Eldridge, and Forsyth Streets, measuring 375 by 200 feet, housed 2,628
people; another, between Stanton, Houston, Attorney, and Ridge, at
200 by 300 feet, held 2,244. Two years later, a block bounded by
Avenues B and C and Second and Third Streets contained over 3,500,
while a smaller one off Houston Street held 3,000, which comes to a
density of 1,562 per acre, or a million per square mile.

The successive waves of immigration from Europe had brought so many people, particularly in the last twenty years of the nineteenth century, and had dumped them in such dire conditions, that as many as four or five families were routinely housed in apartments intended for one.[7] Yet even these could count themselves as provisionally fortunate. Less so were the numbers of homeless, dispossessed, or those who had never found lodging, who were legion. The least lucky were those forced into the barracks located in the cellars of police stations. Such accommodations were originally intended for emergencies, but a permanent state of emergency soon took hold. These rooms, with planks for bedding, no ventilation of any kind, and the inhibiting presence, passing for protection, of the police, were inns of last resort. They were not used much except in winter, but then they were often wildly crowded; they also possessed the distinction of being among the few temporary lodgings open to women who were not actively or passively prostitutes. Police Commissioner Theodore Roosevelt, prompted by Jacob Riis, finally shuttered all such rooms on February 15, 1896, but no provisions were made for the accommodation of their former tenants—and this was the dead of winter.[8]

The next step up was flophouses, which were numerous and varied. The tariff rates can be established with a degree of specificity for circa 1890: twenty-five cents bought the use of a cot, a locker, and a screen; fifteen cents paid for just the cot and the locker; ten cents for just the cot; seven cents for a hammock-like canvas strap hung above the floor; five cents for a spot on the floor itself. Some houses offered the full range of options; many others restricted themselves to the last one or two.[9] Many flops contained bars as well, which sold various forms of rotgut or "smoke," or stale beer needled with ingredients that included denatured alcohol, malt residue, camphor, and benzene, so that at least some of the guests must have become permanent, if not eternal. One writer of the time described the clientele of these houses as "runaway boys, truant apprentices, and drunken mechanics," but this assessment once again presses the moral point, and in fact the range of unfortunates was probably a good deal wider.

Boardinghouses were the next level of amenity. Many accommodated

women, and some even constituted a square deal. In 1892, a working
person could expect to pay $2 a week for a room and between $3 and
$5 for board per week in a house of the middle level of refinement.
To be bedded and fed for $24 per month could be considered a solid
bargain. By contrast, a lower-middle-class family of the time would
pay between $25 and $50 a month for the rental of an unfurnished
five- or six-room flat. Anything above $50 would include such em-
bellishments as marble mantels, oak wainscoting, dumbwaiters. At the
same period a three-room tenement apartment might run nearly $20
a month if situated in the front of the building; three dark rooms in
the rear would still cost in excess of $10. Riis cites further examples:
a windowless back-building room at $6 a month; an identical chamber
with a hole knocked through the exterior wall, $6.50. He found a
Russian Jewish family living in a hutch under a staircase in a tenement
on Orchard Street who paid $8 a month for the privilege. Around this
time the minimal legal space allowance, which formerly had been 600
cubic feet per person, was "realistically" reduced to 400 for adults,
200 for children. Airless rooms were finally outlawed in 1894, but this
only prevented the construction of new ones; they continued to be
found for decades afterward, and in fact some still exist today.

However unenforceable or flawed such legal measures were, they at
least represented piecemeal improvements. Many laws passed after
1890 are the direct result of the campaign of Jacob Riis, through his
journalism, books, and photographs. As a one-man band of social
reform, Riis altered the outlook of the whole city, and eventually the
nation. It is easy enough to find fault with his writings and deeds
today: he was a moralist who ignored economic causes and who did
not hesitate to judge the people he was helping by the same lofty
standards of conduct he applied to those whom he reproved; he was
a sentimentalist who, even as he made capital use of sentiment as a
weapon in his cause, was vulnerable to rosy and unworkable solutions,
discarding the skepticism and canniness he brought to problems. He
was no great thinker, but he was well endowed with determination
and energy, and he had a genius for publicity. What Riis achieved was

a campaign of public persuasion on social issues that would set the standard for such crusades and exposés well into the following century. Riis finally convinced the average reader of newspapers that the poor were not so by choice; that the dangerous and unhygienic conditions in which they lived were imposed, rather than the result of loose moral standards; that the slums were something that needed to be fixed, rather than gaped at or shunned.

Riis was born in southern Denmark in 1849 and came to America in 1870. He spent seven years in migration and want, a period which had a profound influence on his later work, and then he became a reporter on the *New York Tribune* in 1877, eventually becoming police reporter. He joined the staff of the *Evening Sun* in 1890, the same year that he published his groundbreaking first book, *How the Other Half Lives*. After 1901 and until his death in 1914, he lectured professionally. He was directly responsible for the demolition of Mulberry Bend, a large block of horrifying rookeries—Bottle Alley, Bandits' Roost, Bone Alley, Thieves' Alley, Ragpickers' Row, Kerosene Row—between Mulberry and Baxter, Bayard and Park Streets, which was replaced by a park. He argued for and supervised the demolition of numerous rear tenements, the closing of police lodging rooms, and the construction of settlement houses, one of which was named after him in 1901. He supported the building of model tenements, and licensing and rent control for lower-class housing. He was a firm believer in supervised leisure activity for the young, in the beneficial effects of nature in the form of parks, in the assimilation of ethnic groups. This latter is one of his least attractive qualities; he was the sort of immigrant who becomes a rabid nationalist in his adopted country, and will brook no deviance. He was the least helpful to those ethnic enclaves that were most faithful in keeping up their traditions and language—in particular the Chinese, whom he loathed.

His photographs speak more eloquently today than his vaguely anecdotal, often cloying prose. Riis's camera, like that of Lewis Hine after him, generally permits his subjects to compose themselves, to establish the terms of their own portraiture. He, naturally, faced some hostility in this pursuit, so his best subjects are often children: the little girls of Baxter Street Alley, the boys of Mullins's Alley. They stand foursquare, hands on hips, even grinning. But his pictures of adults, dangerous adults at that, are no less forthright. The inhabitants of Bandits' Roost look out from under the brims of their hats with more than a small measure of pride, and even the Short Tail Gang, photographed under the Jackson Street pier from a police boat as they squat among a pile of tin cans, give anything but the impression of having been captured and pinned. That Riis was a humanist rather than a collector of miseries is evident from the fact that his pictures are nearly all composed like frames, or like theatrical spaces in which the people hold the stage, and this is true even of the "flash and run" work he engaged in early in his career, when he would briefly surprise needled-beer drinkers in dives or sleepers in nickel lodging houses. These photographs, for all the quality of invasion inherent in their method, do not reduce or degrade their subjects, but feature them like actors. Even an 1890 picture of boys stealing apples from a pushcart, which was taken hastily on the street, has a theatrical suggestion, although in this case looking forward to the early movies in its depiction of antic movement against a static background. As social documents, Riis's photographs have the effect, through valuing their human centers, of denying any picturesque quality to the squalor in which they are set. Dimensions are accurately captured, light or the lack thereof is noted, debris appears as itself. The human does not adorn or ennoble this setting, he or she appears superimposed on it, as in a montage of grotesquely juxtaposed elements. The vibrant faces look all wrong against the dirt. The mismatch cries out for rectification.

This denial of the picturesque was quite pointed, because at the time there was a vogue among the intellectual classes for treating the slums as an exotic locale. High-minded tourists could go to the East Side and take in the street life, staring at patriarchal bearded Jews and Italian women with bundles on their heads, treating themselves to the sights of the Grand Tour without the concurrent expense, then go home and write rapturous articles about the splendid colors of poverty and the true happiness of the slum dwellers. In *A Hazard of New Fortunes* (1890), William Dean Howells gives his character Basil March, a magazine editor, fairly typical musings in this vein:

> [*He*] *descended the station stairs at Chatham Square, with a sense of the neglected opportunities of painters in that locality. He said to himself that if one of those fellows were to see in Naples that turmoil of cars, trucks, and teams of every sort, intershot with foot passengers going and coming to and from the crowded pavements, under the web of the railroad tracks overhead and amidst the spectacular approach of the streets that open into the square, he would have it down in his sketchbook at once.*[10]

Even as Mulberry Bend was slated for demolition, the novelist Edward W. Townsend, in *A Daughter of the Tenements* (1895), already regretted its passing:

> *For the sunlight and air introduced into that neighborhood we shall all feel appropriately proud of our share in the achievement, yet I cannot but regret even with all the deliberation our rulers may exercise in this matter, the transformation of the Bend into the park which will have taken place before any American painter shall have found time from working up his "Naples sketches" and elaborating his "scenes from Cairo streets" into ambitious canvases, to step over into the Bend and preserve its distinctive color and action for those of us who care. He might even conceal his indiscretion by labelling his picture "Street Scene in an Italian Town," and sell it, i' faith!*[11]

Long after Riis's crusade, and at a time when reform of housing conditions was not gigantically advanced from its state in 1895, there were

those who could go on mourning the old slum, such as the aesthete
James Gibbons Huneker, in *The New Cosmopolis*, 1915:

> *An East Side there was in those hardy times, and it was
> still virginal to settlement-workers, sociological cranks, im-
> pertinent reformers, self-advertising politicians, billionaire
> socialists, and the ubiquitous newspaperman. Magazine
> writers had not topsyturvied the ideas of the tenement dwell-
> ers, nor were the street-cleaner, the Board of Health, and
> other destroyers of the picturesque in evidence. It was the
> dear old dirty, often disreputable, though never dull East
> Side; while now the sentimentalist feels a heart pang to
> see the order, the cleanliness, the wide streets, the play-
> grounds, the big boulevards, the absence of indigence that
> have spoiled the most interesting part of New York City.*[12]

These testaments, respectively wanly tasteful, bizarrely protectivist, and
cynically decadent, do, of course, have some truth to them. Housing
reform does tend toward the expedient, the homogenized, the bland.
Nevertheless, such arguments from the vantage of the voyeur must be
viewed in context as a convenient cover for the point of view of the
landlord. The slums were interesting, but they were also ghastly; the
failure of reformers to come up with solutions that were equally interesting scarcely invalidates the pressing need for dwellings that were
at least tolerable. Even Riis's complacent-sounding proposals for parks,
those tiny, constricted zones of turf and feeble trees, filled a real need:
there were no open spaces on the Lower East Side. It was not as if
New York at the time could be said to contain an old section in need
of preservation. It was not Naples or Cairo; it was not Paris, and reform
was not Haussmannization. The Lower East Side was not threatened
with the ramming through of grand boulevards until Andrew J. Thomas's proposal for a Chrystie-Forsyth Parkway in 1931, a futuristic specter
of double-decked roadways and middle-class high-rises. Luckily, this
plan got no further than the more Riisian Sara D. Roosevelt Parkway,

which involved the razing of seven tenement blocks between Chrystie and Forsyth Streets below Houston and their being replaced with a bona-fide neighborhood park.

Riis's work merely tapped the surface, needless to say. In 1908, a magazine writer finally called public attention to the vast slum holdings of venerable Trinity Church on the Lower West Side. This was a warren of nearly five hundred tenement buildings between Greenwich Village and Canal Street, an assemblage of ancient frame dwellings that collectively resembled a shantytown built from rubbish. Their inhabitants were mostly native-born Anglo-Saxons, and the area failed to qualify as exotica. The church had owned and administered these properties for a century, during which time they had gone to seed and had been thereafter totally neglected by their owner, not even made beneficiary of Trinity's official charity, established in 1857. Publicity embarrassed the church; and it duly razed the tenements, soon to replace them with office buildings and warehouses. Seldom did the process work quite that neatly. Most slumlords could not be embarrassed, even when they did not hold their property in secret or under a shield of corporation names.

Meanwhile, efforts to improve tenement design had been on going for some time, beginning with an 1867 law that required fire escapes, banisters on stairs, a water closet or outside privy for every two inhabitants, and a transom above the door of each inner room, although the last provision was delayed until 1874 by epidemics of cholera and smallpox and the consequent need to isolate the afflicted. Improvements like these were quite necessary, but what was really needed was a thorough redesign. The "dumbbell" form, proposed in the 1870s, was the first major step, and it was to be the dominant idea in tenement design from 1887 until the end of the century. The dumbbell eliminated the windowless interior room by providing for air shafts—in most cases, a barely adequate three feet or so in depth—running down the center of the buildings' flanks. Architectural renditions of the time grossly exaggerate the beneficial qualities of these vertical tunnels, representing them as courtyards dense with greenery, looking like the atria of Roman villas. While the air shaft undeniably introduced a minimum of oxygen into the blind areas of buildings, it did little else. Even when two adjacent houses were so equipped and their shafts happened to be contiguously positioned, the resulting hole was laterally no more than the size of a large man's coffin, and the pathway from sky to window was so constrained that sunlight could not make its way below the top story except at high noon. Furthermore, the seldom accessible lower depths of the shaft would quickly become a garbage dump, and even the windowsills on intervening floors would be heaped with guano from the already increasing profusion of avian vermin. To put all this in the past tense is misleading; thousands of dumbbell tenements and their air shafts remain, by now caked with a century of soot. In any event, it is important to recognize that, at the time of their construction, the same principle obtained in the building of the early middle-class apartments. The petit-bourgeois pioneers of the French flat often had only a three-foot vista out their bedroom windows.

Various alternative designs, most of them involving side courts, were briefly tried, but these too often impinged on profit by limiting the number of rooms that could be built per floor, so nothing much was done until the early twentieth century, when multiple tenements began to be erected. These edifices, built on double- or triple- or quadruple-sized lots (figured in multiples of 25 feet across), could feature interior courts of reasonable size without sacrificing the maximum concentration of rooms or their symmetrical disposition. By "reasonable size" is meant something on the order of a hundred or so feet square, nothing to inspire ceremonial fountains or formal gardens. Still, it was an improvement. Lower floors might get an hour or two of sunlight during the day, and wash lines could be discreetly hung within the building's confines, instead of indecorously festooning the public street.

The wash line was the flag of the tenement, and it survives in urban folklore as the horizontal totem of the Old Neighborhood. Such ropes, hung with the inevitable underwear, pajamas, housedresses, and sheets, garlanded the fronts, backs, and sides of buildings, stretched across side streets, billowing in the wind and collecting ambient fallout

The flags of the tenements, circa 1910. Photograph by Brown Brothers

Visiting nurse on Hester Street, traveling over the rooftops. Photograph by Jessie Tarbox Beals

A couple in their
tenement home,
evidently under the
eaves, photographed
by Jacob Riis

The new-law airshaft:
a scene shot by Riis in
the 1890s that could
just as easily have
been taken yesterday

from factory smokestacks, and they were useful in many ways besides drying laundry: for running messages and cups of sugar from one apartment to another, or—stretched diagonally down to the ground— for conveying groceries to the elderly infirm or growlers of beer up from the corner saloon. They were characteristic of the way life stretched, by necessity, out of the interiors of tenement apartments as far as possible into the public spaces beyond.

Tenement dwellers made full use of every available part of their building. Fire escapes, once they became mandatory and then common, were given such a range of employment that they effectively became extra rooms. People slept on them in the hot months, not without some risk—restless sleepers on imperfectly constructed scaffolds might well roll over into the void. Roofs played a similar role, and had an even broader range, able to hold parties and gatherings too large for any apartment. Roofs were honeycombed with pigeon coops, in the days when the keeping of homing birds was a popular and inexpensive proletarian sport. They could act as an alternative sidewalk, too, on streets dominated by rows of identically scaled tenements. In this capacity they were used by rent collectors, census takers, traveling salesmen, and anyone else whose job involved working methodically from apartment to apartment along a street; by police reporters scooping the competition by arriving first on the scene of fire or murder; and by visiting nurses and other social workers whose duties took them to the domiciles of the very poorest, who invariably lived on the upper stories after the eradication of cellar lodgings. This hierarchy held for walk-ups, but was reversed in elevator-equipped buildings. As one former tenement dweller reminisced: "The higher you lived, the poorer you were, and consequently the farther down the social scale. The church missionary went from house to house via the roofs, because most of the people of her church lived at the top of the tenements. The more prosperous the East Side family became, the less they attended church."[13]

Indoors, the tenements were sparse and cramped at once, overfurnished and underequipped. In the mid-nineteenth century, slum dwellers often possessed no furniture at all, but as the century went on, an industry sprang up that manufactured cheap beds and tables and chairs from weak woods or reconstituted sawdust or the lesser metallic alloys, and thus flats could be stuffed with mammoth, space-hogging pieces in emulation of the overdressed domiciles of the more prosperous, but within constricted spaces that made a mockery of scale. Rooms were dominated by beds, whether the huge metal cages of the better-off or the barracks' worth of rolled mattresses in the apartments of those forced to take in boarders. Closets were not introduced into the lower ranks of housing in New York until well into the twentieth century, so more space was taken up by unwieldy armoires and foot-lockers (the very poor resorted to pegs and nails). When the refinement of plumbing brought sinks into each flat, these tended to be galvanized-steel vats that had at least the ability to double as tubs (if a bit un-comfortably for full-bodied adults); when actual tubs came in, they were generally placed in the kitchen, no provision having been made for bathrooms in the layout. Figuring in the centrally located stove, and at least one table, there was not, as Riis put it, "room enough to swing the proverbial cat," and this without accounting for the bur-densome equipment of the home workshop, the sewing machines and cigar-rolling setups and paper-flower assemblies that occupied a large chunk of numerous apartments. There was no room for a settee, for example, even assuming such a thing could be afforded by the inhab-itants, let alone the omnipresent piano of the middle-class lodging.

It is therefore poignant to look at photographs by Riis or Hine or Jessie Tarbox Beals and see how, when they could afford to, tenement dwellers fixed up their hovels with curtains, bureau scarves, flounced runners along the edges of shelves, ormolu-framed ancestral portraits and certificates and chromolithographs, and bibelots and souvenirs of the past and of trips to Coney Island. The fiction of gentility in the tenement begins in nineteenth-century legends of forgotten duchesses and cast-off victims of primogeniture expiring in grimy attics—there being no surer way to the hearts of the middle class than by the revelation of noble blood—and over the decades moves little by little into the domain of commodities, finally culminating in those improbable tenement flats seen in movies of the 1930s—the ones the Bowery Boys might share with their noble elder sisters, for example—that might be the kitchens and parlors of real houses on Main Street, only with a skyscraper visible though the window. The tidy furnishings were a literal embodiment of virtue, of the pure heart misplaced in the slums. To most minds, the slums were a wilderness, as inevitable as forest or desert, in which vice and crime were natural conditions. The task of extracting goodness fell to the liberal—"I like a dirty slum; not because I am naturally unclean . . . but because I generally find a certain sediment of philosophy precipitated in its gutters," Fitz-James O'Brien wrote in 1859—or to the sentimental temperament:

> *A little side street, such as often you meet*
> *Where the boys of a Sunday night rally;*
> *Though it's not very wide, and it's dismal beside*
> *Yet they call the place Paradise Alley.*
> *But a maiden so sweet lives in that little street,*
> *She's the daughter of Widow O'Malley;*
> *She has bright golden hair and the boys all declare*
> *She's the sunshine of Paradise Alley.*

In actual fact, the tenement was many things: a beehive or rabbit warren of interconnected residential cubicles, any of which could function on the side as a workshop, a boardinghouse, a meeting room, a whorehouse, a dive, a social club (this last brought to its apogee by the institutional rent parties of Harlem in the 1920s and thirties). The cubicles shared a roof with the street-level storefronts occupied by grocery stores or dry-goods establishments or pre-Volstead Act saloons. The whole comprised an organic unit of intense concentration, heat, temper, volatility, heterogeneity, secrecy (the unknown people upstairs), and transparency (the gossip telegraph, the wash lines, the thin walls). It was a leveler of character, a mold that made diverse temperaments and personalities subject to the same diseases, the same water shortages or power outages, the same forces of landlord malice or structural deficiency or natural hazard. No one knew when a wall might collapse, having been made of plaster eked out with sawdust in the first place, and then weakened by years of weather, so that the inhabitants of all floors would be exposed like the occupants of an ant farm—in their nightshirts, in their baths, eating, screwing, reading the funnies, coughing blood. In his book of New York sketches, *The Color of a Great City* (1925), Theodore Dreiser describes how a fire, begun in a basement leased by a dealer in paints and chemicals, spreads to reveal and link the inhabitants of a row of tenements in a relay of disastrous contagion:

> *And yet the fire continues to burn. It catches a dressmaker who has occupied the rear rooms of the third floor of the building, two doors away from that of the paint-dealer's shop, and while she is still waving frantically for aid she is enveloped with a glorious golden shroud of fire which hides her completely. It rushes to where a lame flower-maker, Ziltman, is groping agonizedly before his windows on the fifth floor of another tenement, and sends into his nostrils a volume of thick smoke which smothers him entirely. It sends long streamers of flame licking about doorposts and window frames of still other buildings, filling stairways and arealandings with great dark clouds of vapor and bursting forth in lurid, sinister flashes from nooks and corners where up to now fire has not been suspected. It appears to be an all-devouring Nemesis, feeding as a hungry lion upon this ruck of wooden provender and this wealth of human life.*[14]

The tenements began dying in large numbers about a third of the way into the present century, as model housing came in: the Amalgamated Houses of Grand Street in 1930, the First Houses of Avenue A and East Third Street in 1935, and after World War II such ambitious undertakings as Stuyvesant Town and Peter Cooper Village, which between them supplanted the old Gas House district, and then the Al Smith, La Guardia, Baruch, Lilian Wald, and Jacob Riis Houses, which combined to redetermine the face of the Lower East Side waterfront.

After death, tenements might have a fate oddly congruent with their purpose in life. In Lower New York Bay, below the Verrazano Bridge, there is an artificial ledge known as New Grounds, or Doorknob Grounds, made up from the wreckage of tenements. As Joseph Mitchell described it in 1951:

> There are bricks and brownstone blocks and plaster and broken glass from hundreds upon hundreds of condemned tenements in the New Grounds. The ruins of the somber old red-brick houses in the Lung Block, which were torn down to make way for Knickerbocker Village, lie there. In the first half of the nineteenth century, these houses were occupied by well-to-do families; from around 1890 until around 1905, most of them were brothels for sailors; from around 1905 until they were torn down, in 1933, they were rented to the poorest of the poor, and the tuberculosis death rate was higher in that block than in any block in the city. All the organisms that grow on wrecks grow on the hills of rubble and rubbish in [. . .] the New Grounds.[15]

Such organisms, Mitchell points out, are particularly attractive to fish, which makes New Grounds an especially rich fishing site. Even in the extreme of dereliction, the tenement continues as a spawning ground. The most hostile environment proves the most fecund: having nurtured humans, causes, stray cats, bacilli, it now breeds bluefish and fluke, all in the soil of decay.

3 · STREETS

IT HAS BEEN NOTED THAT AL-
THOUGH NEW YORK ENVISAGED IT-
SELF EARLY, AND VERY PROPERLY, AS
A GREAT HARBOR, ITS AMBITION AS
a city lagged some steps behind. In consequence of this, it was for the most part meanly
proportioned. There was a distinct absence
of grand boulevards and parkways in the
original plans, and even the major thoroughfares were essentially corridors, their purpose
not to lead anywhere in particular so much
as to house the maximum in cubic bulk along
both sides. They were, of course, crowded
down the middle and along their walks as
well; a heavy concentration of wheeled and
pedestrian traffic has been constant for two
hundred years.

Until automobile traffic in the current century necessitated the widening of streets and
the gradual introduction of macadam surfac-

ing, sidewalks tended to be exceptionally broad on avenues and major cross streets, and the streets themselves were cobbled, in a hierarchy of surfaces that ran from the rutted brick-like blocks of the lesser concourses to the Russ pavement used on the most important arteries. Russ pavement was an expensive innovation of the mid-nineteenth century consisting of granite blocks set on a bed of cobblestones and cement. As with most such municipal improvements, it was first laid on Broadway adjacent to City Hall, and gradually came to cover the rest of that thoroughfare. Even this elaborate preparation, however, was not immune to the many deficiencies of the road surface in the era of block paving. The stones wore away at their edges, causing the hard wheels of carts and carriages to jounce, making for incessant rattle and din. In 1844 Edgar Allan Poe was complaining of cobblestones that "a more ingenious contrivance for driving men mad through sheer noise, was undoubtedly never invented," and he went on to plead the case for "stereatomic" wooden pavement, consisting of boards marinated in corrosive sublimate so as to produce "metallic hardness and texture," the ideal in "cheapness, freedom from noise, ease of cleaning, pleasantness to the hoof . . ."[1] His proposal does not appear to have been seriously considered.

Traffic, as well as being dense, was chaotic and completely unregulated. Broadway was quite unmanageable well before the middle of the nineteenth century; it was the central avenue of commerce and fashion as well as the most direct route between the Battery and important uptown locations. Thus, it was plied by every sort of truck, wagon, cart, and coach, although the bulk of traffic was made up of the all-purpose two-wheeled delivery carts driven by white-smocked carmen that were the terror of all. The function of the police was to untangle the mess when flow came to a dead halt, to quell right-of-way disputes with the aid of their clubs, and, quite literally, to help old ladies across the street. The very idea of traffic regulation is a comparatively recent development. In 1902 alternating cross traffic was established at major intersections, starting on Fifth Avenue, and this was followed in 1905 by a rotary plan for Columbus Circle, and in 1906 by pedestrian "isles of safety" at the more hazardous crossings; all these innovations were viewed as revolutionary undertakings. One-way streets started coming in gradually in the early 1910s, and traffic lights in the twenties, but it would take many more decades for either phenomenon to be widely established.

The major victims of the primeval condition of traffic were the horses, who were beaten, ridden to exhaustion, trampled upon by each other, and left to die at the curbs. The Society for the Prevention of Cruelty to Animals and the Horse Aid Society were both formed to try to stem the appalling abuse of dray animals and to provide them with some very basic amenities, such as watering stations. Besides dying inconveniently, horses added to the squalor of the streets by their excretions. One estimate from the turn of the century posited an average of 2.5 million pounds of manure and 60,000 gallons of urine on the streets every day. In 1895 Colonel George E. Waring was brought to the city from Rhode Island to manage the cleaning up of the streets, and he began by ridding the city of horse carts left out overnight, making it a law that horses be lodged in livery stables. He, furthermore, tackled the problem of sweeping, which had formerly been done on an irregular basis by a ragtag army of the unemployed or, in wealthier districts, by privately hired cleaners, by establishing the Street Cleaning Department, a disciplined corps with an operetta-military look involving white uniforms, pith helmets, and wheeled carts. Photographs of slum streets before the advent of Waring show a scarcely credible accumulation of refuse, piled up to a foot or two high. Waring even seems to have managed the city's hibernal cloaca of blackened snow, a remarkable feat before motor-driven plows. The snow was packed into trucks and unloaded directly into the rivers. The horse carcasses were sold to glue factories; most of the manure was sold for fertilizer. The remaining refuse was sent to dumps along the waterfront, where it was picked over by rag dealers who salvaged any article conceivably fit for reuse. At the time, this could take in virtually everything, not excepting ashes and bones.

For some years the congestion in the streets was paralleled by congestion overhead. The telephone was introduced to New York City in 1877, with 252 subscribers listed in the first directory, and the first exchange opened on Nassau Street in 1879. Within a few years, however, the new device was so popular that, combined with the telegraph and the increasing presence of electric lighting, it created a city dense with poles hung with as many as twenty-five crosspieces, from which wires were garlanded in an unbelievable profusion. The situation was so bad that all above-ground wires were banned in 1884, even though subterranean conduits were not laid until 1886; and even so the law was generally ignored. Then the great blizzard of 1888 toppled poles and broke wires. All cables were buried the following year.

Until then, telegraph wires had even stretched across the river, the ones leading to New Jersey departing the Manhattan shore at Fifty-ninth Street and extending straight to Weehawken. At the time, this was some distance from the city's commercial waterfront. In the last decades of the nineteenth century, twenty-two miles of docks fanned along Manhattan's bottom and sides, approximately seventy piers on each of the rivers. The North River side ran up to Little West Twelfth Street, until the increasing volume of transatlantic shipping, in concert with the growth of the city, extended the line up to Fifty-ninth Street, where it was continued by several additional miles of railroad wharves. On this front the transatlantic vessels were joined by mercantile and passenger-carrying steamers, by the oyster trade, and by ferries and railroad barges that ran to New Jersey. The East River front, which at this period extended up to Eleventh Street, provided for sailing ships, coal barges, floating docks, and the canal barges which plied from the Erie to the Gowanus and on which whole families lived, as well as the numerous ferry lines to Brooklyn. There were more than a dozen of these before the bridges began to be built, and the last line, to Greenpoint, was not eliminated until the La Guardia administration. New York never had a particularly modern or well-organized waterfront, its piers being for the most part wooden, irregular, and in various states of dilapidation. The streets near the water were usually among the dirtiest and most vice-ridden as well, so it is not surprising that

waterside residence was distinctly unfashionable during the century
and a half of New York's maritime peak years. Fifth Avenue was, after
all, the farthest one could get from either river.

Stagecoaches were the first means of inland public transportation,
running up the Boston Post Road and the Bloomingdale Road, connecting the lower city with its dependent hamlets. From these evolved
the Broadway omnibuses, the first form of mass transit, celebrated by
Whitman: "The Yellow-birds, the Red-birds, the original Broadway,
the Fourth Avenue, the Knickerbocker, and a dozen others . . ."[2] These
flourished all over downtown until the advent of the streetcar, after
which they remained solely on Broadway, where merchants and property owners held out against any transport innovations. The department-store tycoon A. T. Stewart declared himself willing to spend
$1 million to insure against the development of a Broadway streetcar
line and its hypothetical attendant dirt, vice, and overcrowding. Broadway gave way to progress by the 1890s, however, and at the century's
turn the omnibus was relegated to service as a tourist attraction and
patrician gesture along Fifth Avenue. The streetcar itself developed as
a refinement of the street railway, which in turn made its debut on
Fourth Avenue in 1831. The New York and Harlem Railway began at
Twenty-third Street, inched its way to Yorkville, then Harlem, and
down to Chambers Street within a few years. Complaints of noise
and fracas were not slow in coming, however, even for this genteel
and lumbering string of adapted stagecoaches, and before long, they
had ceased running south of Forty-second Street. By the latter half of
the century they had become the New York Central and by 1910 it ran
underground as far as Harlem. The streetcars got around the law
prohibiting engines below Forty-second Street by being horse-drawn,
and so they remained until the belated local introduction of cables,
which on some lines did not occur until 1917.

The first elevated railroad was experimentally established by Charles
Harvey in 1867, along Greenwich Street between the Battery and
Twenty-ninth Street. This system, consisting of small cars drawn on
a wire rope by a stationary engine, was doomed to failure by its expense,

inefficiency, noise, and widely rumored danger. The company folded in 1870. Interest was revived some five years later when the influence of the Tweed Ring obtained variances to permit the use of locomotives, and in 1879 a system was begun that consisted of four lines. The New York Elevated Railroad ran tracks along Second and Sixth Avenues; the Metropolitan Elevated Railway extended Harvey's line up Ninth and opened another on Third Avenue.

The elevated trains were enormously popular: they nearly halved the transit time of the horsecars, and they had the virtue of being well ventilated. At least, this was true at night; during commuting hours, conductors had a reputation for packing the cars to bursting before allowing the train to leave a station. Their placement at third-story height received mixed notices. Passengers enjoyed the opportunity to peer in, feasting their eyes on endless rows of tableaux vivants featuring men in undershirts and women in housedresses, but at the same time this feature made such rooms distinctly harder to let out. (The wag Wilson Mizener was once given a hotel room that had an El line running directly outside it. He angrily phoned the desk: "What time does this goddamn room get to Chicago?") On the other hand, perhaps third-story occupancy did have its dubious pleasures, if one is to believe the 1882 *Police Gazette* illustration entitled "Shooting at the Elevated," which shows a soubrette in a hotel room aiming a revolver out the window. The train would certainly not have been very difficult to hit, particularly if it was one of the El lines of the New York company, which ran on separate pillars down either side of the street, hanging over the sidewalk. The Metropolitan lines, by contrast, ran their tracks together in the avenue's middle, supported by open elliptic arch girders, with the exception of the Third Avenue's stretch on the Bowery.

The El quickly became a landmark and a tourist attraction, its most picturesque or characteristic spots recorded as standard views on postcards of the early 1900s: the Bowery looking north, as seen from the Grand Street station by day or by night, taking in streetcars and delivery wagons in profusion in the portion of the street exposed between the tracks, as well as signs advertising theaters, dime museums, and jewelry concerns; the dramatic convergence of the Second and Third Avenue lines at Chatham Square, their tracks briefly double-decked; the point where the uptown and downtown Third Avenue tracks joined sweepingly together, just in front of Cooper Union; the high curved trestle between Ninth and Tenth Avenues at 110th Street, admired by de Lesseps himself; the dizzying double curve at Coenties Slip. The voyeuristic opportunity afforded by the El could be taken as a particularly uplifting anthropological sightseeing experience, as attested by two characters in Howells's *A Hazard of New Fortunes*:

> She . . . said that the night transit was even more interesting than the day, and that the fleeting intimacy you formed with people in second- and third-floor interiors, while all the usual street life went on underneath, had a domestic intensity mixed with a perfect repose that was the last effect of good society with all its security and exclusiveness. He said it was better than the theater, of which it reminded him, to see those people through their windows: a family party of workfolk at a late tea, some of the men in their shirtsleeves; a woman sewing by a lamp; a mother laying her child in its cradle; a man with his head fallen on his hands upon a table; a girl and her lover leaning over the windowsill together. What suggestion! What drama! What infinite interest![3]

The human cargo of the trains themselves offered a spectacle no less edifying:

> He found the variety of people in the car as unfailingly entertaining as ever. He rather preferred the East Side to the West Side lines, because they offered more nationalities, characters, and conditions to his inspection. They draw not only from the uptown American region, but from all the vast hive of populations swarming between them and the East River.

The Thalia Theater and the Atlantic Garden, seen over the El tracks near the present-day Manhattan Bridge entrance

The Second Avenue El, photographed not long after its opening on a random stretch of tenement blocks, actually near Seventy-fourth Street

Before George Waring's tenure in the Sanitation
Department. Varick Street, photographed by Riis, with a
typical four-foot accumulation of offal in the gutter

During Waring's reign: snow removal on Longacre Square in
the blizzard of 1899. Photograph by Byron

*[. . . T]he East offered him continual entertainment . . . For
short distances the lowest poverty, the hardest pressed labor
must walk; but March never entered a car without encoun-
tering some interesting shape of shabby adversity, which is
almost always of foreign birth.*[4]

The El was democratic in a way that no other means of transport
had been: higher-priced luxury streetcars ran on Third Avenue for
many years, and for a while the Sixth Avenue surface line even maintained Jim Crow wagons. The El mixed everybody up together; it is
clear from context, for example, that Howells's hero, a magazine editor
who could certainly afford to take cabs, actually preferred the Elevated
as a means of transport and not merely as entertainment. When the
lines were dismantled between 1940 and 1955, the city was deprived
of a major portion of its transit system that was never quite replaced,
not to mention that it was denied the sight of the cheerfully eccentric
El stations, little pitch-roofed wooden cabins invariably likened to
Swiss chalets.

The notion of an underground railway had been bruited about since
the Civil War and given elaboration in A. P. Robinson's impressively
detailed plan of 1864. The charter plan for the company that was to
build the subway was defeated in the state senate, however, and it was
not until 1870 that a prototype was built. Unlike Robinson's conception,
which bore some resemblance to a conventional railroad, having been
modeled on the London Underground, this system, devised and built
by Alfred Ely Beach, was based on the ingenious but ultimately im-
practicable notion of pneumatic power. The tunnel was eight feet in
diameter, and it stretched along Broadway from Warren Street to a
little below Murray; cars were propelled by an air machine, like a giant
version of the pneumatic-tube system then in use as an alternative to
local mail and still employed as an intramural means of communication
in older department stores. Although Beach insisted his method would
be capable of moving 20,000 passengers per hour each way, the plan
fizzled. Various other designs were discussed over the following

quarter-century, including one for an "Arcade railway" that would have opened a lower level of shops along the cutting through which the trains ran, the whole being roofed over with glass. The reason for the long delay between initial proposals and ultimate execution had less to do with a shortage of ideas or of engineers than with the issue of ownership, particularly in the tangled web of patronage scandals bequeathed the city by the Tweed Ring. In 1894, the state legislature passed the (Second) Rapid Transit Act, which established public ownership and created a Board of Commissioners; this cleared the way in principle, but matters of contract and financing held up work for another seven years. Construction of the first subway line, the portion of what is now the Lexington Avenue line from the Battery to Forty-second Street, with a hook over to Times Square, finally began in 1901 and was completed in 1904, a full forty years after the first moves were made. Additional lines were built between 1908 (the Brooklyn extension) and the 1920s and thirties (in the outer boroughs and to replace some elevated service). By World War I, Manhattan was serviced within and without by a wide range of public transportation: several kinds of streetcars, elevated trains, subways, as well as horse-drawn and motorized cabs, long-distance railroad trains, ferryboats, steamships, and, within a few years, air-shuttle services to shore points on Long Island and in New Jersey. By then, the streetcar system alone was so well realized and interlinked that one could ride far out into the Long Island, Westchester, and New Jersey suburbs at minimal cost. Nothing remotely comparable exists today.

As the city grew through the course of the nineteenth century, it became a babel of competing voices. There was none of the gradual layering, the slow accretion of traditional identities in certain quarters, certain streets, certain habits of commerce and residence that European cities had the leisure to develop. New York did develop traditions, marked neighborhoods, rings of power, but it did so almost instantaneously, almost by fiat, and those habits and rituals and associations were all subject to immediate change. The speed of change was ruthless, but it was more a promise than a threat. Only the upper social bracket felt discomfited, not that the lack of stability caused them actual physical hardship, but it was such a chore to stay ahead of the current. High society was constantly winnowing itself, restricting admission, attempting to enforce ever more specific rules of conduct, criteria ever more difficult to meet. The social arbiter Ward McAllister decreed that persons with actual professions (doctors, lawyers, editors, artists) would not be encouraged by society, that even the most eminent would be invited only on New Year's Day; eventually, he limited society to the now-proverbial four hundred persons (the number who could fit comfortably in Mrs. Vanderbilt's ballroom). Attempting to be continuously on the beachhead of social movement, Delmonico's changed its venue six times in fifty years. At the lower end of the scale, the very poorest were cut off from the flux by poverty, by linguistic handicap, by social patterns that had migrated from the Old World with the group: family relations, trades, hierarchies, traditions of patronage. Such restrictions might last only a generation, however; children attended school or went to work, learned English there and on the street, were everywhere subject to the pressure of assimilation. Soon they might Americanize their names (if that had not already been done without their consent at Ellis Island), leave the family, the neighborhood, become forward-looking and progress-minded, plan to join the millionaires' club.

Between the very rich and the very poor was a large class of people who, while disparate in income and culture, shared a belief in their potential material improvement. The more idealistic among them applied this belief to a whole class, to the entire nation; others became gangsters, slumlords, profiteers. All were engaged in a struggle to be heard, whether this meant to be respected and followed, to have their services engaged or their business patronized. All were attempting to attract attention, to shout each other down. Because of this, New York became a riot of texts, a forest of signs. On the streets hardly any surface existed but that it was thought of as ground for conveying a message. The shacks of the very poorest squatters were virtually the only exception, being the only structures in the city where basic function and availability of materials overwhelmed any other considerations. All other buildings were signs or vehicles for signs, not excepting the dwellings of the upper class, which advertised the taste, learning, and cosmopolitanism of their owners in a frenzy of eclectic style that attempted to gather and harness all the glories of the European past.

That kind of architectural reference filtered down from the houses of the rich in the 1870s and eighties and before long, as we have seen, affected tenements, saloons, warehouses, factories. Gradually, every building became scrolled and ornamented, adorned with crenellations, bas-reliefs, mosaics. An army of immigrant laborers, inexpensive to hire and schooled in the older trades, went to work fabricating terracotta highlights, miniature statuary, small masterpieces of carving, molding, stonemasonry. Cast iron, first tried out as a building material in the 1850s, began to take hold in the 1870s, and massive Palladian temples went up along the downtown avenues to house jobbers, underwriters, import-exporters. Lack of ornamentation became an admission of poverty and therefore shame, so no railing lacked its vegetal curves, no wooden storefront went up without its carved false columns and functionless entablatures, no sign lettering was complete without loops and curlicues and gold paint.

In the street, the buildings were aggressively lined up side by side, each one's details yelling for notice. The white façade with arched windows and decorative brickwork laid out in Gothic verticals might house an oyster saloon on the ground floor, a "painless" dentist upstairs, and a manufacturer of chromolithographs on the top. Next door, a four-story fantasia of uneasily combined rococo and Middle Eastern ornamentation might be home to three floors' worth of patent-medicine wholesalers, with a tobacconist installed on the street level. The look of the buildings did not bear any particular relation to what went on inside them, beyond attesting in a vague way to the aesthetic ideals of the tenants and, more important perhaps, the determination to outflourish any other buildings in view.

Since buildings were of varying sizes, the taller edifices would present blank surfaces on their sides, left for the most part windowless in anticipation of yet taller structures flanking them in the future. Such empty stretches could not be left entirely devoid of function, so they were let out as signboards, the signs being painted directly onto the brick. The signs might indeed pertain to the nature of the building's occupants, listing in illuminated script the sixteen different cloak-and-suiters or photographers or song publishers located within, or they might advertise biscuits or soap or nerve tonics made elsewhere. On the façades of buildings would be more signs, painted boards thrown up against and further populating the confusion of pillars and trefoils and scallops. By the 1890s the profusion of signs had become such that a legal height of two feet was imposed. Commercial tenants of earlier decades had painted their names and specialties right onto the fronts of buildings, then plain enough to hold a good deal of text, so that a dry-goods jobber might list his complete inventory in the interstices between the windows and the floors of a four-story loft structure. This did not accord with the pictorial ideals of the fin de siècle, which preferred seemly frippery to plain statement, although the law was probably intended to prevent one osteopath from taking undue advantage of another by monopolizing the frontage. In any event, an 1892 inventory of commercial signs reveals that what advertisers were denied in height they made up in length: the prize was taken by the "Mechanico Therapeutic and Orthopedic Zander Institute," whose placard stretched 128 feet.

The same survey cites two Broadway businesses, a clothier and an "electric belt" doctor, who put up portraits of each of their firm members in the spaces between windows. Around that time, black-and-gold was becoming the favored combination for sign-painting, over black and white; photographers generally affected logotypes in script (the "signature" of the artist); tavern signs were often supplied by breweries and those of dry-goods stores by makers of collars and cuffs. The main purpose of that inventory, published in *The New York Times*, was to record the surviving "old-style" signs, which still existed in profusion; a new era of advertising paid homage to its ancestry. These were emblematic devices hung perpendicular to a building's façade, like English pub signs, and their language of images drew on a tradition stretching back to the Middle Ages: druggists featured mortars and pestles; shoemakers, gilt boots; hatters, gilt hats; opticians, enormous eyeglasses; sporting-goods dealers, huge guns; locksmiths, keys or saws; tobacconists, meerschaums; wine merchants, demijohns. A cutter would display great scissors; a knitter, a stocking; a sausagemaker, a wurst; a boating supplier, a wheel; an art supplier, a palette; a paint supplier, a pyramid of differently colored barrels. There were cameras for photographers; trumpets, French horns, or violins for musical-instrument vendors; large gilt teeth for dentists; beer steins for saloons; huge rattan sticks for caners; stuffed bears for furriers; tombstones for undertakers. The beehive embellished many banks; the Indian most cigar stores; the three gilt balls of the Medici family crest indicated pawnbrokers, the blue-and-white-striped pole barbershops, the red-and-white-striped globe oyster houses.

In the 1890s, advertising was in flower, taking new and unusual forms, beginning the invasion of the subconscious that was to attain full force in the following century. For some decades, posters were becoming increasingly prominent, getting larger as printing processes developed, appearing on every unoccupied surface. "Belles-lettres in signboards," the novelist Rupert Hughes called them, "romances set up so that he who runs may read, and stop running." Posters appeared on the fences around vacant lots, on the fronts of condemned buildings, on construction hoardings, garbage cans, and ash barrels, even curb-stones and flagpoles. They advertised the whole range of locally avail-able goods and services, as well as theatrical productions, dime museums, electoral campaigns greater and lesser, the outings and pic-nics of chowder clubs and local Tammany fiefdoms, policemen's and firemen's balls, parades. The transport stages had merely featured landscapes painted on their sides, just as moving vans traditionally displayed tableaux from American history, but the construction of the elevated lines opened the way to postering on platforms and in the cars. Color processes were becoming more sophisticated, and image began competing with text. There were teaser campaigns, such as the 1895 series which began with posters announcing "He Is Coming," followed by others asking "Who Is He?"; the whole thing turned out merely to be heralding the appearance of the Hungarian gypsy bandleader Lajos Munczi at the Eden Musée on Twenty-third Street. In the nineties, there was a vogue for fake events, as described by a contemporary:

> *Crowds lining the streets waiting for processions that seemed always late in starting, were given false alarms—"here they come"—by cavalcades of horses which turned out to be drawing vehicles rigged up by safe-makers and other firms. There were also small independent business parades, such as that of a string of Mexicans with pack-laden mules, arranged by the makers of a blood-purifying vegetable compound.*[5]

This trend, and probably most of the others as well, went back to the master of manipulative advertising, P. T. Barnum, who had invented "bulletin wagons," ambulatory hoardings that carried posters for druggists, clothiers, and theaters, as well as for his museum. Among the first of the stunts he contrived to draw attention to his establishment was having an unknown idler make a circuit around the intersection of Ann Street and Broadway, laying down one brick here, one brick there, then on the next pass taking them up again, in between turns entering the museum and walking very slowly through the exhibits. A curious crowd gathered and followed him in, paying admission for the privilege. Barnum's other well-known venues, including the wedding of Colonel Tom Thumb and Lavinia Warren at Grace Church, and the hugely successful American debut of the hitherto unknown Swedish singer Jenny Lind, who was advertised more on the basis of her virtue than of her talent, were masterpieces of something that went beyond advertising and approached conceptual art. While Barnum, indisputably, set out to make money first and foremost, and succeeded in making a great deal of it, he managed to create a new kind of commerce in which product and advertisement were inseparable, often virtually the same thing. Barnum's autobiography, originally *The Life of P. T. Barnum Written by Himself* (1855), and later *Struggles and Triumphs*, was an advertisement not only for himself but also for itself, combining the entertainment, the pitchman's speech promoting it, and the moral derived afterward. He made quite a remunerative trade out of that one book, employing his own teams of salesmen to peddle it door to door in the hinterlands, starting with the second edition of 1869, and periodically adding and subtracting chapters, so that the tome could be sold again as an entirely new version. Barnum embodied a unique combination of the showman, the preacher, the con artist, the speculator, and the politician, the epitome of his era and a model for future generations.

By the early nineteenth century New York was primarily a marketplace. Despite the prevalent pieties about the virtues of home life, only the few streets inhabited by the upper bourgeoisie were solely residential, and these often just temporarily so. The great poem of display—to borrow Balzac's phrase—chanted its many-colored strophes from the Battery to City Hall Park, from the vestry of Trinity to the dives of Cherry Hill, from the homesteads of Greenwich Village to the waysides of the Bloomingdale Road. Formal markets began to be established: Washington Market in 1813, Fulton Market in 1821, Tompkins Market in 1828, and then Catherine, Union, Clinton, Franklin, Centre, Gansevoort, and the great Wallabout Market in Brooklyn, to be followed by private and railroad markets and others that rose and fell with the tides of development. Most of these combined wholesale and retail operations, but even so, they were not adequate to the trade of the slums and were augmented by pushcart markets, large semi-permanent ones on Rivington Street, on Orchard Street, on Mulberry, on Third Avenue in Harlem, on First Avenue both uptown and downtown, on Grand and Hester Streets, on Tenth Avenue in Hell's Kitchen: all the major concentrations of the poor.

But the bulk of the pushcart traffic did not operate in designated markets. Pushcart operators could not afford shop rental, so they invested in wagons equivalent to large wheelbarrows, got up at two or four to buy their stocks at the legitimate markets, and set up at strategic points, whether residential streets or areas of heavy pedestrian flow such as those near train stations, only to suffer the inconvenience of being repeatedly moved along by the police. Typically, the vendors were harassed by the cops even while guides to the city were citing them as points of color and attractive conveniences. The key to this paradox lay, naturally, in the inability of itinerant tradesmen to pay very much in the way of graft.

In spite of this, virtually every kind of inexpensive article was offered for sale on the streets. This trade went on without benefit of advertising, obviously; to orient the expectations of the clientele, certain formal manners had to be initiated, kept up, and gradually altered with the times, like a host of miniature and constantly fluctuating traditions— cries, costumes, locations, the age or sex or race of the vendor, each an indication of what was for sale. At first these signs borrowed from older European models. Up to the Civil War the city was famous for its street cries, which, like those of Dickens's London, made their way into illustrated handbooks and as motifs on kerchiefs and crockery. There was the clam seller: "Here's clams, here's clams, here's clams today / They lately came from Rockaway / They're good to roast, they're good to fry / They're good to make a clam-pot pie / Here they go!" There were chimney sweepers ("Sweep o, sweep o") and ragmen ("Rags, rags, any old rags" or "Old clo', old clo', any old clo' "). Most celebrated were the hot-corn vendors ("Hot corn, hot corn, here's your lily-white hot corn / Hot corn, all hot, just came out of the boiling pot"), who were almost always young girls and sold their wares from baby carriages and children's wagons. The hot-corn girl, barefoot and dressed in layers of calico rags, attained a certain romantic status as the semi-mythic heroine of sentimental tales and popular ballads, representing a middle-class idealization of poverty. She stood for virtuous striving not unmixed with a sexy aura of availability, a sort of bowdlerized prostitution, and the trade prospered accordingly. Not that the hot-corn girl herself stood to profit, for the commerce also resembled prostitution in that it was controlled behind the scenes by husbands and ponces.[6] It was a perfectly legal hustle that sold roasting ears to men who fancied they were buying something more.

The wares sold by street criers give a fair indication of the sorts of comestibles most enjoyed at mid-century, the range of fast food of the time: oysters, fish, buns, hot spiced gingerbread, strawberries, ice cream, baked pears, a wholesome-sounding list. The criers occasioned much sentimentalizing and few complaints, although the cantankerous Poe typically registered his objections:

> *How often does it happen that where two individuals are*
> *transacting business of vital importance, where fate hangs*
> *upon every syllable and upon every moment—how frequently*
> *does it occur that all conversation is delayed, for five or even*
> *ten minutes at a time, until these devils'-triangles [charcoal*
> *wagons] have got out of hearing, or until the leathern*
> *throats of the clam-and-cat-fish vendors have been hallooed,*
> *and shrieked, and yelled, into a temporary hoarseness and*
> *silence!*[7]

Competition with the increasing general noise level of the city is presumably what drove the criers out of business, as little is heard from them after about 1860, with the notable exception of their heirs, the newsboys.

Meanwhile, other readily identifiable customs were being developed by street vendors. Song sellers displayed penny ballads on strings hung from the railing around City Hall Park, until the fence was removed, under orders from Boss Tweed. Strawmen clothed their horses' legs in trousers and their bodies in mosquito netting. Ragpickers hung rows of bells on their pushcarts, jangling them by agitating the handles as they pushed. Scissor and knife grinders blew bugles to announce themselves. Old-clothes men wore towering piles of hats. Selling became minutely particularized in the middle nineteenth century, as commercial turf lines were drawn up by various groups. As of the 1880s, for example: Irishwomen (popularly identified as smoking pipes) sold apples, "George Washington pie,"[8] St.-John's-bread, and flat ginger-bread cakes called "bolivars"; Chinese men sold candy and cigars. Men in general sold tobacco, socks, suspenders, hose, yarn, and gloves. Women sold most of the food, although, after the era of the hot-corn girl, roasted ears were almost always sold by black men. Boys sold ties, pocketbooks, pocketbook straps, and photographs. Little girls sold matches, toothpicks, songs, and flowers. After the Civil War, lame soldiers held the monopoly on shoestrings, and they also sold ties and a lesser rank of books and magazines. Italians dispensed ice cream; Germans dealt in sausages.

Locations for vendors became fixed as well: toys were sold just above Canal Street; newsstands at the time were collected in the financial district and around City Hall and the ferry stations; the Chinese cigar vendors worked outside major hotels, as did dog and bird men. In residential areas there were, in addition, itinerant umbrella menders, tinkers, whitewashers, washtub menders, glaziers, paviors, hod car-riers, excrement carriers, odd-job men identifiable by their square paper caps. Ballad vendors and encyclopedia salesmen likewise worked the doors. In the slums there were public letter and visiting-card writers. Orange vendors sold their wares in bundles hung from yokes. Street photographers plied the main arteries with samples of their work mounted on boards. Hackmen waited at stands outside train and ferry stations, calling "Keb, keb, keb." Newsboys were everywhere, fighting for territory, hitching rides on horsecars, yelling "Extra!"

In the Bowery, Chatham Square, and the nearby region, another mercantile style prevailed. Many of the shops were run by "cheap Johns" selling shoddy goods, but even the more respectable merchants behaved with frenzied aggressiveness. In contrast with shopkeepers anywhere else in the city, they displayed the bulk of their stock in stalls and boxes on the sidewalk in front, and they were constantly putting on fire sales that had not been occasioned by fire and going-out-of-business sales that might go on for years at a stretch. The local haberdashers were probably the champions of combative merchandising, relying as they did on "pullers-in" to hook innocent passersby and not let them go until they had made a purchase. The suckers were subjected to a rapid-fire hard sell—"It fits like der paper on der vall," as the fitter gathered the slack behind the customer's back and displayed a head-on mirror view—loaded up with as many items of a wardrobe as possible, regardless of whether they matched or fit, and then separated from their money. The clothes were usually made of rag ends in dubious sweatshops and not infrequently fell apart as soon as the customer got home.[9] In the Bowery's laboratory of low-level greed the study of suckers was refined daily. The "Peter Funk" auctioneers specialized in bait-and-switch routines, in auctioning off, say, a dozen socks for a dollar, which the mark would discover meant a dollar apiece. Blind auctions of unredeemed pledges were another favorite; suckers would let their imaginations ascribe value to pawn tickets just because they were pawn tickets, but they would invariably turn out to redeem tin watches or phony stock certificates.

Everything on the Bowery was loaded and short-counted. Even the pushcarts sold bad fruit, cutlery made of scrap that broke at first use, used ink bottles filled with water. In this atmosphere, creative salesmanship was everything, and sometimes the hustle was even more creative than it was fraudulent. The spiel, for example, may not have been conceived on the Bowery, but it was certainly refined there, as a rhetorical art that combined elements of the carny barker's routine and the preacher's harangue, the confidence man's patter and a sort of stream-of-consciousness poetry. In other ways, too, local advertising became a form of entertainment. The London and Liverpool Clothing Company, at Bowery and Hester, began by importing four constables from County Cork to pull in the Irish trade, and went on to use a live male model in the window, gotten up in the mode of the neighborhood swells of the nineties (loud plaid suit, pearl-gray derby, patent-leather shoes, rattan stick), and then used even more theatrical setups as window displays: the magician's illusion of a woman sawn in half; a snow scene that featured a live black bear (who, unfortunately, ate the rock salt used for snow, became ill, and had to be removed).

The Bowery had its own economics and its own laws. The Sunday closing law, for example, was essentially defunct there as early as 1870, while it was still being enforced in other parts of town for decades afterward. There were also businesses that could hardly be found anywhere else: tattoo parlors, for instance, which flourished around Chatham Square until the 1950s, and black-eye fixers, who were essentially makeup artists, and whose ability to maintain sufficient trade to set themselves up in storefronts, while only occasionally keeping a second line in something more workaday like barbering, is a testament to the continuous violence of the neighborhood. For a century, the area was also virtually the only place where pawnshops could be found. The first were noted on Park Row around 1822, and they quickly spread through Catherine Street and East Broadway. Early on, laws were passed to regulate the industry, but they were seldom if ever enforced, so that, while legally a pawnbroker could charge a maximum annual interest of 25 percent on the value of a pledged article, the average broker extracted 10 percent a month, as well as additional fees for "storage." The pawnshops of the nineteenth century dealt not merely in watches and musical instruments but in a range of goods that included umbrellas, eyeglasses, coats, boots, shirts, handkerchiefs. Some brokers employed a scam that involved conspicuously dropping pawn tickets on the streets and then charging the marks a fee to see the ticketed item, which was never, needless to say, anything worthwhile. Some pawnbrokers doubled as fences, but not many, as the legitimate profession carried enough risks of its own. Most fences fronted as tradesmen in more innocent fields, such as groceries or furniture.

The lowest level of commerce was the rag trade. Ragpickers worked the city's ash heaps and garbage dumps and solicited door-to-door in residential areas, collecting unwanted, broken, or superannuated articles of every description. A ragman's den visited in the 1870s yielded up

bones, broken dishes, rags, bits of furniture, cinders, old tin,
useless lamps, decaying vegetables, ribbons, cloths, legless
chairs, and carrion, all mixed together and heaped up
nearly to the ceiling, leaving barely enough room for a bed
on the floor.[10]

Ragpickers either reconditioned and repaired items salvaged from the refuse or gathered and resold bulk items like newspapers, wood, bones, and tin back to industry.[11] They hawked wares on the streets or, if they were lucky and industrious enough, opened shops, and the slums were full of them until a blow was struck in the early twentieth century by the intrusion of organized charities, who centralized the old-clothes and second-hand furniture traffic. The antiques craze that hit gentrifying Greenwich Village just before World War I floated a number of junk-men, but a bit over a decade later the Depression overloaded the market with sellers. Barter markets sprang up in Harlem and on the Bowery, but the stakes were lower than ever. The cleaning-up of the Bowery, which had coincided with the start of World War I, had destroyed the city's major thieves' market, the Little Stock Exchange at Bowery and Bayard, where hot goods had been disposed of at extremely low prices, a bona-fide diamond (it was said) sometimes changing hands for a dollar. After that, such trade had no established location; the barter markets of the 1930s and later were more likely to deal in odd shoes.

Junkmen and ragpickers, however reduced their circumstances, are still tradesmen. It is their responsibility to maintain an inventory of some kind of stock, to obtain more of it, to guard it at night, to carry it to market, to talk it up, set prices, make change. There remained another commercial level below theirs, this one consisting of persons needing to do nothing but be ambulatory, in however rudimentary a fashion. These were the men (they were always men) who were used as vehicles for advertising, and who were known as sandwich men, because most of them wore signboards yoked front and back over their shoulders, which enclosed them like halves of a sandwich. The boards were not an absolute feature; the men sometimes wore signs affixed to their hats, and an enterprising tradesman might rig out his men in appropriate costumes, as trappers or Indians to promote a fur business, for example. This tradition began somewhere in the mists, probably just after the Civil War, and hit several peaks coinciding with periods of economic recession, from the depression of the 1870s to that of the 1930s. The status of sandwich man was universally understood to be the very lowest, undertaken solely by those so far gone with disease or alcoholism that they could do nothing else, unless hard times wiped out every other possible field of endeavor. Sandwich men were presumably invisible behind their signs, as their appearance could scarcely be thought conducive to trade. The irony was not lost on Theodore Dreiser:

> *To send forth an anaemic, hollow-eyed, gaunt-bodied man*
> *carrying the announcement of a good dinner, for instance.*
> *Imagine. Or a cure-all. Or a beauty powder. Or a good suit*
> *of clothes. Or a sound pair of shoes. And these with their*
> *toes or their naked bodies all but exposed to the world. An*
> *overcoatless man advertising a warm overcoat in winter.*
> *One from whom all and even the possibility of joy had fled,*
> *displaying a notice of joy in the shape of a sign for a dance-*
> *hall, a theater, a moving-picture even. The thick-witted*
> *thoughtlessness of the trade-vulgarian who could permit*
> *this!*[12]

Then again, if the miserable half went unnoticed as they lay wrapped in newspapers or as they trudged through the snow without hats or coats, they stood a slim chance of being visible behind a brightly colored signboard. They were thus reduced to competing with the architecture that likewise seemed primarily intended to support signs. In such a competition, the human being was fated to lose.

P A R T 2.

[· Sporting Life ·]

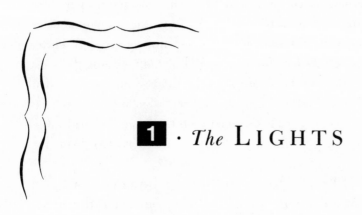

1 · *The* LIGHTS

MANHATTAN WAS A THEATER FROM THE FIRST. WHEN, EARLY ON, IT WAS A WALLED CITY, AND FURTHER SUR-ROUNDED BY A FOREST OF MASTS, IT enclosed in its ring a small universe. This enclosure is the model of cities as it is of theaters, as can be seen when one compares old representations of fortress cities and of Greek amphitheaters and later theaters like the Globe. In Manhattan, social stratification followed a course in which the waterfront and the area environs near it became undesirable, became like the galleries, while the dead center, Fifth Avenue, would be the orchestra stalls. What, then, would be the stage? There are two answers. One of them is contained in the image of the city as a theater, consisting of rings, loge, and parquet, in which there is no stage per se but where the audience is the object of its own contemplation. Manhattan has eternally been fascinated by itself, its pursuit of its own regard epitomized in hundreds of ways, from the numerous scale representations of the city built in the nineteenth century—E. Porter Belden's 20-foot-by-24-foot wooden model of 1845–46 was the most impressive[1]—to the fact that beatniks in the 1950s would refer to their territory in Villages West and East as the "Set." The other answer has to do with the street that runs diagonally up the island—Broadway—putting itself on display and carrying in its train its dark twin, the Bowery.

The duality of Broadway and anti-Broadway began in the mists of New York's theatrical history, around the end of the eighteenth century. It quickly came to stand for a class distinction, in regard both to money (cost of tickets, wages paid to actors, production budgets, structural and land values of theaters) and to a perceived idea of quality (art vs. entertainment, sometimes; at other times, merely the slick vs. the rough-cut). Broadway was the theater of the bourgeoisie, the standard, the temple, while the Bowery was the circus of the masses. The scenery-chewing productions of Shakespeare typical of the nineteenth century might be viewed by the press and by memoirists as art if they were produced on Broadway, as stunts if they played to the Bowery mechanics. When the Bowery finally folded as an entertainment venue just before World War I, Broadway nominally had the game all to itself, but actually the opposition merely changed its name and setting. There has consistently been some kind of dichotomy ever since: stage plays countered by moving pictures, the legitimate theater countered by vaudeville and burlesque, the native drama by ethnic drama, "big" theater by little theater, Broadway by Off-Broadway, Off-Broadway by Off-Off-Broadway. Although some of these contrasts may appear to be of an innocuously practical nature, each of them also exemplifies the assumption of the standard of official culture by one party and the challenge to that standard by another.

Oddly enough, the Broadway–Bowery polarity first came to light with the opponents playing each other's roles. Entertainment of the most popular sort was born on Broadway, in the form of the circus.

New York's first circus was a menagerie briefly set up, at some un-
specified date a few years after the Revolution, in the marshes above
the Collect Pond, near the present-day intersection of Broadway and
Broome. The first permanent circus was Pepe and Beschard's, which
opened at Broadway and Worth Street in 1808, and the second, which
ran for at least a decade, was West's, at Broadway's juncture with
Canal. Meanwhile, the city's first important theater was the Park,
opened in 1798 on Chatham Street, later known as Park Row, which
in the cosmology of Manhattan is, with Pearl Street, one of the two
southern extensions, physical and symbolic, of the Bowery.

The Park Theater was built on the model of the London stage, with
a repertoire that naturally ran heavily to Shakespeare, as well as featuring the work of such successful comic playwrights as Colly Cibber
and Richard Brinsley Sheridan. It was expensive for its time, with
prices up to fifty cents for pit seats and a dollar for boxes. On its
boards walked a collection of actors imported and domestic, many of
whose names are familiar even now: Junius Brutus Booth, Edwin
Forrest, Charles Kean, Ellen Tree, George Frederick Cooke, Thomas
S. Hamblin, Tyrone Power (great-grandfather of the movie star), Charlotte Cushman, the Wallacks, Henry and James William, and the Kem-
bles, Fanny and Charles. The Park was not merely the cynosure; for
years it had no competition at all. It may have been elite, but it was
scarcely exclusive, as the cheaper gallery seats filled up every evening
with the families of "mechanics" (this was the common term at the
time for working men). In those days, and for another couple of
decades, "le tout New York" would be literally that.

The Park set another trend by burning to the ground in 1820—ever
afterward, major New York theaters were to incinerate with alarming
and somewhat suspicious regularity (there were at least thirty-seven
major theater fires in New York in the nineteenth century). The Park
was soon rebuilt, but in 1848 burned again and was abandoned. In
the meantime, competition developed in the form of the Bowery Theater, a singularly robust institution which opened in 1826 at the corner
of Canal Street and, in spite of four devastating fires (1828, 1836, 1838,

1845), lasted more than a century. At the Bowery, more even than at the Park, the character of the New York stage was determined. The stars moved there gradually—Booth, Forrest, Kean, Hamblin—and were featured in the Shakespearean crowd-pleasers—*Lear, Othello, Hamlet, Richard III*—staged as stiff-legged oratorical displays interspersed with swordplay. Booth, increasingly a drunk, was noted with hilarious approval for his insistence on really fighting the staged duels, on at least one occasion refusing to die even though his part clearly called for it.

This approval came from a changing audience. By the 1830s the middle classes were making their way to Castle Garden, the former Castle Clinton at the Battery, and the following decade they began to go up to Broadway, to Tripler Hall, Niblo's, and Brougham's Lyceum Theater, among others. In the 1830s the Bowery Theater was a working-class entertainment, its arena recalled years later by Walt Whitman as

> *pack'd from ceiling to pit with its audience mainly of alert,*
> *well-dress'd, full-blooded young and middle-aged men, the*
> *best average of American-born mechanics—the emotional na-*
> *ture of the whole mass arous'd by the power and magnetism*
> *of as mighty mimes as ever trod the stage—the whole audito-*
> *rium, and what seeth'd in it, and flush'd from its faces and*
> *eyes, to me as much a part of the show as any—bursting*
> *forth in one of those long-kept-up tempests of hand-clapping*
> *peculiar to the Bowery—no dainty kid-glove business, but*
> *electric force and muscle from perhaps 2000 full-sinew'd*
> *men . . .*[2]

The pit, at least, was an exclusively male domain. Formerly (and again now) the second rank of seating (after the boxes) under its more formal designation of "orchestra" or "parquet," the pit at the Bowery and the other theaters on that street was among the cheapest areas, and it was a tumult. It was furnished with benches, backless and uncushioned, and regulars would save seats for their friends, so that the whole was

a close-packed carpet of toughs who would toss out unsuspecting intruders head-first. This audience alternated unpredictably between
rapt and critical attention to the stage business and utter lack of interest.
On holidays, for example, the play went on as mere background color
to the festivities taking place on the floor. Routinely the men, and boys
when they came of age, would chew tobacco and eat peanuts and throw
the shells at each other, but they would be just as likely to throw the
shells and whatever other impedimenta were lying at hand at the stage
if the play, staging, or interpretation met with their disapproval. Meanwhile, the "gallery gods," as the newsboys and young gang members
came to be known who sat in the upper tier as long as they were too
young or too poor to join the pit, threw pennies on the stage as a mark
of their displeasure. The women, children, and whole families seated
in the galleries were hardly more decorous. Apples, oranges, and ginger
beer were sold throughout the theater at all points of the show, and
families brought their own suppers. Foreign visitors were aghast to see
mothers of families gnawing bones up on the balconies and discarding
them over the sides, where they would bounce off the hats of the pit
audience. Mrs. Trollope, in her *Domestic Manners of the Americans*
(1832), particularly deplored the habit of those in the front ranks of
the galleries of dangling their boots over the edge; when word of her
disapproval got back to the Bowery, the men in the pit seats went on
the alert, and would loudly shout "Trollope!" or "Boots!" at offending
parties upstairs. The audiences were nothing if not interactive, whis-
tling, yelling, singing, stamping their feet, shouting "H'ist dat rag!"
if the curtain was slow in rising, loudly vocalizing their assessment of
the occurrences on stage.

"Awhile after 1840, the character of the Bowery . . . completely
changed," noted Whitman sadly. "Cheap prices and vulgar pro-
grammes came in." What happened is that the theater managers left
off programming their houses as if they were still addressing the mixed
and at least partly educated audiences of the 1820s and earlier, and
instead began consciously catering to the immigrant mechanics who
were their actual patrons. Nuance and drawing-room wit went by the

boards, and in their place came spectacle. Whitman himself mentions such pageants as *The Last Days of Pompeii* and *The Lion-Doom'd*, giant set-pieces that depended far more on the deployment of stage machinery than on acting or writing. They were the ancestors of colossal cinema, the pure show of great scale and violent motion that has been a twentieth-century staple mostly during periods of prosperity: everything from the original *Ben-Hur* and *Cabiria* to the applications of Cinerama and Sensurround. The financial scale of the 1840s must be kept in mind to appreciate fully the success of these spectacles. At a time when a very decent room and board might cost a single person $15 a week, *The Earthquake*, which featured rattling furniture, falling walls, and collapsing flats, grossed $8,000 in its first week; *The Last Days of Pompeii*, graced by more of the same plus an animated volcano, took in $10,000 for its initial week not long after. Even before there was any serious competition in the form of other comparable theaters on the street, the management of the Bowery Theater was struggling to top itself every few weeks. On the Fourth of July 1840 they introduced the first "tank drama," *The Pirates' Signal*. Tank dramas involved the use of a large pool of water, taking up most of the stage, on which were mobilized entire ships, rendered in miniature but large enough to hold a dozen actors. *The Pirates' Signal* featured one full-rigged ship; two weeks later *Yankees in China* opened, boasting two of them. The quest for eye-popping scale became ever more relentless. Soon there was a staging of *Richard III* in which most of the principals appeared on horseback; a *Battle of Waterloo* featured fifty horses and more than two hundred supernumeraries. Troupes of trained dogs began appearing in specially written plays, such as *The Butcher's Dog of Ghent*. In 1849 the managers of the Bowery hit on a new gimmick, one that was just as crowd-pleasing as the spectacles without costing nearly as much to produce: they engaged the well-known saloonkeeper, gang leader, and boxer Tom Hyer to appear in a play called *Tom and Jerry*, thereby making him the first actor to be employed as a consequence of non-theatrical celebrity, a move that was to have major

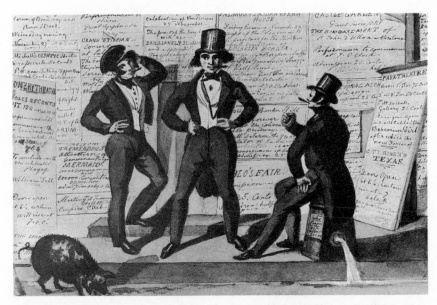

Soap-locks and butt-enders, probably cleaner and more dudish than their models, depicted by Nicolino Calyo, 1840s

The Bowery melodrama in its late phase, 1904

A dime-museum performer, photographed by Byron, 1897.
One can only surmise the nature of her act

The Grand Street Theater, featuring Jacob Adler as King
Lear. Mr. and Mrs. Adler can be seen standing by the door
farthest to the right in the colonnade. Photograph by Byron

repercussions in the future of Bowery drama and on the history of American entertainment in general.

It did not take long for the Bowery audiences of the 1830s and forties to be recognized abroad as conforming to a type. This was the Bowery Boy or (following the Irish pronunciation) B'hoy, the essence of the proletariat, of the "soap-locks, butt-enders, and subterraneans." The Bowery B'hoy, his essential figure distilled from a thousand variations, wore a red woolen shirt which buttoned on the side, a black or brightly colored silk cravat knotted around his neck, black broadcloth trousers either tucked into high-heeled boots or flaring bell-bottomed over them. He grew a tuft of whiskers on his chin, combed his hair straight forward toward the brow and glued it down with soap ("soap-locks"), and kept a cigar butt in his mouth at all times ("butt-enders"). (The "subterranean" moniker alluded to the radical Democrat Mike Walsh, whose Spartan Association defied Tammany Hall and the supporters of Martin Van Buren alike, and whose newspaper, *The Subterranean*, represented itself as the voice of "subterranean democracy.") On his head the b'hoy wore a plug hat, which his friends mashed down on his forehead by way of friendly greeting.

Around his neck the b'hoy wore a large gold or brass medallion bearing the number of his fire company. Nearly every "full-blooded" Bowery male, whether immigrant or native-born, laborer or artisan, belonged to a fire company. These volunteer organizations were para-political, para-fraternal entities, organized by neighborhood, by ancestry, by religion, by party registration. Like army divisions, they were formally numbered but were actually known by allusive nicknames: Big Six (famous for being Boss Tweed's company), Black Joke, Old Rock, Charter Oak, Americus, White Ghost, Shad Belly, Dry Bones, Red Rover, Hay Wagon, Bean Soup, Old Junk. They were fiercely competitive, racing each other to the scenes of conflagrations, now and then duking it out for the privilege of extinguishing the blaze and letting the unlucky building char and crumble as the fight raged on. Until the municipal fire service was established in 1865, however, they were the only firemen in town, and all chroniclers agree that what they lacked in professionalism they made up in enthusiasm.

The myth of the Bowery fireman was embodied by Mose, New York's own version of Paul Bunyan or Pecos Bill. Mose had his origin in a real person, Moses Humphreys, a *Sun* printer (or possibly a butcher) and a member of Number 40, Lady Washington Engine.[3] He was a huge man of fearsome attributes, but in 1838 he was bested in a company fight against Number 15 (Old Wreath of Roses) and subsequently disappeared, rumored thereafter to be operating a pool hall in Honolulu. Once he was gone, the real Mose could be replaced by Mose the legend. This paragon stood eight feet tall, possessed hands the size of hams and arms so long he could scratch his kneecap while standing erect. He could beat up his rivals with an uprooted tree or lamppost. Mose saved beleaguered ships by blowing his cigar smoke at their sails, drank whole drayloads of beer at one sitting, swam the Hudson in two strokes, jumped from Manhattan to Brooklyn in one bound, carried horsecars on his shoulders. Legend further has it that he personally so depleted the cherry trees of Cherry Hill and the mulberry trees of Mulberry Street that they disappeared. He came equipped with a sweetheart, Lize, who became the epitome of the Bowery Girl, or G'hal. The prototypical g'hal dressed in layers of multicolored calico, wore a heavily ornamented poke bonnet perched on the side of her head, bore a parasol in one hand, and swung the other hand free. She, too, sometimes smoked cigars.

The culture and the language of the b'hoys and g'hals was sometimes known as "flash." Many flash terms have since entered the language: bender, blarney, blow-out, chum, coppers (for policemen), jimmy (a crowbar), kicking the bucket, lark, pal, swell (as a noun), square, sponge (as a verb), swag, swell-head, spot (as in to notice or recognize). "Dust" was money; "mountain dew" was whiskey, particularly Scotch; to "peach" was to tell on or inform against. As the majority element and strongest force in the Bowery audience, the b'hoys began to have a real say in what was staged at the eponymous theater and its eventual rivals, voting with their feet for their favorite actors, who in the 1840s were Ned Forrest, Tom Hamblin, and John R. (Jack) Scott. In 1834 the Bowery put on the first play to feature its best customers as characters, *Beulah Spa, or Two of the B'hoys*, which one outside commentator dismissed as "a sop to the pit." In the late 1840s, however, the b'hoys really came into their own with the appearance of the first Mose drama, *A Glance at New York*, by Benjamin Baker, which was staged at the Olympia on the Bowery in February or March of 1848. The second, *New York As It Is*, followed at the Chatham in April. In these plays, New York's fascination with itself was first explicitly realized on the stage.

The man who received most of the credit for the Mose cycle was Edward Z. C. Judson, who wrote under the name Ned Buntline. As Buntline, he was one of the first and most prolific of the authors of dime novels, churning out hundreds of pulp romances, both Westerns and what might be called Easterns. As Judson, he was a prominent political thug, the adjutant of the gang leader and politico Isaiah Rynders. In January 1848 he published the first installment of what was eventually to be a five-volume colossus, *Mysteries and Miseries of New York: A Story of Real Life*. This repetitive, cliché-ridden saga, which was issued in magazine-sized sections twenty-five cents a pop, the last of which included a glossary of flash terminology, went on to sell a reputed one hundred thousand copies, and was followed by two equally voluminous sequels, *B'hoys of New York* (1849–50) and *G'hals of New York* (1850). The adventures of Mose, Lize, and their pal Sykesy were lifted directly for the stage from the novels, although Judson's biographer, Jay Monaghan, notes that theatrical demand outran Judson's inspiration, so that by the fourth and fifth volumes of the *Mysteries* he reversed the process and filched his plots from new theatrical sequels.

Onstage, Mose was incarnated by Frank Chanfrau, who ironically enough was the younger brother of Henry (Hen) Chanfrau, the very member of Old Wreath of Roses who had given the real Moses Humphreys his final ducking only five years earlier. Chanfrau first played Mose in a brief skit called *New York in 1848*, put on as part of a benefit program at Mitchell's Olympic Theater. He appeared on stage in full b'hoy regalia, and the audience, dumbfounded by this representation of themselves, received him with total silence. Then he took the cigar out of his mouth, spat, and said, "I ain't a-goin' to run wid dat mercheen no more!" By this he meant that he was quitting his fire company, but it was not the line's literal meaning that furnished its import. The New York stage historian T. Allston Brown reported:

> *Instantly there arose such a yell of recognition as had never been heard in the little house before. Pit and galleries joined in the outcry. It was renewed several times, and Mose was compelled to stand, shifting his coat from one arm to the other, bowing and waiting. Every man, woman and child recognized . . . all the distinctive external characteristics of the class.*[4]

The Mose cycle went on for years, and playwrights and producers were kept busy figuring out new variations, sending Mose to California and even to China in their efforts to disguise the essential monotony of the one-note plot, in which, invariably, a danger arose and Mose met it by beating somebody up, after which peace was restored. The fiction did little more than hold up a mirror to the most superficial aspects of Bowery life, but this in itself was so gratifying that no one questioned the lack of story or substance, except the responsible parties. Judson's pretext to the world at large was that his pulp epic somehow constituted a "moral crusade," a phrase meant to carry an implied leer, but the Mose series could not even be accused of raciness. What the plays and novels actually did was to shift the focus of representation from the noble and heroic, the exotic and bygone, to the swaggering, unashamed proletarian present.

Around the same time, another long-term fixture of the stage was being born, this one possessing even greater longevity and adaptability: the black-face minstrel show. The deep origins of this pantomime of racial caricature remain somewhat obscure, but as far as New York goes, it can be determined that at some point in the mid-1830s a man named T. D. Rice was appearing in a show at the Park Theater in which he was made up with burnt cork, played the banjo, and went by the sobriquet of Jim Crow. A decade or so later, one George Washington Dixon had an enduring hit with a song called "Old Zip Coon," the tune of which has survived to the present day, although as "Turkey in the Straw." This song, in its original form, was a standby and for years an icon of Americanism. During one of the several theater riots of the mid-nineteenth century, one at least superficially prompted by Irish resentment of the star status of English actors, the only way the house manager found to calm down the audience was to send out a singer, clutching Old Glory in each fist, to do a rendition of "Old Zip Coon." The first appearance of a minstrel show in New York, in the form that was to last nearly a century more, was in 1843, when the Virginia Minstrels, featuring Dan Emmett on fiddle and three other blackened white men on banjo, tambourine, and bones, appeared at the Branch Hotel on the Bowery and quickly moved to the more spacious Chatham Theater on Park Row. This same Dan Emmett went on to "develop" (which is to say, to adapt, collect, or some similar operation, rather than "write") the fateful song "Dixie" in 1859, as a member of the most famous minstrel troupe of all, that of Dan and Neil Bryant. Minstrelsy may have originated on a folk level somewhere down South, but it was in New York that it became professional entertainment, an unquestioned, unprotested, seemingly innocuous diversion. It should be noted that, while all this was going on, New York was hardly wanting for bona-fide African-American musical talent. Blacks, who throughout the early history of the city were present in large numbers and yet are scarcely mentioned by their contemporaries except when they figure at the center of some fracas, had provided the primary pool of musical virtuosity on the extra-professional level since the eighteenth century. Black performers seldom if ever appeared in formal stage shows before the Civil War, but black bands played in every Five Points dive and every Bowery resort that was not dominated by the Germans, who insisted on their own oom-pah outfits. Black bands played at dances, in concert saloons, and on the street, most often in quartets dominated by fiddle and banjo, and an idea of what songs they played can be gotten from the well-known minstrel tunes, nearly all of which were stolen from them. After the Civil War, shifting attitudes brought about a curious phenomenon: Afro-Americans themselves joined minstrel shows, sometimes blacking up if their skin tones happened to be light. This stereotypical medium had the ironic, and interestingly subversive, function of opening the door to black expression.

A not unrelated development was the unbelievable enduring popularity of the stage adaptation of *Uncle Tom's Cabin*. The first version, written by Charles Weston Taylor, appeared at the Bowery's National Theater just five months after the novel's publication, in 1852, but Taylor was so earnest about the story's theme that he forgot the drama and entirely omitted the characters of Little Eva and Topsy. It closed after eleven performances. Later that year a more consciously melodramatic adaptation opened at the Chatham and enjoyed immediate success, lasting a then exceptional 325 straight performances, after which it toured all over the North and West, returning to the Bowery for intermittent but lengthy tenures. As a road-show standard, it had a nearly continuous run that lasted well into the twentieth century. Its productions might be stark, or they might be so elaborate as to involve mechanical ice floes and trained dog packs, but in any guise, *Uncle Tom's Cabin* was so firmly established in the American subconscious that it would be referred to and parodied in various theatrical formats for the next century.

Race relations at mid-century were not uppermost in the minds of the b'hoys, however. They were racist in a relatively passive way, primarily because blacks were so completely powerless that they did not pose a threat. As we shall see, however, radical Democrats did succeed in manipulating the b'hoys' insecurities, resulting in such frays as the anti-Abolitionist riot of 1834. The major ethnic component of the Bowery subculture was Irish (with German a strong second) and this factor, combined with a sensitive memory of 1812 in their native-born counterparts, made for a distinct anti-English sentiment. As has been noted, this tension was frequently expressed in the form of theater riots, since English actors were the closest thing to English aristocrats in the Bowery universe. The worst such debacle occurred in 1849 at the Astor Place Opera House, which had opened just two years earlier. This affair, as so often happens, had a complicated reality that was overtaken by a tidy legend. As the legend goes, the actor and b'hoy idol Ned Forrest had a rather one-sided feud going with a prominent English actor named George Macready. It seems that Forrest had once been hissed at in London and believed that it was done at Macready's instigation. When Macready was scheduled to appear in *Macbeth* at the Astor Place, Forrest's dim-witted jealousy merged handily with anti-English sentiments and with the rabble-rousing hooliganism of Isaiah Rynders and his lieutenant Judson. Forrest, who was coincidentally also playing Macbeth at the Bowery, chose a night before Macready's debut uptown to broadly emphasize the line "What rhubarb, senna or what purgative drug would scour these English hence?" and the house responded with cheers. When Macready took the stage on a later night, he was met with a shower of eggs and garbage, including a bottle of asafetida that broke at his feet. Scenes that did not feature Macready passed without incident, but whenever he set foot on stage, hurled objects and catcalls followed, so that the play had to be stopped partway through the second act. A second performance took place the following night, and actually went its course, but not without a fracas between the b'hoys and the police and militia. Edwin Forrest, meanwhile, nominally emerged as victor of the fray, but fallout from the incident dogged his later career. As a widely bruited story had it, he went on to stage a public breakdown. His marriage was breaking up acrimoniously, and his wife managed to enlist the sympathies of many of their friends. When Forrest's closest friend, Nathaniel Willis, took her side in the pages of his magazine, *The Home Journal*, it was said, Forrest snapped, and each night stepped in front of the curtain at the close of whatever play he was appearing in to deliver a lengthy diatribe against wife and friend, such displays becoming something of a tourist attraction. The story has proved apocryphal, but it sullied Forrest's reputation before and after his death.

The story could be believed with little difficulty, since actors were generally viewed as freaks capable of all sorts of antics. In 1851 the notorious Lola Montez, exotic dancer and quondam mistress of the King of Bavaria, arrived in New York to a tumultuous reception and a great success on the Broadway stage, playing to an audience almost exclusively male. Her next production, *Lola Montez in Bavaria*, its sensationalism captured in its title, nevertheless fell victim to whim or reform and flopped resoundingly. The actress was shrewd enough to pack up the production and move it to the Bowery, where it thrived and she enjoyed a series of successes. A few years later, however, she abruptly quit her career and dropped from sight, devoting the rest of her days, so it was said, to good works. She died in 1861 and was buried in Brooklyn's Green-Wood Cemetery under her real name, Eliza Gilbert; it turned out she had been born in that borough, of dully respectable stock. Even so, her reputation adhered not to her birth name but to her pseudonym, and that moniker stood long afterward as a sort of metonymy for whoredom. For that matter, one of New York's most hackneyed stories concerns the marriage of the actor George Holland, turned down, it is said, by a Fifth Avenue church because of his profession, so that he was advised to stage his nuptials at a church so obscure that it was known by size and location (Little, Around the Corner) rather than by its true designation (the Transfiguration); this occurred in the late 1860s.

In both the Broadway and the Bowery theaters, melodrama was the ascendant form in the 1850s and throughout the next two decades. While Broadway unveiled such once and future chestnuts as Dion Boucicault's *The Octoroon* and *The Streets of New York* and Augustine Daly's *Under the Gaslight* and *After Dark*, the Bowery reveled in obscurely authored epics like *H—l on Earth, or Good and Evil; The Last Nail, or the Drunkard's Doom*; and *Ambition, or the Throne, the Scaffold, and the Tomb*. The stalwart *Ten Nights in a Bar-Room*, fodder for an endless succession of parodists to come, dates from this period. It belonged to the sub-genre of melodramas of sentiment; there were also melodramas of action, known as the "blood and thunder" genre after their most notable special effects. These latter were a favorite of the b'hoys and their successors, who were particularly devoted to *Six Degrees of Crime* (and its star, J. Hudson Kirby) and *The Three Fast Men, or New York by Daylight and Gaslight*. The eventual success of a play could be just about determined in advance by the size of the pile of corpses that would litter the stage at the close. The era rivaled the Jacobean in this feature, if scarcely in the use of language; the plays, when they can be traced, prove virtually unreadable. Multiple roles and quick changes were another sure-fire draw of the period; on Broadway, for example, the veteran actress Charlotte Cushman was playing in *Henry VIII*, alternating performances as Catherine of Aragon and as Cardinal Wolsey. Actors on the Bowery were now increasingly given to audience-directed asides; soliloquies would be punctuated by patter and queries on the order of "Isn't that so?" Audiences, for their part, were developing special cheers for particular performers, not unlike those directed to specific baseball players in later years. The great hit of the time, quite transcending any other melodrama in its appeal, was *Mazeppa*, a routine action feature that had been around, not very noticeably, for some years before 1859, when Charlotte Crampton became the first woman to play the title role of the seventeenth-century Cossack leader. The casting of a woman had its major payoff in the central scene, in which the hero is lashed naked (or "naked") to a horse. Later that same year, the feminist and bohemian Adah Isaacs Menken took over the part, and went on to make a career of it, eventually touring this masterpiece to every wayside on the continent.

A very different sort of theater was being born not far away from the Old Bowery. Tony Pastor, who had apprenticed at various theaters on the thoroughfare, in 1864 acquired the lease to one of the many institutions that willed themselves Opera Houses, his being located between Rivington and Delancey. His mainstay at first was minstrelsy, which he compiled in variety shows, and his gambit was to run a clean house: he abolished the bar, outlawed smoking, admitted women free on Fridays, and on Saturdays raffled off hams, turkeys, half barrels of flour, half tons of coal, and dress patterns. If the whole act, from song-and-dance to raffles, is rather reminiscent of the Depression, this is surely no accident, since the decade after the Civil War was not an especially prosperous one on the Lower East Side. Pastor had such success with his entertainment package that in 1875 he was given the chance to move uptown and into, as it were, the pocket. In 1869 Tammany Hall had opened a new headquarters, on Fourteenth Street, right next door to the Academy of Music, the operatic bastion of the city's old guard. The sachems happened to have a large ground-floor space for which they had no use; Pastor took the lease and occupied the premises until his death in 1910. Although Pastor, unaccountably, failed to die a rich man, he did possess an acute commercial canniness and great luck. The minstrel show, as he gradually rehabilitated it, softening the edges of his acts and combining them serially into reviews, led to the first outlines of what came to be known as vaudeville.[5] Furthermore, back on the Bowery in 1872, he had been among the first managers to employ a burgeoning song-and-dance team named Harrigan and Hart. The theatrical world was beginning to turn to musical comedy.

In 1866 a piece made its debut at Niblo's Garden on Broadway that was to be the greatest hit of the century, as well as the most preposterous concatenation of ill-fitting elements in an era of strong competition. *The Black Crook* was perhaps not the first American musical, but it may as well have been, and it was many other things besides: it was a formless mishmash of fantastic plot elements ranging from *Faust* and *Der Freischütz* to sundry fairy tales and myths; it was a showcase for scores of singers, dancers, and musicians; and it was five and a half hours long. The corps de ballet, scantily clad, for the time, in tights and ballet skirts, was unquestionably the main attraction, as well as the principal focus of the play's denunciation from pulpits, which added to the attraction. About a hundred young women appeared in the production on any given night. The ranking system can best be conveyed by its economics: premières de ballet, who passed themselves off as French or Italian whether they were or not, were paid $150 a week; secondas got from $50 to $100; coryphées received between $25 and $30; the first, second, and third lines made from $10 to $30, depending on position; those used only in processions got $8. By comparison, a "ballet girl" of any rank, when the song-and-dance fever took hold a year or two later (and it must be remembered that at the time little distinction was drawn between ballet and any other sort of theatrical dance), was elsewhere paid an average of $12 a week, approximately the same wage as a doorkeeper. *The Black Crook* ran for a record 474 performances and was thereafter revived with extraordinary frequency until the turn of the century.

The influence of *The Black Crook* was felt in numerous ways: it spawned many imitations; it inspired the taste for light opera, or opéra bouffe; it prepared the climate for burlesque, in both of its meanings, as a song-and-dance farce and as a (highly circumspect) skin show. Among the beneficiaries of this extraordinarily influential work were Ned Harrigan and Tony Hart. Their genius, however, was of a very different order; they both sang and danced, and they were wildly sentimental, but they were fundamentally realists. The depiction of the Bowery scene by and for its habitués had never quite gone out of vogue since the "Mose" days, although it had meanwhile mutated in form, from the broad comic-heroics of the original to the Grand Guignol of melodrama. Exceptions could occasionally be found, such as the play that had run in 1856 at the Stadt Theater (which alternated productions in English and in German), called *Life in New York, or Tom and Jerry on a Visit*, which was noted for its set realistically depicting Centre Street on a Saturday night, with its fruit stands, weight machines, and "lung testers," its quoit games, its peddlers and beggars. Harrigan and Hart took this sort of direct observation and faithful reproduction, wrapped fairly original plots around it, and garlanded the whole with songs and dances that bore an actual relation to both plot and setting.

Hart, an enormously gifted singer, dancer, and actor, was the star; Harrigan, who also performed, was the writer; and the latter's father-in-law, a conductor named David Braham, was the composer. Their shows were heavy on local color, sometimes slopping over into reasonably good-natured ethnic caricature, usually about the Irish, as in the Mulligan series (*The Mulligan Guard Ball, The Mulligan Guard Nominee, Mulligan's Silver Wedding*), and sometimes concerned with actual topical issues, as in *Squatter Sovereignty*, which was based on the war waged in the 1870s between the occupants and the owners of a rocky stretch of land on the East River at Seventy-second Street. Minute particularization of detail is what made their songs more than merely sentimental; their songs were wildly popular across nearly all classes in New York, but, unsurprisingly perhaps, they had very little impact outside the city. Hart died young, in 1891, of tertiary syphilis, after nearly a decade of hospitalization, but Harrigan's popularity continued unabated. Along with Braham, he turned out shows and songs for another two decades, his work laying a foundation for the twentieth-century musical, forming a bridge between the operatic fripperies of *The Black Crook* and the sophistication of later generations animated by the likes of Jerome Kern.

Harrigan and Hart also brought the Bowery to Broadway; by 1882 they were installed in their own theater, on Broadway near Waverly Place. The "tough guy" fad of the nineties was largely their doing, and in the middle of the decade Harrigan introduced a new wrinkle: the Tough Girl, in the person of Ada Lewis, whom he had discovered in California and brought back for *Reilly and the 400*. Lewis was rather awe-inspiring: dressed all in black, shoulders hunched forward, arms dangling apelike, her body tilted slightly to one side, her face distorted into a fearsome sneer. She announced herself in song: "You see in me a dead tough girl / Who's known to all de gang."

In the eighties and nineties, theater became a major industry in New York. It was the period of Lillie Langtry and her scandals, of Lillian Russell and Diamond Jim Brady, of the first American tours by Sarah Bernhardt. Playwrights became producers and theater owners: Augustine Daly, David Belasco, Henry D. DeMille. In the eighties the stretch of Fourteenth Street at Union Square opposite the statue of Washington became known as the Slave Market because of the hundreds of actors milling around, like so many longshoremen at a shape-up, looking for engagements at the numerous theaters in the district. In 1883 the Metropolitan Opera opened for the benefit of the nouveaux riches who could not obtain boxes at the old-line Academy of Music. In this case the old guard did surrender, and the Academy closed a mere two years later, in spite of having secured the exclusive services of the home-grown operatic phenomenon Adelina Patti, and it eventually jumped class altogether by becoming a vaudeville theater. By the 1890s the Broadway center had migrated northward, and the term the Gay White Way came into currency, at that time defining an area from the Hoffman House at Twenty-sixth Street to Rector's, between Forty-third and Forty-fourth Streets. Broadway became the territory of a newly organized motley public: the burghers and their families were still present, but now they mingled with playboys, reporters, gamblers, bohemians, jockeys, boxers, chorus girls, soubrettes, pimps, thugs, opium merchants, as well as the inevitable millionaires and aristocrats. The whole mob swayed from Child's (the original fast-food emporium) to lobster palaces, from cigar stores to saloon bars, under the eye of the pickpocket and the fly cop, to the tune of the Salvation Army Band.

The Bowery, facing such competition, was slowly beginning to pall. Melodramas plodded on, now and then augmented by dramatizations of current events, such as the 1879 *Life of Custer* presented at the Old Bowery, in which the Battle of Little Big Horn was immediately succeeded by Sitting Bull's death at the hands of a character called Daring Bill. There was, besides, a scattering of guest appearances: Buffalo Bill Cody appeared in *The Scout of the Plains* and *The Prairie Wolf* some years before the debut of his Wild West Show; Jim Corbett starred at the People's Theater in the melodrama *After Dark*, in 1891, immediately after his knockout of John L. Sullivan. Old favorite Frank Chanfrau, of Mose fame, appeared in a new role as Kit, the Arkansaw Traveler, and he played it until he became too infirm for the role, at which time he was succeeded by his son Henry. The young William S. Hart appeared at the very start of his career in *The Man in the Iron*

Mask. As ever, the old blood-and-thunder tradition rolled on: *The Waifs of New York, The Outcasts of a Great City*.

Melodrama, with its semi-abstracted urban settings, its extreme character types, and its ritualized violence, had become the slums' own. The extent to which this truncated and exaggerated form of theater had become the favorite vehicle for self-dramatization by urban fringe elements can be illustrated by the case of the Grand Duke's Theater. This house, located in the basement of dives first, around 1882, on Baxter Street and subsequently on Water Street, was operated by a youth gang called the Baxter Street Dudes, led by one Baby-Face Willie. The theater was not only owned, managed, and operated by adolescent boys; its casts, crews, corps of playwrights and, for the most part, audiences were likewise made up of boys ranging in age from three to twenty. Just as the sets were improvised from found and stolen materials, so was the house's physical equipment similarly scavenged: six kerosene lamps made up the footlights, the stalls were benches, two sawdust-stuffed red plush lounges were the boxes, and stepladders and piled boxes functioned as the gallery. Such makeshift was forced not only by the impecuniousness of the youths but by the provisional nature of their establishment: it was under constant attack—bombardment with bricks and stones—by rival gangs. Not surprisingly, blood-and-thunder was the main fare, with a light sprinkling of variety. The admission scale ran from a nickel to a quarter.

By the 1890s, Bowery theater no longer held the franchise on popular entertainment, and it looked as if it might soon die out. The tank dramas and horseback operas of yore paled in comparison to what the vast spaces of Madison Square Garden could offer: Buffalo Bill's Wild West Show featured hundreds of horses, whole battles, a replication of the Rough Riders' charge up San Juan Hill; the annual Sportsmen's Show was staged in landscapes with real trees and such topographical features as a 150-foot tank—complete with an island in the center—for the canoe races, logrolling contests, and water-polo matches. Pageants at the Garden ran the gamut from the annual Cake Walk and Carnival that presumed to represent all of "colored society" to the

Six-Day Bicycle Race, also a yearly event, which survived until World War II.

What saved the Bowery from obsolescence were two factors. The first was the arrival of new ethnic forces, with their own talents and their own audiences. In much the same way that slum neighborhoods were periodically regenerated by new blood, so was the theater. The most important of these forces was the Yiddish theater. Drama in the Yiddish tongue was not exactly a tradition before the first American production around 1882—public manifestations by Jews in Russia and the Eastern European countries were too restricted or assimilated for that—so the Bowery and its analogues became its real home. The vigorous life of the Yiddish theater began for real in 1889, when the great Jacob Adler—the "Yiddish Salvini"[6]—began to appear in translated productions of Shakespeare and later Ibsen, many of them put on by Jacob Gordin—the "Yiddish Shakespeare." Gordin soon began to write his own plays, such as *The Wild Man* and *God, Man and the Devil*, and then he was joined by increasing numbers of competitors. One theater after another on the Bowery became a Yiddish house: the Windsor and the Thalia in the middle nineties; the People's, in 1899. Yiddish theater gradually crept uptown, taking over somnolent German theaters on Second Avenue—which became known as the Yiddish Rialto—and extending up to the Amberg, later the Irving Place, on Fifteenth Street.[7]

In an analogous development, a crack Russian troupe led by Paul Orleneff and Alla Nazimova arrived with a certain amount of fanfare in the mid-nineties at Broadway's Herald Square Theater, where they promptly failed, not being sufficiently close to the mainstream. It was a committee of immigrants, including, among others, Emma Goldman, which raised money to install them at the Third Avenue Theater—on that spiritual extension of the Bowery—at Thirty-first Street. The patronage of immigrants was sufficiently remunerative that within a decade Nazimova had her own theater, on Thirty-ninth.

The other factor responsible for staving off the Bowery's doom was variety, what in later years would be termed vaudeville. Variety was a city-wide attraction by the nineties, but the Bowery's version had its particular flavor as well as its own laws. Theaters all over town were bound by Sunday closing laws until 1907, but Bowery theaters, under the protection of Tammany chieftains, blithely operated seven days a week. (These laws, long a bone of contention in the entertainment industry, began to be generally ignored around the turn of the century. In 1907 Mayor George B. McClellan decided to enforce them. The result was that all theaters in the city closed in protest for several days, and the producer Percy Williams sued the city, arguing restraint of trade. The State Supreme Court ruled in his favor.)

Variety, after all, had been born on the Bowery, as far back as the 1840s, the issue of the marriage between minstrelsy and specialized magic and ventriloquistic acts that had been consecrated by the likes of Tony Pastor. Variety began to infiltrate not only minstrel shows but the entr'actes of legitimate plays, and the Bowery was treated to such spectacles as the first roller-skating exhibition, in 1866, at the New Bowery Theater. By the nineties the major venue was Miner's Theater, home to such nascent legends as the young dialect-comedy duo Weber and Fields (now forgotten, but for decades a byword in American entertainment) and the Four Cohans, from which George M. eventually graduated. Sharing the stage were such luminaries as the male impersonators Ella Wesner and Vesta Tilley; Maggie Cline, who made her name with the Harrigan and Hart tune "T'row 'im down Mc-Cluskey"; the jig dancer Pat Rooney, known for his catch phrase, "Are yez all lookin'?" Up to 1900, variety at Miner's consisted of a two-tier program followed by a melodrama—this last part was presently to disappear.

What made Miner's absolutely unique for a time, however, was Amateur Night, held on alternate Fridays. All contestants were paid a dollar just to appear, which naturally prompted many to show up just to claim that sum, regardless of lack of talent or even lack of any idea what to do. Winners might get a watch or $5 in gold for first place, a wallet or $3 in bills for second. A 1905 account outlines a typical night's fare: a juggler, buck-and-wing dancers, a blackface comedian

in a red plaid suit, a clay modeler (incredibly, arts-and-crafts demonstrations carried off with a certain amount of panache and speed went
over with the roughest crowds), a quartet of singing newsboys. As
entertaining as the acts on stage might be, people often came to Amateur
Nights at Miner's to take in the audience reaction, which could be
brutal. On this night "The Black Shakespeare," florid and halting by
turns, failed miserably to win the gallery crowd, but, a few moments
later, their sympathy was aroused by the Armless Wonder, who, per
tradition, was showered with coins. Acts by the halt and the maimed
were a nearly unfailing sympathy draw, but even they could be subjected to whistles and catcalls (the Bronx cheer was not developed
until some two or three decades later; the rhythmic colonial clap was
in its infancy). The eventual winner that night was a singing newsboy,
also scarcely exceptional, since newsboys held both the sympathy card
and the talent-in-the-making advantage; boxers, too, were often former
newsboys, or at least they said they were.

Since the procession of semi-talented and utterly untalented hopefuls
could be painful, not to mention boring, an enterprising stage manager
at Miner's came up with a way of policing the lengths of unsuccessful
acts: the hook. The first one, apparently, was a stage-prop shepherd's
crook lashed to a pole. Before long, hooks were being manufactured.
The hook appeared in theaters all over the world, entered the language,
and on at least one occasion was called for by the members of the
French Chambre de Députés during a particularly agonizing speech.
Back at Miner's, "Give 'im the hook" took barely twenty-four hours
to establish itself as the crowd's favorite line. Soon it was a cliché, and
stage managers were kept busy hatching entertaining alternatives: dous-
ing performers with selzer from spray bottles, carrying them out on
stretchers manned by burly stagehands. The hook and its variations
became a reliable source of audience jollification at theaters everywhere,
so that managers began to engage in something like inverse talent hunts,
as truly disastrous acts achieved perverse renown. Among celebrated
bombs, few quite reached the depths of infamy plumbed by Sadakichi
Hartmann, a half-German, half-Japanese bohemian-about-town re-

membered today for his avant-garde plays and even more for his pres-
cient theoretical writings on photography. Hartmann's act, which he
pursued with evident sincerity and lack of comic intention, involved
a contraption of his own invention that dispensed floral perfumes in
combinations controlled by him. He conceived of the performance as
analogous to music, a symphony of scents, but he remained unaware
both of the unprepossessing visual and auditory aspects—one silent
man crouched behind a machine—and of the effect of the dense clouds
of perfume that, especially in combination, were by all accounts nau-
seating. In the popular mind Hartmann became the man who put on
the worst show anyone had ever seen, while his literary talent was
known only to the cognoscenti.

What killed off the Bowery as a viable entertainment center was a
series of political events just before World War I (to which we shall
return). By then, variety in that precinct had become rather moribund,
ironclad in format, an unchanging ritual. It staggered on at such institutions as the Bowery Follies, which ran until during the Depression
as an endlessly repetitive menu of chorus girls (markedly less attractive
than their uptown rivals), kick lines, blackout routines, baggy-pants
comedians, Irish tenors, "Oriental" set pieces. Rather than pursuing
its own tradition of vigorous irreverence, the Bowery sank to an imitation, years after the fact, of uptown successes. Generations of Bowery
chorus lines continued to imitate the *Floradora* Sextette—six beautiful
young women who put on an entire show of songs, dances, and comedy
routines to an audience of champagne-guzzling boulevardiers of the
nineties—both Stanford White and his eventual murderer, Harry K.
Thaw, were enthusiasts—and who launched the enduring catch phrase
"Are there any more at home like you?" Comedians imitated Weber
and Fields, individual chorines tried to ape the charms of Miss Frankie
Bailey—she of the World's Greatest Legs—and of Anna Held, famous
for her onstage milk bath. Every promoter and producer fancied himself a rival of the indestructible Florenz Ziegfeld, although few had
anything like his imagination and none could begin to approach his
resources.

Variety had numerous offspring; burlesque and striptease derive there-from, and they can be seen in a very early form in the 1885 appearance at Koster and Bial's Tenderloin establishment of the Spanish dancer Carmencita, who was noted for wearing her corsets on the outside of her dress. Little Egypt, the exotic belly-dancing prodigy of the 1892 Chicago Columbia Exposition (she is said to have been born in St. Louis, for all her Oriental pretensions), became the metonymic rep-resentative of the forbidden throughout the nineties. Society orgy scan-dals of the period tend to revolve around her, metaphorically or in the flesh. There was the dinner given at Sherry's by Herbert Barnum Seeley, nephew of P. T. Barnum, at which, it was alleged in advance, Little Egypt would dance the hootchy-kootchy in the nude. The police, led by a certain Captain Chapman, raided the dinner and found Little Egypt, having apparently already executed her performance, clad in lace drawers and a Zouave jacket. The dinner given by Stanford White at his Madison Square Garden studio in honor of Diamond Jim Brady was the subject of even more scandalized speculation: evidently, an immense Jack Horner pie was brought out and, when the top was lifted, a naked sylph presented herself as Brady's party favor. The rumor remained unconfirmed, but the tradition penetrated unto thou-sands of stag parties and plumbing-sales conventions in the following century.

After 1900, variety was giving way among the cognoscenti to cabaret. The birthplace of this form of entertainment was probably Marshall's, a black hotel on West Fifty-third Street, where there was a bar of a type then common, one that catered to entertainment professionals, where actors played for other actors and musicians played for other musicians. At Marshall's, black singers, dancers, musicians, and com-posers entertained each other after their stage shows were over, and the company included such major figures of the day as the singer Ada Overton Walker; the songwriters Alex Rogers and Will Marion Cook; Bob Cole and J. Rosamond Johnson, composers of "Under the Bamboo Tree"; the bandleaders Ford Dabney and James Reese Europe; the comedian Bert Williams; the "dancing conductor" Will Dixon; and the trick drummer Buddy Gilmore. Gradually, in the course of the decade, white show people, composers, and songwriters began to drop by, absorbing the musical innovations that came through from the South and West, and the influences began to show up in their work, initially and notably in Irving Berlin's first great hit, "Alexander's Ragtime Band," which introduced the world at large to ragtime.[8] Not long after, around 1910, Blossom Seeley, appearing on Broadway in *The Hen Pecks*, unveiled a new kind of song (new, that is, to white New York audiences), "Toddling the Todolo," and a new kind of dance to go with it, the Texas Tommy. The effect was immediate and overwhelming. Soon the dance craze was on, and the usual motley crowd of financiers, gigolos, gangsters, heiresses, prostitutes, pimps, actors, and ward bosses began practicing the steps of the bunny hug, the grizzly bear, the turkey trot, the one-step, and that import from the slums of Buenos Aires, the tango. Soon the established Broadway lobster palaces began converting their premises to allow for large dance floors. Churchill's began the fad, and then Bustanoby's, Maxim's, Murray's Roman Gardens, the Café Madrid followed suit. The proprietor of Rector's couldn't manage it in his space, so he opened a huge new place on Columbus Circle called the Bal Tabarin. Efforts were made around 1913 to suppress dancing under what remained of the old blue laws, but nothing much came of it. Chinese restaurants, heretofore noted only as a raffish thrill for sophisticates slumming around Chatham Square, began a new era of popularity when the proprietors of such uptown establishments as the Pekin and the Tokio (apparently a Chinese restaurant in spite of its name) started hiring jazz bands to play during meals, a bizarre tradition that endured among midtown Chinese boîtes until the 1950s. Dancing went on at restaurants even after Prohibition came along and shuttered most of the pioneers, so that in 1923 a journalist could note: "You can dance at almost every restaurant except Child's and the Automat."

All this was far from the Bowery. By then, that thoroughfare was beginning to fall back on its last resource of popular entertainment: the dime museum. This peculiar institution probably had its origin in the back rooms of eighteenth-century taverns, where curiosities, anatomical anomalies, and the like were exhibited on an irregular basis. The man who made it into an institution was P. T. Barnum, who started in 1835 by exhibiting an ancient black woman named Joice Heth, who, he alleged, was 161 years old and had been George Washington's wet nurse. Barnum showed her in daily sessions in a coffee house at Bowery and Division to great popular acclaim, until she died several months after her debut. Barnum next staged diverse attractions at the Vauxhall Saloon, near Astor Place, from 1840 until, in 1842, he had accumulated the capital to purchase the old American Museum, a staid exhibition hall of elegant white marble, at Broadway and Ann Street. There he showed wax figures, "human wonders," a menagerie, dioramas, edifying dramas, mechanical contrivances, panoramic views, and sundry frauds, and was legendarily successful at it. He continued in the trade throughout the century, even after his museums succumbed to fire, first the one on Ann Street in 1865, then the one on Broadway between Prince and Spring in 1868, after which he removed to the theatrical nexus of Fourteenth Street and later became a partner in the grand hall called Gilbert's Garden, eventually renamed Madison Square Garden.

The museum format, which Barnum did not invent but which he broadened in appeal, was widely imitated. In 1867 the moniker was established when, as a result of a price war, admissions were reduced to a dime. The first to reach this mark was Bunnell's Museum on the Bowery, which boasted—besides its tattooed man, its "double-brained" child, and the like—a "Dante's Inferno" that featured wax figures of widely despised living figures (Boss Tweed, Henry Ward Beecher, Jay Gould, Victoria Woodhull) writhing in eternal torment. For an additional five cents the visitor could venture downstairs and take in a drama. Nevertheless, Bunnell's major attraction for the year 1879 was a grand poultry show. Around the Bowery there were scores of emulators: Worth's, Alexander's, the New York, the Gaiety, each with its waxworks, its "moral dramas," its mechanical wonders, its panoramas. Slightly risqué tableaux and set pieces began showing up in abundance. The Mazeppa craze launched dozens of miniature Mazeppa-lashed-to-the-horse interludes. Everywhere, the museums whispered of "spicy French sensations," "secrets of artists' models," "secrets of the seraglio," "beautiful minuet dancers from the Jardin Mabille," "bewitching female bathers in real water."

On the Bowery, dense as it was with such diversions as nickel shooting galleries featuring animated, noise-making figures, such lures hardly stood out, but by the 1880s they were creeping uptown. The Eden Musée, on Twenty-third Street diagonally across from Mc-Creery's Department Store, featured the usual retinue of freaks, midgets, fire eaters, sword swallowers, waxworks, a Chamber of Horrors, and "Ajeeb, the chess mystery," a pseudo-automaton of the sort described by Poe in "Von Mälzel's Chess-Player," consisting of a hollow figurine inhabited by a child dwarf. At Huber's Dime Museum on East Fourteenth Street, patrons would be regaled by the spiel of the barker, a formidable gentleman in evening dress, with pomaded hair and waxed mustaches, who intoned: "Ladies and gents / for only ten cents / you can see all the sights / and there on your right / is the great fat lady. / She's a healthy baby / weighing 300 pounds. / She's six feet around. / Her husband is the living / skeleton—see him shivering. / The dog-faced boy / will give you all joy / and the tattooed man / does the best he can. / The human horse / is wonderful of course. / And I'll show to you / the baby kangaroo. / The lady lion tamer / will please every stranger," and so on. This worthy is said later to have killed himself "when his muse ceased to be appreciated."

Elsewhere, there were mermaids (usually, dead manatees in a tank), two-headed calves, four-legged chickens, calculating horses, dwarves, giants, bearded ladies, armless wonders, wild men of Borneo, "Circassian princesses" possessing incredibly long hair and usually surrounded by snakes, snake charmers, Indian rubber men, glass eaters, mental marvels, ossified girls, legless ladies, men-fish, "iron-skulled" men, men "who will not smile," men "who cannot stop walking," geeks, living half-men, human pincushions, human clawhammers, human anvils, egg cranks (who could eat something like 120 of them at a sitting), idiot-savant calculators, tattooed marvels ("ninety thousand stabs and for every stab a tear," at Barnum's Museum). Inarticulate minor celebrities were also thus displayed, such as Bob and Charlie Ford, when they made their Eastern tour after killing Jesse James.

Bowery museums were the true underworld of entertainment, and their compass could include anything too shoddy, too risqué, too vile, too sad, too marginal, too disgusting, too pointless to be displayed elsewhere. They could even be romantic, in a way: one memorialist of the nineties recalls the aftermath of a raid on the Palace of Illusions, at 257 Bowery, when Lady Mephistopheles, done up in red doublet, tights, horns, and tail, was led away by the police. For the inmates, life in the museums was no doubt rather boring and workaday. At Bunnell's, renamed the Globe, George the Turtle Boy played cards between shows with Laloo the East Indian Enigma, who had a small head growing out of his side. Then, every hour on the hour, the Professor (the compere at such establishments was so called, as inevitably as the piano player in a whorehouse) lectured on the exhibits. Meanwhile, an extra nickel would allow one downstairs for the melodrama or variety (Al Jolson, for one, got his start in such a venue). Twelve or fifteen shows went on daily, during which the freaks had to stand around and assume typical poses, although when the immortal Jo-Jo the Dog-Faced Boy hit the Bowery his draw was so great that the schedule was expanded to twenty-three shows daily.

Mostly the museums were desperately cheap and small-time. A great number of them lacked even the resources to put on shows or to hire human oddities, and so instead displayed any rag end they could get their hands on and elevate in stature through imaginative labeling: old coins, old musical instruments, old furniture, spearheads, Civil War rifles. On the Bowery was continued the medieval practice of trading on pieces of the True Cross, or at least shards of wood from the Mount of Olives. Worth's Museum claimed to display the pickled head of Guiteau, President Garfield's assassin; three separate Bowery museums insisted they possessed the club with which Captain Cook was killed in the South Pacific. Museums would be plastered with signs warning

"For Men Only; No Minors Admitted" and then turn out to contain a scattering of old newspapers, yellowed envelopes, peepholes admitting views of ordinary chromolithographs, slot machines, waxen masks, maybe a fake on the order of the Cardiff Giant. One such establishment was destroyed in 1899 by a group of soldiers returning from the Spanish-American War, enraged at finding no actual sex or depravity.

Depravity was there to be had, of course, in various forms, at places like the Grand Museum, owned and operated by one Broken-Nose Burke and variously characterized (although not fully described) as "in bad taste" and "obscene." There were "living picture" emporia, which featured tableaux vivants by women clad only in flesh-colored tights. There were joints that promised "nude women" and delivered (after the sucker had paid two or three separate admissions to sanctums within sanctums within the museum) a single unadorned showroom dummy, or possibly an embryo in a jar. There were "anatomical museums," which displayed wax models of organs and vaguely obscene charts detailing the "secrets of a successful marriage," and where "professors," who claimed to have lately come from Berlin or Paris, droned on while showing lantern slides of horrifying venereal deformities in the faces of victims of tertiary syphilis. There were places where visitors were encouraged to test their powers on a machine that was rigged to give them an electric shock, after which they were made to pay extra for "treatment." There were outfits where blood-pressure tests or lung exams or phrenological observations or palm readings were administered apparently gratis, but then were interrupted in the middle by the sudden appearance of a sign indicating the price of the session (usually a then excessive two dollars).

Shortchanging was nothing new on the Bowery, either. During the era when the three-cent piece, only slightly smaller than a dime, was current, cashiers were always palming customers' admissions and then displaying a threepenny coin, claiming they had been shortchanged, and they were equally quick at handing over one of these units along with a nickel as change for a quarter.

Around the start of World War I, the museums and their cousins the auction rooms had vanished from the Bowery, although for decades afterward they could be found engaging in many of the same pursuits in uptown honky-tonk districts such as Herald and Times Squares;[9] today they survive in vestigial form as pinball and video-game arcades around Times Square, many of which literally evolved from the museums that had formerly occupied their sites.

Around the turn of the century, the museums briefly found a new occupation for themselves. Until the movies became respected and had to be shown on a larger scale, which happened around 1910 or so, they were considered a freakish novelty and were thus relegated to museums or to disused storefronts. The first kinetoscope parlor opened on Broadway in 1894, but the first screen show in New York was held April 20, 1896, at Koster and Bial's on Twenty-third Street. On that occasion, twelve short subjects ranging from "Sea Waves" to "The Butterfly Dance" and from "Burlesque Boxing" to "Kaiser Wilhelm Reviewing His Troops" were shown on a variety program that also included a Russian clown, an eccentric dancer, a pair of gymnastic comedians, a pair of French duettists, and a Cockney music-hall team. The films were hand-tinted, and some of them, to judge from "The Butterfly Dance," which has survived, were quite beautiful. "Sea Waves" was noted for having upset the audience in that early way, apparently persuading them that an actual wall of water was heading toward them. But the novelty did not take long to dissipate; very soon movies were adjudged unfit even for variety. "Store shows" was the moniker given to the disreputable early movie circuit; the movies themselves were known as the "tape." The shows were usually held in museums or converted stores that seated 299—three hundred would have required an amusement license. Some twelve to eighteen shows were given every day, and bouncers emptied the house on the half hour. At this time, the fodder consisted of very crude fictions and literary adaptations, little more than tableaux vivants, as well as boxing pictures, bullfight pictures, and that old Bowery standby: re-creations of current events. The Russo–Japanese War was reenacted with models;

Harry K. Thaw played himself in *Harry K. Thaw's Fight for Freedom* (which was denounced from pulpits as an example of how the movies glorified crime); in the wake of one of the era's most resounding scandals, the three gangsters who testified against Police Lieutenant Charles Becker—Bald Jack Rose, Sam Schepps, and Harry Vallon—starred in *The Wages of Sin* after Becker went to the chair.

Nickelodeons, which specialized in hand-cranked machines that showed movies to one viewer at a time—basically an adaptation of the kinetoscope—went a long way toward establishing the commercial viability of the movies. In 1904 there were no nickelodeons to speak of; by 1907 their attendance averaged two million a day, half of that children. The future kings of the movie industry got their start in this market; William Fox, for example, owned fifteen of them, and his rivals included the former fur traders Marcus Loew and Adolph Zukor. The greatest of the nickelodeons was the Automatic Vaudeville, on Fourteenth Street near Union Square, which had scores of machines laid out in rows like a large coin-operated laundry. Nickelodeons only rarely showed movies on screens—they were less popular and furthermore suffered from a disreputable aura—although some cut peepholes in a back wall to permit the viewing of films projected in a room beyond, to which there was no admission.

In 1908 the reform Mayor George B. McClellan, who the year before had lost his fight to enforce the blue laws governing theaters, took after nickelodeons and movie houses. With the support of church leaders and vice crusaders, including the ubiquitous Anthony Comstock and Reverend Charles H. Parkhurst, he issued an order shutting down all such places of exhibition. The argument had to do with, among other things, the fact that the exits of movie houses often adjoined saloon entrances, thus enabling one vice to lead to another. On Christmas Day, all 550 of the city's exhibition sites were shuttered. Managers were permitted to reopen upon their acquisition of a license, which in turn was obtained by signing a pledge not to open on Sundays and to refrain from showing films that would "undermine the morals of the community." McClellan's successor, the more genuinely reform-

The movies come to Union Square. The greatest of all the
nickelodeons, Automatic Vaudeville, circa 1910. Photograph
by Brown Brothers

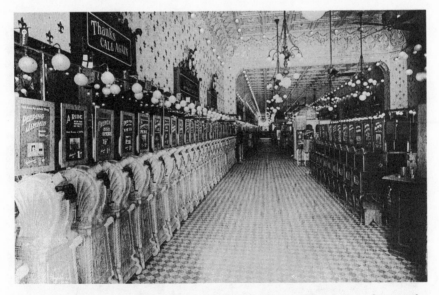

The interior of the same establishment. The focus is on the
slightly louche: ''Peeping Jimmy,'' ''French High Kickers,''
''The Soubrettes' Picnic.'' Photograph by Byron

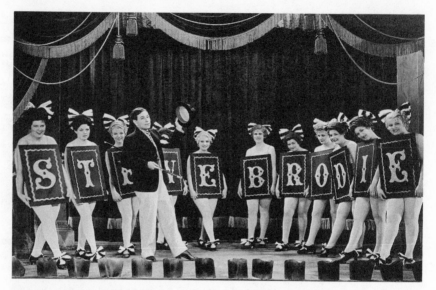

The Bowery seen by Hollywood: George Raft as Steve
Brodie, his saloon inflated into a nightclub in Raoul Walsh's
The Bowery, 1933

The cinematic Chuck Connors (Wallace Beery) confronts
Carry Nation and her troops (also from *The Bowery*)

minded William J. Gaynor, rescinded the law shortly after taking office in 1910.

Around this time New York was still the movie capital. Biograph Studios had been operating out of a brownstone on East Fourteenth Street since 1906, and there, in 1908, D. W. Griffith directed his first film, *The Adventures of Dollie*. Meanwhile, Vitagraph had been renting studios on Nassau Street since the late 1890s (eventually moving to Flatbush); Kalem established itself on Twenty-first Street in 1907 (although most of its films were shot at studios in Fort Lee, N.J.); in 1914 Zukor's Famous Players set up shop in a former armory on Twenty-sixth Street. While most movies were shot in studios, location work on the rooftops and even in the streets and subways of New York began early. Biograph's Billy Bitzer, for example, documented a ride on the East Side IRT from Fourteenth to Forty-second Street in 1905, and in *The Black Hand*, 1906, broke up the studio scenes with shots taken along Seventh Avenue with a hidden camera. Another cinematic pioneer, Edwin S. Porter, made a number of shorts entirely in outdoor locations, notably *What Happened on Twenty-third Street, New York City* (1901).

Over the course of a century, New York had not tired of seeing itself represented, and of course it still has not today. If New York, like Paris, was a city of lights, a harbor beacon for the American empire as well as a lurid midway of cheap attractions, the lights that were brightest and best-known were those of the theatrical nexus. In this way, as well as by virtue of containing the greatest spectacles in a city that was itself a spectacle, the theater and its popular accomplices could be said to be more New York than New York, to be New York redoubled.

2 · SALOON CULTURE

THE SALOON LOOMS LARGE IN THE HISTORY AND FOLKLORE OF NEW YORK. BUT ITS ORIGINS ARE CONCEALED IN THE MURK OF THE Dutch and English past when things like taverns were neither licensed nor regulated and anyone could sell grog informally. Both before and after the Revolution, there were countless inns and taverns and wineshops and breweries and rumshops; the saloon did not begin to acquire its mythic character until reform came along to complain about it, and in the eighteenth century the voice of reform was still pitched rather low. Even in 1786, though, a year before the end of the Revolution, there were those who complained about the city's estimated eight hundred taverns; since the population, according to the census of 1790, was 340,120, this works out to one groggery for every 425 inhabitants, which is not an extraordinary figure. By 1826 the count had been reduced to six hundred, but this figure takes in only legitimate taverns and fails to account for the hundreds of tippling shops and other quasi-clandestine outlets. In 1870 there were, indisputably, 7,071 licensed suppliers of liquor by the drink in Manhattan, but, again, the count fails to include the proportionately vast number of illegal dives, blind tigers, needled-beer cellars, and the like, which flourished mostly in the slums. An 1897 survey, which more sensibly attempted to list every place of sale and consumption of alcohol, but limited itself to the district bounded by East Houston and Hester Streets, and the Bowery and Essex Street, found 237 saloons, dives, and blind pigs (illegal dives with innocuous fronts), or one for every 208 men, women, and children.

Saloon culture naturally gravitated around the people's delirium, the Republic of the Bowery. Things began slowly enough there. The first Bowery tavern was probably Cornelis Aertszen's inn at Bowery Village, established in 1665. During the street's century or so of relative respectability, a number of such institutions arose, mostly in the form of travelers' relays, most notably the Bull's Head Tavern at Bowery and Broome, which opened sometime in the mid-eighteenth century and prospered uninterruptedly until the 1820s, when its formerly rural site was suddenly in the way of the wedge of urban construction.[1] The saloon, as it came to be known, loved, and reviled, was born several blocks to the east, in the area of the Five Points. Here unlicensed grogshops grew up in the back rooms of grocery stores, which in turn appeared on every corner, four to an intersection. The demand for groceries was not so great as to warrant such a boom in shops; in fact, the stores were so closely associated in everyone's mind with the grog-geries for which they fronted that for a time "grocery" became a popular euphemism for groggery. The first, or at least the most celebrated, of these, around 1825, was Rosetta Peer's, on Centre Street near Anthony (later Worth), and it doubled—or tripled—as the headquarters of New York's first recorded armed gang, the Forty Thieves. An ordinance of 1841 legalized the grocery saloons blanket-fashion, and, not long after, the greengrocers themselves removed to the middles of blocks, leaving the corners in undisputed possession of their former sub-tenants. Around then, these began to be called, for the first time, saloons, an obvious corruption of the word "salon."

On the Bowery itself, where the fashion of the time was heavily influenced if not actually dictated by the prominent German contingent, beer gardens predominated. Among these were the Volksgarten, which in one form or another lasted more than half a century, and the Atlantic Garden, next door to the Old Bowery Theater. The Atlantic seated over a thousand on two floors, and consumption by its patrons was such that two four-horse drays were kept in constant rotation to the brewery and back for ten hours a day. It was a familial sort of place, where burghers could come in with their entire broods and be entertained by the music of pianos, harps, violins, drums, and brasses, or where men could play cards, dominoes, or dice, or even engage in the occasional target shoot with rifles, all the while nursing large mugs that went for a nickel apiece. In the early days, before the Civil War, the owner went so far as to hire barmaids, aged between twelve and sixteen, clad in short dresses and red boots with bells that dangled from tassels, a uniform that would shortly be taken up by waterfront prostitutes. These barmaids were the first and last female help to be seen in drinking establishments in the environs who were not themselves offered for sale.

The low-class Bowery dives just emerging featured a novelty: no glasses. Drinks, at three cents per, were served from barrels stacked behind the bar via thin rubber tubes, the stipulation being that the customer could drink all he wanted until he had to stop for a breath. Needless to say, there were many who developed deep lung capacity and tricks of circular respiration in order to outwit the system.[2] In the decades before the Civil War the worst dives were located on the waterfront, and they traded with a highly elastic clientele of sailors. Sailors were free spenders, rootless, and halfway untraceable; they were marks of the first order. The street most overrun by sailors was Water Street, and there some of the tenements managed to boast a saloon, brothel, or dance hall on every floor. Notable were John Allen's saloon-cum-whorehouse and Kit Burns's Sportsmen's Hall, which was an entire three-story building in which every variety of vice was pursued, but none so famously as its matches to the death between terriers and rats, held in a pit in its first-floor amphitheater, hence the resort's more common name, the Rat Pit. Commerce was aided by the fact that, whether through fluke or graft, Kit Burns's was the terminus for one of the early stage transit lines.

Rat-baiting was the premier betting sport of the nineteenth century. Its prestige can be gauged in economic terms, circa 1875: admission to a then illegal prizefight between humans cost fifty cents, to dogfights and cockfights $2, while a fight pitting a dog against rats ran anywhere from $1.50 if the dog faced five rats or fewer, up to $5, in proportion to the number of rats. In the eighteenth century the biggest draw had been bearbaiting, but that sport gradually dissipated as the number of available bears decreased, although matches continued to be held up to the Civil War, notably in McLaughlin's bear pit at First Avenue and Tenth Street. For a while, dog-vs.-raccoon contests were popular, but rats were so readily available that they came to dominate the scene; boys were paid to catch them, at a rate of five to twelve cents a head. The dogs were always fox terriers, and they were trained for six months before being sent out at a year and a half, retaining the status of novice until they reached two years of age. The pits, at Kit Burns's and elsewhere, were unscreened boxes, with zinc-lined wooden walls eight feet long and four and a half feet high. Matches typically drew no fewer than a hundred betting spectators, from all walks of life, with purses starting at $125. A good rat dog could kill a hundred rats in half an hour to forty-five minutes, although the modern record was set by Jack Underhill, a terrier belonging to one Billy Fagan, who slew his hundred in eleven and a half minutes at Secaucus, N.J., in 1885. Late in the century it briefly became popular to pit rats against men wearing heavy boots. The ASPCA finally drove the game out of the city in the early 1890s.

At the intersection of Dover Street stood the Hole-in-the-Wall, a brawling den run by a well-known crook, One-Armed Charley Monell, and his female adjutants, Gallus Mag and Kate Flannery. On Cherry Street, not far away, were the domiciles of the crimps, operators who specialized in drugging and robbing sailors, sometimes arranging for them to be shanghaied aboard tramp boats, if they survived.[3] At least one place, the Fourth Ward Hotel, had convenient trapdoors through which corpses could be disposed directly into the East River. This hostelry later became famous as the site of the murder of a local woman of uncertain age but dire condition, who was popularly nicknamed Shakespeare because for the price of a drink she could recite all the speeches of the major female roles in *The Merchant of Venice, Hamlet, Macbeth*, and *King Lear*. This talent naturally led to wild speculations about her origins, with most of the locals maintaining that she was of noble birth, and the newspapers capitalized on such rumors. Likewise, her murder, never solved, was exoticized by being attributed to Jack the Ripper, come to New York on vacation.

The crimps refined the art of the knockout. They used laudanum at first, but this proved inefficient in the long run. A man named Peter Sawyer came from California in the 1850s and became so proficient an artist that for a while all members of his profession were known as "peter players." He is said to have used snuff at first, odd though that may sound, and occasionally employed morphine for a particularly tough or important hit. Then either he or one of his colleagues introduced chloral hydrate around 1866, and it was to remain the drug of choice for many years. Up to twenty grains or so were normally used for medicinal purposes, but the peter players habitually administered between thirty and forty, or up to sixty for an especially robust customer. Care had to be employed, because the physical action of chloral hydrate (soon permanently dubbed "knockout drops") was to decelerate the action of the heart, and an overdose would paralyze the heart and lungs. The chemical was originally very expensive for the time, running from two to five dollars per half-dram vial, but the market opened up and by the 1880s a dose cost twenty-five cents. The taste was detectable by anyone of sound mind and body, so the victim needed to be thoroughly drunk before he could be thus clobbered. Then he would be robbed, perhaps stripped as well, and dumped in an obscure alley. Some dives maintained an arrangement with the police, whereby knocked-out customers would be brought to a convenient location so that the cops could remove their lifeless bodies to the precinct house, where they would eventually be charged with public intoxication. Sometime during the nineties, technology finally brought a refinement to the art, in the form of the Mickey Finn. This concoction was named after the proprietor of Chicago's Lone Star and Palm Saloons, who supposedly bought the recipe from New Orleans voodoo operators, and then went on to sell it to other saloonkeepers around the country. The trouble is that no one can seem to agree on exactly what a Mickey Finn was. Some believe it to have been a complex recipe effective only when mixed with alcohol and water; the effect of cigar ashes in beer has also been cited, a dubious possibility. It was often described as being more volatile and more potentially lethal, if more effective, than chloral hydrate. To further complicate matters, in later years a Mickey Finn could also be a rapid physic administered to suckers by confidence men after bathroom doors had been locked, paralyzing them while the sharpers fled.

After the Civil War, vice came into its own, ascending from the gutter to become an institution. Epitomizing this ascendancy was the success of Harry Hill's concert saloon at Houston and Mulberry Streets, which lasted almost two decades. Hill's was officially sanctioned as a tourist attraction, the den of vice to which cab drivers steered strangers in search of the louche, but at the same time it was a real den of vice. It announced its presence by means of a huge red-and-blue globular lantern; it had, after the fashion of joints everywhere, two doors: a free entrance for women, who were understood to be one sort of prostitute or another if they visited Hill's, and the other for men, who were charged twenty-five cents. The main hall was composed of a series of rooms from which the partitions had been removed, but which retained their varying heights and surface finishes. A bar stood at one end, and at the other was a stage. On this stage, farces were sometimes mounted, or Punch and Judy shows in a box set, or, by and by, boxing matches: there John L. Sullivan made his first New York appearance, knocking out Steve Taylor in two and a half minutes on March 31, 1881. On most evenings, however, the stage held an orchestra consisting of piano, violin, and bass viol, and patrons were expected either to dance to it with paid female partners or else to leave. This was the major tourist-trap component of Hill's. Actual prostitution was always present, but not alluded to publicly; arrangements were to be made in private and the johns taken elsewhere. Exceptions to the dancing rules had to be unusually big spenders, or they had to be known to the management, in order to be permitted to congregate with the drinking crowd on the bar side. This element included the usual roughnecks and gangsters, as well as politicians, high-stakes gamblers, society figures, authors, off-duty cops. Order and discrimination were maintained by Hill himself, backed by a squad of bouncers. Hill was flamboyant in his role of protector of peace: he enjoyed intervening in what seemed to be incidents of roughhousing—usually staged for the rubbernecker trade; he often spent all evening dramatically shouting for quiet and order. His rules were posted in rhyme on the wall, forbidding drunkenness, profanity, lack of chivalry toward women, stinting on drinks.[4] Meanwhile, in the basement was a more conventional dive, featuring crooked games, knockout artists, and the like. By the mid-1880s, Hill's profits were estimated at $50,000 a year. By this time, he was a full member of middle-class society, distinguished from mere businessmen only by the adjective "colorful."

Hill's was known as a concert saloon, but concert saloons were actually a specific and distinct phenomenon. These establishments began springing up after the Civil War, along the Bowery mostly, and in cellars along the stretch of Broadway between Spring and Fourth Streets. Their modus operandi was a prostitution tease, one that has survived into the present day at topless bars and the like. Outside, the concert saloons displayed painted transparencies of twenty or thirty women, who, it was given to understand, were employees of the place, although the pictures were usually bought at random in job lots from photograph dealers, and often included well-known actresses of the day among the assortment. Inside, women were employed as waiter girls—in the parlance of the time—and other women would be just sitting around looking vaguely like customers. The sucker would be strongly encouraged to buy numerous drinks for himself and for a minimum of one female companion, whose drinks would be heavily watered or consist simply of colored water, and which would cost twice as much as the man's, which were themselves expensive for the time, from fifteen to twenty-five cents. The women did not receive wages but worked on a percentage basis. Sex did not occur on the premises, and in fact usually did not occur at all; obstreperous customers were treated to knockout drops. The concert saloons derived their name from the fact that some sort of excuse for music, probably three drunks on strings and piano, could be found somewhere on the premises. These houses also usually maintained a sideline in house-controlled gambling, not infrequently a side room devoted to keno. These places succeeded despite the fact that their clientele consisted almost exclusively of tourists and straying squares. In 1866, for example, there were seventy-five such houses, employing 745 waitresses, according to a police estimate.

If the concert saloons traded in sham vice, there was real vice lurking on the side streets nearby. On Hester Street, for example, was Billy McGlory's Armory Hall, a dive described as "perhaps the worst in New York's history." The place was all menace, scarcely bothering with the obeisance to good taste made by most dives. Its double doors opened onto a long, pitch-black hallway. Customers had to make their way through in utter darkness to the opaque door that led to the bar, beyond which was the dance hall. Murder was an everyday occurrence at the Armory, if we are to believe contemporary descriptions. It seems that if one flashed a roll on the premises one was more than likely to be set upon by half a dozen goons right at the table. In the dance hall was the usual sodden trio—piano, violin, and cornet—and a floor show of transvestite singers and dancers who doubled as waitresses. Upon being seated, customers would be visited by a flock of waitresses of either sex who would sit on their laps. If the mark did not want matters to go further, he would put a quarter in his visitor's stocking for luck. If he did, the twain could repair to one of the curtained boxes in the balcony, which were reserved for what was referred to as "private can-can exhibitions." In either case, nobody was expected to leave in possession of his wallet.

The majority of dives featured one or another variation of the basic setup: bar, dance floor, private boxes, prostitution, robbery. At least, this was the pattern of the 1870s; later decades would dispense with the dancing and entertainment components in favor of a more stream-lined approach. In this period, vice was also famously on display at the American Mabille, on Bleecker Street, run by The. Allen, who was popularly known as the "wickedest man in New York," a fortunate bit of publicity encouraged by Allen himself; Allen was also known for having been raided 113 times without a conviction (he was, as we shall see, very well connected politically). Frank Stephenson was a dive proprietor who specialized in exotica. The Slide on Bleecker Street was probably the very first—and until recent times the last—open and undisguised gay bar in New York. It is all but impossible to get an idea of what it was like, unfortunately; the loud distaste of contem-porary chroniclers made them incapable of turning in an actual de-scription. Stephenson's Black and Tan, also on Bleecker, differed from the average dive in that all the women were white and all the men were something else: African-Americans as well as American Indians, East Indians, Chinese, Malays, Lascars. This may well have been the entire extent of its depravity, but reports of the time suggest that non-whites were in any event just as likely to be cold-cocked and fleeced as visiting farmers from upstate.

It was often noted that by some peculiarity the very worst dives were situated within proximity of the police headquarters on Mulberry Street. One of these was kept by a fence named Mike Kerrigan, also known as Johnny Dobbs, who, when asked the reason for his location, answered, "The nearer the church, the closer to God." Nearby were the House of Lords and the Bunch of Grapes, at Crosby and Houston

Streets, both of which catered to enclaves of English crooks, as well as Owney Geoghegan's Hurdy Gurdy, on the Bowery. Geoghegan, retired leader of the well-known Gas House Gang, was the first to introduce boxing matches—known as "free and easys," although the term also referred to a crude sort of whorehouse—in a small ring in the middle of the dance floor. Raw whiskey was distilled on the premises and sold for a rather steep ten cents per glass. The place was a favorite of pickpockets and lush-workers, as well as a rendezvous for professional mendicants, who would stow their canes, dark glasses, and fake prostheses in lockers in the back room. When things got a bit slow, the giant waiters would stage their own bare-knuckle boxing matches, fighting for a five-dollar purse. There was the Morgue on the Bowery, headquarters of the Whyo gang. And there was the place on Mercer and Houston run by one Johnny Camphene, whose specialty drink included the chemical from which he took his moniker, otherwise known as rectified oil of turpentine, a popular varnish solvent and lamp fuel which, it is claimed, blinded scores or maybe hundreds of customers. Another feature of the time was the boys' dive. There were a number of these on Worth, Mott, Mulberry, and Baxter Streets, catering to newsboys, bootblacks, and members of youth gangs. There they could purchase three-cent whiskies as well as the favors of little girls. Once again, the records fail us, so far as description is concerned, the chroniclers of the era being so blinded by moral outrage that they failed to note physical particulars. We can expect that these dives would have borne only a very general similarity to what we have become accustomed to thinking of as decor. There would be a lamp, a counter, maybe a bench. Chairs and tables would be discretionary. The floor would be wood, maybe, or maybe packed dirt. There might be chromos on the walls, but probably not. There would certainly be a peephole, a guard at the door. There would be nearly a zero level of amenity. Between poverty and drink, nobody would notice anyway.

In the late 1870s, vice began moving uptown, specifically to Sixth Avenue in the thirties, a region that became known as the Tenderloin, or, per clergymen and reformers, Satan's Circus. As the song went:

Lobsters! Rarebits! Plenty of Pilsener beer!
Plenty of girls to help you drink the best of cheer;
Dark girls, blonde girls, and never a one that's true;
You get them all in the Tenderloin when the clock strikes two.

The establishment that set the tone was the Haymarket Dance Hall, on Sixth Avenue just south of Thirtieth Street. It opened in 1872 as the Argyle and was originally meant to house variety programs, but it could not compete with the immense popularity of such places as Tony Pastor's. The following year its owner, William McMahon, changed its name to the Haymarket after a famous old roistering institution in London, and removed the seats to make it a fully operative dance hall. It did, apparently, feature good music, but its major attraction was as a rendezvous spot between middle-class married men and prostitutes. McMahon sought to attract this sort of straying husband, and so he endeavored to foster an atmosphere of respectable vice. He hired a bouncer-cum-manager called Big Bill, who threw out the "trimmers," as thieving prostitutes were known, prohibited close dancing, and even expelled women for displaying their ankles. Customers could be barred for life for using "vile and abusive language." It was a large three-story edifice painted yellow; an evocative painting by John Sloan shows it near the end of its existence, decaying after the turn of the century, but still lurid. Like most such places, it admitted women for free and men for twenty-five cents, and it, too, featured cubicles curtained off for the presentation of those intimate dances; for that matter, it had a tunnel conduit to an adjacent hotel. The Haymarket paid the fairly minimal sum of $250 a week for protection, probably because police officials were among its steadiest customers.

Nearby, the streets were filled with similar places: the Cairo and Bohemia Dance Halls, on Twenty-seventh and Twenty-ninth Streets, respectively, Buckingham Palace on Twenty-seventh, and the Cremorne Garden, notable because it charged no admission fee, on Thirty-second Street. The Tivoli on Thirty-fifth Street was a clip joint that went for the short payoff, by means of watered drinks, shortchanging, and the like, indifferent to repeat business. The Heart of Maryland and the Tuxedo soon opened on Twenty-seventh, then the Stag Café, owned by one Dan the Dude, then Paddy the Pig's and the Burnt Rag. These places ran the gamut from modified blind tigers to such an amusement park as the Buckingham Palace, a single room two stories high that had crammed into its confines a shooting gallery, a full-scale restaurant, and, via the omnipresent curtained booths, a brothel. As time went by the area became stratified: Twenty-ninth was the street of whorehouses, Twenty-eighth stood for high-end gambling, and Twenty-seventh for the low end. There were saloons on every corner, each with its Ladies' Entrance, and houses of assignation (meaning, in current parlance, hot-sheet hotels) on every block. The raids on whorehouses were so frequent that in the 1890s a night court was established nearby to handle the traffic. The Haymarket itself survived raids, crackdowns, closings (during reform administrations, changes in police hierarchy, and as a bargaining point in payoff negotiations), and a seven-year tenure as Worth's Museum. In 1897 it was bought by Eddie Gray, who had complex blood ties to important members of the police department, and he, nominally at least, tried to run it as a clean joint— for example, by not allowing women to smoke. He fatally assumed, however, that this respectability made him immune to the necessity for protection; as a result, the cops began raiding him constantly for violating the ban on Sunday-night dancing. He finally quit in 1903, having, as his records claimed, seen 1,900,000 admissions in his six years. Others bought it, brought back the tarnish and the baksheesh, and kept it going until 1913, when it was demolished.

Between the Civil War and World War I, reform and racket administrations succeeded each other in New York with the regularity of crop rotation. Tammany Hall affiliations were generally indicative of a mayor's willingness to tolerate vice, but not necessarily. When Abram S. Hewitt was elected in 1887 on a Tammany platform, he nevertheless began wielding the broom, and among his first actions was to shut down McGlory's, the Black and Tan, Harry Hill's, the American Mabille, the Haymarket, the Cairo, the Bohemia, and others of the more egregiously disreputable joints. The sweep was merely temporary show, however. There was such an outcry that Hewitt's successor, Hugh Grant, allowed most of them to be reopened when he took office in 1889. The Bowery and adjacent areas immediately became filled with new places, some of them even worse. If Gombossy's Crystal Palace, which was known mostly for its piano player, Will Fox, who sometimes played wearing boxing gloves, sounds rather tame, there was Bismarck Hall on Pearl and Chatham Streets, which in its basement had a catacomb-like bagnio, consisting of dozens of featureless cubicles. Gunther's Pavilion was similar; there, so the legend went, Grand Duke Alexis of Russia paid an incognito visit and recognized one of the waiter girls as a Russian countess fallen on hard times, so he bought her freedom and arranged for her repatriation. There was Paddy Martin's, with its basement opium den; Hell Gate and the Chain and Locker on Baxter Street; Milligan's Hell on Broome Street; the Tombs on Center Street near the real Tombs; the Ruins, run by one Boiled Oysters Malloy, who served at cut rate: three whiskies for a dime. The House of Commons was haunted by a character called Ludwig the Bloodsucker, who, according to contemporary accounts, had hair growing "from every orifice" and was said to be a vampire.

It should be emphasized that not all saloons were dives. At this period, mixology (as it was already known) came to be practiced as an art. The inspiration came from the famous bartender Jerry Thomas, who invented the Blue Blazer and the Tom and Jerry, and is credited with having originated the very concept of the cocktail. He worked at various places on Broadway, including one he owned at Twenty-second Street that featured a gallery in the back room where the works of Thomas Nast were first exhibited. Harry Johnson ran his Little Jumbo on the Bowery for many years in perfect tranquillity, and in the Tenderloin there was Billy Patterson, at the Star and Garter, who created personalized concoctions for preferred customers, keeping the ingredients secret from everyone else. The Bowery possessed other more-or-less respectable institutions, such as Mike Lyons's, between Stanton and Houston, which was known less for its bar than for its restaurant.

It ran for thirty-seven years, the last thirty of them without a minute's closing, and served a wide spectrum of city types, from cops to bohemians and from politicians to beggars. The Bowery nostalgia that can be found in the memoirs of the prominent published between 1920 and 1950 is often dependent on memories of colorful and safe places like Lyons's, where the Bowery mix was displayed as benevolent and toothless, which is not to say that they were necessarily artificial.

Another such place, Diamond Dan O'Rourke's, on Park Row at Pearl Street, was so durable it reopened after Prohibition and succumbed only in the late 1950s. O'Rourke was a locality mayor—the Mayor of Park Row. This unofficial but meaningful title accrued on fixers and natural leaders in neighborhoods, who did not tend to be strongmen so much as peacemakers. There were, for example, mayors for Avenues A, B, and C, for Mott, Elizabeth, and Mulberry Streets, for nearly every one of the streets east of the Bowery. Some of these positions lasted until very recently. These mayors tended to be shopkeepers, usually bartenders or barbers, who had the ear of the ward heeler, the district boss, and the precinct chief, and could get erring sons out of jail, arrange for permits and variances to fly easily through the machine, and could take on spokesman tasks, such as with the press, for the neighborhood at large. It was a vestige of the village life that underpinned the order of neighborhoods, and when the neighborhoods disintegrated slowly, between roughly 1950 and the early 1970s, the role was one of the items that vanished.[5] O'Rourke was a popular man, therefore, and his saloon attracted a clientele of boxers, reporters, and politicians—three professions whose headquarters were conveniently located nearby. O'Rourke's was the first saloon in the general area of the Bowery since the Atlantic Gardens to feature the owner's daughters as barmaids. It did not bar women, either, which was unusual for a non-sporting establishment; among its regulars was the globe-trotting journalist Nellie Bly.

Silver Dollar Smith (né Charles Solomon) kept an equally popular establishment on Essex Street. He acquired his moniker from the fact that its floor was studded with thousands of the coins, which the riffraff would sometimes attempt to dislodge with cold chisels, but to no avail. The roster of habitués at Smith's is an amusingly evocative list of the sorts of handles men commonly went by at the time who were not members of the business class. There was Slippery Johnny Leipziger, so called because he once traveled by train to and from a Democratic convention in Kansas City without paying any fare; small political notables like Cross-Eyed Murphy, Mustache Ike Witkoski, Big Feet Louie Gorden; the marriage broker Schatchen Max Hahn; Stitch McCarthy, otherwise known as Samuel Rothberg, the Mayor of Grand Street; and of course boxers: John L. Sullivan, Jake Kilrain, Tom Sharkey, Jack Dempsey the Nonpareil ("the original," as distinct from the champion of the 1920s). Although Smith's place was basically aboveboard, Smith himself was not. He was a member of the Max Hochstim Association, also known as the Essex Market Court Gang, whose front, at least, was as a bail-bond firm for prostitutes, but which was generally supposed to engage in that terror of the times, white slavery.

The average Bowery saloon was not a terrible place. It was avoided by women who thought themselves respectable, and businesses catering to families tried not to rent locations adjacent to saloons. Women who didn't care what the neighbors thought drank in a fair number of these places, though some would not allow females in even to fill a growler with take-out beer, making them wait on the sidewalk in front. Then, too, Salvation Army girls were known or thought to make their biggest collections in saloons. The average saloon had a sawdust-covered floor, a potbellied stove, a wall covered with mirrors, nudes, framed newspaper clippings, chromos of boxers and horses. In some places a stein of beer was drawn and dumped in front of you the minute you sat down. Beer was the blood. Meanwhile, stale-beer salesmen would come by and drain the lees from kegs through bungholes, and then they would take the stuff and sell it to the cellar dives around Mulberry Bend that catered to the truly gone. A saloon was a club and a home. Men tended to avoid their own homes, and they herded together in trade and ethnic organizations, in political clubs, in shooting and singing societies. It was the heyday of the fraternal orders: the Elks (founded as the Jolly Corks on Elm Street, later renamed Elk Street), the Red Men, the Knights of Pythias, the Woodmen of the World, the Masons, the Odd Fellows, the Royal Neighbors of America, the Tribe of Ben Hur, the Druids, the Gleaners, the Moose. Many of these met in the back rooms of saloons. Likewise, saloons functioned as the equivalent of those orders for those too marginal to join them, or who lacked the funds to pay dues. Men could play cards or pool; they could hold union or political meetings in the back room, or argue politics and labor, or horses or baseball, in the front. They could trust the bartender, who would be their confessor, business adviser, political mentor, gossipmonger. And there was the free lunch, or, as an unwritten law had it, free after two nickel beers: cold meats, salted and pickled fish, cheese, pickles, rye bread. Everybody used the same fork, but then everybody also used the same towel hanging from the bar to wipe beer foam from his mustache. In the 1890s the Bowery itself claimed over half the saloons and pawnshops south of Fourteenth Street; an 1891 survey revealed an odd imbalance: the east side of the Bowery featured seventeen saloons, while the west side boasted sixty-five.

By popular accord, the very worst dive on the Bowery in the 1890s was McGurk's Suicide Hall, on the East Side just above Houston Street (the building is still standing), and it did not conduct its business in secrecy, since it possessed one of the first electric signs on the avenue. John McGurk, an Irish immigrant, had arrived on the Bowery via Boston in 1883 and opened the Mug, which featured waiters armed with knockout drops. When the Hewitt administration closed him down, he opened a clip joint catering to seafarers called Sailors' Snug Harbor. When this, too, was shut down, he moved up Third Avenue and opened a dive called the Merrimac, but it was shuttered as well, this time by the anti-corruption movement occurring in the wake of the Lexow Committee. In 1895 he opened McGurk's. It was four stories tall, with a deep interior and a large back room, with a direct entry to the barroom for gents and one through a long corridor for women. Entertainment consisted of singing waiters and a small band; the customers were, as ever, mostly sailors. "It was said," noted a contemporary, "that his business card reached every seaport in the world." Per habit as well, the waiters, led by headwaiter Short-Change Charley, were equipped with chloral hydrate, and they were reinforced by a formidable bouncer, a mayhem specialist named Eat-'Em-Up Jack McManus. These enforced the house rules, such as that if women were observed stealing from men, they were subjected to spot searches. McGurk's was nearly the lowest rung for prostitutes, having taken over that position from the waterfront dance houses of the previous generation; hence the suicide craze that gave it its name and, incidentally, its grisly lure as a tourist attraction. Figures are unreliable or uncertain on the total number of self-killings that went on there, but in just one sample year, 1899, there were at least six, as well as more than seven attempts. In October of that year, for example, Blonde Madge Davenport and her partner, Big Mame, decided to end it all, and so they bought carbolic acid, the elixir of choice, at a drugstore a few doors away. Blonde Madge was successful in gulping it down, but Big Mame hesitated and succeeded in spilling most of it on her face; the resulting disfiguration resulted only in her getting permanently barred from the place. Suicide attempts were so common that the waiters, upon getting an indication of same, would form a flying wedge and hustle the party out before she (or occasionally he) succumbed. After a woman named Tina Gordon killed herself, McGurk gave a speech over her body: "Most of the women who come to my place have been on the down grade too long to think of reforming. I just want to say that I never pushed a girl downhill any more than I ever refused a helping hand to one who wanted to climb." This rather chilling bit of equivocation overlooks the fact that by then his business depended on the suicides for a good part of its allure. McGurk was finally shut down once and for all in 1902, and retired to California with an estate supposed to have been in the neighborhood of $500,000. His last heartbreak came when his daughter was denied admission to convent school after those in charge discovered her father's identity.

McGurk's, for all the success of its negative publicity machine, was not actually the worst, of course, and neither was its close rival across Houston Street, Chick Tricker's Flea Bag. Some suicide candidates might go to the Three Deuces, a horror on Chrystie Street, instead. Otherwise, there were plenty of options for those who preferred to kill themselves by degrees. There were "shock houses," which catered chiefly to black people, and were also known as "block and fall joints," because "you'd get a shock, walk a block, and fall in the gutter." There were places that sold liquor mixed with liquid camphor, and those that sold a punch composed of whiskey, hot rum, camphor, benzene, and cocaine sweepings, for six cents a glass. Customers most assuredly knew what they were getting into; sometimes the attraction was the low price, more often it was oblivion. On Park Row there was the Doctor's, which gave away a premium coupon after every sixth drink that entitled the bearer to a free refill. Impostor cripples hung out there, deposited their imitation prostheses in lockers, and slept on and under the benches for a nickel.[6] The Billy Goat nearby had a two-drinks-for-five-cents special between 5 and 5:30 a.m., which made for long lines that had to be patrolled by the cops to prevent mob action. There were the Hell Hole, the Harp House, the Cripples' Home on Park Row; the Dump on the Bowery; the Inferno on Worth Street; the Workingman's Friend on Mott Street; Mother Woods's on Water Street; Cob Dock on Hester, all of them selling adulterated liquor to doomed addicts almost all dependent on beggary.

The Raines Hotel Law, passed in 1896, declared it illegal to sell liquor by the drink on Sundays, except with meals in hotels. Ostensibly a reform move, this was actually a boondoggle. Any dive that could muster ten rooms or a semblance thereof came to call itself a hotel. A meal might consist of a sandwich, according to the law, so these joints would make inedible sandwiches, sometimes consisting of a rock or a brick between two slices of bread, and leave one on each table, where, as weeks went by, the bread would develop a mold. Notable establishments which became hotels included McGurk's, the Tivoli, the Senate, the prostitutes-only bar the Rosedale, Bertha Hertz's notorious Dry Dock, as well as a host of more respectable outfits. This law actually

troubled no one, although it did have the unfortunate side effect of
virtually eliminating the free lunch, for which two cents was charged
in most places thereafter (it should, however, be noted that the two
coppers would buy one a bowl of soup, a frankfurter, and a side of
sauerkraut). Such innovations occurred all at once, courtesy of such
enforcing units as the Liquor Dealers' Association, which was fundamentally a police-protection racket.

It was around this time, the middle of the 1890s, that the Bowery
attained the height of its legend. For this it was mostly indebted to
two characters, Chuck Connors and Steve Brodie. The latter, a local
boy, had inconspicuous beginnings as a newsboy and bootblack, staking
out the Manhattan end of the Brooklyn Bridge as his territory immediately after its 1883 opening. A few years later he began announcing
to friends that, as a sort of dare, he planned to jump off the bridge.
One of his friends was a printer named Tom Brennan, who had numerous connections in the newspaper world, and so word spread fast.
At length, an East Side liquor dealer, Moritz Herzberg, came forward
and offered to back Brodie in a saloon if he carried out the stunt. On
July 23, 1886, Brodie jumped. Or did he? Nobody ever actually saw
him do it, or at least no impartial figure did. The alleged feat made
the front page of every newspaper in town. One reporter, Ernest Jarrold
(whose pseudonym was Mickey Finn), tracked down every individual
in any way connected with the event, but the results of his investigation
remained equivocal. Only members of Brodie's team claimed actually
to have seen it. Word eventually got around that, on the night in
question, a confederate on the bridge, upon receiving a signal from
the Dover Street dock, had dropped a dummy loaded with iron sash
weights into the water, after which a tout planted on shore began
yelling "There he goes!" Brodie, meanwhile, was lurking under a pier
in a junkman's rowboat, and when he heard the signal he swam un-
derwater to the spot where the dummy had hit the surface. Given the
vagueness of Brodie's story and the inability of anybody to provide
hard proof of the occurrence, this is probably what actually happened.
Nevertheless, it is remarkable that nobody among the numbers who

would have been involved in some capacity ever tipped his mitt. The fact is that people very much wanted to believe the story, regardless of its improbability. It became legend very quickly, and thus joined that body of lore which nobody cares to upset, since, after all, the literal truth hardly matters. As late as 1933, Raoul Walsh's raucously entertaining and totally ahistorical movie *The Bowery* did its part to cement the legend. In the film version Brodie, played by George Raft, at the last minute can't locate the dummy, which has been stolen by a pair of ruffians, so he is forced actually to make the dive.

Brodie's jump, real or fake, made him a star. For a while he appeared as an exhibit at Alexander's Museum. He staged a number of stunts similar to the jump, mostly other jumps from prominent heights that were always reported after the fact, until at one point he circulated the news of his death, waited for the announcement to sink in, and then appeared on the Bowery in triumph. After that, the newspapers refused to give him any more space. In 1888 he allowed himself to be persuaded to swim the rapids of Niagara in winter. Although he was dressed in a rubber suit, the cold and the current were too much for him; he would not let go of the rope by which he was dropped into the water, and begged to be hoisted up. If he had gotten to the point where he believed his own story, this seems to have disabused him, not that it made him own up or become humble.[7] In 1890 he finally opened a saloon, at 114 Bowery near Grand Street, that was to become a prime tourist attraction of the area, and stayed open for some years after his death from diabetes in 1901. His bar, which banned pickpockets and sailors, was popular with the usual crowd of sportsmen, and when John L. Sullivan, Jim Jeffries, Peter Maher, Jim Corbett, Tom Sharkey, Terry McGovern et al. were not present, barflies were pressed into impersonating them for the benefit of the sightseers. Tour buses would stop at the door, and even the quick jaunts would have guides intoning, "Ladies and gentlemen, to the left you see one of the great historical scenes of this great city. That, ladies and gentlemen, is Steve Brodie's famous saloon. You have all heard of Steve Brodie, the man who made that terrible leap for life from the Brooklyn Bridge

to the river below and lived to tell about it." Brodie capitalized relentlessly on his legend: his saloon featured an enormous oil painting
depicting the stunt that was officially offered as proof that the thing had
really happened. Occasionally, Brodie would wear an aged and battered
suit of clothes that he claimed was the outfit he had worn to make the
jump. The saloon was a three-room affair, the two rear of which were
reserved for his pugilist and reporter friends. Above the bar in the
front hung a profusion of signs, with legends such as "The Clock Is
Never Right" and "We Cash Checks for Everyone" and "If You Don't
See What You Want, Steal It" and "$10,000 in the Safe to Be Given
Away to the Poor; Ask the Bartender for What You Want." Brodie's
gift for publicity continued to serve him in new ways; one of his ploys
was to distribute free umbrellas to working girls during rainstorms,
and it was predictably covered in the newspapers.

Brodie's career attained new heights when, in 1894, a play called
On the Bowery began rehearsals. The lead role was originally intended
for the local boxer Swipes the Newsboy, but he killed somebody in
the ring and had to be replaced. The part was offered to Brodie, who
accepted with alacrity, and the plot was altered to suit him. The play
opened in Philadelphia, as was already traditional, and moved to
Brooklyn, and then finally to the People's Theater in October 1894.
Brodie was given a hero's welcome home, complete with banners
draped over the avenue and across the front of the theater, and a
profusion of floral tributes began arriving, including a massive replica
of the Brooklyn Bridge contrived entirely from flowers. The play itself
was an undistinguished hodgepodge melodrama with songs, its plot
concerning the ineffectual young aristocrat Hobart, who keeps making
a mess of things. True hero Steve continually has to cover for him,
rescue him from arrest, and eventually jump off the Brooklyn Bridge to
save the beleaguered heroine Blanche, who has been hurled off by the
villain Thurlow Bleeckman. The plot was of less interest at the time
than details of the production such as the setting of Act II, apparently
a faithful reproduction of the interior of Brodie's saloon. There were
songs galore: an aria sung in "Bowery Italian," a moral ballad sung

Steve Brodie and friends, hoisting short beers in his back room. Photograph by Brown Brothers

Chuck Connors (dancing, with cigar) at one of his Tammany Hall rackets. Photograph by Brown Brothers

A murder in a saloon, probably one of the blind-pig variety.
NYPD evidence photo

A typical saloon, albeit one populated by cops and
plainclothesmen. NYPD evidence photograph, circa 1915

by the bridge sweeper, and the centerpiece, Brodie's rendition of "My Pearl":

> *My Pearl is a Bowery girl,*
> *She's all the world to me.*
> *She's in it with any the girls 'round the town,*
> *And a corking good looker, see?*
> *At Walhalla Hall she kills them all*
> *As waltzing together we twirl.*
> *She sets them all crazy, a spieler, a daisy,*
> *My Pearl's a Bowery girl.*

For full effect, of course, this should be imagined as sung in the Bowery accent that was then just beginning to stand for New York in the American popular mind: "My Poil's a Bowery goil," etc. As an encore, Brodie sang Hoyt's "The Bowery," which, by all accounts, positively slew his audiences; it had apparently not yet come to possess the negative connotations it later acquired when local merchants blamed its refrain ("I'll never go there any more") for the street's decline. In the play the famous bridge leap was rendered without a tank; Brodie merely jumped through a trap as stagehands threw handfuls of rock salt in the air to simulate the splash. After the play had enjoyed a long and successful run, Brodie began dressing like a star, with a five-carat diamond ring, diamond studs in his shirtfront, a gold watch and chain, a fur coat. He went back to his saloon to garner more profits than ever before, and continued making a good living from letting the world know that he was a crook and a faker, if not in so many words. The tiny glasses of beer he would drink with insistent customers proved to be the agents of his death, as diabetes killed him before he reached the age of forty.

Perhaps even more emblematic of the time and the place was George Washington "Chuck" Connors, who became famous simply for his day-to-day behavior. He claimed to have been born on Mott Street but probably arrived there as an infant from Providence, R. I., and acquired his lifelong nickname (thereby shedding an earlier one, "Insect") from a childhood fondness for cooking chuck steaks on the end of a stick over small fires he built in the street. He grew up loose on the bricks, worked as a newsboy, a small-time boxer, a clog dancer at the Gaiety Museum. As a child, he was fond of tormenting the local Chinese, pulling their pigtails and throwing rocks at their windows, but came to like them and eventually enjoyed a special relationship with them, to the point of learning the rudiments of their language. He thus avoided the fate of local tough Big Mike Abrams, who boasted of having decapitated numerous Chinese with his clasp knife, and certainly did kill two or three. He was finally killed himself, the weapon being a thin rubber tube leading from a hallway gas jet into the keyhole of his room, and the murder was generally ascribed to one or another of the tongs, although some believed Connors had carried it out as a favor.

Connors worked as a bouncer and factotum at various dives; he idolized and imitated Scotchy Lavelle, an old river pirate who had settled down and taken a job as a bouncer before opening his own saloon on Doyers Street.[8] Connors in early adulthood briefly attempted to lead the straight life: he got married; his wife taught him to read and write; he got a job as a driver on the Third Avenue El. The wife soon died, though, and after her death Connors, who had returned to the drinking life, got shanghaied aboard a boat bound for London. He made the most of his exile, finding his way to Whitechapel and absorbing the style of the costermongers. When he returned to the Bowery a few months later, he was decked out in full coster regalia: bell-bottomed trousers, a blue striped shirt, a bright silk scarf, a pea jacket, and big pearl buttons everywhere, down the front of the coat and the seams of the pants. He had a jingle to go with the getup:

> *Pearlies on my shirt front*
> *Pearlies on my coat*
> *Little bitta dicer, stuck up on my nut*

If you don't think I'm de real t'ing
Why, tut, tut, tut

The "little bitta dicer" was a very small, tight-fitting derby, which he wore in place of the coster cap, because in America caps were then worn only by boys, baseball players, and bicycle riders, and the style was just not in keeping with Connors's personality.

After that, Connors became a character, a semi-fictitious invention. He made for endless newspaper copy and would stand for anything he was quoted as saying, even if many of the tales and saws attributed to him were the work of two reporters in particular, Roy L. McCardell of the *World* and Frank Ward O'Malley of the *Sun* (the latter has been credited with the invention of the word "brunch," as well as the catch-phrase complaint "Life is just one damned thing after another"). Connors did tell stories of his own, with flourishes in German, Yiddish, Chinese, and Cockney and Irish dialects. He held office at Barney Flynn's Old Tree House on Bowery and Pell Street (around the corner from Professor O'Reilly, World Champion Tattooer). He lived in a row of flats on Dover Street owned by *Police Gazette* publisher Richard K. Fox, who, rumor had it, let Connors live rent-free for more than two decades. Connors was called the Bowery Philosopher and the Sage of Doyers Street; he is said to have originated such catch phrases as "the real thing," "oh, good night," "oh, forget it," and "under the table" (meaning drunk). In 1904 Fox published a collection of Connors's routines, *Bowery Life*; its cover identified the author as Mayor of Chinatown, which he most assuredly was not, that distinction being reserved for Connors's friend Tom Lee, head of the On Leong tong. The booklet, which was included in a series that otherwise ran mostly to boxing, wrestling, club-swinging, and poker manuals, was illustrated with photographs of Chuck in typical costume striking typical poses (cigar in corner of mouth; one hand pointing forward with index or back with thumb; the other hand in coat pocket with thumb sticking out; legs set apart, one forward, one back; pail of beer at the ready), as well as a few Chinatown street scenes. The text is fairly lugubrious dialect comedy; a New York equivalent of the Arkansaw Traveler line (those Southern-talk joke books that were best-sellers in train stations for over a century). Here, for example, is Connors congratulating himself on having written a book:

> *Here's to me new graft. I'm one of dose guys now wot gits ink all over his flippers and looks wise. Say, it's a cinch, and I've got some of dem blokes wot writes books skinned a mile.*

And Chuck imagining himself a millionaire:

> *Me headqua'ters would be de Waldorf, but I would hev a telephone station in Chinatown, so I could git a hot chop suey w'en I wanted it quick. Ev'ry mornin' at 10 o'clock—or near dere—I'd call up me Chat'am Square agent an' tell him ter give cologne ter der gals an' segars an' free lunch ter der gorillas. Ev'ry bloke dat wuz hungry would have a feed bag an w'enever he wanted it. How does dat grab yer?*[9]

Connors's principal occupation in the nineties was as a "lobbygow," a pidgin Chinese term for tour guide. Connors would take parties of slummers around the Bowery, where he had a certain amount of competition, and through Chinatown, where he had the field all to himself. Chinatown was his turf. He knew the people and enough of the language to make for a veneer of verisimilitude on a spiel that was principally fable. He would point out innocent-looking pedestrians and identify them as notorious tong hatchet men, while any woman—Chinese or Caucasian—glimpsed in an upstairs window was liable to be labeled a "slave wife." His prize exhibit was a spurious opium den, a tenement flat haphazardly furnished and occupied by a white woman named Lulu and a half-Chinese man named Georgie Yee, who posed as addicts. The high point of the tour would occur when Yee would start dancing around, singing "Sweet Sixteen" or something identified at the time as "Allee Samee Jimmie Doyle," whereupon Connors would gravely announce that the man had become crazed from the drug's effects. Connors would not, of course, escort just anyone on these tours. Ordinary pikers could take the "haywagons" or "rubberneck wagons" that plied down from Times Square. Connors was much in demand as a guide for celebrities. He gave tours to such notables as Sir Thomas Lipton, Chauncey Depew, the novelists Israel Zangwill and Hall Caine, theater personalities Henry Irving, Ellen Terry, and Anna Held, and members of German and Swedish royalty. When he showed the French *diseuse* Yvette Guilbert around, he refused her tip, as a professional courtesy. Following Brodie's lead and his own natural inclination, he began appearing on the stage, in a gradual way. He began with a dance act that paired him with Nellie Noonan, the "Belle of the Seventh Ward," at the American Theater, and soon was coupled with the great Anna Held herself in an act staged at Oscar Hammerstein's theater on Broadway. In 1896 he appeared in a quasi-autobiographical sketch oddly called "From Broadway to the Bowery," also mounted at Hammerstein's. He was graduating in style from advanced barfly to roughneck boulevardier. At this point he was dividing his time among three women, occasionally squiring all of them at once. They were respectively known as the Rummager, the Truck (so called for her build), and Chinatown Nellie, described by a contemporary as a "regular busted doll."[10]

Late in the nineties, he began a major trend by founding the Chuck Connors Association, the sole purpose of which was to hold an annual ball, an affair that could guarantee a sizable profit from ticket sales and bar take, and whose profits were transmitted directly to Chuck's pocket. As well connected as Connors was, he had no trouble coming up with a roster of honorary members that included prominent politicians, actors, artists, and writers, as well as such raffish personalities as George F. Train (the ex-millionaire former Union Pacific Railroad promoter and Crédit Mobilier manipulator who passed through phases of dissolution and bohemianism before ending up busted and living at the Mills Hotel shelter on Bleecker Street), plus the mayors of the Bowery,

Avenue C, Poverty Hollow, and Chinatown. The first ball, held like its eventual successors at Tammany Hall on Fourteenth Street, featured music by two bands, Professor Wolf's Orchestra and Professor Yee Wah Lung's Chinese Orchestra. It drew representatives from clubs uptown—the Princeton, the New York Athletic, the Knickerbocker, the Hasty Pudding (imported from Cambridge), the Racquet and Tennis—and downtown—the Knickerbocker Icemen, the Lady Truckers, the Desperate Seven, the Bartenders' Club, the Lee Hung Fat Club, the Stuffed Club, the Sweet Sixteen Club, the French Cooks, the Girl Getters. His 1903 ball is noted for having been raided by Carry Nation, the temperance agitator, who was in town on one of her East Coast swings. She swept bottles and glasses off tables, snatched cigars and cigarettes from lips, and made her way to the podium, where she began reading a letter from a disconsolate mother whose daughter was alleged to be lost in the wilderness of the Bowery. At this point a wild local girl called Pickles threw a bottle and some epithets at the crusader, who retaliated by unsheathing her ever-present hatchet and chasing Pickles around the room with it. The ball exploded into a pandemonium of police whistles, shouts, screams, and fistfights among the guests, which stopped when Connors collared the reformer and personally ejected her from the building.

Connors's scheme launched a thousand imitations. Before long, the Bowery was thick with associations and clubs of one or two or ten or a hundred, all of which gave annual balls, so many that in the winter there was usually at least one every night. At Tammany Hall, the Walhalla, the Everett, the New Irving, the Arlington, such bodies as the Limburger Roarers, the Soup Greens, the Lady Locusts, the Lady Barkers, the Lady Flashers, the Crescent Coterie, the Bowery Indians, the East Side Crashers, the Plug Hats, the Jolly 48 held forth, their officers' names poetic in the period style: Mixed-Ale this and Bug that, Slimmy and Fatty and Peg-Leg and Limpy. The balls at first inspired great decorum. Prostitutes would wait patiently at the door for unaccompanied gentlemen to escort them in. Fights did break out every now and then, usually of a gallant nature, seldom at first anything very serious. Besides being surefire profit-making schemes in the area of ticket sales, the balls were also a way to beat the excise laws prohibiting after-hours liquor vending, and saloonkeepers were not slow to realize it. The Arbor Dance Hall on Fifty-second Street near Seventh Avenue, formerly the Eldorado, formed its own club, the Dave Hyson Association, and all its waiters held balls one after the other, making it a de facto after-hours night spot.

By this time the late Bowery Boy style had been established: the pearl-gray or brown derby tilted over one ear, the suit in loud checks with a tight coat, worn over a pink striped shirt, with a flaring box overcoat thrown on top in winter. The "mug," who might refer to himself as "me steady," would clinch his female partner—"me rag" or "me bundle"—herself clad in a tight jacket with a corseted waist, a long, somewhat bedraggled skirt, a nondescript hat perched on top and perhaps ornamented with a feather, typically a broken one. The two had a swagger that became a routine, known as the "hard walk," and it became a promenading dance at the balls and its execution the subject of contests that sometimes ended in riots. Dancing became known as "spieling" and it was practiced at private affairs or on the liners that sailed to Coney Island. The men all smoked Sweet Caporal cigarettes—the ones that came with baseball cards or pictures of actresses—and the women all chewed gum.

The language and the accent were what became thought of as New York talk by the rest of the country after being circulated in novels like Edward Townsend's *Chimmie Fadden* and Stephen Crane's *Maggie*, as well as in the testimony given by the hapless Chinatown crook Georgie Appo to the Lexow Committee in 1894, which was widely reported in the newspapers. Appo's speech and body language could be found reproduced almost note for note in any Warner Brothers B-movie of the 1930s: the "dese, dem, and dose," expressions like "youse guys," "dead game sport," "chase yerself," "wot t'hell," "hully gee" (or "chee"), the refrain of "see?," the lateral slicing motion made with the hand palm down, the crook talk of come-ons and come-backs, of "easy marks," the admission "he trun a scare into 'im."

The balls became known as rackets and became increasingly insti-
tutionalized and politicized. The ball of the saloonkeeper and bagman
Harry Oxford was an inevitability on Washington's Birthday, and Larry
Mulligan's was likewise on the eve of St. Patrick's; they held their affairs
at the Terrace Garden or Tammany Hall. The gangster and dive owner
Biff Ellison formed the Biff Ellison Association right on the heels of
Connors's innovation, and before long he was so formidable he could
command as many as three annual balls at the Tammany Wigwam.
The affairs were very quickly controlled by politicians, and attendance
at some of them was de rigueur for anyone seeking to obtain or keep
a license or a piece of turf for liquor sales or gambling or a contract
for city work. Connors died in 1913, having in his last years lost his
grip, due to a combination of alcohol and ill health, and become a
mere loafer. He was made to endure the combined tribute and indignity
of seeing a young Italian bootblack, Frank Salvatore, formerly known
as Mike the Dago, rename himself Young Chuck Connors (as boxers
would style themselves after their models) and form the Young Chuck
Connors Association. What made this more poisonous was that the
ball committee listed the original Connors second only in rank, the
first position being reserved for Jim Jeffries, even if he did outrank Jim
Corbett.[11]

Some of the balls kept going for years, even after Bowery culture
had been damaged by the shoot-'em-up outside the Lenny & Dyke
Association ball at Arlington Hall in January 1914, after it had been
all but destroyed by the subsequent reform sweep and finished off by
World War I. The *New Yorker* writer Joseph Mitchell found a character
called Commodore Dutch in the 1940s who was up to his fortieth
annual ball, the "Annual Party Affair, Soiree and Gala Naval Ball of the
Original Commodore Dutch Association." The breakdown Mitchell
gives of this event provides a glimpse into ball mechanics as refined
over the decades. The card advertising the gala listed such names as
Al Smith, Herbert Lehman, and Robert Wagner, Sr., as well as monikers on the order of Big Yaffie, Little Yaffie, Gin Buck, Senator Gut, Eddie
the Plague, Johnny Basketball, and Swiss Cheese, most of which were

borne by professional horseplayers, although also in attendance were saloonkeepers, fight managers, nightclub proprietors, tip-sheet publishers, bail bondsmen, and Turkish-bath attendants. These worthies were all given titles: Dutch himself was Founder and Standard Bearer; others were Head President, Assistant Head President, Second Assistant Head President, Admiral, Rear Admiral, Front Admiral, Judge Advocate, Field Marshal, Overseer, Master of Fox Hounds. Dutch, who was sixty-two years old at the time of the interview, had refined this sort of racketeering into a métier, and earned most of his living from it. He claimed to have been instructed by Connors and Silver Dollar Smith (in the 1940s those names were still legendary on the Lower East Side), to have apprenticed as a lobbygow and worked as a steerer for McGurk's, and to have been awarded the racket franchise by Tammany strongman Big Tim Sullivan in lieu of a requested loan. His rackets had been held at Everett Hall on East Fourth Street until 1912, when they outgrew the house and moved to Tammany Hall, upon which occasion the free beer was discontinued. The Fourteenth Street Tammany Hall was torn down in 1928, so the affair was transferred to the back rooms of various Third Avenue speakeasies and then their legal equivalents after Repeal. By the time the piece was written, few people actually bothered to attend the balls, but a large number bought tickets nevertheless.[12]

Commodore Dutch inherited the scene by outliving it. At the height of the Bowery as an institution he would have been lost in the crowd of characters. Connors and Brodie inspired hundreds of imitators; a forgotten showman named Charles B. Ward attempted to corner the market, calling himself the Original Bowery Boy, and singing "Only a Bowery Boy," a fair success even if he himself wasn't, in a show called *McFadden's Elopement Company*. There were famous panhandlers: Tennyson, so called because he was said to resemble the laureate; Shakespeare, who quoted the Bard at all occasions and is not to be confused with the murdered female Shakespeare mentioned earlier; his boon companion Daddy Ward, who claimed to have been ruined on Wall Street and who was always aiming curses at the captains of industry, and was known, too, for his costume of collar, cuffs, frock coat buttoned high, and no shirt. There was Doc Shuffield, said to have once been a fellow of the Royal Medical Society, who ministered to the penniless on the Bowery and died in a blizzard on his way to a call.

The turn of the century saw a number of fairly profound changes. The 1902 election of the reform mayor Seth Low brought about the closings of many notorious dives, like McGurk's and the Rosedale. The Williamsburg Bridge opened in 1903, and Delancey Street was widened and Kenmare Street cut through. The Manhattan Bridge opened in 1909, with a sweeping entrance plaza off Canal Street, for which a number of institutions, such as the Windsor Theater, were razed. At the same time the avenue was getting generally tougher and less whimsical. By 1902 the Bowery was called the "paradise of the criminal" and in 1905 there were reports of conductors on the Grand Street cars fighting among themselves for the right to pick passengers' pockets. During George McClellan's more lenient, if not outright corrupt, administration, as of 1904, the new places that opened in the wake of the dives closed by Low were more unabashedly criminal. The killer Louie (the Lump) Piaggi opened a joint on Doyers Street; the former dog thief and later opium boss Bridgie Webber opened the Sans Souci Music Hall up on Third Avenue. They, as well as such underworld luminaries as Chick Tricker, Kid Twist, Jack Sirocco, Big Jack Zelig, Julius Morello, Charlie Torti, and the gambler Bald Jack Rose hung out at Callahan's Dance Hall Saloon and the Chatham Club on Doyers Street, at Jimmy Kelly's Mandarin Club on Doyers and at Nigger Mike Saulter's the Pelham on Pell Street.

Oddly enough, these places eventually gained renown, but for something other than the criminal activities they housed and supported. Nigger Mike (who was Jewish) opened his dive in a space that had been the original site of the Chinatown Music Hall, the first Chinese theater in the Eastern states, and he himself brought in music, hiring a pianist named Blind Tom and occasionally supplementing him with a busker named Blind Sol. The Chatham Club was said to have the best piano player, one Louie Gass, who often accompanied the tenor Johnny Doyle. Soon Saulter's and Callahan's began hiring singing waiters, and a certain spirit of competition arose among the dives. The waiters at Callahan's included the two Yoelson brothers, who changed their name to Jolson; the younger was named Al. At Saulter's the most melodious of the waiters was young Izzy Baline, who when he left that seedy milieu behind changed his name to Irving Berlin. The kind of song that went over best with the thieves, murderers, extortionists, and their assorted muscle was the sentimental ballad. The tune that supposedly launched Izzy Baline's career at Saulter's was Arthur Lamb and Harry von Tilzer's "The Mansion of Aching Hearts":

> She lives in a mansion of aching hearts,
> She's one of the restless throng;
> The diamonds that glitter around her throat,
> They speak both of sorrow and song;
> The smile on her face is only a mask
> And many's the tear that starts,
> For sadder it seems, when of mother she dreams,
> In the mansion of aching hearts.

The repertoire was topheavy with such laments of the strayed remembering their kindly old mothers. There was James Thornton's "She May Have Seen Better Days":

> While strolling along with the city's vast throng,
> On a night that was bitterly cold,
> I noticed a crowd who were laughing aloud
> At something they chanc'd to behold.
> I stopped for to see what the object could be,
> And there, on a doorstep, lay
> A woman in tears from the crowd's angry jeers,
> And then I heard somebody say:

> *She may have seen better days, when she was in her*
>   *prime;*
> *She may have seen better days, once upon a time.*
> *Tho' by the wayside she fell, she may yet mend her ways.*
> *Some poor old mother is waiting for her who has seen*
>   *better days.*

And Charles Graham's "The Picture That Is Turned Toward the Wall":

> *There's a name that's never spoken,*
> *And a mother's heart half broken,*
> *There is just another missing from the old home, that's all;*
> *There is still a mem'ry living,*
> *There's a father unforgiving,*
> *And a picture that is turn'd toward the wall.*

And William B. Gray's "She Is More to Be Pitied Than Censured":

> *At the old concert hall on the Bowery,*
> *'Round the table were seated one night*
> *A crowd of young fellows carousing,*
> *With them life seemed cheerful and bright.*
> *At the very next table was seated*
> *A girl who had fallen to shame;*
> *All the young fellows jeered at her weakness,*
> *Till they heard an old woman exclaim:*
>   *She is more to be pitied than censured,*
>   *She is more to be helped than despised,*
>   *She is only a lassie who ventured*
>   *On life's stormy path, ill advised.*
>   *Do not scorn her with words fierce and bitter,*
>   *Do not laugh at her shame and downfall;*
>   *For a moment just stop and consider*
>   *That a man was the cause of it all.*

And "Just Tell Them That You Saw Me," by Paul Dresser, Theodore Dreiser's older brother; the lachrymose "Just Break the News to Mother," of Civil War vintage; "A Violet for His Mother's Grave"; "A Bird in a Gilded Cage," about the sorrows of a kept woman; "My Mother Was a Lady, or If Only Jack Were Here"; "Gold Will Buy 'Most Anything but a True Girl's Heart"; "Heaven Will Protect the Working Girl"; "With All Her Faults I Love Her Still"; "Just for the Sake of Our Daughter"; "You Made Me What I Am Today—I Hope You're Satisfied"; and the immortal "Teach Our Baby That I'm Dead." These songs must have performed some sort of expiatory function; the mind boggles at the spectacle of garrote artists weeping at songs about shame, white slavers sobbing at the tribulations of white slaves, ear-chewers remembering their white-haired mothers.

The ambience of these dives was set down rather caustically in 1904 by the novelist Rupert Hughes, describing a "subterranean grotto" near Chatham Square, its "sloppy" saloon leading to a back room filled with

> *soldiers, sailors, workingmen, cooks, ladies of the pavement and the impresarios who live upon their earnings. At a rickety piano sat a hardworking mechanic in shirt sleeves, whose most artistic effect was a so-called mandolin attachment, which gave the decrepit instrument a still tinnier sound. A youth in a striped sweater stood alongside and roared out dismal melodies in a saturated voice.*[13]

Many of these places were shut down in 1912, following the scandal caused by the murder of the gambler Herman Rosenthal and the subsequent revelation that his killing had been ordered by the corrupt police lieutenant Charles Becker. By this time the Bowery was well into its decline. An 1890 estimate had supposed there were nine thousand homeless in the region; by 1909 this was updated to around 25,000 living on park benches, in doorways, and in flophouses along the Bowery, Park Row, and adjacent areas. It had also become strictly a man's world. The avenue contained 115 men's clothing stores, but not a single purveyor of women's articles. Of 560 buildings on Park Row (it was then considerably longer than it is now), 425 were occupied by businesses catering exclusively or almost exclusively to men: saloons, cigar stores, flophouses, clothing stores. A few years later, in 1917, a survey of the Bowery conducted by the *Herald* turned up sixty-three saloons, fifty-one flophouses, fourteen theaters and (by then in the majority) movie houses, forty-one cheap restaurants, nine pawnshops, twenty-one labor agencies, and five missions. It was around this time that a movement arose to change the name of the avenue to something less tainted: Fourth Avenue South, Peter Cooper Street, Hewitt Avenue, Central Broadway, even Parkhurst Avenue, after the reformer.

Any remaining life in the area was killed off by the passage of the Volstead Act in 1919. After the sixty-three saloons closed, speakeasies began opening, but not at first on the Bowery. The drinking trade went to the ground floors of West Side brownstones, to inner sanctums in East Side town houses, to upstairs joints along Broadway, and the bars of third-class hotels on side streets. Herbert Asbury quotes an item from the *New York Telegram* in 1929:

> *Where on Manhattan Island can you buy liquor?*
> Answer: *In open saloons, restaurants, nightclubs, bars behind a peephole, dancing academies, drugstores, delicatessens, cigar stores, confectionaries, soda fountains, behind partitions of shoeshine parlors, back rooms of barber shops, from hotel bellhops, from hotel headwaiters, from hotel day clerks, night clerks, in express offices, in motorcycle delivery agencies, paint stores, malt shops, cider stubes, fruit stands, vegetable markets, taxi drivers, groceries, smoke shops, athletic clubs, grillrooms, taverns, chophouses, importing firms, tearooms, moving-van companies, spaghetti houses, boarding houses, Republican clubs, Democratic clubs, laundries, social clubs, newspapermen's associations* . . .[14]

Dives continued to exist near the Bowery, and on the old avenue itself, back rooms operated where hustlers sold smoke to the desperate, but the saloon culture that had its center there was dead once and for all.[15] Drinking had stopped being a sub-culture and become mainstream; illegality made it respectable as well as open to women. Then, too, many among the riffraff who were running Bowery joints in the oughts and early teens used Prohibition as a ladder to success, exchanging the lumpen clientele of the saloons for the better class they mixed with as bootleggers.

The Bowery itself had fallen into desuetude. Without the super-structure of gin mill and dance hall, all the attendant businesses collapsed. By the mid-1920s, wholesalers were buying buildings on the cheap, and so were petty manufacturers and distributors whose services did not require elegant presentation. The avenue was populated by the immobile victims of earlier times, by dipsomaniacs who rotated among the missions, the flophouses, the greasy spoons, the barber colleges (there was a stretch of them north of Houston Street, famous for asymmetrical haircuts), the labor agencies, the rag vendors, and the dealers in smoke. After Repeal, nostalgia came in, briefly, but the physical plant had decayed too much for anyone to make much serious effort to revive the old-time atmosphere. Otherwise, the principal difference made by the end of Prohibition was that neon-lit joints serving bad wine came in as a somewhat safer alternative to the smoke trade.

Characters of a sort continued to haunt the Bowery, the most memorable of the champion bums being Joe Gould, who had graduated from Harvard, had gone on to measure the heads of thousands of Mandan Indians as part of an anthropological expedition, and was apparently keeping somewhere the untold pages of a manuscript of an Oral History of Mankind—and who imitated a seagull for drinks. He was a figure not only on the Bowery but around most of Lower Manhattan from the twenties to the forties; he consorted with poets, philosophers, politicians, and movie stars. His Oral History was a city legend, speculated upon in print numerous times, until Joseph Mitchell in 1964 proved that it had been a chimera, its substance consisting of a pile of notebooks in which Gould had written a few reminiscences over and over again.

Bowery characters acquired a professional venue at Sammy's Bowery Follies, which opened at number 267, on the site of some notorious dives of the past, such as McGurk's the Mug. There, slummers could feast their eyes on a collection of old-timers, eccentrics, geeks, and the more presentable of the bums, who carried on in a mild and pathetic way; its atmosphere of good-natured decay was chronicled in photographs by Weegee (Arthur Fellig). The proprietor became the last Mayor of the Bowery, and his place was the only one by then to possess a cabaret license and present a floor show. A certain ambience did grow around the place, mostly of a nostalgic and toothless sort: there was a Bowery Chamber of Commerce, which handed out such honors as Miss Hitchhiker at an annual ceremony; a man named Harry Baronian published *The Bowery News*. In 1955 the El was torn down, and the suddenly exposed street looked naked and empty. Today all that remains of the Bowery's heritage are a number of missions and, at last count, two bars.

3 · HOP

A SORT OF HISTORICAL AMNESIA
GOVERNS THE POPULAR VIEW OF
THE USE OF DRUGS, MAKING IT SEEM
LIKE A RECENT PHENOMENON AND
obliterating its deep roots in American culture. Drugs came into American life in a
substantial way at the beginning of the nineteenth century, when Boston-based traders
broke the monopoly on opium exportation
that had formerly been held by the British
Levant Company out of Anatolia, Turkey,
and the British East India Company out of
China. At first the trade was mainly confined
to intra-Asian routes, but amounts of the
product had been gradually making their way
back to the United States, and its popularity
kept growing. By 1840 an estimated 24,000
pounds were coming into the country every
year, and a duty imposed by the government
that year raised the price to $1.40 per pound.

By 1860 the amount had grown to 105,000 pounds and the price had risen to $4.50. In 1870 half a million pounds were coming in, and the duty alone was $2.50 per pound. The period immediately after the Civil War brought drug use and its perfectly legal traffic new avenues of enterprise: cheap, quality-controlled cocaine hydrochloride was available in drugstores, as was cannabis indica extract. Before long, morphine, the chief active ingredient in opium, was extracted and made available for ready sale. In that early period, drugs were a fancy of the middle class; the poor simply didn't know about them, lacking the sorts of fashionable medicos who might prescribe them for ailments often of a neurotic or psychosomatic kind. The pattern usually involved a patient obtaining a prescription, often a temporary one to relieve symptoms, renewing the prescription with little trouble from his local druggist, and soon developing an addiction as the process was repeated long after the initial malady had gone away.

Something happened in the 1870s, however, to give drugs greater notoriety and correspondingly greater popularity. Some blamed the habit on the use of morphine to relieve pain from wounds in the Civil War. The vice crusader Anthony Comstock, when he received his mandate as a Postal Censor from Congress in 1874, made it his business to go after drug traffickers as well as purveyors of indecent literature, but at that point he seems to have been concerned mostly with contraceptives and abortifacients, and did not begin seriously to pursue opiates and psychotoxins until the 1890s. The democratization of opium appears to have been rooted in its use by the Chinese, who came to the West Coast in large numbers as laborers on the construction of the transcontinental railroad. The Chinese, of course, owed their addictions largely to the marketing expertise of the British East India Company, and they were discreet and peaceable users. What turned the tide against opium was a wave of prejudice against the Chinese that began in the West and spread eastward, and which fastened onto objects, habits, and peculiarities connected with them. One of the most conspicuous of these secondary attachments was, once the press had gotten hold of it, opium use. In this connection it should be recalled that in 1874 Samuel Gompers, future founder of the American Federation of Labor, persuaded a consortium of California cigar manufacturers to apply to their product the first union label—one that proclaimed the cigar to have been untouched by Chinese labor.

The Chinese came relatively late to New York City. In 1858 one Ah Ken moved into a house on Mott Street and opened a cigar store on Park Row. He was followed by a sailor, Lou Hoy Sing, in 1862, and, around the same time, by the first Chinese immigrant to acquire notoriety in the press, a man who went by the improbable name of Quimbo Appo. Appo was quite evidently deranged—he killed his wife and then a neighbor for no apparent reason—but his racial heritage made his condition and his acts appear to be moral choices to the eyes of the ignorant city. His son, Georgie, continued the lineage; he was a luckless sort who kept taking the fall for a gang of mostly Irish cargo thieves with whom he hung out on James Street.

In 1868 a man named Wah Kee came to town and opened a store on Pell Street where he sold vegetables, dried fruit, and what are inevitably referred to in accounts of the time as curios; he also kept a room upstairs which had facilities for gambling and for opium smoking. A few years later, in 1870, there might have been anywhere from twenty-five to seventy-five Chinese in New York, such was the gap between the census and the unofficial estimates. By that time there was an opium den established in a sailors' boardinghouse on Baxter Street and another one on Mott Street. Observers had then begun to notice that these houses were frequented by white customers, mostly prostitutes. One unverifiable—and spectacularly unlikely—estimate of the time counted 90,000 opium smokers and eaters in the city, or a tenth of the population of Manhattan.

In 1880 there were said to be seven hundred Chinese in the city; in 1890 there were supposed to be between 12,000 and 13,000. With such an increase in numbers, and with a population largely isolated by culture and language, it was inevitable that some force would come along to control the movements of the masses. Sure enough, by 1880, the first tong had been established. The tongs, a form of Chinese organized criminal society dealing in rackets and protection, were entirely an American phenomenon, the first one having been started in the California goldfields around 1860. In New York the tongs controlled gambling, especially fan-tan and lotteries, settled local disputes, handled relations with cops and politicians, and promoted and directed opium sales and consumption (the diversity of operations is strikingly reminiscent of later consortiums, such as the Mafia). Soon there were opium dens of a minimal sort ensconced everywhere, in basements, back rooms, and upstairs holes. The Chinese, it should be emphasized, were more sinned against than sinning; the remoteness of their language to Western ears and their tendency not to assimilate made them a readily available subject for any invention of the sensational press. By the late 1870s it had become routine for cub reporters on newspapers everywhere to turn in their "horrors of Chinatown" piece soon after being hired. These reports were largely fictitious, drawing on the sexual fantasies of the white middle classes, and using a certain propensity of the early Chinese settlers for marrying Irish women, as a loose basis for involved tales of white slavery and the forcibly induced drug addiction of white girls. In actuality, most of the Chinese in New York were working stiffs, and not very colorful, although baffling to Caucasians. An 1890s poll shows that a disproportionate number worked as laundrymen—there were about eight hundred in the metropolis—and the same poll records precisely three prostitutes, or female slaves.[1] By that time there could not have been very many Chinese women around at all; they were kept out by the Chinese Exclusion Act, which went into effect in 1896 and was not lifted until it became strategically advisable for the United States to do so, in 1942. Also kept from entering the country by its provisions were Chinese men except proven scholars, highly qualified professionals, and, of course, the rich.

The Chinese were thought of as threatening and unworldly because of a large number of signs and attributes only semi-intelligible to Westerners. There was their food, for example, which was much more nutritious and lower in fat than the Western diet of the time, but which initially struck those of European extraction as repulsive. Then there was their music, which resembled no Western music in any way, and their theater, which became a novelty attraction because of its strangeness to uninitiated eyes. New Yorkers were baffled by a drama that made no pretense of realism, and in which the prompter, the director, and actors not in the scene being staged nevertheless remained onstage, eating, smoking, and walking around as the action went on, and where props were moved and costumes changed without so much as a dimming of the lights. For that matter, Chinese audiences were equally casual about smoking, eating, and walking in and out during the course of the play (no one seems to have remembered that American audiences behaved similarly in the days of the Old Bowery Theater). The Chinese also had an incomprehensible religion, and the many rubberneckers who visited the Joss House on Mott Street could not interpret the complex symbology of the decorations and assumed that every figure depicted was some sort of deity and that the scenes they were shown engaging in were to be understood literally. The Chinese, it was averred, did not even walk side by side when in conversation, but one behind the other. And opium was seen everywhere by observers who mistook the water pipes commonly used to smoke tobacco for more exotic layouts. One writer of the 1890s broke down the nationalities by their odors (that sort of pigeonholing was popular at the time): the French smelled of garlic; the Germans of sauerkraut and beer; the English of roast beef and ale; the Americans of corn cakes and pork and beans; the Chinese of opium, cigars, and dried fish.

Further complicating matters, to outside eyes, was the complicated structure of Chinatown's governing body, or bodies. Was the assembly, transliterated as Chong Wah Gong Shaw, independent of the tongs? And for that matter, which of the tongs (innocuously described as "merchants' associations") had the real power—the Hip Sings or the On Leongs? The balance of power shifted constantly, until the end of the tong wars, which did not occur until around the time of World War I (and a vestige of the rivalry continues to the present day). In any event, someone was taking care of the opium dens, arranging graft with the police; in the nineties the sum was said to be $17.50 per week per house. Someone was also doing the importing. At the height of opium's popularity there were as many as six major brands and numerous minor ones. Leading the field locally were Fook Yuen (Fountain of Happiness) and Li Yuen (Fountain of Beauty); just behind were the four labels that came via British Columbia: Ti Yuen, Ti Sin, Wing Chong, and Quan Kai.

"Opium smoking in this country," Stephen Crane reported in 1896, "is believed to be more particularly a pastime of the Chinese, but in truth the greater number of the smokers are white men and white women. Chinatown furnishes the pipe, lamp, and yen-hock, but let a man once possess a 'layout' and a common American drugstore furnishes him with the opium, and afterward China is discernible only in the traditions that cling to the habit."[2] These habits mainly concerned form and nomenclature. There were the darkened rooms, the pallets, the disposition of bunks, the rituals affected by even serious users. The only American terms in use were very broad ones, and they have come down to the present day in only slightly altered form: the pipe was a "joint," probably because it was made from jointed stalks of bamboo; the goo itself was called "dope," a term that, according to the boulevardier James L. Ford, derived from daub, the axle grease applied to the prairie schooners, which resembled cooked opium in color and texture.[3]

The nearly sacramental instruments of the opium ritual, however, were called by their Chinese names, or an approximation thereof: the pipe or gong was, properly speaking, "yen tsiang"; "ow," the bowl; the "yen hock" was the dipping needle, the "yen hop," the box that contained the paraphernalia; "yen dong" was the lamp; "kiao tsien" were the scissors for cutting the bricks up into pills; "sui dow" was the sponge for cleaning the pipe; "dao" was the knife; "yen tau har" was the table on which the bowl was set; "yen shee hop" was the box that held the ashes known as "yen shee" (these were saved for a rainy day or perhaps sold down to needier addicts as "rooster brand" or "san lo"). The pill itself was the "yen pock," while the residue that

A morphine addict skin-popping, circa 1910. Photograph by
Brown Brothers

An opium den in Chinatown, late 1880s. Photograph by
Richard Hoe Lawrence

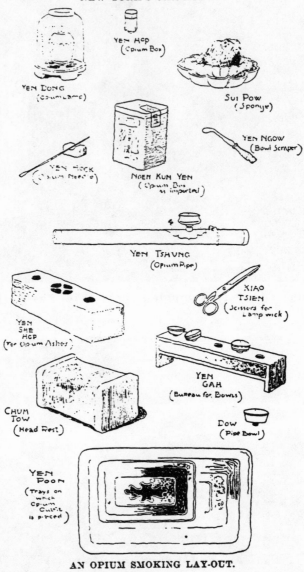

Opium paraphernalia, from *New York's Chinatown*, by Louis J. Beck, 1899

collected in the pipe stem was "gee yen," and it was removed by means of a scraper called "yen shee gow." "Yen shee kwoi," or users, were divided into distinct classes. There were the big users, who would go after the "li yuen," the good stuff that came in "high-hats," large pills that went for a dollar apiece, that is, per draw. Common users had to settle their "yen yen," or craving, with "pen yen," the generic opium that came in "pin-head" pills that cost a quarter. Lower down the scale, users might be reduced to rooster brand or, if they were really hard up, to a "bunk yen," meaning to hang around the den without possessing the wherewithal to bang the gong, and thus having to attempt a make-do high by inhaling ambient fumes. All these types had only contempt for "ice cream eaters," who had "chippy habits," which they would indulge occasionally and for thrills.

By the 1890s, opium dens were to be found concentrated not only in Chinatown but also in the Tenderloin, and until Comstock and associates began cracking down later in the decade, there were whole strips of dens where one could go without being introduced. Opium was popular among a certain class that dwelt along the common fringe between the underworld and show business. As Crane wrote: "Cheap actors, race track touts, gamblers and the different kinds of confidence men took to it generally,"[4] and it was equally in vogue among prostitutes and showgirls. A con artist, say, would make a big score, a hundred dollars or so, and then would repair to his favorite den, where he would hole up for weeks. There was no shortage of wealthy users, either. Some of them came in with their own equipment, pieces made of gold, silver, and ivory. At one point there was a house on Forty-sixth Street near Seventh Avenue that catered exclusively to the hophead gentry. It was run by two crooks, Harry Hamburger and Sammy Goldstein, and was said to be bankrolled by a bank robber named Jim McNally. The house had heavy curtains, a piano at which sat a rotating staff of entertainers, and elaborately embroidered cushions and bunks. The newspapers generated a steady stream of blind items that alluded to various celebrities seen entering the house, the women disguised by heavy veils. Hop use was simultaneously condemned and glamorized by the press, and its popularity grew steadily. At the time Crane published his report, in 1896, he estimated there were 25,000 regular users in the city; another writer of the same period guessed a far less plausible 500,000.

By the late nineties, cocaine was also on the ascendant, although it prompted less condemnation, less glamorization, and very little press feature, because its use required fewer props and was generally far less colorful. Of course, opium and cocaine tended to attract many of the same people, and to the uninitiated they were indistinguishable. If anything, cocaine, available in drugstores for a pittance and consumable anywhere in secrecy, was a poor man's high at the time. The full version of the anonymous "Willie the Weeper" evokes the drug culture of the fin de siècle in all its confusion:

Did you ever hear about Willie the Weeper,
Willie the Weeper, yes, the chimney sweeper,
Had the dope habit and had it bad,
Listen and I'll tell you 'bout the dream he had.

'Round the lay-out a couple of dope-fiends lay,
Listen and I'll tell you what they had to say,
Tales of money they were going to make,
And faro banks that they were going to break.

I heard one big hop fiend say,
"Grand scheme I got on today,
Got an interest in a silver mine,
Left to me by a friend of mine.

"Got a ruby-bush, a diamond-mine,
An emerald-tree, a sapphire-vine,
Hundreds of railroads that run for miles,
A thousand dollars' worth of coke stacked up in piles."

They started off in a Pullman car,
Did not get so very far.
In their minds they had the railroad clinched;
They woke up in the morning, found the joint was pinched.

They marched them off to a station-house,
Meek as a lamb, quiet as a mouse;
"What's the charge?" the judge then said,
"Hittin' up the hypo," and the fiend dropped dead.

"But I beg to differ," said the other smoker,
"The cop is kidding, he's quite a joker.
I'm the King, the land of poppies is my home."
"Twenty-three," said the judge. "Show the King his throne."

They went to a land called Kankantee,
Bought a million cans of hop and had a jubilee,
Visited the neighbors for miles around,
Presented the King with a bottle of Crown.

He went to Monte Carlo where he played roulette,
Won every penny and he never lost a bet.
Played every night till the bank went broke.
Laid himself down and took another smoke.

This is the tale of Willie the Weeper,
Willie the Weeper, yes, the chimney sweeper,
Fell asleep on his hall-room cot,
Dreamed he had a million dollars' worth of hop.

But in the morning, where am I at?
I thought that I was in my sweet baby's flat.
But in the morning I'm right in line.
Mister Hop Sing Toy you're no friend of mine.[5]

The song is unmistakably black in origin, but it turned up in minstrel shows and was translated to the white novelty market. Just on the face of it, there would seem to have been so many additions, corrections, and alterations made to the text that it is a jumble of disparate elements: the narrative contradicts itself in the middle, seems to become a different song at least four times, and it contains a moralistic last verse that has the sound of a very different voice. It is probably older than its single datable element, the "twenty-three," which refers to a slang term that grew out of the police move-along of loiterers around the Flatiron Building (built 1901). It shows how intertwined were the use of opium and that of cocaine, since it seems to blur the effects of the two. It also shows how rooted in poverty drug use was by that time; it is a slum version of Baudelaire's "Les Paradis Artificiels."

Cocaine was generally injected with needles in the nineteenth century, but around the turn of the century, ingesting it via the nose became a fad; crystallized cocaine was for a while called "burny" or "bernice" and snorters were known as "burny blowers." According to the reminiscences of the policeman Cornelius Willemse, the Lafayette Hotel, a Tenderloin fixture at Fortieth Street and Seventh Avenue, was so popular with users that it featured in its back room a potted tree called the Burny Tree, its branches garlanded with hundreds of lengths of the black rubber tubing used for snorting. Cocaine was to become ever more popular in the following decades, and increasingly identified with the criminal population. Cannabis and its derivatives were known, but their use seems to have been largely restricted to rural areas, especially among blacks, until a combination of Prohibition's effects and widespread black migration northward to the cities made it the drug of choice in the 1920s and thirties.[6] On the horizon was heroin, then merely the brand name for the diacetylmorphine solution synthesized by Bayer, the German inventors and manufacturers of aspirin, in 1896. It was marketed as a cough suppressant around the turn of the century, and caught on quickly, so that by 1916 it was estimated that one-third of the city's habitual drug users were addicted to it.

Meanwhile, the various reform drives continued apace. As soon as dens and distributorships were closed down, graft would make it possible for them to reopen elsewhere. On the national level, restrictions on imports had by 1890 reduced to 93,667 pounds the amount of opium brought in legally, and an 1891 tariff law made legal importation prohibitively expensive. This did not, of course, affect illegal traffic except to raise prices. The wholesale banning of narcotics was discussed as early as the beginning of the nineties, but it was delayed for nearly a quarter of a century because of the horse-trading that went on between the anti-drug forces and the alcohol-prohibition movement; the latter, Midwestern in origin, was largely ignorant of drug use. Not until 1914 was the Harrison Act, which forbade the sale of narcotics without prescription, passed in Congress. Even then, the use of recreational drugs continued in open and aboveboard fashion until the 1930s' crusade by Harry Anslinger, of the Bureau of Narcotics and Dangerous Drugs.

4 · CHANCE

NEW YORK CITY REPRESENTED A GAMBLE FOR NEARLY EVERYBODY WHO ARRIVED VOLUNTARILY. THE ODDS VARIED SOMEWHAT: FOR IM- migrants from impoverished nations, for example, the stakes may have appeared high, but the outcome virtually had to be better than what they started with. For those coming to the city from other parts of the United States the odds were longer, because the decision involved parlaying a modest future against the big take of ambition, and chances were few. New York displayed the full range of possible outcomes, laying heaviest emphasis on big prizes and vast fortunes on the one hand and utter destitution on the other; as an advertisement for itself, it only shrank from publicizing the mediocre mid-range settlement. If life was a gamble, gambling was an essential part of life, and gambling permeated every masculine gathering in every station of the social and economic range. This was no more nor less true in a general way for New York than for any other part of America at the end of the nineteenth and the beginning of the twentieth century, a time when the main chance seemed open to all, and its capture a mysterious process that could be as much a matter of pure random luck as of the hard work so esteemed in retrospect by the winners. In New York, though, while fortunes might not be made and lost as precipitately as in the goldfields of California, fortune was a constant promise rather than a seasonal fever, and poverty was just as constant a threat. While gambling fads did not come around as frequently or as inventively as in New Orleans, there was a greater range of ways to lose one's shirt. While New York was not filled with innocent rubes for the sharper to prey upon, it was, however, filled with sophisticates who thought themselves impervious to flimflammery and who could thus throw away common sense in the name of hubris.

Gambling always existed in New York, but it took the nineteenth century to make it into a real business. Prior to that, it had been small change: euchre and whist in taverns, betting on cockfights and dog-fights, and a ubiquitous feature of early America—the lottery. In the eighteenth century, this was an eminently respectable pursuit, its man-ifestations mostly local; many were the churches built on lottery pro-ceeds (which in the following century would preach fervently against gambling and its ill-gotten gains). It is worth noting that the construc-tion of both Harvard and Yale was assisted by lotteries, and that a scheme to help finance the Continental Congress in 1776 by means of a country-wide lottery was abandoned only because of the difficulty of selling tickets at that troubled time. Lotteries increased in number, size, and reach after the Revolution, but it was not until the end of the War of 1812 that crooks entered the business in substantial numbers.

Soon fraudulent lotteries were displacing the honest ones, and by 1819 the situation was such that New York State passed a measure requiring licenses, procurable for a fee of $250 a year. This proved less than effectual; two years later a provision was added to the State

Constitution banning them altogether. There was, however, a loophole that permitted already extant lotteries to continue functioning, so that the state continued to possess legal lotteries until 1834. Another loophole kept the racket alive long after that; there was nothing illegal about running agencies for out-of-state lotteries, and the very crooked ones in some Southern and Western states thrived for decades afterward. Lotteries were ridiculously easy to establish, and even simpler to rig, so that they amounted to the proverbial license to mint money. For that matter, the lottery did not even have to exist; a rented office and a few printed signs and tickets would suffice. There was, after all, no shortage of customers. An 1826 handbill for the New York Consolidated Lottery, one of the post-1821 holdovers, features a cartoon of an upstate rustic who is shown saying: "How darnayshun tickled I am to see our Debbyties at Olbyna tryon to stop fokes from byen tikkets—they mite just as well hold a live eal by the tale, without having an old mitten on there hand with ashes out."

Policy, which is to say, a system of wagering on figures that most often represented combinations derived from the numbers of winning lottery tickets, existed in the eighteenth century as a form of side bet among sporting gentlemen, but not notably among the poor. Its name derived from an earlier denomination, "lottery insurance," that survived until the 1830s. Policy became so popular that in time it threatened to outdraw the lotteries themselves, which was no hardship, since they were often controlled by the same people. In 1818 it was said that a single New York City lottery office made a profit of $31,000 on policy alone in one three-day period. After the New York lotteries were finally suppressed, policy drew its figures from the New Jersey state drawing, until that, too, was banned in 1840. Then the action switched to the shady Southern lotteries, particularly the Kentucky Literature Lottery, the Kentucky State Lottery, and the Frankfort Lottery of Kentucky, taking the story up to well after the Civil War. In more recent times, policy (or numbers, as it has come to be called) has based its figures on the outcomes of horse races or stock-market totals. Bettors of policy in the nineteenth century were not confined to simple three- or four-number combinations, but could choose from a menu of complex combinations similar to horse-playing boxes and sets. Up to four numbers could be played, to appear either anywhere on the board or in fixed positions. These combinations bore names redolent of horse racing: Gig, Saddle, Horse; the Gig (three numbers anywhere) evolved into the standard numbers play, and even its magic figure—4-11-44—was handed down.

The fact that neither lotteries nor policy lent themselves to any kind of system play gave rise in the early nineteenth century to the use of dream books, and some are in print today with only minor alterations over almost two centuries. The standard dream book, then as now, is based on a classic model of dream interpretation from the tradition of soothsaying. It records a list of persons, objects, and situations that might occur in a dream—a Turk, a clock, a wedding, say—but in addition to assigning them a meaning it gives a number to be played, often followed by instructions as to whether the number should be played fixed or floating, and whether the wager should be heavy or light. Policy increased in popularity and influence with every passing decade in the nineteenth century. When the game was run by Reuben Parsons as banker and John Frink as manager, from 1840 to the 1860s, the pair controlled nearly 350 shops around Manhattan. After the Civil War, Zachariah Simmons became the boss, backed by the Tweed Ring. He ran about three-quarters of the six hundred or seven hundred operations in the city at that time and opened franchises as far west as Milwaukee and as far south as Richmond. Albert J. Adams, once a runner for Simmons, took the baton in the 1880s and ran things until 1901. He dispensed with drawings altogether, and paid out strictly on numbers that had been bet low, or not bet at all, and nevertheless saw the policy shops in the city increase to around eight hundred, with a million regular players. Reform and raids finally dampened matters, and policy began to decline around 1905, becoming defunct by 1915. Prohibition changed the city's temper once again, however, and the game was reborn in 1923, particularly in Harlem, as numbers.

On-site betting operations were for many years a feature of taverns, and their play was generally modest and did not necessarily occur on a regular basis. It was not until the late 1820s that properly constituted gambling houses began to appear in New York. The development was inevitable, as specialization and then consolidation followed a general pattern in commerce in the city at the time, when New York was becoming a full-fledged urban center. The example of Kit Burns's Sportsmen's Hall, or Rat Pit, mentioned earlier, is particularly illustrative, as it took the ancient brutal sports of alleys and farmyards and turned them into a steady proposition. The phenomenon really represented an adaptation to the new industrial era of pursuits that seem almost medieval. Even members of the merchant class did not consider it beneath them to bet on fights to the death between rats and dogs. Meanwhile, on the Bowery, men like Charley Mook, Slab Baker, Shell Burrell, and the b'hoy George Rice were opening rooms that were entirely devoted to table games, which at this time were most prominently represented by roulette, twenty-one, chuck-a-luck, and faro.

Faro, now nearly forgotten, was the gambling pursuit that seized and held the imagination of the country for more than a century. From dim origins in the middle ages, it spread gradually through Europe, first receiving wide notice in France during the *ancien régime*, probably getting its name at the same time: Pharao, or Pharaon, from the Egyptian images printed on the backs of the cards. Louis XIV banned the game in 1691, but the Duc d'Orléans revived it in 1715, and it was popularized a few years later by John Law, the legendary Scottish gambler and confidence man who lived in Paris in the eighteenth century. It made its way to North America by way of French settlers in New Orleans and Mobile around the end of the century, and in the decade after the Louisiana Purchase spread all over the United States.

It was set up on a table, behind which sat the dealer and his assistant. On the table itself was the layout, which consisted of a suit of thirteen cards, usually spades, pasted or painted on an enameled oilcloth. The cards on the layout were set out in two parallel rows, with the odd card—the seven—between and at the end of the rows to the right from the players' point of view. The row nearest the players consisted of the king, queen, jack, ten, nine, and eight; that nearest to the dealer had the ace, deuce, trey, four, five, and six. The dealer shuffled and cut and inserted the cards into a box with an open top, then he proceeded to draw them two at a time, first disposing of the top card, considered dead (as was the last card). Of each pair, the first card counted for the house, the second for the players, and they were put into two piles—the winners going on top of the dead card, unless, as happened later in unscrupulous houses, that counted for the house as well. In more decorous places, bettors waited for the draw of the dead card before placing their wagers on the remaining spaces. Each draw of the cards was called a turn, and there were twenty-five of these in a game. Bettors played single cards or combinations: king, queen, and jack made up the big figure; ace, deuce, and trey the little figure; six, seven, and eight were the pot; king, queen, ace, deuce made up the grand square; jack, three, four, ten the jack square; nine, eight, six, five the nine square. The bank paid four to one for a winner, unless two cards of the same denomination were drawn in a single turn, which was called a split and which would occur on average about three times in two games; then the house would split the bet with the players. While the dealer was drawing, his assistant would be manipulating a device called a case-keeper, a miniature of the layout in a box, which would establish what had already been drawn so that the house could keep track of what cards were left. On the last turn, additional bets were made on the order of extraction, and for many players this became the whole point of the game.

Up until the middle of the nineteenth century, faro was considered the fairest game of all time, with an advantage to the bank generally estimated at a mere one and a half to three percent. It was never permitted at Monte Carlo, possibly because of its relative unprofitability for the house if played honestly. Indeed, in a scrupulous game, the player could achieve a disadvantage only through his own efforts, and then by playing a "running limit" or "going paroli"—a term that evolved into the word "parlay"—that is to say, running up winnings, consolidating them, and then risking the whole sum on one turn, usually the last. Of course, the game never was played honestly, and the methods of rigging became more elaborate as the years went by. Dealing was the first element to be affected. In the early days the deck had been dealt from a face-down position in the dealer's left hand. In 1822 an anonymous American introduced the dealing box, made of brass, half an inch wider and a little longer than the deck, covered on top with a single thumbhole, used to push the cards out through a side slit, with a spring keeping the rest in line. The open-top model came in a few years later. Soon, however, the market was deluged with rigged boxes of all sorts, with devices that in some cases can be imagined from their names: the gaff, the tongue-tell, the sand-tell, the top-sight-tell, the needle squeeze, the end squeeze, the horse box, the screw box, the lever movement, the coffee mill. All sorts of ingenious contraptions were fitted into these small instruments—springs, levers, sliding plates—to inform the dealer of the order in advance and to allow him to alter it invisibly and at will.

In addition to this, there were a variety of trimmed and marked cards and cards manufactured in such a way that any two could be made to stick together. What is remarkable is that these devices were all sold very openly, advertised in newspapers as "advantage tools," and in at least one case carried on the shelves of a specialized shop around the corner from the Bowery, so that any gambler not straight from the woods would know that the chances of his being swindled were overwhelming. (Other wares included loaded dice, crooked roulette wheels, cutters and trimmers for preparing cards, poker rings for marking cards during a game, hold-outs for concealing cards in vests, sleeves, and under the table at poker, and shiners, little mirrors that enabled the artful cheater to read the hands of his opponents.) But such is the faith of the gambler. Even with these tools, adept dealing at faro was a profession that demanded great skill, and paid accordingly. In mid-century the top practitioners, known as "mechanics" or "artists," might earn several hundred dollars a week, in addition to a cut of the profits.

Faro was popular across the country and with every class. One measure of its influence is the number of terms specific to it that have entered the language in a general way: "tabs" were sheets annotated by players to keep track of cards already dealt, hence "keeping tabs"; "losing out" meant to lose four times on the same card, and "winning out" was its opposite; "piking" was to place small bets all over the board, and a practitioner was known as a piker; to "break even" was to play a system; to "string along" was to play all odd cards or all evens; a "square deal" was one made not with round-cornered but with square-edged cards, which were harder to adulterate; a "sleeper" was a bet made on a dead card (which might be carried over to the next game); a "pigeon" was the victim of a leg—a sharper—and a "stool pigeon" was a shill; a "shoe string" involved parlaying a small bankroll into big winnings; the last card was said to be "in hock" because the first card was called "soda," after the expression "soda to hock" (hock was dry white wine). Faro generally was known as the "Tiger," from the image of a Bengal tiger, of obscure origin, that was used to indicate a house where a faro bank could be found, and to play the game was to "buck the Tiger." The tiger signs were sometimes used by players to communicate the relative honesty of the house by means of a sort of hobo alphabet that involved minute scratches in a prearranged pattern. A particularly unscrupulous house (they were all unscrupulous to some degree) was called a brace house; a very fixed game, a brace game.

Variations on faro popped up every now and again: short faro and rolling faro both enjoyed brief vogues. The legendary shyster lawyers Howe and Hummel, in their 1886 guidebook to New York vice, *In Danger*, mention something called skin faro, in which the mark was assigned the role of dealer and given a deck with a pinhole through it. The players, employees of the skin house at which the game was played, could then clean him out on the final turn; Howe and Hummel tactfully refrain from specifying how this was accomplished. The most successful variant was stuss, or Jewish faro, which completely domi-nated play east of the Bowery from the last decade of the nineteenth century up to World War I, although it failed to spread much outside the neighborhood. The major gangsters of the period, such as Monk Eastman, Johnny Spanish, and Kid Twist, all kept a sideline in stuss at some point. The game was a simplification of faro that literally stacked the deck in the bank's favor. After bets were made—and they could be made only on single cards—the deck was shuffled, cut, and turned over. The first card was the house's, and so were all splits. Even without the various palming, reading, and counting methods employed by dealers, the house advantage was considerably increased. All these games were moribund from around World War I; they did not fully disappear until after World War II.

The other popular game in the early Bowery hells was chuck-a-luck, also known as sweat or sweat-cloth. It was the only dice game played on the East Coast until craps came along in the early 1890s and rapidly dominated the scene. The early houses might also feature such games as loo, all-fours, seven-up, pitch, hearts, euchre, ecarté, cassino, rouge et noir, Boston, and whist, some of them ancient, some soon to achieve respectability. Keno, which did not outlast the century except in a bowdlerized boardwalk version, was essentially the same as bingo, although cards were sold at rates that varied from a dime in the slums to a hundred dollars in the high-class joints; for the dealers it was as much of a fish-in-the-barrel as the ersatz lotteries. Monte, not to be confused with three-card monte, was played with a deck of forty or forty-four (the eights, nines, and sometimes the tens were removed). The top two and the bottom two cards of the deck were set in two layouts, top and bottom, and then players would bet on matching the face or suit of cards as they were drawn against the layout cards. Needless to say, it, too, was extremely easy to manipulate. Its heyday came in the wake of the Mexican War.

By the middle of the nineteenth century Manhattan was awash in gaming houses. The reformed gambler Jonathan H. Green, who had written exposés of the generalized cheating and rigging practices of the houses across the country and had become the general executive agent of the New York Association for the Suppression of Gambling, was commissioned by this body in 1850 to take a survey of local

conditions. When he presented his findings at the Broadway Tabernacle early in 1851, he reported the existence of six thousand gambling
houses in New York City, two hundred of them of the first class, and
this not even counting lotteries, policy, or raffles. Although the figure
sounds wildly exaggerated, it should be noted that it works out to the
not unreasonable average of one house for every eighty-five inhabitants.
At the time it was elsewhere estimated that 25,000 men, or one-
twentieth of the city's population, depended on gambling for their
livelihood.

The classes and degrees of houses were numerous. The first-class
joints of the time were clustered on Park Row, Park Place, lower
Broadway, and Liberty, Vesey, and Barclay Streets. Some of these were
veritable mansions, where every amenity was observed. The truth was
that they were skinning houses not fundamentally different from the
lower orders, but to persuade the prosperous—often the newly prosperous—to separate themselves from their bankrolls, a stage set was
required that would suggest that the proprietors did not need the cash,
that they were sporting gentlemen who wagered for the sheer love of
the pursuit. Thus, these places might feature huge mirrors in gilt
frames, Old Master paintings (a much more loosely defined category
at that time than now), rosewood furniture upholstered in satin and
velvet, elaborate crystal chandeliers. They would serve lavish dinners
to all parties as a perquisite, with costly viands laid out on silver and
gold plate and esteemed vintages decanted in cut glass. Even clients
who recognized the polite fiction involved might be moved to refrain
from an overly close examination of the hands of the faro mechanic.
Nestled among these arriviste houses were the day houses that catered
to messengers and clerks, keeping regular business hours and expe-
riencing their heaviest trade at lunchtime. Both sorts of establishments
tended to be run by the same people: Jim Bartolf and Frank Stuart on
Park Place, the b'hoy Handsome Sam Suydam and Harry Colton on
Barclay, a certain Hillman on Liberty, Orlando Moore on Broadway.
Jack Wallis, who was said to be Chinese, won his house, so legend
had it, from French José and Jimmy Berry in a coin toss. For that

matter, Pat Herne, established on Broadway, was so much of a gambler himself that he lost his house's take more than once, and eventually the house itself. Many houses of all grades were bankrolled by one man, the lottery king Reuben Parsons, who eventually became known as the Great American Faro Banker.

Ann and Barclay Streets at the time were a lurid gaming locus halfway between the Bowery and Wall Street, and bridging the two. Ann Street, crowned on its Broadway corner by Barnum's American Museum, was a mecca of lower-class hells, saloons, and hash houses popular with a milieu of b'hoys, firemen, thieves and footpads of all stripes, pickpockets, gangsters, and Tammany shoulder-hitters, as well as with brokerage house and express-office employees. Its particular feature were the wolf-traps, also known as snap houses, or ten percent houses, or deadfalls. These were rooms, possessing no amenities or centralized bank, that let out space to individual gamblers who got up their own games, in return for a ten percent cut. Such bazaars were totally unpredictable, since a dealer of relative honesty might set up cheek-by-jowl with the most rapacious skinner. The biggest wolf-trap of them all was the Tapi Franc, at 10 Ann, which boasted the only roulette wheel in such an establishment, as well as twenty-one, chuck-a-luck, and twenty-four-hour faro action. Here low-limit games—called snaps—set a minimum wager of $25, while the high-rolling games had bottoms of as much as $500 or $1,000. At the Tapi Franc the crowd was said to be even more lawless than the dealers; fights broke out regularly and pickpockets operated without restrictions. Only a handful of bouncers kept the peace, since cops, by common agreement assisted by graft, were nowhere to be seen. Not that the police ever did much to protect the average sucker: a story of 1849 had it that one time, when a mark complained to the authorities about his treatment in a skinning joint, these worthies told him that his motives for visiting the place were "less than honorable," and then jailed him as a material witness.

There were two main classes of professional gamblers in the mid-nineteenth century, distinguished not by income but by life-style.

There were the fashionable dandies called blacklegs, who were described as pursuing an unvarying daily schedule: strolling on Broadway in the morning, driving on Fifth Avenue in the afternoon, attending the opera in the evening, and then cheating on Park Row until 5 a.m. The other class was proletarian in origin, and connected to the interlaced worlds of boxing and politics, both of which were, of course, forms of gambling themselves. Bets were made on boxing matches as on elections; politicians sponsored boxers and fixed their fights; boxers would move into either gambling or politics or both when they retired from the ring. The same names crop up again and again in chronicles of gambling, boxing, and politics of the time. In 1842, for example, Chris Lilly, who was both a member of Isaiah Rynders's clique and an employee of Jack Wallis's hell (odd for a Nativist to be working for a Chinese), was matched against one Tom McCoy in a bout at Hastings, N.Y. The fight lasted 119 rounds, over two hours and forty-three minutes, during which time McCoy was knocked down eighty-one times; the fight stopped only with McCoy's death. Lilly fled the country, but soon returned under Rynders's protection; thereafter, he went into politics, setting out for New Orleans in 1848 to spread repeat voting and other New York niceties among the local electorate.

The two unbeatable local champions were Tom Hyer and Yankee Sullivan. Both were identified with the Nativist cause (in spite of the fact that Sullivan, whose real name was James Ambrose, was Australian), and both were professional gamblers: Hyer as a roper (a tout) and shill at Frank Stuart's on Park Place, and Sullivan as proprietor of his own joint, the Sawdust House on Water Street. What was needed was a Tammany champion to uphold the honor of the Irish. That man, it turned out, was John Morrissey, known as Old Smoke, born in Ireland and brought up in Troy, N.Y. When Morrissey came to town, he worked as a freelance troublemaker, originally as a Tammany shoulder-hitter. He beat a Know-Nothing champion called Bill Poole (who subsequently was shot and killed by Morrissey associate Lew Baker) and led at least one raid on Rynders's Empire Club. Rynders was sufficiently impressed by Morrissey's prowess to offer him a job, but the vicissitudes of party political enforcement were limiting for a man of Morrissey's ambitions, and in 1851 he lit out for California. There he defeated a Western champion, George Thompson, familiarly known as Pete Crawley's Big Un, in a nineteen-minute bout, and afterward called himself Champion of America.

When he got back to New York, he found to his chagrin that this title cut no ice with the natives, so he set about becoming champion of the East. He wanted to fight Hyer, but the latter demanded a $10,000 cash bet as his condition, and Morrissey couldn't raise the sum. Instead, he settled for fighting Sullivan, and beat him in a fifty-three-round affair at Boston Four Corners, N.Y., in 1853. After that, Hyer lost his crown to Tom Heenan, known as the Benicia Boy, and then Morrissey finally claimed his title by beating Heenan—who went on to marry the storied Mazeppa, Adah Isaacs Menken—in a twenty-one-minute match at Long Point, Canada. It should be noted that in those days the fights—which were, incidentally, illegal—were fought under London Prize Ring rules: a round ended when a fighter fell, was knocked down, or was thrown; the match ended when a fighter was unable to come to scratch at the beginning of a round. The bare-knuckle fights were brutal and often lethal; one of the standard corner jobs at the time was that of bloodsucker.

After their respective defeats, Hyer seems to have faded into obscurity. Sullivan slunk off to San Francisco, where he got himself arrested by the Vigilantes and ultimately committed suicide. Morrissey, on the other hand, rose steadily in the world. He opened saloons on Broadway and on Leonard Street, and began acquiring gambling houses. Morrissey had accumulated sufficient respect and goodwill over the years that his houses were thought of as considerably more square than they actually were, a reputation that was perhaps boosted by the story of the night that Benjamin Wood, brother of Mayor Fernando Wood, won $124,000 from Morrissey's house on Twenty-fourth Street. His other two houses, both of which had existed before he bought them and continued after he had sold them, were two of the longest-lived and most celebrated hells in the city's history. The one at 818 Broadway endured at least thirty years, and was famous for its imperviousness to raids. Under Morrissey's ownership, it was raided only twice, once in 1867 by an anti-gambling society, whose members were mollified with a bribe, and again in 1873 as a result of a political grudge, although this incident too, seems to have passed without much damage done. After Morrissey retired his interest in 1877, the house was raided with greater frequency, since later owners lacked his connections and charisma, but nothing was ever found of much consequence. This was thanks to an ingenious basement vault, not publicly revealed until the building was slated for demolition in the nineties, that permitted all the gambling apparatus and the bank to be hidden rapidly behind a false wall. Morrissey's other house, at 8 Barclay, was operated continuously as a gambling den from 1859 to 1902. The longevity of these places and their relatively untroubled existence attest to Morrissey's wits and political skills. All around, gambling houses rose and fell with alacrity. One of Morrissey's associates, a man named Bill Mike Murray, opened a large, "comprehensive" house on Eighth Street east of Broadway in the early 1870s, but a plague of raids forced him to shut it after a few years. Thereafter, he moved his operation to a smaller establishment on West Twenty-eighth, but that house was also visited by ill luck: one night a local character named Jim Murphy ran faro for a few hours and then shot himself right on the floor, effectively hexing the house and driving business away for good.

But Morrissey's continued prosperity was not to be attributed simply to luck. His energy and enterprise were formidable. His Tweed Ring connections got him elected to Congress in 1866 and reelected two years later. He then turned on Tweed and became a leader of the opposition group Young Democracy in 1870, and on that ticket was twice elected to the state senate. Meanwhile, he began to invest in the upstate resort, Saratoga, at that time a genteel and rather dull place. He began with a Club House in 1861, added the still-extant race track two years later, and then continued adding casinos and buying properties until he was in virtual control of the resort. At the height of his powers Morrissey's holdings were estimated at over a million dollars.

Unfortunately, he met up with a sharper far slicker than himself, in the person of Commodore Cornelius Vanderbilt, who, for whatever reasons, counseled him to make investments of an imprudent sort, and Morrissey's estate began to dwindle. He lost $500,000 on Black Friday in 1869 alone. At the same time he spent lavishly, trying to establish himself and his wife in upstate high society, when he was perceived as a low-born gambler, and the more he spent, the more he was jeered. By the time he died of pneumonia in 1878, his fortune was down to $78,000.

The golden age of gambling in New York lasted from shortly after the Civil War until just after the turn of the century. During that time, there were untold hundreds of gambling houses of all sorts for all classes and for every specialty. A particular feature of the 1880s was the gambling resort catering exclusively to women, offering them roulette, faro, and poker amid elegant furnishings. Such places were entirely bourgeois and were found in strictly respectable neighborhoods. The period also saw cheating and fakery achieve new heights. Three-card monte and its cousin, thimble rig, now better known as the shell game, blew in from the West and flourished; they are believed to be the only major gambling games actually invented in the United States. More elaborate schemes were developed as well; the era was the heyday of the confidence man.

The confidence game took many forms, but its underlying principle was always the same: to let the mark beat himself, using his cupidity as the motor of his doom. What was perhaps the ultimate refinement of this principle did not actually manifest itself until the beginning of the twentieth century, in the form of the game called Klondike, or Canfield: the john was sold a deck of cards for $52 which he would use to play solitaire; at the conclusion the house would pay $5 for every pip on the ace pile (in this version, kings counted as thirteen, queens as twelve, jacks as eleven). There was simply no way to so much as break even. The most famous of all sucker games, however, was the one that arrived in New York in the late 1860s: banco. This game had been known for some time in England, where it was called eight dice cloth, and it was first imported to San Francisco, where it was christened banco, or bunco; the term soon entered the language as a synonym for fraud, hence the usage "bunco squad" and H. L. Mencken's celebrated expletive, "buncombe.[1]" The game was played variously with eight dice or eight numbered cards; the layout for dice contained fourteen spaces, for cards forty-three, of which forty-two were numbered, thirteen of them additionally bearing stars, and one was blank. A throw of the dice or a draw of the cards would add up to a figure that corresponded to one of the spaces on the layout. On the card layout the unstarred numbers represented cash prizes from $2 to $5,000, while those with stars allowed the player to draw again for more money. The player would be allowed to win steadily up to a certain point and then he would be dealt a hand totaling twenty-seven, the number corresponding to a space on the board called a "conditional." This meant that, to proceed further, the player would have to put up in cash a sum equal to his total bank winnings thus far. If he did so—and he invariably did—the only way he could lose would be to hit one of the two spaces covered with metal caps, called "banco." The mark did so without fail. The pattern was unvarying: the doe was led to intoxicate himself with his own greed, winning a sum that the operators would calculate represented the limit of his ready capital, and then he would rapidly be led to unpocket himself.

The games were played in elaborate setups called banco skins, usually hotel rooms or rooms in financial-district buildings made up to look like bustling business offices. The marks were usually newcomers to the city, prosperous visiting farmers being the best targets. The skins employed a pair of touts to lure them: the feeler and the catcher. The feeler would hang around hotels, identifying wealthy rubes and tourists, and would research details of their hometowns, professions, family lives, hobbies. He would then pass this information along to the catcher, who would feign acquaintance or kinship with the mark, who could usually be induced to believe that he simply failed to recall his old army buddy or second cousin, and the camaraderie thus fired would lead to an evening on the town, complete with roistering and

entertainments of varyingly risqué nature. As the hour grew late, the
roper would propose one last bit of jollity, a visit to a friendly game
gotten up by friends of his, and he would steer the pigeon to the banco
skin. As the mark lost, the tout would be losing as well, and would
accompany his loss with such a theatrical display of bad sportsmanship
that the embarrassed target would temporarily be distracted from his
own misfortune. The most famous catcher was Hungry Joe Lewis; his
most famous catch was Oscar Wilde, on the latter's 1882 tour of the
United States. Hungry Joe took the dramatist for $5,000, but was
trusting enough to let him pay with a check. When Wilde figured out
that he had been swindled, he simply stopped payment. Wilde refused
to prosecute, however, so Hungry Joe was not finally stopped until
1888, when he was arrested for a $5,000 catch in Baltimore. Before
that time, Hungry Joe was reckoned to be the greatest banco artist of
them all, prodigiously successful and prolific in his swindles; his fatal
flaw was that, according to Police Captain Thomas Byrnes, he was "a
terrible talker," so unable to stop gabbing that he very nearly gave the
operation away more than once. He ultimately wound up in the laundry
business. The upper rank of the banco circuit also included Tom
O'Brien and Charles P. Miller, both at various times called King of
the Banco Men, and Peter Lake, aka Grand Central Pete, all of whom
endured in their profession well into the 1890s. Amazingly enough,
banco survives into the present day; the late 1980s saw a banco skin
as elemental as any of those of the previous century setting up at various
locations—hardware stores, multi-vendor bazaars—around SoHo,
possibly in some of the very same buildings.

Even more elaborate than the banco setups were those skinning
houses, to all outward respects ordinary gambling halls, that in the
1870s and eighties were established for the exclusive purpose of rooking
one chump at a time. These would be located in the back rooms of
saloons and pool halls, be rigged out with all the conventional trap-
pings, and would employ dozens of steerers, shills, and supernumer-
aries. The standard premise was that employed in three-card monte:

the shill won again and again as the sucker watched; the sucker would imagine that the dealer was slow-witted and vulnerable; then the sucker would play big and lose everything. The mise-en-scène was soon adapted for even more ambitious play: what came to be called the big con, the large-scale confidence game. An itinerant sharper named Ben Marks can be regarded as the father of this pursuit. A few years after the Civil War he set up a front called the Dollar Store in Cheyenne, Wyoming. The store featured display windows full of quality merchandise, all of it priced at one dollar. The johns brought in by this lure would be dissuaded from buying by a swift line of patter which would steer them instead to gambling, and then they would be fleeced in short order.

In the next few decades the principle of the Big Store was refined into its principal variations: the wire, rag, and pay-off stores. All these had several main points in common; they involved a fraudulent business location, usually a betting parlor for horse races, appropriately furnished and manned by shills, ropers, and stand-ins, and one well-heeled pigeon at a time would be brought in for the play. This involved stringing the mark along over a period of days, convincing him that he was getting in on the ground floor of an enterprise making quick money by defrauding others, getting him to pour substantial and increasing amounts of cash into the operation, with the idea that the more he put in, the more he could extract, and then, when all his liquid resources were exhausted, quickly lowering the boom and skipping town. These cons were as complex and as highly organized as any legitimate business, and they involved a network of connections oiled by graft that in a smaller city might take in the whole police department and most of the municipal administration. Although one might expect such games to flourish largely in the more pliable provincial towns, there were important stores in New York which were protected by the ever-corruptible cops and politicians. There as elsewhere the suckers were imported from the outside, and it was made certain that they were properly disoriented and vulnerable. Beginning around the turn of the century, major stores were set up by such characters as Christ Tracy, Larry the Lug, Limehouse Chappie, and 102nd Street George.

The dazzling variety of short con games in the late nineteenth century ranged from such acting exercises as the Spanish prisoner swindle (a grieving wife and children would be toured around, pleading for funds to release a prisoner of conscience from foreign confinement) to vaudeville routines like the pedigreed-dog swindle. This con would begin with a man entering a saloon, accompanied by a dog. Over a drink, he would explain to the bartender that the mutt was a prize winner, an extremely valuable specimen of some mythical breed. Then he would ask the bartender to watch the dog for half an hour while he attended to a crucial matter of business, possibly sweetening the deal by giving the bartender a small tip. While the dog owner was away, another man would come in, spot the dog, exclaim over it, and then ask the bartender if he was willing to sell. When the bartender refused, the man would pretend that the bartender was simply being canny, and he would offer greater and greater sums. Finally, just as the bartender was beginning to weaken, the man would give up and leave, adding as an afterthought that he might come back later in case the bartender had changed his mind. Soon after that, the dog's owner would return, looking distraught, announcing that he had been ruined. After accepting the bartender's sympathy, he might allow himself to think of selling the dog, and the bartender, not wanting to seem too eager, would name a smallish but still sizable figure. The dog owner would look both stricken and relieved, accept the money, and leave with tears in his eyes. The accomplice, needless to say, would never return.[2]

The gold-brick scheme, which has given the language the term "goldbricker," was invented around the time of the Civil War by a man named Reed Waddell. He manufactured gold-plated lead bricks, stamped with the initials "U.S." after the practice of the U.S. Assayer's Office, and sold them as solid gold. His display brick contained a slug of real gold, which he would dig out to show to the scoffers. Meanwhile, an accomplice posing as an assayer would pretend to test the brick. Waddell sold the first brick he made for $4,000 and never afterward sold one for less than $3,500, and is said to have made more than $250,000 in his first few years in the business. He was a versatile con man who was also a major banco artist, and he was eventually killed by the banco king Tom O'Brien in Paris in 1895. The green goods swindle, also known as the sawdust game, arrived on the scene in 1869. Waddell dabbled in this enterprise as well, along with such legendary swindlers as Pete Conlish, George Post, and the immortal Yellow Kid Weil. The con took several forms. There was a bait-and-switch routine that involved showing suckers a bag of bills which they would be told were counterfeit; when the bait was taken and money exchanged, the saps would find themselves holding a sack of clippings or sawdust. Some operators sold a machine allegedly capable of turning out fake money; they would introduce a genuine bill, turn a crank, and two perfect copies would emerge. Still others ran the scheme as a mail fraud, buying address lists of lottery subscribers and sending them circulars that announced: "For $1200 in my goods (assorted) I charge $100," and so on, up to $10,000 counterfeit for $600. Sometimes these brochures would be illustrated with pictures of notes purported to be fakes. Buyers would either be bilked long-distance or be lured to a New York hotel room. As usual, the scheme preyed on the suckers' own lawlessness, and one of the resounding advantages of this was that they could not take their complaint to the police upon discovery of the swindle.

As the century drew to a close, the swindling and gambling establishments became larger and more intricate, and civil corruption became an art in itself. At the upper level of gambling in New York was Richard Canfield (who had nothing whatsoever to do with the aforementioned short-con card game named after him). His house on East Forty-fourth Street was the most refined, ambitiously decorated, exquisitely catered, and his police protection for more than two decades was the finest and most discreet. Canfield serviced the richest and most socially prominent gamblers, heirs, and tycoons. His sole rival in this field was the House with the Bronze Door, an elegant institution that lasted from 1891 to around 1917 in a town house on West Thirty-third Street remodeled in the late 1890s by Stanford White. At both this house and at Canfield's, the stories of rich men dropping enormous sums in a single evening kept topping each other, so that the phenomenon almost comes to seem like a version of potlatch, in which wealth is proven by the ability to shed it. The House was owned by a syndicate, the makeup of which was never thoroughly established, but which was known to be headed by a gambler named Frank Farrell. Farrell's partner in other enterprises was a policeman called Big Bill Devery, one of the many claimants for the distinction of most crooked cop of the era, and also known as the "meanest gambler in New York." In 1903 he and Farrell bought an American League baseball franchise they moved to town and called the New York Highlanders, which they sold in 1912 to Colonel Jacob Ruppert and Tillinghast Houston, who renamed the franchise the Yankees.

Farrell and Devery, along with Tammany boss Big Tim Sullivan, made up a syndicate that handled protection services for gambling establishments. *The New York Times*, responding in 1900 to the failure of the 1899 Mazet Committee to examine properly the state of gambling in the city, published an exposé of this syndicate that gave a breakdown of its income: 400 pool rooms at $300 per month apiece, adding up to $120,000 per year; 500 crap games at $150, $75,000 annually; 200 small gambling houses at $150 per month, $30,000; 20 large gambling houses at $1,000 per month, $20,000; 50 envelope games [pawnshop swindles] at $50 per month, $2,500; policy operations at $125,000 per annum. The whole added up to a grand total of $3,095,000 per year. The scheme was airtight, since between Sullivan's and Devery's positions, the syndicate comprised the powers of the police, the state senate, and the State Gambling Commission. The man behind this report was William Travers Jerome, who had assumed as a personal mission the abolition of gambling.

Before he could do much, however, Jerome had to wait out the administration of Tammany Mayor Robert Van Wyck (1898–1901), who let gambling houses run wide open all over town. Broadway and the Bowery were both chockablock with joints offering "high play at cards," roulette, dice, off-track betting, and wagering on prizefights, cockfights, and dogfights, while in Chinatown there were scores of places specializing in fan-tan and pi-gow. The boxing situation was completely out of control. Whereas, under some earlier reform administrations, matches had been held in an atmosphere of high secrecy and sometimes in complete silence, now the sport flourished as if it were legal.[3] The only problem was the turf war over control of the graft, a matter contested by the Manhattan-based Farrell–Devery–Sullivan axis and the McCarren–McLaughlin syndicate in Brooklyn. On the night Van Wyck took office a match was stopped in the middle because both factions claimed the payoff. Eventually, the matter was settled, Farrell and company being awarded the state minus Brooklyn. They kept such a tight rein on the sport that even the venerable New York Athletic Club was unable to stage bouts. It was not until 1910 that the Frawley Law permitted legal ten-round matches in New York City, although it made decisions non-binding.

Reformers had their work cut out for them. Jerome was elected district attorney in November 1901, in the same election that brought reform mayoral candidate Seth Low to office. Jerome immediately began staging raids on gambling houses, ensuring the maximum publicity angle by inviting reporters to come along, and by personally wielding a hatchet to break down doors. Early in 1902, the Reverend Charles H. Parkhurst's Society for the Prevention of Crime raided the headquarters of Al Adams, the widely disliked policy king who also owned two breweries, about a hundred saloons, $2 million in real estate, and allegedly a stake in every gambling house between the Battery and 110th Street. He was arrested on evidence that linked him to eighty-two policy shops, was sentenced to twelve to eighteen months in Sing Sing, and emerged from prison a broken man. Jerome's men raided Canfield's establishment that same year, although some months after Canfield had shut the place down himself, but there were enough gambling rigs stowed in the closets to make a case. Ironically, the matter spurred

Canfield to get back into business, and he kept reopening until a 1904 conviction proved conclusive. His bad luck continued: in 1907 he was forced to shut down his Saratoga Club House, and the same year lost at least half of his $13 million fortune in the stock-market panic, and he began to sell off the remainder of his property, including his collection of paintings by Whistler. When he died in 1914 of a fractured skull resulting from a fall in the Fourteenth Street subway station, his estate was assessed at $814,485.

Jerome had less luck with the resilient Honest John Kelly. Kelly was not related to the identically named and monikered Tammany politician, but acquired his sobriquet in 1888 when he refused a $10,000 bribe while serving as umpire in a pennant game between Boston and Providence. In 1890 he and the baseball star Mike Kelly opened a Tenderloin saloon that offered faro as a sideline, and in 1895 he opened a gambling house on West Forty-first Street that ran for seventeen years. This house featured a saloon on the ground floor, gambling on the second, and Kelly's domicile on the third; it was the hell of choice among boxers and their backers. Kelly was an independent, genuinely defiant of the syndicates. He steadfastly refused to pay protection, so his house was constantly raided. He acted as referee for prizefights in his spare time and was noted for calling off all bets if he sensed a fix. He did this at an important 1898 fight between Jim Corbett and Tom Sharkey, despite a warning from Big Tim Sullivan, who had a $13,000 bet riding on Sharkey. The very next day Kelly's house was raided and ransacked by the police. He promptly reopened. Many more raids followed, but it was not until 1912, when cops broke all his furniture, windows, and mirrors, and damaged the building itself, that he was compelled to announce his retirement. A month later he opened the Club Vendome on West Forty-fourth, which lasted until 1922 and grossed over a million, mostly from poker, in its last year of existence; in its last four years a uniformed cop was posted in front of the door, day and night. Kelly, despite his nickname an old-fashioned skinner, died peacefully in the Bahamas several years later.

Among the small-time gamblers downtown, chaos prevailed. Such

"Hooking a Victim": from the *Police Gazette*, circa 1850,
one of the very few iconographic representations of
prostitution in nineteenth-century New York. The location
may be Broadway and Canal Street

Frank Stephenson's Black and Tan, Thompson Street, late
1880s. Photograph by Richard Hoe Lawrence

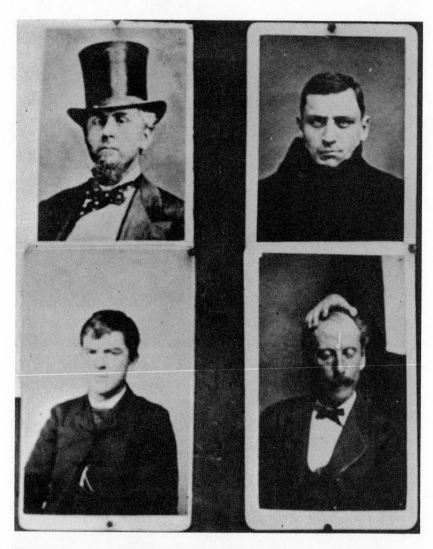

Four banco operators immortalized in Rogues' Gallery: (clockwise from top left) "Old Ike" Vail, Joseph "Hungry Joe" Lewis, Joseph "Paper Collar Joe" Bond, James "The Kid" Fitzgerald. Photograph by Jacob Riis

operators as Herman "Beansy" Rosenthal, Bald Jack Rose, Bridgie Webber, and Sam Schepps were constantly feuding among themselves and with their police protectors. Rosenthal, for example, closed his house in Far Rockaway because of persistent raids instigated by a rival, then opened the Hesper Club on lower Second Avenue, which swiftly failed because of the success of Webber's nearby Sans Souci, then opened a house on West 116th Street that was soon closed by the police, then opened one on West Forty-fifth that was raided innumerable times and firebombed twice. His luck changed dramatically when he took on Lieutenant Charles H. Becker of the Gambling Squad as his partner. Becker, who extorted from prostitutes and pursued a bitter vendetta against the novelist Stephen Crane, who had exposed him in print, was called the "crookedest cop who ever stood behind a shield," which was certainly a distinction in such a crowded field. Rosenthal's security was short-lived, however. In March 1912 Rosenthal failed to contribute $500 toward the legal defense of Becker's press agent, who was charged with a killing in the course of a raid on a dice game, and the following month Becker retaliated by arranging for a raid on Rosenthal's house. When Rosenthal then threatened to spill all he knew about protection rackets to District Attorney Charles Whitman, other gamblers became alarmed and threatened Rosenthal. In June of that year the gangster Big Jack Zelig was approached in the Tombs and offered his freedom in return for disposing of Rosenthal. Zelig commissioned four of his hoods, Gyp the Blood, Lefty Louie, Dago Frank, and Whitey Lewis, to do the job. They set out to execute it in early July at the Garden Café on Seventh Avenue, but somehow suffered a collective failure of nerve. A week or two later Rosenthal published an affidavit in the *World* naming Becker as his partner at 20 percent of the cut in illegal gambling operations, and that same day was summoned to appear before the D.A. The following evening he was called away from dinner at the Hotel Metropole on West Forty-fifth by the message that a man wanted to see him outside, and Rosenthal, incredibly, complied. The minute he hit the pavement he went down in a shower of bullets fired by four men in a car. Gyp, Lefty, Dago, and Whitey were arrested almost immediately. Zelig turned state's evidence and was scheduled to testify in the trial that autumn that the execution order came from Becker, but before he could appear in court he was gunned down while boarding the Second Avenue streetcar at Thirteenth Street. Enough evidence linking Becker to the Rosenthal killing was obtained, however, and the cop and the four hoods were convicted and sentenced to the electric chair. The gunmen were executed at Sing Sing in the spring of 1913, while Becker began an appeal for clemency. Unfortunately for him, the governor whose decision it happened to be was none other than former D.A. Charles Whitman. Becker was put to death in the summer of 1915. His widow had his tombstone engraved with the words "Murdered by Governor Whitman," but later had them erased when threatened with a criminal libel suit.

The Becker case opened a can of worms that finally led to the collapse of the city's gambling establishment. By that time Sullivan was dead and Devery was in the real-estate business, and Mayor John Purroy Mitchell's reform administration was undertaking an unprecedentedly thorough sweep of gangs and vice. Gambling was reduced to a small-time clandestine activity, and it remained so for nearly a decade, until the bootlegging success of such new mobs as those of Owney Madden and Dutch Schultz inspired them to expand into such operations as policy and wire rooms. After Repeal, their successors continued these sidelines, and ran them for some thirty-five years, until legalization and state control ruined the trade in the city, or at least did so by official reckoning, since bookmaking, numbers, and many other grafts continue in spite of it all.

5 · *The* LOST SISTERHOOD

IN THE NINETEENTH CENTURY, A
YOUNG MAN BORN INTO A POOR FAM-
ILY, PERHAPS ARRIVED IN NEW YORK
AS AN IMMIGRANT, MIGHT NURSE
ambitions of wealth and status. If he was
sufficiently enterprising, there were a number
of avenues he could take. In the approved
scenario of achievement, he could practice
thrift, save his salary, buy a store, save his
earnings, buy another store, keep saving and
earning until he had a number of stores or
one large store. Or, given that workers' salaries in general were barely enough to live
on, let alone save to any appreciable degree,
and that acquiring the wherewithal to buy
just one store could take decades, he might
become a burglar, a footpad, a shoulder-
hitter, a gambling-house shill, a saloon runner, a swindler of immigrants, a poisoner of
horses, a mayhem specialist for hire, a river

pirate, a crimp, a dip, a ghoul. Then, with sufficient skill, and luck, and drive, and ferocity, he might come to lead his own gang, and from there, if he managed not to get himself killed, he could be launched into politics, or saloonkeeping, or real-estate management, or the business end of the entertainment industry. Connections were made this way; men with a degree of power were always looking for younger men with organizational ability and muscle. A poor young woman who harbored similar ambitions generally had only one route open to her: prostitution.

Young women became whores in any number of ways and for any number of reasons. Prostitution went along with careers on the lower levels of the theater; it was one of the few means for women of the lower class to meet men of a higher station; it gave the appearance of being a way to avoid the drudgery of housework or sweatshop labor; it fostered the illusion of allowing a woman independent enterprise; it dealt in the outward manifestations of a better life, such as fancy clothes and jewelry; it was associated in the popular mind with the realm of leisure, with the pursuit of pleasure. A young woman might be drawn to prostitution by the attraction of any of these, or any combination thereof. Or it might happen that if she was solitary—an orphan, for example—that life might be the only possible one for her. Or she might be lured into it by an older sibling already in the profession, or be procured by a lover or a male acquaintance who sought to establish himself as a pimp, or she might be offered money for favors on the street by a stranger who would probably be aware that he was displaying a sum greater than she might otherwise make in a week, or she might, indeed, be sold into the trade by her own parents. After all, no family below the middle class could afford to support children past the age of twelve; few could support them past the age of eight, and many not past infancy. Girls went to work as early as boys, employed as pieceworkers in "light" manufacturing or as shop assistants. "For many reasons . . . the tone of morality among store girls in this city is not high," observed Howe and Hummel disingenuously in 1886, a time when shop girls were seldom paid more than a dollar and a half per week, not enough to pay for lodging above the flophouse level.

So a young woman not actually seduced or sold into the profession might start by freelancing. Opportunities were manifold for comely women in their teens and twenties. There were men on the street, on public conveyances, at places of amusement, who could spare a dollar or two for a rapid sexual fix. Any woman by herself was fair game, and two together might be thought a team. Any woman out after dark would be assumed to be a whore. The temptation of money would be hard to refuse, and perhaps the associated link to a higher class would be an added inducement. Perhaps the young woman could get away with doing this every so often to supplement her income. Too often, however, hazards would intrude. She might very well contract a venereal disease from a man who got around, and in the nineteenth century a poor woman who contracted syphilis or gonorrhea, quite apart from the mortal danger posed by the diseases themselves, would find herself barred from conventional society: she could never marry, and any medical treatment would usually be reported to the police and get her branded. Even without this risk, chances are that, in the smaller and more socially claustrophobic order that then prevailed in the city, someone would spot her with a man not of her class, and word would spread. Then she would be ostracized by such relations and acquaintances as thought themselves respectable, and she would be prey to the threats and manipulations of pimps, and the fresh quality that made her attractive to strange men would be spoiled, and she would need to solicit. A young woman who entered a brothel, where her earnings would be taken by the madam, who would pay her only a meager allowance, and where her movements and activities would be as closely monitored as if she were in a nunnery, could nevertheless count herself fortunate, since the alternatives were so much worse.

If she worked on the street, she would find herself progressively devalued, a prey to vultures who would pimp her and rob her and beat her, a prey to the police, who would rob her and demand favors for free and periodically arrest her in any case, a prey to bad liquor, to drugs, disease, malnutrition, and the elements. Her face would be known and filed away by prospective clients, who would soon consider her tarnished and backdated merchandise, and she would have to chase business by going from district to district, invariably downward, from the choice corners on or near Broadway to the side streets, and from the side streets to the Bowery, and from the Bowery to the strip on Canal Street, and from there to the waterfront, which was the end. A policeman was quoted in 1909 as referring to "generations" of whores; by a generation he meant two years.

It was not entirely inconceivable that she could survive and flourish. She might, after all, be tough and smart enough to become a madam, or determined enough to pursue a career on the stage before it became too late, or lucky enough to meet a patron who would keep her, and might be nice to her and not discard her too quickly. But such cases were the exception. The outcome in the majority of cases was death: death from disease, from beatings, from rough usage, from misadventure, from drinking, from exposure, or murder, or suicide. Even without the attendant mortal hazards, prostitution was not a very good bet economically. A survey conducted in the late 1870s, around the same time that the median weekly wage for shop girls was $1.50, indicated that fully a quarter of the whores questioned made only one dollar a week, and a sixth made two dollars, a tenth made three dollars, a twentieth made four dollars, and so on. Starvation was another possible outcome.

New York being a port city, prostitution was probably there from the beginning, in waterfront groggeries and sailors' hostels, and in the dance houses and groceries that grew up around the Collect Pond and then the Five Points. Whenever early writers refer to "immorality," as in the immorality of shared dwellings, they are using a shorthand for prostitution, explicit mention of which was taboo in the polite press; unorthodox living situations were assumed to be the product of or the breeding ground for prostitution. Likewise, their mentions of race mixing in the slums (and such mentions are plentiful in the 1830s and forties); to their minds, it was an exceptional depravity, and clear evidence of prostitution, since no other reason for such liaisons could be imagined. The restrictions against mentioning prostitution, against thinking about it seriously as a social and economic fact, which continued in some sectors through the century and into the next, made people absolutely preoccupied with it. They saw it everywhere. And it *was* everywhere, but not for the reasons they imagined or in the ways they thought. It is telling, for example, that at this period, when prostitution was detected everywhere and everywhere alluded to, no one appears to have seen or at least to have commented in print on the sexual trade inherent in the phenomenon of the hot-corn girls. Figuratively, at least, it was the girls and not the ears of corn that were being sold. As in literal prostitution, the girls depended for their livelihood on their youthfulness, attractiveness, and relative novelty; they passed their earnings into the hands of a sponsor; they walked around displaying themselves to men of superior social standing. But the hot-corn girls could be idealized, and therefore exempt from tarnish. They represented the promise of sex without its consummation.

Before the Civil War, brothels—called bagnios, or disorderly houses, or free-and-easys—were largely restricted to the waterfront and the slums, to Cherry and Water Streets, to the Five Points and the Bowery. Dance houses, by contrast, were multi-purpose establishments in the same districts that might collect a saloon, a hotel, and a bordello under the same roof, with overlapping amenities, personnel, and clients. The most prominent and notorious of these was the house of John Allen at 304 Water Street. Allen came from a family of divines; two of his brothers were Presbyterian ministers, and a third was a Baptist preacher. He himself had been a divinity student at the Union Theological Seminary but had somehow taken a turn in the road, and with his wife he came to open his house of ill-repute around 1850. The place, which catered to sailors in a manner just a notch above the practice of the crimps, was nevertheless flamboyant in outward expression, and it was said to have netted $100,000 in about a decade. His staff of twenty girls were arrayed in costumes consisting of low black satin bodices, scarlet skirts and stockings, and red-topped boots festooned with little bells.[1] The house featured an additional wrinkle that contributed a certain piquancy: Allen ornamented his facilities with religious trappings. Three days each week he led whores and bartenders in a Bible reading at noon, just before the house opened for business, and even during hours of operation he might gather his employees and lead them in hymns from a collection called *The Little Wanderers' Friend*. The bagnio's cubicles were furnished with Bibles; the tables of the saloon were strewn with devotional journals and Christian newspapers; the walls were decorated with sacred chromos; on special occasions Allen would give away New Testaments to his customers. None of this kept the popular press from dubbing Allen the "wickedest man in New York" (an appellation that was soon to pass to the divekeeper The. Allen, who was no relation).

Allen's penchant for the sacred led to his downfall. In May 1868 a clergyman named A. C. Arnold, who ran the nearby Howard Mission, came to Allen's house and found him dead drunk. He took advantage of the situation to persuade Allen to let him begin holding prayer meetings at the house. The services were at first an amusing novelty for Allen's customers, but they got tired of them after a while and stayed away. By August, Arnold and other preachers announced that the joint was closed, that Allen's "Magdalenes" were available for hire as servants in Christian households, and that Allen himself had been converted and reformed. Meanwhile, ministers were having a similarly magical effect upon other dens of vice in the neighborhood, including Kit Burns's Rat Pit, and for a while these places attracted the city's devout, who would come for services and incidentally to gape at the remaining signs of dissipation (reporters who attended meetings at Burns's could not help noticing the stench from the cadavers of dogs and rats buried in the dirt under the pit's bleachers). Finally, *The New York Times* published an exposé, in which it claimed that the miraculous reform was a fraud, that the clergymen were paying Allen $350 a month for the privilege of converting his house and himself, and that similar graft had been distributed to other landlords, including $150 per month to Burns. They furthermore asserted that the congregations assembled for services in those houses consisted entirely of respectable members of the middle class, and did not include any—beyond the principals—of the vicious, fallen sorts who were the targets of reform. This certainly has the ring of truth, although the question remains as to whether $350 a month could really have made up for the loss of Allen's trade, or $150 for Burns's. Perhaps the area was falling into decline, and they saw this odd publicity stunt as the only chance they had to continue in business, for however brief a term. In any case, the *Times* report had the effect of driving the preachers away, but the old customers did not return, and so Allen was left without resources. In December of the same year he, his wife, and several of his girls were arraigned on the charge of robbing a sailor of fifteen dollars. Allen's last public statement before he slipped into obscurity was that he had been framed.

Immediately after the Civil War the moral complexion of the city changed, and perhaps this is the real explanation for Allen's woes: prostitution spread all over town. Brothels, now identified by their red doorway lights, sprang up in clusters in the side streets west of Broadway in what was then midtown, and soon all through the Tenderloin. In the Broadway district, there was a literal progression in price and quality as one moved uptown, from the houses near and on Canal Street that catered mostly to sailors to the luxurious establishments around Clinton Place (now called Eighth Street). All of them, regardless of tone or price, were essentially the same: red-brick residential houses, with names painted in white above their doors: the Gem, the Forget-Me-Not, Sinbad the Sailor, the Black Crook. The fanciest, which were called "parlor houses," featured an atmosphere of considerable decorum in their parlors, where liquor was sold and imbibed with sophisticated restraint, and where a pianist, always called Professor, provided a cultural note. Flora's and Lizzie's were among the most famous and expensive of the houses; Josephine Woods's, on Clinton Place between Broadway and University, sold champagne for the then outrageous sum of eight dollars a bottle,[2] and was celebrated for its annual blind-man's-buff party on New Year's Eve and its open house on New Year's Day. Even fancier was Seven Sisters' Row on Twenty-fifth Street near Seventh Avenue, where seven adjacent houses were run by seven women said to be sisters from a small New England village—although it was remarked that they could just as well have gotten their name from an 1860 Laura Keane musical revue. The sisters ran tidy, expensive houses, with parlors in which their young ladies, as well schooled as if they had been convent-reared, which in a sense they were, played the guitar and practiced the art of refined conversation. They attracted customers by sending engraved invitations to important businessmen staying at Fifth Avenue hotels. On certain nights each week, clients were admitted only if they were attired in evening dress and bore bouquets for the girls. The total proceeds from the Christmas Eve trade were donated to charity, and this fact was given considerable publicity in the press.

Meanwhile, in the lower strata, one curious phenomenon, which was to continue for at least thirty years, was the "cigar store battery." Ostensibly, these were tobacco shops, but an uninitiated customer who entered would find a very meager stock of cigars and a shopkeeper, often female, who did not appear interested in selling them.[3] The knowing client, on the other hand, would be directed to the brothel in the rear or upstairs. These flourished near Canal Street, mostly on Greene Street, and kept day hours, with a business peak around lunchtime. Not far away were the concert saloons, which derived the bulk of their trade from sailors. The first of these, the Melodeon, was established on Broadway in 1860, and soon there were dozens, many of them carrying names like the Sailor's Welcome Home, the Sailor's Retreat, the Jolly Tar, the Flowing Sea Inn. The female employees, who were sometimes attired in "Turkish" costumes, with harem pants, were principally what today would be called B-girls. They spent most of their time urging customers to drink, receiving a one-third cut on inflated prices, such as $5 bottles of wine, and if they wished to pursue the interaction past that stage, had to do it off the premises and on their own time. Further down the scale were the streetwalkers, or "cruisers," who at this period mostly worked the parks (Washington Square, Union

Square, Madison Square), but gradually moved to the corners and eventually onto Broadway itself. Meanwhile, there was the Tenderloin, where anything went.

In an 1866 address at Cooper Union, the Methodist Bishop Matthew Simpson complained that prostitutes were as numerous as Methodists in the city. A bit later, preaching at St. Paul's Methodist Episcopal Church, he cited figures. There were, he declared, 20,000 whores—equivalent to one-fortieth of the city's population—along with 30,000 thieves, 3,000 saloons, and 2,000 gambling houses. The numbers caused a sensation when they were reported by the press, but the police insisted they were vastly exaggerated. By their count, there were merely 2,670 whores (or maybe 3,300; reports differ) at 621 brothels and 99 assignation houses, and these figures did not include the 747 waiter girls in the concert saloons. These totals might still seem large, although the police might equally be suspected of trimming their statistics.

Nevertheless, judging by accounts from the period, those numbers could plausibly apply to the Tenderloin alone. In the blocks between Twenty-fourth and Fortieth Streets, and between Fifth and Seventh Avenues—sometimes also called Satan's Circus—there clustered an incredible profusion and variety of manifestations of the sex trade, in and among other institutions of vice (by 1885 it was estimated that half the buildings in the district were entirely given over to some kind of immorality). In this area, where turf was carefully divided up between specialties—where Twenty-eighth Street, for example, was devoted to high-end gambling houses and Twenty-seventh Street to pool rooms with bookmaking operations—the streets reserved for whorehouses were Twenty-fourth, Twenty-fifth, Thirty-first, Thirty-second, and Thirty-fifth, and that was not counting the houses of assignation that sprang up everywhere. The houses ranged in tone from the Sisters' down to places where sex was incidental and robbery uppermost.

There were the panel houses, for example, where, once a john was safely occupied in bed, a male house employee called a creeper would silently push through a detachable panel in the wainscoting and make for the pockets of the pants hung conveniently on a nearby chair. More sophisticated was the badger game. The gangster Shang Draper, for example, ran a saloon on Sixth Avenue and Twenty-ninth Street where clients were, by fair means or foul, gotten very drunk. When a customer was sufficiently intoxicated, he would be lured by one of the staff of forty female employees down to a whorehouse on Prince and Wooster Streets. Very near the climactic moment of his encounter with the woman, an angry man would burst in through the door. He was, he would declare, the woman's husband. Enraged by the evidence of adultery, he would threaten to beat the customer senseless, to kill him, to take him to court. But perhaps, he would hint, he could be mollified, for a significant financial consideration. Identical scenes would meanwhile be taking place in every other room in the joint. Another of Draper's houses employed girls nine to fourteen years of age. In this variation the "parents" would burst in, the mother would hit the girl in the face so hard her nose would bleed, and the father would shake down the john. It was estimated that a hundred men were taken this way every month. Perhaps the all-time champion of the badger game was a Tenderloin operator named Kate Phillips, who one night landed a visiting coffee-and-tea dealer from St. Louis. In the throes of their clinch a "policeman" appeared, who "arrested" the merchant and took him to "court," where a "judge" fined him $15,000 for adultery. Kate, according to reports, got the money, and the man was never seen again.

The demand for new girls by brothelkeepers was such that the procurer's trade became a lucrative specialty in its own right. In the 1870s the principal figures in this field were Red Light Lizzie and Hester Jane Haskins (known as Jane the Grabber). Each of them controlled a staff of "cadets," who went out into the suburbs and the countryside to seduce and inveigle young women and recruit them for the New York whorehouse trade. Both women owned brothels themselves, beyond stocking a roster of others, and they maintained reputations for exclusively supplying daughters of good families. Procurers often would recruit very young girls as well, and these were sold to people who ostensibly employed them to sell flowers in hotel lobbies and on the avenues. Other pre-adolescent girls would solicit trade by approaching men on the street and asking plaintively for a penny. For that matter, there were dives in streets near the Bowery and Chatham Square that specialized in female children, who were sequestered in back rooms.

Such practices thrived at the very height of Victorian morality, when suggestions of indecency of the most remote and allusive sort in literature, in couture, and on the stage were vigorously decried from pulpits and in the press. The same newspapers that might denounce the suggestiveness of Lola Montez's dance routines might meanwhile carry discreetly coded advertisements in the classified pages for houses of assignation, for freelance whores who established themselves in residential hotels, and for abortionists. Abortion was considered so far beyond the pale in polite society that it was, paradoxically, relatively safe and protected. All this changed at some point in the 1870s when the reputation of one abortionist, a certain Madame Restell, became known to one and all. Born Ann Trow around 1820, she immigrated to New York from England, and when she was sixteen years old married a quack practitioner, "Doctor" Charles Lohman, from whom she learned the rudiments of medicine. By 1850, she was running an abortion practice of her own, which she advertised in classified listings that described her as a "professor of midwifery," offered "infallible French female pills," and guaranteed "a cure at one interview." She began calling herself Mme Restell because of the popular belief that intimate physical matters were best known to the French. She was canny enough to make the acquaintance of Tammany figures, and pay them pecuniary tribute. Soon she was charging from $500 to $1,000 for a consultation, specializing in the mistresses of prominent men, who often put her on retainer to see to their ever-changing roster of sex partners. Her practice was secure enough that she acquired a four-story brownstone on Fifth Avenue and Fifty-second Street (outbidding the Catholic Archbishop John Hughes, who sought it for his episcopal residence), while maintaining offices at the prime downtown business intersection of Chambers and Greenwich Streets. At some point, word of her trade leaked out, and it was rumored that she had been charged with murder but had squelched the indictment with a total of $100,000 in bribes. It was reported that little boys began to run beside her carriage as she drove from home to office, and that they yelled, "Yah! Your house is built on babies' skulls!" and called her, as their parents began to call her, "Madame Killer." Finally, in 1878, she was arrested by Anthony Comstock, the omnipresent, partly self-employed vice crusader, who might have been responsible for leaking the rumors in the first place, and who came to her office posing as a worried husband. He later claimed that, on their way to Jefferson Market Police Court, she offered him a $40,000 bribe. She was remanded to the Tombs, but got out on bail, went home, drew a bath, and slit her throat. James Gordon Bennett, the righteous publisher of the *New York Herald*, announced that he would publish her client lists in his paper. This led to considerable panic among the quality, and, not surprisingly, the lists mysteriously vanished before they could be typeset. The abortion trade was driven further underground and became generally more dangerous for all concerned after that; by the 1890s it was reported that women were resorting to the use of calisaya, a commercially available quinine extract with apparent abortifacient properties.

By the beginning of the 1880s the focus of sexual entertainment had shifted away from the brothel and toward the sort of place that combined saloon and dance hall and that invariably featured private, curtained cubicles where patrons could be visited by dancers and waitresses. In the Tenderloin there were, among others, the Cremorne, the Strand, the Idlewile, the French Madame's, all in the vicinity of Thirty-first Street and Sixth Avenue. The French madame herself was actually French, a fat, bewhiskered Alsatian woman named Matilda Hermann, who was usually to be found sitting on a high stool next to the cashier. The cops called her the "French gold mine," as well they might, since she paid out an estimated $30,000 in bribes over a period of six years. Along with the other keepers of these establishments, she pretended to run a restaurant, but actually only dispensed liquor and black coffee, music supplied by a three-piece band, and, of course, the

cancan. A nude dance on the floor by an employee cost the customer
one dollar; private exhibitions were more expensive, but negotiable.
The scene was much the same, perhaps a little rougher around the
edges, at downtown venues like The. Allen's American Mabille and
his St. Bernard's Hotel at Prince and Mercer Streets, and, perhaps
most notoriously, at Billy McGlory's Armory Hall, at Mott and Hester
Streets. The scene here was described in such awestruck tones by a
reporter for the *Cincinnati Enquirer* that Howe and Hummel saw fit
to reprint it in their pamphlet-length advertisement for New York vice,
In Danger:

> *There are five hundred men in the immense hall. There are*
> *a hundred females—it would be mockery to call them*
> *women. The first we hear of them is when half a dozen in-*
> *vade our box, plump themselves on our laps and begin to beg*
> *that we put quarters in their stockings for luck. There are*
> *some shapely limbs generously and immodestly shown in con-*
> *nection with this invitation. One young woman startles the*
> *crowd by announcing that she will dance the cancan for half*
> *a dollar. The music starts up just then, and she determines*
> *to do the cancan and risk the collection afterward. She seizes*
> *her skirts between her limbs with one hand, kicks away a*
> *chair or two, and is soon throwing her feet in the air in a*
> *way that endangers every hat in the box. The men about the*
> *hall are all craning their necks to get a sight of what is*
> *going on in the box, as they hear the cries of "Hoop-la!"*
> *from the girls there.*
>
> *Some of my companions have been drawn into one of the*
> *little boxes adjoining ours. They come back now to tell of*
> *what depravity was exhibited to them for a fee. The piano*
> *gives a bang and a crash. The gray light is beginning to*
> *stream through the windows. There is a hurrying and a*
> *scurrying among the females, and there are a precious lot of*
> *young fellows, with low brows and plug-ugly looks, gathering*

on the floor. There are twenty-odd women with them, mostly
young, none good-looking, most bearing marks of a life that
kills. The band strikes up a fantastic air. The whole place
is attention at once. The sleepy beer-bummers rouse up. The
persons on the balcony hang over the railings. The figures on
the floor go reeling off in a mixture of dancing and by-play as
fantastic as the music. The pianist seems to get excited and
to want to prove himself a Hans von Bülow of rapid execu-
tion. The fiddler weaves excitedly over his fiddle. The cornet-
ist toots in a screech like a car-engine whistle. The
movements of the dancers grow licentious and more and
more rapid. They have begun the cancan. Feet go up. Legs
are exhibited in wild abandon. Hats fly off. There are occa-
sional exhibitions of nature that would put Adam and Eve
to shame. The draperies of modest costumes for a time cover
the wanton forms, but as the performers grow heated wraps
are thrown off. The music assumes a hideous wildness. The
hangers-on about the place pat their hands and stamp and
shout. The females on the floor are excited to the wildest
movements. They no longer make any attempt to conceal their
persons. Their action is shameful beyond relation. It is cli-
maxed by the sudden movement of eight or ten of them. As if
by concerted arrangement they denude their lower limbs and
raising their skirts in their hands above their waists go
whirling round and round in a lascivious mix of ballet and
cancan. It is all done in an instant, and with a bang the
music stops. Several of the girls have already fallen ex-
hausted on the floor. The lights go out in a twinkling.[4]

Such an account cannot but raise a large question mark in the modern
mind. The author's obvious enjoyment of the scene, along with his
rather unconvincing professions of moral outrage, seems at odds with
the horrors one might expect from the flesh trade of the times. It all
seems rather tame: the "universal cancan upon the floor," the room

filled with swells and "country cousins," the room foggy with cigar smoke but "ablaze with light," the women laughing, smoking cigarettes, plunking themselves down on the men's knees. It certainly sounds more spontaneous and more enjoyable to its female participants than the goings-on at, say, a present-day go-go bar. It is possible that, in the skewed vision of sexual matters that prevailed a century ago, license and abuse were thought of as scarcely differing. While it is true that McGlory's was a clip joint where out-of-towners were set up to be robbed, it seems positively carnivalesque, and hardly on a par with a place like McGurk's, where women were treated like animals.

A relatively clear view of the city's *louche* districts in 1890 can be had from a curious publication called *Vices of a Big City*, published under the auspices of the *New York Press*. Like Howe and Hummel's book, this pamphlet poses as a warning, as a sort of index of areas to avoid or to redeem, while it is unmistakably a vade mecum for visitors seeking action. Its listings of whorehouses, concert saloons, dance houses, and the like are exhaustive and impressively detailed. The listings are organized geographically and by specialty. On the Bowery, for example, at number 207 is Bertrand Myer's concert saloon: "The place is crowded with women nightly, who smoke cigarettes and drink gin." At number 41 is Herzberg's saloon, "a large store where all liquors, and even a so-called champagne, are sold at 5¢ a glass; the door is kept locked at night, but a man stationed on the outside has a key and will open it for anyone." There are "Rum Holes" on Baxter Street; disorderly houses on Canal, three of which are "cigar store" houses (number 117, the New Jersey House; number 119, the New York House; and number 121, the Brooklyn House). On Water Street between James Street and Catherine Slip are "very low" whorehouses, while those on Cherry Street are of "a little higher order." Those on Thirteenth Street are "ignored by reformers." "Elizabeth Street, between Hester and Grand, is almost entirely given up to disorderly women," and this is said to be the legacy of McGlory's, by then closed. The portions of Hester and Bayard Streets east of the Bowery feature women sitting on stoops. Meanwhile, Frank Stephenson's aforementioned the Slide, at 157 Bleecker, is described as "the lowest and most disgusting place. The place is filled nightly with from one hundred to three hundred people, most of whom are males, but are unworthy the name of men. They are effeminate, degraded, and addicted to vices which are inhuman and unnatural." Presumably, the homophilic tourist of the time would take such rhetoric in his stride.[5] The most anomalous of the places listed is Catherine Vogt's saloon, at West Fourth and Thompson Streets, with a clientele consisting entirely of "degraded" middle-aged women of all races, which may have been a local for superannuated prostitutes. At the end is a chapter purporting to describe the "success of the crusade," which is useful for informing potential customers about houses that have been shut down.[6] What is most interesting about the guidebook is the way that its reformist pretext forces it willy-nilly to represent all persuasions and every degree of vice, without favoritism.

A few years later, things began a turn for the worse, with the most obvious victims being the prostitutes. The price of protection went up, and the ponces and madams took the difference out of the girls' allowances. Opium addiction became widespread among whores, with devastating results; in 1894, when the efforts of the Lexow Committee began to send large numbers of women to jail for substantial sentences, the prisons were filled with hundreds of whores suffering withdrawal symptoms. Emma Goldman, who was then a trusty in charge of medicine in the Blackwell's Island infirmary, noted in her memoirs that nearly all the prostitutes who arrived were thus afflicted. A few years later the Raines Law, which permitted dozens of dives to serve liquor on Sundays provided they called themselves hotels, forced brothels to close. Or, not close exactly so much as turn into houses whose inmates were made to solicit on the streets in any sort of weather, bring the john into what had been the parlor and persuade him to drink so that they could make their cut, and to be permitted upstairs finally only with a sodden customer. By such standards, the sort of vice that had dominated the Tenderloin and the Bowery a decade earlier might seem positively arcadian. Streetwalking, drug addiction, the overwhelming presence of pimps, ever-increasing graft, and persecution and regular prison sentences in the name of reform were to be the staples of the whore's lot for decades afterward. Prohibition, which relaxed some of the so-called moral standards, did not make life easier, either, since it introduced new and much bigger syndicates which controlled the sex trade as gougingly and impersonally as liquor or gambling.

PART 3.

[: *The Arm* ·]

1. · GANGLAND

THE BASIC UNIT OF SOCIAL LIFE
AMONG YOUNG MALES IN NEW YORK
IN THE NINETEENTH CENTURY WAS
(AS IT PERHAPS IS STILL AND EVER
more shall be) the gang. However this unit
functioned and whatever its reasons for existing in other times and places, in the Manhattan of the immigrants it served as an
important marker, a sort of social stake driven
in which allowed the offspring of the various
races and nationalities and sects and liveli-
hoods and districts to differentiate themselves
from their heterogeneous peers. Gangs, it
should be recalled, were not always criminal.
They engaged in violence, but violence was
a normal part of life in their always-contested
environment; turf warfare was a condition of
the neighborhood. As a social unit, the gang
closely resembled such organizations as the
fire company, the fraternal order, and the

political club, and all these formations variously overlapped; gangs might serve as the farm league or the strong-arm squad for the other entities. It was not until rather late in the century that gangs grew independent of their communities and became criminal outfits solely set on plunder, as a result of increasing population and worsening economic conditions. It is axiomatic that the more sophisticated the gangs became, the more violent they grew as well.

The earliest identifiable gangs date from the years immediately after the Revolution. In the late eighteenth century there were five major groups; records of the time are sufficiently imprecise that we cannot know for sure whether they all existed at the same time. The Smith's Vly gang, the Bowery Boys, and the Broadway Boys were white groups; the Fly Boys and the Long Bridge Boys were black.[1] Both the Fly Boys and the Smith's Vly outfit owed their names to the Fly Market, at the foot of Maiden Lane, which in turn derived its title from the Dutch *vly*, meaning valley. (It should be pointed out that the late-nineteenth-century use of "fly," as in "fly cops," meaning undercover policemen, has a very different and more obvious etymology, and that the black usage in our own time, often applied to gang members, has yet a third source, being derived from the movie character Superfly.) These early gang members were definitely not criminals, and nearly all of them were gainfully employed as laborers of one sort or another, with a high proportion of butchers as well as mechanics, carpenters, and shipyard workers. There was evidently only a small percentage among them who followed the less morally august professions, such as gambling and tavernkeeping. The age range, then as later, was relatively broad, from early teens well into the twenties. The principal pastime of these bands was warring with each other over definitions of territory. Their weapons were stones and slung shots (not a sling shot, but an ancestor of the blackjack, consisting of a weight of shot with a flexible strap or handle), their battlefield the swamp area that later became the Five Points, with clashes occasionally extending down Pearl Street or over to Maiden Lane. Some truly epic fights between the Smith's Vly and Broadway gangs were staged on a rise of the present Grand Street between Mott and Broadway that was known as Bunker Hill, on which occasions the gangs might muster as many as fifty members each. These conditions lasted a couple of decades into the nineteenth century, the picture only slightly changing with the rise of such additional gangs as the Spring Streeters and the Grand Streeters.

With the development of the slums in the area centering on the drained Collect Pond, the Lower East Side lost most of what remained of its rural innocence. The squalor and overcrowding of this area, known as the Five Points or, in a more general way, the Bloody Ould Sixth Ward, seemed to come almost immediately, and made it a natural terrain for competition that took the form of crime. The corner groceries, which hardly concealed the groggeries that were their true business, were the social centers, so it is natural that the area's gangs were born in them. Around 1825, the first important and decisively dangerous gang of the quarter, the Forty Thieves, captained by Edward Coleman,[2] came forth from Rosetta Peer's grocery on Centre Street near Anthony. This front also, perhaps a bit later, was home to the Kerryonians, an outfit whose members might be guessed to have originally come from County Kerry in Ireland. The Sixth Ward gangs whose lore has survived were apparently all Irish; it is, unfortunately, unrecorded whether their membership equally reflected the substantial black population of the district. In the late 1820s and early 1830s the gang roster of the neighborhood was further swelled by the Chichesters, the Roach Guards, the Plug Uglies, and the Shirt Tails. The latter were, as might be expected, distinguished by the fact that they refrained from tucking their shirts into their pants. The Plug Uglies wore oversized plug hats stuffed with leather and wool; in frays they would mash them down over their ears like helmets—a good idea at a time when the major weapons were clubs and brickbats, and blows were likely to be to the head. The gangs also favored hobnail boots, for effective kicking.

The Roach Guards, named after Ted Roach, the liquor dealer who backed them, suffered a factional dispute some time in the early 1830s. During the argument a member of one feuding sector evidently threw a rabbit carcass into the assemblage of the other. These recognized a potent symbol when they saw one and hoisted the corpse as their banner. Henceforth they called themselves the Dead Rabbits, an epithet whose pungency was not diminished by the fact that in flash lingo "dead" was an intensifier meaning "best" and a "rabbit" was a tough guy. Further distancing themselves from their former parent body, the Dead Rabbits sewed red stripes down the outer seams of their pants legs; the Roach Guards continued to sport blue ones.

This period saw the formation of numerous gangs all over the city. They varied greatly in strength, importance, and raison d'être. Some were, like fire companies, occupational: there was a band of butcher's boys known as the Hide-Binders, their name also rendered as High-Binders[3] (a term that in some manner now lost came to be applied exclusively to Chinese tong warriors); and a gang of bookbinders' apprentices and printers' devils called the Old Slippers, a name that perhaps sounds less than fierce—although it probably meant they came from Old Slip. The Slippers were opposed by the White Hallers, whose trade is unknown but who presumably lived on Whitehall Street; the Hallers once made news by capturing two Slippers and dipping them first in molasses, then in sand.

Midway in seriousness between these amateurs and the Five Points outfits were the agglomeration of gangs that grew up along the Bowery. These were led by the Bowery Boys, by then a venerable institution, and included the O'Connell Guards, the Atlantic Guards, the American Guards, and the True Blue Americans. What these gangs had in common were their neighborhood and their enmity toward the Five Points gangs. Otherwise, they were a heterogeneous mix: the O'Connell Guards were Irish to the hilt, for example, while the American Guards and the True Blues made much of their allegiance to Old Glory. They could find common ground as well in an opposition to all things English, but friction soon developed as a result of the political rivalry between the Irish-oriented Tammany Hall and the Nativist Party, or Know-Nothings. Still, at first such ethnic divisions were probably not all that serious; the True Blue Americans, paper tigers who were known mostly for wearing black frock coats buttoned up to their chins and for darkly scheming against the English while striking terror into the heart of no one, were, in fact, Irish. Most of the Bowery Boys were employed and reasonably prosperous by contrast with their Five Points counterparts; most were butchers' or mechanics' apprentices, and many belonged to fire companies as well. In the crudest sociological terms, it could be said that the Bowery gangs represented the working poor, and the Sixth Ward gangs were the underclass. On either side of the fence, the gangs all rumbled with each other and kept constant intramural spats going—Shirt Tails vs. Plug Uglies, O'Connells vs. Atlantics—but joined forces to fight neighborhood against neighborhood. Later in their careers they would prove themselves capable of all uniting in common cause against the police.

The major outfits in both these milieux endured until the events surrounding the Draft Riots in 1863 changed the face of the area. The Bowery Boys and the Dead Rabbits in particular grew in size, ferocity, and renown until they were recognized as units of military effectiveness, unstoppable by ordinary means. Their conventional battles, which in the early days were still held at Bunker Hill, as if by formal designation, were bad enough. These battles lasted for days at a time, with the amalgamated gangs massed behind barricades of piled carts and paving stones, fighting with every weapon then available: fists, feet, teeth, bludgeons, brickbats, rocks, knives, pistols, muskets, on several occasions even cannons. More than once, the city had to call out the National Guard or the 27th Regiment to cool things down. As vocational schools, the two gangs had their different specialties. The Dead Rabbits turned out numerous keepers of dives (for example, Kit Burns, Shang Allen, Tommy Hedden), and enforcers, shoulder-hitters, mayhem artists; Hell-Cat Maggie (it was, in the early days, common enough for the gangs to have female members) filed her front teeth to points and wore artificial brass fingernails, and went on to make an independent career of saloon brawling. The Bowery Boys, on the other hand, specialized in supplying bodies to political entities, for poll fixing, poll guarding, repeat voting, and any number of other activities. The clash between Tammany and Nativist factions constantly threatened the stability of the gang, which somehow always survived, although internecine battles were common. One particularly serious fray occurred in June 1835 when the O'Connell Guards and the American Guards battled for two days, beginning at Grand and Crosby Streets and spreading eastward into the Sixth Ward, where the Five Points gangs joined in, fighting impartially against both sides.

The extraordinary longevity of the Dead Rabbits and the Bowery Boys was matched by the longevity of their dispute. Their enmity survived both fracases in which they sided together, such as the anti-Abolitionist riots of 1833, the general looting after the fire of 1835, the Astor Place Opera House riot of 1849, and endless disputes in which they butted heads. The Bowery Boys would assure the cooperation of their pacific Bowery neighbors by spreading rumors that the Dead Rabbits planned to sack shops along the avenue; the Dead Rabbits would enlist the aid of all the Irish by spreading rumors that the Bowery Boys planned to assist Nativists and Republicans in burning St. Patrick's Cathedral (the old one on Mott Street) to the ground. Sometimes ethnic loyalties overrode neighborhood affiliation, as when Orangemen from the Five Points allied themselves with the Bowery Boys against the Dead Rabbits.

Both gangs possibly reached their apex in the summer of 1857. At the time the city had two competing police forces, the Municipal Force and the Metropolitan Force, as a result of political machinations (we shall return to this strange phenomenon), and as rival cops showed more interest in fighting each other than in curtailing crime, the city was virtually unpatrolled. On the night of July 4th a large party of Dead Rabbits and Plug Uglies raided the clubhouse of the Bowery Boys and the Atlantic Guards at 42 Bowery. An all-night battle ensued during which the Bowery side appeared to prevail. The next day, fighting continued around Pearl and Chatham Streets, during which some passing Municipal cops were beaten up; the Metropolitans steered clear of the area. The Roach Guards joined the Rabbits and the Uglies in an attack on a Broome Street dive called the Green Dragon, which they demolished with iron bars and paving stones while drinking up the entire stock of liquor. The Bowery gangs hastened to the scene, and another large battle began near the corner of Bayard Street, during which a Metropolitan cop who made a foolhardy attempt to intervene was beaten up and sent back to the White Street headquarters in his underwear. This prompted a detachment of Metropolitans to come marching up Centre Street in quest of revenge, but the combined action of all the gangs sent them away in defeat. The riot swelled as reinforcements for both sides arrived from all over the city. It was noted that whenever the noise of the fighting abated, the Five Points women could be heard taunting their men, accusing them of cowardice. Looting and vandalism took place on the fringes, while inhabitants of nearby buildings assisted by pelting the rioters indiscriminately with rocks. The police of both forces would make sporadic arrests, which had no effect whatsoever, and finally agreed with each other long enough to bring in the aging gangster and political boss Isaiah Rynders, who pleaded for a halt to the fighting. The gangsters jeered at him and beat him up as well. Rynders then made his way to the Police Commissioner's office to demand that he call out the army. Three National Guard regiments arrived late in the evening, and the fighting stopped, probably more on account of the rioters' exhaustion than for any other reason. The toll was officially set at eight dead and over a hundred wounded, but these figures seemed absurdly low; it was widely rumored that the gangs had taken away their own dead and secretly buried them in alleys and tunnels. The following day, as scattered fighting broke out in fringe areas as far as the German neighborhoods along Avenues A and B, north to Fourteenth Street and east to the river, *The New York Times* ran the following notice:

> *We are requested by the Dead Rabbits to state that the Dead Rabbit club members are not thieves, that they did not participate in the riot with the Bowery Boys, and that the fight in Mulberry street was between the Roach Guards of Mulberry street and the Atlantic Guards of the Bowery. The*

Dead Rabbits are sensitive on points of honor, we are as-
sured, and wouldn't allow a thief to live on their beat,
much less be a member of their club.[4]

The riot, as bad as it was, would turn out to be a mere dress rehearsal for the Draft Riots six years later, in which 70,000 to 80,000 people fought, with some individual mobs comprising as many as 10,000.

In the era before the Civil War, the only other significant concentration of gangs was along the waterfront, where gangs were much more singlemindedly criminal, and divided their attention between prey in the form of dive patrons and that represented by the harbor shipping. An 1850 report to the mayor by Police Chief George W. Matsell estimated that there were between four hundred and five hundred river pirates in the Fourth Ward, divided among about fifty gangs, whose numbers were sometimes augmented by thieves commuting from Brooklyn, New Jersey, or Staten Island. The major gangs included the Daybreak Boys, the Buckaroos, the Hookers, the Swamp Angels, the Slaughter Housers, the Short Tails, the Patsy Conroys, and the Border Gang.

Mugging was done by all these units as well as by ad hoc bands of thieves. Scorning such refinements as knockout drops, they developed a simple routine in which a well-dressed intruder, sailor, or, indeed, nearly anybody else walking by would be lured under a window, a female accomplice would dump ashes on him from above, and the gang would drag him to a cellar where he would be stripped, robbed, beaten, and often killed. A zone grew up between the southern docks (in what is now the financial district) and Corlears Hook, into which cops allegedly never ventured in groups of fewer than six. In the late 1860s it was estimated that, on Cherry Street alone, 15,000 sailors were robbed each year to the tune of about $2 million.

The first of the great East River gangs was the Daybreak Boys, who were headquartered at a saloon run by one Pete Williams at Slaughter House Point, the old name for the intersection of James and Water Streets in the territory that since the days of the Dutch had been associated with tanneries. They specialized in robbing ships at anchor and derived their name from their practice of working the hours around dawn. Their captains were Nicholas Saul and William Howlett; other members included Slobbery Jim, Patsy the Barber, Sow Madden, and Cowlegged Sam McCarthy. All were under twenty years of age at the height of their careers. In their heyday they were said to have stolen property worth in excess of $100,000 in two years. On an August night in 1852, detectives followed Saul and Howlett out to the brig *William Watson*, where they bungled a robbery, fatally shot the watchman, and then fled. The two were hanged in the Tombs yard the following January before a crowd of more than two hundred spectators. Shortly thereafter Slobbery Jim and Patsy the Barber had an epochal fight over the division of twelve cents from the pockets of a German immigrant they had killed, in the course of which Jim murdered Patsy; he was never seen again. Then Daybreaker associate Bill Lourie, owner of the saloon the Rising States on Water Street, was arrested for robbery along with Sam McCarthy. Police Roundsman Blair and Patrolmen Spratt and Gilbert reported killing twelve Daybreakers in 1858, and that same year Detective Sergeant Edwin O'Brien arrested fifty-seven gang members, variously Daybreak Boys, Short Tails, and Border Gangsters. What was left of these three gangs faded from view along with the Swamp Angels[5] and the Hookers. In view of such accounts, one might wonder about the disparity between the bloodthirstiness of these gangs and their obvious lack of sophistication and brains. Or perhaps the police were simply superior in equipment and in reasoning, and older and stronger as well. A diet of ale and mash would probably tend to make one both violent and rather vulnerable.[6]

The only gang of note at this period on the less frequented West Side docks was the Charlton Street Gang, which worked the North River in rowboats. In 1869 they were joined and soon commanded by Sadie the Goat, a former East Side barfly best known for having had an ear chewed off in a fight by the formidable Gallus Mag, of the Hole-in-the-Wall. The ear was later returned to her, and she was said to wear it in a locket around her neck. Her own preferred method of engagement was the head butt, hence her moniker. Under Sadie, the gang grew more ambitious. They stole a sloop, flew the Jolly Roger from its mast, and ranged up the river as far as Poughkeepsie, robbing villages and outlying houses. Like Tom Sawyer, Sadie was evidently up on her pirate lore; she made captives walk the plank, and directed her gang in kidnappings after learning that Julius Caesar had once been held for ransom by pirates. Their career fell victim to their notoriety; once word of their exploits got around, Hudson Valley farmers began keeping firearms in sight, and one welcoming committee eventually defeated the gang.

The most famous pirate of the time was a middle-aged crook named Albert E. Hicks, who in 1860 was shanghaied by a Cherry Street crimp and woke up aboard the sloop *E. A. Johnson*, bound for Virginia to pick up a shipment of oysters. Five days later the boat was discovered drifting off the coast of New Jersey, empty and with signs of bloodshed. Inquiring policemen found that Hicks had been seen in Manhattan with a great deal of money on his person. He skipped town, but was arrested in Providence, R.I., carrying a variety of effects that included a watch and a daguerreotype which could be traced to the ship's officers. The U.S. Circuit Court found him guilty of murder and piracy on the high seas, and he eventually confessed to having killed all hands with an ax. The case received maximum publicity and achieved enduring fame when P. T. Barnum acquired a life mask of Hicks as well as all his clothes for $25 and two boxes of cigars. Hicks was hanged a mere four months after his deed, on Bedloe's Island (the future site of the Statue of Liberty), to much pomp.

The dives around Corlears Hook grew their own species of crook. In the Tub of Blood, the Hell's Kitchen, the Snug Harbor, Swain's Castle, Cat Alley, and the Lava Beds thrived such gangsters as Skinner Meehan, Dutch Hen, Brian Boru, Sweeney the Boy, Hop-Along Peter, and Jack Cody. Hop-Along was a half-wit who was said to go berserk whenever he saw a police uniform, Sweeney and Boru were legendary for having slept in a marble yard for twenty years; one night (according to Frank Moss's account) Boru got so drunk he was eaten by rats. The river pirates of the area's later period featured the Patsy Conroys, who ranged all the way from the Fourth Ward to the Hook. The membership included such worthies as Joseph Gayles, known as Sacco the Bracer; Scotchy Lavelle, who much later was to employ Irving Berlin as a singing waiter at a dive on Doyers Street; Mike Kerrigan, who was to become well known as a bank robber under the name Johnny Dobbs; and such impressive if forgotten names as Kid Shanahan, Pugsey Hurley, Wreck Donovan, Tom the Mick, Nigger Wallace, Beany Kane, and Piggy Noles. They sprang up in the early 1870s and flagged by 1873, when Sacco was killed by cops in a fight on the river, and a number of the others were arrested for robbing the brig *Mattan*, anchored off Castle Garden. Their mantle was assumed by the Hook Gang, led by Suds Merrick and Terry Le Strange. The Hook Gang was diversified, with a hand in activities ranging from piracy to burglary to picking pockets. Piggy Noles, who joined the Hooks after the demise of the Conroys, became famous for having stolen a rowboat, repainted it, and sold it back to its original owner, a legend later to circulate concerning many a car thief. Another member of the gang, Slipsey Ward, got his comeuppance while attempting the extraordinarily brazen, or stupid, task of single-handedly taking over a schooner.

The gangs had been driven away from the Fourth Ward by 1865 by concerted police action, and in 1876 the Steamboat Squad was formed to clean up Corlears Hook. The river dives were a thing of the past by 1890 (one reason being that most shipping had by then moved to the North River side), and the last of the gangs dissolved by 1900. The waterfront was therefore relatively unmolested until after World War I, when a major gang called the White Hands arose on the Brooklyn shore of the East River and, captained by Dinny Meehan and Wild Bill Lovett, controlled a block of territory that ran up both banks from Red Hook to the Brooklyn Bridge. Their major occupation, in that more sophisticated time, was extorting protection money from barge owners. In one form or another this gang limped through two decades of bloody wars of succession. According to one authority, who unfortunately does not provide substantiation, the White Hands were a direct outgrowth of the Swamp Angels, who would have had to lay low for some forty years.

The 1860s and 1870s were the grand era of bank robberies. James L. Ford wrote in his memoirs fifty years later: "Such operations as bank burglary were held in much higher esteem during the 'sixties and 'seventies than at present, and the most distinguished members of the craft were known by sight and pointed out to strangers."[7] The district gangs of the time were mere pikers and barroom brawlers compared with such an outfit as that put together by George Leonidas Leslie, also known as Western George and referred to in the press as King of the Bank Robbers. His gang was made up of veterans of various gangs, including Jimmy Hope, Jimmy Brady, Abe Coakley, Red Leary, Shang Draper (the panel-house king), Johnny Dobbs, Worcester Sam Perris, and Banjo Pete Emerson. According to George W. Walling, who was Police Superintendent from 1874 to 1885, the Leslie gang was responsible for 80 percent of the bank robberies in New York between the Civil War and Leslie's death in 1884; estimates of their total take ranged between $7 million and $12 million. Such statistics must be viewed with suspicion as sounding entirely too convenient; one set of devious masterminds, after all, does less to damage police prestige than a whole town full of bank robbers. Nevertheless, there is no denying Leslie's prowess. He was perhaps responsible, for example, for the June 1869 robbery of the Ocean National Bank at Greenwich and Fulton Streets, which netted at least $786,879. His gang also sacked the Manhattan Savings Bank at Bleecker and Broadway, in October 1878, to the tune of $2,747,000, but despite its impressive profile, this job was not an unqualified success. The heist was some three years in the planning, but even so, the planning proved fallible, and, contrary to Leslie's usual caution, force was used, rather than bribery, to subdue the bank's janitor, which led to the gang's being identified. Not only that, but the take turned out to be principally composed of non-negotiable bonds, so that the business end of the haul amounted to a relatively paltry $11,000 in cash and $300,000 in negotiable securities, of which latter the bank eventually recovered $257,000. Arrests in the

A low character in Raoul Walsh's *Regeneration*, 1915, one of the few Bowery crime dramas to be shot (in part) on location

Murder in a blind tiger, taken from the point of view of the gunman. NYPD evidence photo, circa 1915

Weapons and miscellanea seized by the police. Photograph
by Jacob Riis

Pool-hall murder. NYPD evidence photo

case began in May 1879. Only John Hope, son of Jimmy, and strongman Bill Kelly actually went to jail, though, as Coakley and Emerson were acquitted and the indictment against Leslie was dismissed for lack of evidence. Afterward, Leslie became a freelance consultant, advising other gangs on strategy and tactics, for a cut of their proceeds. In June 1884 his body was found at the base of Tramp's Rock, a landmark that formerly stood somewhere on the boundary between the Bronx and Westchester County. He was said to have been murdered by accomplices, but the case was never solved, perhaps intentionally.

Even the 1869 Ocean National Bank job might not have been entirely to Leslie's credit. It is a measure of the deliberate confusion surrounding municipal affairs manipulated by Boss Tweed and associates that to this day the amount taken and the ultimate responsibility for that job cannot be established in any definite way. Other sources, who round off the amount of the take to $2,750,000, credit the Bliss Bank Ring, a gang organized by George Miles Bliss and Mark Shinburn, and among the proponents of this theory there is disagreement over the exact composition of the ring. It was alleged by Thomas F. Byrnes, who acceded to the leadership of the Detective Bureau in 1880, that the Bliss Ring had pulled off the job with the assistance of numerous bribed police officials, who then pinned the deed on Leslie to protect themselves. Conveniently, Bliss was finally caught in an attempt to rob the Barre Bank, in Vermont, in 1875; Shinburn was arrested for a robbery in Belgium in 1883, after which events their respective trails vanished. It is a measure of the political and judicial chaos of the period that even within Byrnes's account there are contradictions as to the year of the robbery, the amount taken, and just who was involved. Even in such an apparently well-publicized case, the border between lore and fact is extremely hazy, so the prospects for factual certainty in the murkier strata of crime is correspondingly dimmer.

Fences in the mid-nineteenth century were powerful enough, and perhaps sufficiently liberal with bribes, to operate with a degree of openness. Maybe the most effective among them chose to retain anonymity, such as the nameless genius who succeeded in handling $50,000 worth of needles and thread stolen from the H. B. Claflin warehouse in the 1870s. A thief who had goods to dispose of would not have had to look very hard to find takers. For many years the Eighth Ward Thieves' Exchange, at Bowery and Houston, ran a sort of fence supermarket, and it was eventually succeeded by the Bowery's Little Stock Exchange, the one at which it was rumored that real diamonds had changed hands for a mere dollar. Before the Civil War, there had been, for example, Joe Erich on Maiden Lane and Ephraim "Old" Snow on Grand and Allen, who was said to have disposed of an entire flock of sheep. Later there was Old Unger's on Eldridge Street, and Little Alexander and Bill Johnson on the Bowery, the latter of whom fronted as a dry-goods retailer. After the Civil War, the major names were John D. Grady, aka Travelling Mike, and the formidable Marm Mandelbaum. Frederika Mandelbaum, an impressive, narrow-eyed figure, secure in her 250-pound bulk, had a three-story building on the corner of Clinton and Rivington Streets where she ran a fencing operation with the assistance of her husband, Wolfe, and their son and two daughters, under the guise of a haberdashery. Her first listing in police records dates to 1862, and over the next twenty years she is said to have passed between $5 million and $10 million in goods through her mill. She was also alleged to have operated a Fagin school on Grand Street, but this very popular allegation was bandied around so carelessly in the decades after the appearance of Dickens's novel that such tales should be viewed with caution. Mandelbaum, whose house was said to be furnished as opulently as any Vanderbilt's with goods liberated from uptown mansions, was the social leader of the female criminal set. Her friends included such prominent sneak thieves and blackmailers as Big Mary, Ellen Clegg, Queen Liz, Little Annie, Old Mother Hubbard, Kid Glove Rosey, the con woman Sophie Lyons, and Black Lena Kleinschmidt. Black Lena was an uncommonly successful pickpocket and moll-buzzer who was undone by her taste for social climbing. After saving her money for years, she finally moved to the then fashionable suburb of Hackensack, N.J., and began entertaining a straight crowd. Legend has it that her end came when, at one of her lunches, a guest recognized a diamond ring Lena was wearing as her own unique piece, stolen years before. Marm Mandelbaum, for her part, was indicted for grand larceny by the district attorney in 1884, but jumped bail and fled to Canada. She had the last laugh, as her bondsmen succeeded in transferring the property pledged for her bail to her possession by means of back-dated documents.

Mandelbaum was represented by the era's paramount criminal lawyers, William Howe and Abraham Hummel, to whom she paid a retainer of $5,000 a year. This pair were very nearly a law unto themselves, and were so much a part of the New York scene, both high and low, in the latter half of the nineteenth century that they can hardly be discussed without the use of superlatives. In their forty-odd-year career they were said to have represented more than a thousand defendants in murder and manslaughter cases alone, with Howe personally pleading more than 650 of these. The firm was established in 1861 by Howe, a corpulent, flashily dressed practitioner noted for his overwhelmingly theatrical manner, in particular much given to weeping in the courtroom. His partner, the canny, diminutive Hummel, joined as an office boy in 1863 and was elevated by Howe to equal status within a few years. They redefined the word "shyster" (which originated when a lawyer named Scheuster so often irritated Justice Osborne of the Essex Market Court that the latter began accusing other obstreporous attorneys of "scheuster" practices). Their offices were in a building on Leonard and Centre Streets, directly across from the Tombs, that was ornamented with a forty-foot sign advertising their practice. Their cable address was LENIENT. They sometimes obtained the minutes of successful trials, had them reprinted, and distributed them as publicity. They owned reporters at most of the daily papers and kept a regular stable of professional witnesses. Hummel once got 250 of the little more than 300 prisoners on Blackwell's Island released all at once on a technicality. They kept no records.

The mainstay of Howe and Hummel's practice was the breach-of-promise blackmail suit, which they effectively worked on both sides, representing showgirls who had had affairs with society figures and then been dropped, and at the same time being kept on retainer by many of these playboys as protection against further suits. Their client list virtually defined the newsworthy part of Manhattan society in the last thirty years of the nineteenth century. In the criminal world they represented entire gangs, such as "General" Abe Greenthal's national pickpocket ring, the Sheeny Mob, the forgers of Chester McLaughlin's Valentine Ring, and the foremost downtown gang of their day, the Whyos. They worked for George Leslie (receiving $90,000 from him in the wake of the 1878 Manhattan Savings fiasco, for many years afterward the largest legal fee on record), the counterfeiter Charles O. Brockway, the major bookmaker Peter De Lacey, the procuresses Hattie Adams and the French Madame, the abortionist Madame Restell, the Tammany boss Richard Croker, the banco artists Hungry Joe and Kid Miller, the dive owners Harry Hill and Billy McGlory, and such once-famous murderers as Dr. Jakob Rosenzweig (the Hackensack Mad Monster), Annie Walden the Man-Killing Race-Track Girl, and Ned Stokes, who shot Jim Fisk. In civil cases of various sorts they represented bridge-jumper Steve Brodie, *Police Gazette* publisher Richard K. Fox, song-and-dance man Ned Harrigan, exotic dancer Little Egypt, music-hall proprietor Tony Pastor, the anarchist Johann Most, the bohemian feminists Victoria Woodhull and Tennessee Claflin, the eccentric George F. Train, and a slew of theatrical figures that included P. T. Barnum, Edwin Booth, John Drew, John Barrymore, and Lillie Langtry. Their industry did not flag until Howe died in 1902 and Hummel was chased from the country by the reform crusader William Travers Jerome, dying in London in 1926.

Some of the flavor of their ambiguous attitude toward the law can be derived from their sole published work, the 1888 *In Danger*. It begins with their citing as an inspiration a sermon by one Dr. Guthrie, "The City, Its Sins and Its Sorrows," which they quote at length:

> *"It had been well for many an honest lad and unsuspecting*
> *country girl that they had never turned their steps cityward*
> *nor turned them from the simplicity of their country home*

*toward the snares and pitfalls of crime and vice that await
the unwary in New York . . ."*

And they proceed to describe the temptations in mouth-watering detail:

> *. . . elegant storehouses, crowded with the choicest and most
> costly goods, great banks whose vaults and safes contain more
> bullion than could be transported by the largest ships, colos-
> sal establishments teeming with diamonds, jewelry, and pre-
> cious stones gathered from all the known and uncivilized
> portions of the globe—all this countless wealth, in some
> cases so insecurely guarded.*

And go on to discuss the ease and convenience of crime in New York:

> *All the latest developments in science and skill are being
> successfully pressed into the service of the modern criminal
> . . . the traveling bag with false, quickly-opening sides . . .
> the shop-lifters' muff . . . the lady thieves' corsets . . .*

Under the guise of alerting the public to the dangers of big-city crime, they offer explicit directions for making burglars' tools, explain the logistics of skin games, and give formulas for rigging cards. The booklet is, in fact, an advertisement for crime, couched in all the subtlety known to the science of publicity at the time. Having instructed the potential criminal on how to pursue the profession, they detail its rewards: the unbridled nightlife available at Harry Hill's and Billy McGlory's, the monetary advantages of blackmailing and quackery, and, of course, the fact that anyone could do it.

> *In no particular can the female shop-lifter be distinguished
> from other members of her sex except perhaps that in most
> cases she is rather more richly and attractively dressed.*[8]

Howe and Hummel bring nineteenth-century Manhattan into relief as a wide-open town dominated by two industries: larceny and entertainment, which often overlap. The corruption of minors, the bribery of witnesses and officials, the generalized suborning of the system of justice: they practiced all of these, and they also, like artists, gave a coherent shape to the chaos of their times, tying its many ends together, showing the common thread that linked P. T. Barnum and faro mechanics, Tammany ward-heelers and The. Allen, Western George and sideshow freaks, trunk murderers and the French Madame. It was often bruited about that they were criminal masterminds who set up jobs for their clients and then got them off at the other end if they were caught, and this is not entirely beyond the pale of speculation, but they scarcely needed to compromise themselves in such barefaced fashion when they had made themselves indispensable to the city's many layers of cupidity. Howe and Hummel, it might be said, were the truest realists of their time, by their example sweeping away the cant of moralists and the hypocrisy of journalists. They saw the inhabitants of New York City as one class, united under the single standard of greed.

Howe and Hummel's clients the Whyos were the most powerful downtown gang between the Civil War and the 1890s, a huge group who ranged all over Lower Manhattan, having (so Asbury theorizes) emerged from the Chichesters, one of the first but thereafter least publicized of the original Five Points outfits. They had numerous headquarters over the years: "Dry Dollar" Sullivan's saloon on Chrystie Street (he was later to become the preeminent Tammany politician of his day), various niches within Mulberry Bend, a churchyard at Park and Mott Streets, an Italian dive at Worth and Mulberry, and the saloon called the Morgue, on the Bowery. Their membership, whose most prominent figures included such colorful names as Hoggy Walsh, Fig McGerald, Bull Hurley, Googy Corcoran, Baboon Dooley, Red Rocks Farrell, Slops Connolly, Piker Ryan, Dorsey Doyle, and Big Josh Hynes, variously worked as pickpockets, sneak thieves, dive owners, and brothel and panel-house keepers. Hines claimed his berth in history by being the first man ever to hold up a session of the newly invented game of stuss (robbing stuss setups soon became nearly as popular, and certainly more remunerative, than trying one's luck at playing the game). Mike McGloin, who was hanged in the Tombs in 1883 for the murder of a saloonkeeper, articulated what might have been the Whyos' motto: "A guy ain't tough until he has knocked his man out."[9] Piker Ryan made his mark by getting himself arrested while carrying a take-out menu of Whyo services:

Punching	*. $2*
Both eyes blacked	*. $4*
Nose and jaw broke	*. $10*
Jacked out	*. $15*
Ear chawed off	*. $15*
Leg or arm broke	*. $19*
Shot in leg	*. $25*
Stab	*. $25*
Doing the big job	*. . . . . $100 and up*

Dandy Johnny Nolan was enshrined in memory for his invention of a copper eye-gouger that could easily be slipped over the thumb (although, if truth be told, this does not sound so very different from Hell-Cat Maggie's artificial brass fingernails); he was also noted for embedding sections of ax blades in the soles of his boots. The Whyos' longest-lived captains were Danny Lyons and Danny Driscoll; both ended up getting hanged in the Tombs yard. Driscoll got his for accidentally shooting and killing a young female bystander in the course of a quarrel. Lyons was a whoremaster whose stable included Bunty Kate, Gentle Maggie, and Lizzie the Dove (Maggie eventually stabbed the Dove in the throat with a cheese knife in the course of a bar brawl). He added Pretty Kitty McGown to the string, but her former lover tracked Lyons down; Lyons killed him and was arrested soon after.

Lesser gangs in this period included the Hartley Mob, centered on Broadway and Houston Street, which happened to acquire a hearse and often carried out jobs under cover of mock funerals, staged complete with black drapes on the vehicle, crepe bands for their hats, and a coffin for the swag; the Molasses Gang, which developed the neat but perhaps self-limiting gambit of walking into grocery stores, asking the keeper to fill a derby hat with molasses "on a bet," clapping the hat over the proprietor's head, and emptying the till; the Dutch Mob, including future Western George associate Sheeny Mike Kurtz, which specialized in staging street fights to draw crowds, whose pockets they would pick, in the area from Houston to Fifth Streets east of the Bowery until it was cleaned up by Police Captain Anthony Allaire in 1887; the Mackerelville Crowd, which dominated the neighborhood of that name that once covered the area between Eleventh and Thirteenth Streets, between First Avenue and Avenue C; and the Battle Row Gang, which emerged from the original Battle Row (a title subsequently claimed by numerous Manhattan streets and alleys) on Sixty-third Street between First and Second Avenues, and which was soon unopposed in the semi-rural district that covered the streets numbered in the sixties from river to river.

The middle West Side, which really developed as a neighborhood only after the Civil War, brought forth its first significant mob, the Tenth Avenue Gang, which made its name by jumping a southbound express at Spuyten Duyvil, tying up the personnel, and throwing off cash and securities packed in iron boxes to confederates who stood waiting at trackside as the train approached Forty-second Street. They in turn were absorbed by the Hell's Kitchen Gang, captained by Dutch Heinrichs, which pursued a variety of occupations: mugging, housebreaking, extorting protection money from shopkeepers, and robbing the rail yards at the Hudson River depot on Thirtieth Street. Farther downtown, in the area north of Washington Market then inhabited principally by Turks, Syrians, and Armenians, there were the Stable Gang, which worked out of a Washington Street barn and preyed on recent immigrants; the Silver Gang, a group of burglars also domiciled on Washington Street; and the versatile Potashes, captained by Red Shay Meehan, who derived their name from the Babbit Soap Factory on Washington near Rector Street. The neighborhood's most venerable outfit was the Boodle Gang, which had begun as far back as the 1850s as butcher-cart thieves—a term that actually applied to robbers preying on any sort of vehicles. Installed in a labyrinthine double-tenement block bounded by Greenwich and Washington, Spring and Canal Streets, they divided their time between raiding stores and wagons at the Centre and Washington Markets and waylaying bank messengers.

The history of the city's gangs can be seen as running a close parallel to the progress of commerce. From small, specialized establishments narrowly identified with particular neighborhoods, gangs branched out, diversified, and merged, absorbing smaller and less well-organized units and encompassing ever-larger swaths of territory. After the Whyos, their numbers decimated by jailings and deaths, dissolved in the early 1890s, a small number of very large gangs, organized as umbrella formations made up of smaller entities, came to dominate the scene. There were four such conglomerates operating in the lower part of the island over the better part of the two decades on either side of the turn of the century: the Five Pointers, the Eastmans, the Gophers, and the Hudson Dusters. The Five Pointers (named with a feeling for history, since the neighborhood of that name had, for all intents and purposes, not existed in nearly thirty years) boasted as many as 1,200 members and controlled an area ranging from Broadway to the Bowery, from Fourteenth Street to City Hall Park. They were headquartered at the New Brighton Dance Hall on Great Jones Street, which was owned by their captain, Paul Kelly. The Eastmans were named after their leader, Monk Eastman. From their base in a saloon on Chrystie Street (from which a police raid once removed two wagonloads of slungshots, blackjacks, brass knuckles, and revolvers), they worked the territory from the Bowery east to the river, from Fourteenth to Monroe Streets. Their turf included the East Side brothel district as well as the main share of Bowery dives, which were for some reason concentrated on the east side of the avenue.

The middle West Side of the island was owned by the Gophers (generally pronounced "Goofers," although not derisively), who were centered in the Roaring Forties but ranged from Fourteenth to Forty-second Streets and from Seventh to Eleventh Avenues. Their name derived from their habit of holing up in basements and cellars, and their five hundred-odd members were directed from a saloon run by one Mallet Murphy (famous for using a mallet as his weapon of choice behind the bar) on Thirty-ninth Street between Tenth and Eleventh Avenues, a block also known in its time as Battle Row. The remaining quadrant was the property of the Hudson Dusters, who from various sites on Hudson Street claimed everything south of Thirteenth Street and west of Broadway. Besides these four companies, nearly all the gangs of Lower Manhattan tended to be subsidiary operations, one of the very few exceptions being the Gas House Gang, which arose from the old Gas House district now paved over by Stuyvesant Town and Peter Cooper Village and whose two hundred or so members followed the risky profession of raiding other gangs' turfs. The city's northern reaches were still considered wasteland, so nobody cared very much that the Red Peppers and the Duffy Hills fought over possession of East 102nd Street, or that Rags Riley's Pansies claimed a stretch of the uptown waterfront from their nest at Eighty-first Street and Avenue A (that part is now York Avenue).

One gang was remarkable for its intransigence and for the respect its determination inspired in other outfits. This was a nameless band of contract workers led by Humpty Jackson from a graveyard on the block between Twelfth and Thirteenth Streets, between First and Second Avenues, and it succeeded in remaining independent and relatively unmolested for several decades. Jackson was a hunchback who always carried three guns: one in his pocket, one on his back below his hump, and a third concealed in the crown of his hat. He was also something of an intellectual, an autodidact who always kept a book in his other pocket, was said to have mastered Latin and Greek, and was often seen reading Voltaire, Spencer, Darwin, and Huxley—a syllabus that bears a suggestive similarity to the reading matter favored by the "direct action" anarchists prominent in France around the same time. Jackson was arrested over a hundred times and served at least twenty stints in jail, but always for minor infractions. He kept a peace of unrecorded specifications with the larger gangs, although three overzealous Eastmans, led by a former shoplifter called Crazy Butch, once attempted to hijack him, and failed. His associates included Nigger Ruhl, the Lobster Kid, the Grabber, and Spanish Louie. The latter, also known as Indian Louie, was a theatrical figure given to mysteriously hinting at Mexican and Apache origins and alluding to his adventures in the Indian Wars. He always carried a brace of Colt revolvers as well as two eight-inch dirks, and dressed in an outfit of solid black topped off by a large black sombrero, in which getup he was often to be seen strutting with no fewer than three whores on his arm. After he was killed, he was discovered to have had no police record, and to have amassed a nest egg consisting of $170 in his pocket, $700 in his shoe, and $3,000 in the Bowery Savings Bank. His body was claimed by his father, who turned out to be Jewish and from Brooklyn.

The gangsters of the 1890s had a more sophisticated veneer than their predecessors. According to Asbury's researches, while the Dead Rabbits and even the Whyos had been bruisers, considerable in height and bulk, these new men averaged 5 foot 3 inches and around 130 pounds; they were bantam cocks. Most Eastmans and Five Pointers were dandies, clean-shaven, manicured, their hair pomaded, who decked out in dress suits for their rackets. They used scent liberally— the Five Pointer and crook-of-all-trades Biff Ellison was said to be detectable from a considerable distance. After the 1911 Sullivan Law made possession of firearms an offense punishable with an automatic jail sentence, many hoods had their pockets sewn shut, so that guns could not be planted on them, and were never seen without their women, who would carry the pistols in their purses, or muffs, or hats, or strapped to their arms by rubber bands under leg-of-mutton sleeves, or concealed within the extravagant billows of the hairstyle called the Mikado tuck-up, or buried under the wire mold called the rat that served as a base for the even more towering pompadour.

The gangs grew more sophisticated in their organization as well. The Eastmans at one point actually began requiring their membership to turn in typewritten reports when they executed contract jobs. Modeling themselves on the Tammany practice of operating locally through the fronts provided by neighborhood chowder clubs and baseball teams, the gangs developed farm systems that served as community liaisons as well as nosing out and training potential future gangsters. Such outfits as the Twin Oaks Club, the Yankee Doodle Boys, the Go Aheads, the Liberty Social Club, the Round Back Rangers, the Bowery Indians, the East Side Crashers, the Jolly 48, the Limburger Roarers, the Soup Greens, and the East Side Dramatic and Pleasure Club held balls, organized outings, laundered cash, and concealed traffic as well. Most gangs also had female auxiliaries, most of whose members were redoubtable thieves and fighters in their own right: the Lady Locusts, the Lady Barkers, the Lady Flashers, the Lady Truck Drivers, the Lady Liberties of the Fourth Ward.

Monk Eastman was born Edward Osterman in Williamsburg, Brooklyn, in 1873; he was also known at various times as Joseph Morris, Joseph Marrin, Edward Delancey, and William Delancey. He loved cats and pigeons, and so his father, a Jewish restaurant owner, set him up in a Brooklyn pet shop. He was restless, however, and left in the mid-1890s to become the sheriff, or bouncer, of the New Irving Dance Hall in Manhattan, where he soon developed a reputation as a man equally handy with fists, club, blackjack, and knockout drops, who nevertheless preserved a certain delicacy (he was known never to have hit a woman with a club). Unlike his fellow gangsters of the time, Eastman was so crude in appearance that he could model for the stereotypical crook who has continued to show up in cartoons down to the present day (he had a bullet-shaped head, a broken nose, cauliflower ears, prominently throbbing veins, numerous knife scars, pendulous jowls, and a bull neck, and was usually seen wearing an undershirt, with a small derby perched on the back of his head of longish, unkempt hair). As his leadership manifested itself, and his power in the underworld grew, his passion for birds and felines re-emerged. He was estimated to have owned five hundred pigeons and more than a hundred cats, and both to indulge his devotion and to serve as a convenient cover he eventually opened a pet shop on Broome Street, but business lagged, it was said, because he grew so attached to the animals that he discouraged customers from buying them. He also came to own a bicycle shop. One of the subordinate gangs under his control, an outfit led by Crazy Butch, was called the Squab Wheelmen in honor of his two preoccupations; the Wheelmen were required to rent a bicycle at least once a week. Other free companies under his aegis included the McCarthys, the Cherry Street Gang (a late agglomeration of sometime river pirates), the Fourteenth Street Gang, the Lolly Meyers, the Red Onions, and the Yakey Yakes, who roosted under the Brooklyn Bridge. The Midnight Terrors, lodged in the First Ward, were famous for having their own baseball team. The Batavia Street Gang disgraced themselves. After the Cherry Street Gang, who were known as dandies, announced that they had all gotten new outfits for the ball held by the Batavias, these latter broke a window of Segal's jewelry store on New Chambers Street and stole forty-four gold rings. They were easily apprehended at their tailor's, as they stood being fitted for suits.

Paul Kelly, the leader of the Five Pointers, whose real name was Vacarelli, was said in his prime to resemble a bank clerk or a theology student; he was fluent in French, Spanish, and Italian. His principal lieutenants, who led their own subdivisions as well as working for Kelly, included Biff Ellison, who made a significant career at running rackets on his own behalf and later came to own a short-lived but wide-open homosexual bar on Cooper Square called Paresis Hall (the name apparently derived from a patent-medicine advertisement commonly found in saloon toilets); Eat-'em-up Jack McManus, famed mayhem artist and sheriff of both the New Brighton and McGurk's Suicide Hall; Kid Dropper, whose real name was Nathan Kaplan and whose moniker came from his prowess at the wallet-drop scam;[10] and Johnny Spanish. Spanish, whose real name was Joseph Wayler, had begun as a solo operator, specializing in holdups of stuss games. He usually carried two revolvers in his belt and two in his pockets, as well as a blackjack and brass knuckles. He was still addicted to robbing stuss tables in his gang years, and once, while trying to stick up the mechanic Kid Jigger, met resistance and misfired, killing an eight-year-old girl. He fled town and returned some months later, only to find that his girlfriend, who was pregnant with his child, had taken up with Kid Dropper. Enraged, Spanish hustled her into a taxi and out to Maspeth, where he stood her up against a tree and shot her through the abdomen. In a denouement out of Western legend, she was merely knocked unconscious, and prematurely gave birth to a child who came into the world with three fingers shot off, but otherwise intact. Spanish got seven years.

In the heyday of the gangs the Bowery and Chatham Square constituted the crime district of the city, analogous to the flower market or the garment district. There was a store on Elizabeth Street that served as an underworld one-stop, selling pistols, brass knuckles, stilettos, billy clubs of house manufacture with a lead slug in the end, and its own design of blackjack, a six-inch leather bag filled with shot, ending in a rope handle. Superannuated hoods got into the business of running locals for the members of their trade, such as Red Jack's on Chatham Square, not open to the public. Pickpockets and hired guns had a variety of other places in which to hang out and openly discuss business as well, such as McGurk's. As it was said of the gangsters of the era: "When times are right, they go out every afternoon, just like mechanics going to work."

Both the Eastmans and the Five Pointers were closely tied to Tammany Hall and employed Tammany lawyers and bail bondsmen, as well as returning the favor in incidentals such as repeat voting. In spite of this, the two gangs began to feud around 1901, and the war never really stopped until the outfits were both defunct. The struggle started haphazardly, a matter of a build-up of skirmishes and minor turf disputes, the odd raid of a ball, some scattered gunplay (including some of the earliest drive-by shootings, as soon as gangsters acquired cars), and the inevitable stuss holdups. In August 1903 a party of Five Pointers attacked an Eastman-backed stuss game under the Rivington Street arch of the Second Avenue El on Allen Street. A major gun battle ensued that eventually involved as many as a hundred gangsters; at one point, some passing Gophers, friends of neither side, joined in and began firing indiscriminately at everybody. A company of police-men at length mustered and charged, killing three, wounding seven, and arresting twenty, one of whom was Eastman, who gave a false name and was released the following morning. Tammany politicians intervened and forced the gangs to accept a truce, its terms being hammered out under the eye of the prominent fixer Tom Foley at a meeting held at a notorious Chrystie Street hellhole called the Palm Café. As a result, the strip of turf between the Pelham Café on Pell Street and the Bowery sidewalk a block away was deemed neutral. A grand racket was held and the gangsters danced with each other's girls.

After the feud, the gangs went back to contract jobs, the odd black-jacking or hijacking, and sundry extortions. Late in 1903, however, a dispute which began with an Eastman and a Five Pointer arguing over a point of honor escalated until the gangs were once again at war. This time the solution worked out by the politicians was that the feud should be resolved in a boxing match between Eastman and Kelly. The two men, backed by a previously determined number of followers each, met in a barn in the Bronx on a winter day. Eastman's strength and Kelly's speed and intelligence were well matched, it would seem, be-cause they fought for two solid hours, eventually collapsing on each other from exhaustion, the bout being declared a draw.

Not long after this, in February 1904, Eastman happened to be near Times Square, where he spotted a young man lurching and weaving down the street, watched from a distance by an unsavory character. Eastman assumed that what he was seeing was the classic cat-and-mouse routine of lush-roller and lush, and he went over to the victim, either—depending on who was telling the story—to prop him up and help him along or to get the jump on working his pockets. As it happened, the young man was a rich wastrel and the other was a Pinkerton detective assigned to keep him out of trouble. As Eastman's fingers drew near the man's pockets, the Pinkerton began firing. East-man ran away but fell straight into the arms of a cop stationed in front of the Hotel Knickerbocker, at Broadway and Forty-second Street. Tammany decided to throw him away, and he was sentenced to ten years in Sing Sing.

His demoralized gang was thereupon split by a succession dispute between Eastman's longtime trusted adjutant, Richie Fitzpatrick, and a rising star called Kid Twist (Max Zweibach), a fray that was soon resolved when Twist fatally shot Fitzpatrick in a dive on Chrystie Street. Meanwhile, the Five Pointers were having their own troubles. Bad blood had developed between Kelly and Ellison, who had become ambitious. Ellison joined up with a Gopher called Razor Riley, and the two went to confront Kelly in his own lair, the New Brighton. A gun battle left one Five Pointer dead and Paul Kelly alive but flattened, with three bullets in his body. The gunmen fled, Riley to Hell's Kitchen, where he died of pneumonia before the police could find him, and Ellison to Baltimore, where he succeeded in hiding until 1911, when he was caught and sent up the river for eight to twenty. Kelly, who had gradually been moving his operations farther uptown, found his power eclipsed during his convalescence. When he got out of the hospital, he opened a joint called the Little Naples down the street from the shuttered New Brighton, but it soon failed, and he slipped into obscurity, emerging years later as a reformed character, or so it was said, becoming a real-estate broker and a labor-union business agent.

Meanwhile, on the West Side, the Gophers had been going strong for two decades. Their main industry, following in the footsteps of the West Side gangs before them, was robbing freight cars on Eleventh Avenue sidings and in the depots of the New York Central; eventually, the railroad established a police force just to deal with them. Among their chiefs were Newburg Gallagher, Marty Brennan, Stumpy Malarkey, Goo Goo Knox, One Lung Curran (famous for his habit of stealing policemen's coats to give to his girlfriends), and Happy Jack Mulraney (so called because of a facial rictus due to partial paralysis; he once killed a saloonkeeper called Paddy the Priest for laughing at him). The Gophers had their own free companies: the Gorillas, the

Rhodes Gang, the Parlor Mob, and, not the least of them, the Battle Row Ladies' Social and Athletic Club, also known as the Lady Gophers, which, under the leadership of Battle Annie, played both sides in labor disputes, alternately fighting scabs and working as strikebreakers.

Their neighbors to the south, beginning toward the end of the 1890s, were the Hudson Dusters, who took over the Lower West Side from what remained of the Potashes and the Boodle Gang. The Dusters mostly stayed clear of the disputes going on in other parts of town; they had their own problems defending their turf, the eastern border along Broadway being disputed by the Fashion Plates, and the western docks and waterfront streets fought for by the Marginals and the Pearl Buttons. Kid Yorke and Circular Jack founded the gang along with Goo Goo Knox, who came over from the Gophers in the wake of a schism (though the Dusters and the Gophers subsequently became allies), and included such worthies as Red Farrell, Rickey Harrison, Mike Costello, Rubber Shaw, and Honey Stewart. The Dusters boasted a legendary thief called Ding Dong, who had organized a corps of children who would assist him on his rounds by climbing onto express wagons and throwing parcels down into his waiting arms, after which they would disappear. The Dusters were a colorful bunch, more given to showing off than to mayhem. They were favorites with journalists, to whom they would provide abundant copy; with the dockside prostitutes, with whom they would drink and dance at spontaneous and lengthy bacchanalia; and with the incipient Greenwich Village bohemians of the prewar years. The future Catholic Worker activist Dorothy Day, by her own admission, spent a great deal of time partying with them in her salad days, as did many others, including Eugene O'Neill, at the various Duster headquarters on Hudson and Bethune Streets, houses of merrymaking invariably equipped with pianos and dance floors. One house after another was raided by the cops, and the Dusters would simply pack up and move on.

One of their few acts of violence was apparently so exceptional that it became a major event in Duster lore. A cop named Dennis Sullivan, of the Charles Street station, had long had it in for the Dusters. When he finally attempted an arrest, the gang beat him up severely, stripped him of his weapons, and for good measure stomped on his face. The Gopher One Lung Curran, who was then hospitalized, heard of the beating and immortalized it in verse, which the Dusters had printed up and distributed in barbershops and saloons, while Ding Dong's youthful accomplices sang it in the streets:

> *Says Dinny, "Here's me only chance*
> *To gain meself a name;*
> *I'll clean up the Hudson Dusters,*
> *And reach the hall of fame."*
> *He lost his stick and cannon,*
> *And his shield they took away,*
> *It was then that he remembered*
> *Every dog has got his day.*[11]

The Dusters did have a major problem, from which they might have gotten their name: they were nearly all cocaine addicts. Ultimately, they succumbed to this weakness in one way or another, and were gone from the scene by 1916. Then the Marginals won the fight for the West Side docks, while the Pearl Buttons moved north to make a new turf for themselves in the 100-numbered streets west of Broadway.

While all these various territorial disputes and reorganizations were going on, a completely separate gang war was being fought in China-town, which lay right in the middle of Five Pointer turf but which none of the Caucasian gangs would touch. The Chinese had their own criminal government, in the form of the tongs, which first appeared in New York at an uncertain date sometime after their Californian origin circa 1860. The tongs controlled opium distribution, gambling, and political patronage, much more directly than the Caucasian gangs ran anything, since the latter were usually only enforcers for more powerful and unassailable forces. The tongs merged the functions, resources, and techniques of politicians, police, financiers, and gang-sters, and enforced their levy with no opposition. The tong gambling syndicate, the Bin Ching Union, would extort a tax of 7 percent on all winnings at fan-tan and pi-gow, the tariff increasing to 14 percent on winnings over $25; late payments were assessed an additional fee of $10. There were two tongs by the late 1890s, the On Leongs and the Hip Sings, although at first only the On Leongs mattered. They were captained by Tom Lee, Mayor of Chinatown, who personally controlled nearly all gaming houses as well as the total of six votes assigned to the Chinese community in elections of any sort, which he would vote in a bloc as often as the right party desired. He was made a deputy sheriff of New York County by his political patrons, and thereafter took to wearing a silver star on his chain-mail shirt and walking at all times with either hand resting on the shoulder of a bodyguard. His only opposition came from a man named Wong Get, who failed to earn respect from the population possibly because he wore a Western haircut and suit of clothes.

Around 1900 a man named Mock Duck appeared on the scene (the transliterations of these Chinese names sound like wild guesses). Mock Duck was a lone wolf, a character straight out of *Yojimbo* or *A Fistful of Dollars*. He wore chain mail, habitually carried two .45 revolvers and a hatchet, and was very soon known and feared for his favored fighting technique, which consisted of squatting in the middle of the street, shutting his eyes, and firing both guns in a full circle around him. Quickly he formed an alliance with Wong Get and with the Hip Sings, led by Lem Tong Sing, or Charley Tong, alias Scar Face Charley. Mock Duck festooned his joss, or private altar, with the words "In God We Trust," and eventually, although he was himself a compulsive gambler, overlaid the central icon of the joss with the image of Frank Moss, the attorney for the reform crusader Reverend Charles Parkhurst; indeed, one of Mock Duck's earliest gambits in the war was to give Moss the addresses of the On Leong gambling joints. With the Hip Sings, he burned down an On Leong boardinghouse on Pell Street, and then took over Pell. Doyers Street became the no-man's-land of the war, the turn in its middle earning the designation of the "bloody angle." Mock Duck's emergence seems to have woken up the Hip Sings.

A Western writer chronicling Chinatown in 1901 calls them "high-binders," estimates their number at 450 (probably an overestimate), and says of the typical member: "He is a far worse character than our 'plug-ugly,' 'brigand,' or other lawless villain." Like their opponents, the Hip Sings usually wore chain-mail shirts, carried hatchets and "fighting bars," and kept a .44 or .45 revolver concealed in their sleeves.

The general ignorance of the Chinese language and customs that colors Caucasian journalists' and historians' accounts of Chinatown affairs makes it very difficult to interpret the war, its causes (other than the obvious ones), and its nuances, and to decide how to credit some of the more sensational details reported in its course. The war seems to have lasted a very long time, interrupted by declarations of peace in 1906, 1918, 1921, 1924, 1928, and so on; a city guidebook published in 1948 still cited Pell and Doyers Streets as Hip Sing territory and Mott Street as On Leong. After the Four Brothers tong joined the alliance sometime around 1904, the war stepped up, and Tom Lee was nearly killed on more than one occasion. In 1906 Judge Warren W. Foster of the Court of General Sessions got both sides to agree to a truce, and a treaty was signed. It lasted only a week, until one *boo how doy*, or hatchetman, took a swipe at another. Six months later another treaty was signed, and this one remained in effect until 1909, which turned out to be the bloodiest year of the war, a year marked by such extraordinary incidents as the locked-room murder of the comedian Ah Hoon (although he was guarded by a small army of On Leongs, the Hip Sings managed to kill him by lowering a gunman in a bosun's chair from the roof of the building), the killing of five On Leongs in a crowded theater (five Hip Sings shot them in the Chinese Theater on Doyers Street under cover of firecrackers at a New Year's celebration), and even a war within a war (the abduction and murder of a "slave girl," Bow Kum, or "Sweet Little Flower," allegedly owned by Low Hee Tong of the Hip Sings, was avenged in a spectacular pageant of bloodshed that saw much use of bombs and left fifty dead). It was estimated that 350 Chinatown residents died in the war in that year.

Throughout all this, Mock Duck appeared invulnerable. Although Tom Lee had put a $1,000 bounty on his head, he was shot only once, in 1904, and not very seriously at that. Lee imported two hatchetmen from San Francisco, Sing Dock and Yee Toy, known as "Girl Face," to put him away, but Yee Toy wound up killing Sing Dock in a private quarrel. Mock Duck was arrested various times, with little consequence. At one of his trials, for the murder of an On Leong member, it was reported that someone convinced the presiding judge that the Chinese were required by their culture to take an oath in chicken blood, which oath was duly administered in the boiler room of the Criminal Courts Building. Thereafter, it was reported, all the prosecution witnesses changed their stories and Mock Duck was found not guilty. He was finally convicted of running a policy game in 1912, and was remanded to Sing Sing. Upon his release, he moved to Brooklyn, from whence he was observed to return on state visits, riding in a chauffeured limousine, coincident with times of peace.[12]

In the city outside, things were clearly changing around the end of the first decade of the twentieth century. Monk Eastman got out of jail in 1909 to find all his old cronies and enemies dead or in jail. His activities were desultory thereafter, although he did organize the ragpickers at the East River dumps on 108th Street into a union and led them in a bloody strike. The cops clearly had Eastman marked, however, and in 1912 a party of them broke into his room and found him smoking opium, for which infraction he did eight months. Almost immediately after his next release he was arrested on robbery charges and sent to Dannemora, where he served nearly three years. In 1917 he joined the National Guard, went to France, and so distinguished himself on the battlefield that Al Smith restored his citizenship in 1919 in compensation. A year later he was found dead, with five bullets in his body, in front of the Blue Bird Café on East Fourteenth Street. His killer was a Prohibition agent, who turned out to have been Eastman's partner in a small-time bootlegging and dope-dealing operation.

His old gang, meanwhile, was undergoing yet another crisis of leadership. In May 1908 Kid Twist was killed in Coney Island by Louie

the Lump Pioggi, who used his Tammany connections to pay with a
mere eleven months in Elmira.[13] After the death of Kid Twist, the
Eastmans were inherited by a consortium consisting of the gambler
Big Jack Zelig (William Alberts), who had come up under Crazy Butch,
the saloonkeepers Jack Sirocco and Chick Tricker, and eventually
Pioggi, but they all soon fell to fighting among themselves. Zelig's chief
lieutenants were Gyp the Blood (Harry Horowitz), who commanded
his own gang on Lenox Avenue, was skilled as sheriff, gorilla, and lush-
roller, and had a parlor trick of breaking men's backs over his knee
(he did this at least once on a $2 bet); Lefty Louis (Louis Rosenberg),
a pickpocket; Dago Frank (Frank Cirofici), a gunman for hire; and
Whitey Lewis (Jacob Siedenshner), a blackjack artist. Zelig and his
men divided their time between contract operations and skirmishes
with the Gophers. Zelig's rates, as quoted by an informant, show his
outfit to have been a relatively cut-rate operation:

Slash on cheek	*$1 to $10*
Shot in leg	*$1 to $25*
Shot in arm	*$5 to $25*
Bomb	*$5 to $20*
Murder	*$10 to $100*

Zelig's aides got theirs as a result of the Lieutenant Charles Becker
case, as detailed above, but not before Zelig himself had been fatally
shot in 1911 by an associate of Tricker's, in what was passed off at the
time as fallout from a territorial dispute but more probably resulted
from his own suspicious role in that case. Tricker, meanwhile, was
compiling quite a record as a magnate of low dives. After his Park Row
joint was shuttered in 1910 by the reformist Committee of Fourteen,
he took over Dan the Dude's old Stag Café in the Tenderloin and
renamed it the Café Maryland, at the same time keeping his hand in
the East Side scene by opening his infamous Fleabag on the Bowery.
The Café Maryland was the scene, soon after its opening, of the climax
in a miniature Trojan epic called the Ida the Goose War. The beautiful

Ida, who kept company with a Gopher, was abducted to the Maryland by Tricker's associate Irish Tom Reilly. The ensuing fracas between the Gophers and the Tricker faction of the Eastmans culminated in a shoot-out at the café in which five Trickers fell to four Gophers. Reilly, who had taken refuge behind Ida's voluminous skirts, was rousted forth by the object of his affections, to meet a Gopher slug of his own.

By the teens the gang situation downtown had entered its decadent phase. Gangs were splintering into tiny groups, while bands of juveniles and amateurs were coming up everywhere. On the Lower West Side were gangs which worked the chicken markets, acted as guards for the scabs in labor disputes, and poisoned horses on contract. A rate sheet from one of these, dating from circa 1914, cites what was said to be the upper limit for such jobs:

> *Stealing horse and rig* *$25*
> *Poisoning one horse* *$35*
> *Poisoning team* *$50*
> *Non fatal shooting* *$100*
> *Fatal shooting* *$500*

Uptown, the Bridge Twisters controlled the approaches to the Fifty-ninth Street Bridge, while the slums by the East River around Fortieth Street were the site of endless battles among the Tunnel Gang, the Teddy Reillys, and Corcoran's Roosters. In the Car Barn area (Nine-tieth to 100th Streets, east of Third Avenue) there arose the Car Barn Gang, who specialized in raiding saloons and did so in an increasingly wide span that finally ranged from Fourteenth Street to the Bronx. They were held to be unbeatable and were heavily promoted by the yellow journalists of their day, but their murder of a Bronx bartender led to the executions of several of them, and they had dissolved by World War I.

The last major downtown gang fight occurred in January 1914 at a ball of the Lenny and Dyke Association (Tommy Dyke was a Tricker underling) held at Arlington Hall on St. Mark's Place. The allied gangs of Dopey Benny and Joe the Greaser, who were feuding with a coalition of smaller gangs led by a man named Jewbach, happened to meet some of the latter in front of the hall, and the two sides began a gun battle that raged for some time between the building's steps and the doorways across the street, with no casualties until a passerby named Frederick Strauss was hit and killed by a stray bullet. This Strauss turned out to have been a court clerk with numerous connections in city government, and the event was extremely useful to reform elements. Mayor John Purroy Mitchell suspended the Chief of Police and inaugurated a campaign to sweep up the gangs, which led to the demise of many of them. Tammany, weakened by losses in the past election, was powerless. Several quiet years ensued.

In 1917 Kid Dropper and Johnny Spanish, who had been arrested in a 1910 sweep that also collared Gallagher and Brennan of the Gophers, Willie Jones of the Gas House Gang, Al Rooney of the Fourteenth Street Gang, and Itsky Joe Hickman of the Five Pointers, were released from jail and returned to the Lower East Side, their feud having faded away. Spanish did not fare well, eventually falling in a hail of bullets on Second Avenue in 1919. Dropper, on the other hand, came into an inheritance (or at least what he described as an inheritance), became a dandy (sporting "a belted check suit of extreme cut," according to Asbury, as well as pointy shoes and extravagantly colored and patterned shirts and ties) and renamed himself Jack the Dropper, forming a gang he called the Rough Riders of Jack the Dropper. For some years his outfit operated in the area around Madison, Monroe, and Rutgers Streets, brushing up against such relative newcomers to the profession as Little Augie (Jacob Orgen), Louis Lepke (Lepke Buchalter), and Gurrah (Jacob) Shapiro. Prohibition and the changes and increased competition that went along with it proved too much for an elder such as the Dropper. In 1923 he was shot through the window of a taxi in which cops were taking him away to be booked. Little Augie got himself iced by Lepke and Shapiro, who by then were mainstays of Murder Incorporated, in 1927.

Back around the turn of the century, Italian Harlem, noted for its

Murder Stable on East 125th Street, was overrun by gangs. Ignacio Lupo, redundantly known as Lupo the Wolf, was one of the earliest prominent New York representatives of what later came to be known as La Cosa Nostra, or the Mafia. He was credited with personally having carried out more than sixty murders (an undetermined number of bodies were found with tongues slit, shipped in trunks or stuffed in barrels and baskets) and was a principal force in the extortion racket known as the Black Hand. This scam, which was for years the subject of lively debate as to the actual numbers of people behind it, involved well-to-do persons, usually of Italian extraction, receiving letters from what purported to be a secret society, demanding a payoff, or else. Perhaps the most famous incident occurred when the opera singer Enrico Caruso, who had paid a note in demand of $2,000, soon after received another demanding $15,000, and went to the police; two Italian businessmen were arrested. Lupo's most notorious deed was the long-distance contract he put out on Police Detective Lieutenant Joseph Petrosino, who was killed in 1909 in Palermo, Sicily, where he had gone to collect evidence against the mob. Lupo was finally arrested by the Secret Service in 1920, on charges of importing counterfeit currency from Sicily. He got thirty years, and served a bit over fifteen. He died in 1944, aged almost seventy-five.

The Mafia in its American version is believed to have originated in New Orleans in the 1880s, establishing a New York branch about a decade later. Its early history is obscure, since its criminal range was intra-ethnic and thus was mostly ignored by the police and the press. The Black Hand swindle made noise because of its focus on celebrities and the bourgeoisie, and because its name provided headline writers with an eye-catchingly lurid tag; for years the Black Hand were the alleged perpetrators of choice for any unsolved crime in any wayside around the country. New Yorkers were made aware of the existence of a criminal body called the Mafia by the three-year war that raged, beginning in 1916, between a Manhattan Italian gang, known as the Mafia, and its Brooklyn counterpart, the Camorra. After much bloodshed and many arrests, the two factions consolidated in the early 1920s, just in time for their principals to be forcibly retired by the bootlegging younger bloods, who derisively dubbed them "Mustache Petes."

In the late teens the Gophers had split into three factions, those led by Buck O'Brien and a certain Sullivan fading away shortly thereafter, leaving only the outfit headed by an implacable character named Owney Madden. Madden wasted little time in taking over the rest of the West Side, swallowing the Village and points south after the demise of the Hudson Dusters, and absorbing the Marginals after the death of their leader, Tanner Smith, in 1919. He went on to become one of the foremost bootleggers of the 1920s (he died of natural causes in Hot Springs, Arkansas, in 1964). On the East Side, he was challenged in reputation by the most promising alumni of the Five Pointers. These included Terrible Johnny Torrio, who had come up under Kelly and led his own James Street Gang before moving to Chicago in 1916 to join the newly forming mob structure there (he died of a heart attack in 1957), to be followed by the then obscure Five Pointer trainee Al Capone, who soon became boss of Chicago (he died a broken man in 1947), while their comrades-in-arms Frankie Yale (who was hit on Capone's orders in 1927) and Charles "Lucky" Luciano (who died of a heart attack while in exile in Naples in 1962) remained in New York. They divided up the pie of gangland profiteering in the city in the 1920s with, among others, Madden, Lepke, Shapiro, Little Augie alumnus Jack "Legs" Diamond, and such men of no background as Waxey Gordon and Dutch Schultz.

Thus there appears a genealogy to New York crime, a more or less distinct line of succession that leads from the corner groceries of the 1820s to the present day. The Five Points coughed forth the Chichesters, for example, who begat the Whyos, whose tendrils reached into the incipient Five Pointers, whose line of succession leads to the Gambino family, which is still active. No doubt, other such family trees could be constructed, with suggestive links appearing between generations even when the details are lost to time, hazy memory, and conflicting legends.

Several aspects of the progress of crime through New York's history

are striking: how increasing violence and increasingly businesslike organization seem inexorably linked; how gangsters whose activities and
names are recorded tended to be Irish, and later Jewish and Italian,
with virtually no Germans involved and an odd silence on the activities
of blacks;[14] how much playacting was present in the self-presentation
and whimsical ventures of gangsters whose every day was crowded by
death; how the stories concerning gangs move, over the decades, from
featuring an undifferentiated crowd of faceless thugs to concentrating
on the legends of individuals; how menial and proletarian the early
gangsters were, not profiting by their activities to the extent of even
appearing middle-class until Prohibition brought them the opportunity
of large-scale management; how the gangs seemed to limit their activities to their own sphere, failing, for example, to invade the cotillions
of the Four Hundred, and never behaving on Fifth Avenue as they
would on Third. One conclusion that might be drawn is that the gangs
were permitted to thrive, to kill each other and drink themselves to
death, by authorities who were mostly concerned with containing their
activities and would gladly allow the gangs to act as the agents of
natural selection in the slums. The gangs repaid this courtesy by
demonstrating their mingled respect and derision for the world outside
their turf through parody: parody of order, parody of law, parody of
commerce, parody of progress.

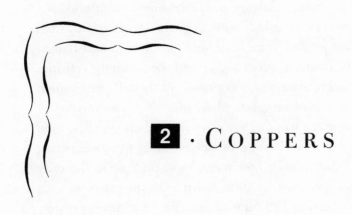

2 · COPPERS

THE HISTORY OF THE NEW YORK
POLICE IS NOT A PARTICULARLY IL-
LUSTRIOUS ONE, AT LEAST IN THE
NINETEENTH AND EARLY TWEN-
tieth centuries, as throughout the period the
law-enforcement agents of the city continually and recurrently demonstrated corruption, complacency, confusion, sloth, and
brutality. Conventionally defined, the police
existed to keep the peace, to protect the population, to enforce the laws that had been
passed for the common good of all. In truth,
however, the police were squeezed by the
city's power structure into a position where
peace was a relative term, where protection
of one part of the population was carried out
at the expense of another, and where the
meaning of laws shifted according to whoever
was in a position to interpret them. Thus,
the police became a repressive and profit-

gathering force halfway between gangsters and politicians, having to serve as interpreters between the two. They were expected to be stern and benevolent at once, or perhaps stern with the poor and benevolent to what was held as the respectable part of society, and this contradiction led to the extremes of viciousness and indolence. They were intended to be the pure element in a system that was corrupt from top to bottom, while simultaneously being underpaid, expected to render financial homage to those who did them favors and to enforce the terms of the graft passed between other levels of society. At times they seemed like gangsters in uniform, and at times, particularly in the slums, like a capricious local government in which they combined the legislative, executive, and judicial branches. Cops felt that they had the choice of inspiring jokes or inspiring fear, of starvation or extortion, of being treated as servants by the rich or as the enemy by the poor, of upholding moral standards or of upholding the standards temporarily raised at the whim of power and fashion. It is not terribly surprising that, in each case, most cops chose the latter option.

For the first two centuries or so of the city's existence the police were managed under the lines of the old Dutch constabulary. There was no outward means of distinguishing them, but in the small city of the time they were known to one and all. Jacob Hays, who served as High Constable in the early nineteenth century, was the first to devise a method of identification for the police, assigning them five-pointed stars—brass ones for patrolmen, silver stars for lieutenants and captains, and a gold star for the office of Commissioner. Sergeants were given a copper star, hence the ancient refrain "Tell it to the copper."[1] Mayor James Harper (1844–45) introduced uniforms to the force, featuring long coats distinguished by brass buttons. These outfits got their premiere at the Bowery Theater fire of 1845, but the b'hoys laughed at them, saying the cops were trying to imitate London bobbies, and the uniforms faded away for another decade, although some compromise was reached by putting leather badges on the cops' hats. Cops were then called "leatherheads," immediately resulting in the phrase "as lazy as a leatherhead." In those days, the police had little effect on the gangs and little impact on the slums. Their major function was to enforce laws of nicety for the benefit of the upper classes. Hence, they spent their time arresting drunks, "lewd women," beggars unless they were disabled, persons sleeping outdoors or in public places, persons driving in the streets in excess of five miles an hour. They also forced street peddlers to obtain licenses. For all this, cops were paid $500 a year.

Policemen were appointed by aldermen and assistant aldermen until 1853, when the legislature formed the Board of Police Commissions, made up of the mayor, the city recorder, and the city judge. The only major difference this made was to determine who would get the graft. The average patrolman paid a $40 bribe to the captain of the precinct he desired to work in, and another $150 to $200 to the politician of his choice. Captains, who were paid up to $1,000 a year, were expected to pay out a minimum of $200 for their appointment. Although it would be decades before reform sweeps and boards of inquiry began to look into the complex economics of the city's system of graft, it should be clear that an investment on such a scale would necessarily require that the profit potential of the job should offset its expense. In addition, cops were expected to serve as bagmen and go-betweens, handling payoffs from businessmen to their superiors, and from their superiors, in turn, to politicians. Joke laws ostensibly governing the duties of the police were passed at various times. In 1846 the first rules of departmental conduct were established, embodied in a ninety-page document that few read and no one, apparently, followed; in 1853 an attempt was made to prohibit cops from taking part in partisan political activities, but nothing came of it.

In the same year the state legislature, alarmed by the degree to which the city had become an independent, semi-feudal regime under Mayor Fernando Wood, passed an act forming a Metropolitan Police Force, which would have jurisdiction over Manhattan, Brooklyn, the Bronx, Staten Island, and Westchester County. Governor Horatio Seymour established a new Police Board, and Frederick Talmage, a former City Recorder, was named Superintendent of the force. Wood was ordered to disband his Municipal Police Force, but he refused. Matters were deadlocked in practice and in the courts until 1857, when the Supreme Court ruled the act forming the new force to be constitutional. Wood continued to stand firm, backed by Municipal Superintendent G. W. Matsell. The powerful Captain George W. Walling, who had formed the Strong Arm Squad and begun the practice of using plain-clothesmen, went over to the Metropolitan camp and began organizing a force. In June, a month after the Supreme Court's decision, both Daniel D. Conover, who had been appointed by Governor John A. King, and Charles Devlin, who had been appointed by Wood for a rumored fee of $50,000, simultaneously attempted to assume the office of State Commissioner. Wood had his cops eject Conover, who in turn obtained a warrant for Wood's arrest. Walling went to serve it, and physically seized Wood and began dragging him out of City Hall, but was intercepted at the door by a party of Municipal cops, who pried him loose from Wood and threw him out. Then a detachment of fifty Metropolitans, in frock coats and plug hats, came marching down Chambers Street from their White Street headquarters, intent on cap-turing Wood. They were met by the Municipals on the front steps of City Hall and a half-hour riot ensued. Before the Metropolitans were turned away, fifty-two cops had been hurt, one of them permanently invalided. Finally, some Metropolitans spotted the Seventh Regiment of the National Guard boarding a boat for Boston and persuaded them to delay their departure. As the troops surrounded City Hall, their commander, Major General Charles Sandford, marched into Wood's office. When Wood looked out the window and saw the military presence, he backed down and let himself be arrested. This did not end the turmoil, however; for the rest of that summer the city was in a state of chaos. Whenever a cop of one force made an arrest, a cop of the other would set the culprit free, and the competing forces routinely raided each other's station houses and freed en masse the prisoners in each other's jails. In the fall the Court of Appeals affirmed the Supreme Court's decision, and Wood was finally compelled to disband his Mu-nicipal force. Around the same time the cops who had been injured in the City Hall riot sued Wood personally for damages, and they were awarded $850 apiece by the court, but Wood never paid, and the city finally had to settle the matter with funds from its treasury. Ultimately, control of the police force was restored to the city by the 1870 charter finagled by the Tweed Ring.

The police force, as it was established in the Tweed years, covered Manhattan and the Bronx, the forces of the other boroughs being amalgamated after those boroughs were annexed in 1898. In the 1870s the force had four commissioners, who included the evergreen Matsell along with three professional politicians. The Superintendent was John Kelso, who, predictably enough, was the brother-in-law of a prominent person, while below him served four inspectors, thirty-two captains, sixty-four roundsmen (a designation more or less interchangeable with lieutenant), 128 sergeants, and 2,085 miscellaneous patrolmen, detectives, doorkeepers, and the like. Each of the thirty-two precincts was headed by a captain; each had two platoons headed by roundsmen, and each platoon was divided into two sections headed by sergeants.

The duties of patrolmen were principally to keep a mental file of the population on their beat; to watch all visitors and intruders; to examine all doors, windows, and gates for proper locks and signs of tampering; and to be aware of all whorehouses and gambling houses and report the identities of parties frequenting them. They were apparently most assiduous at noticing the condition of locks, having in one decade spotted 40,000 houses left open at night. The principal crimes they were assigned to watch out for were public intoxication, maltreatment of animals, interference with telegraph wires, the conducting of dogfights, cockfights, and prizefights, as well as of theatrical entertainments on Sundays, and potential and actual riots. They were not permitted to engage in casual conversation, even with each other. In the winter they were clothed in navy-blue frock coats and trousers, and in summer in sack coats and pants of navy flannel; on their heads they wore glazed caps (later in the decade these were experimentally replaced by high-crowned derbies in winter and Panama straws in summer, these in turn giving way to the high helmets that lasted until caps were restored in the teens). They were armed with revolvers and with billyclubs, which took the form of "day sticks" and the longer "night sticks." These were used not only to threaten potential derelicts and work over suspected malefactors but to summon their colleagues by means of sharp raps on the pavement. They were assigned complex schedules of duty and reserve that frequently kept them on their feet for thirty-six hours at a stretch, never fell the same way two days in succession, and gave them one day and one night off in every eight-day rotation. They went on foot except in the shantytown and semi-rural uptown precincts, where they rode horses. Their pay was meager; from the $500 annual salary of the 1840s, the starting wage had only gotten up to $800 by 1901, and out of this amount cops had to disburse for their own uniforms and equipment and they were additionally expected to contribute to police associations and to politically favored charities.

The motto banner of the 1870s was boldly emblazoned "Faithful Unto Death," and featured vignettes of cops at their various duties: chasing runaway carriage horses, being assaulted by thugs on the street, quelling a riot, arresting a footpad at night, guiding lost children, saving an old woman from a fire, saving a drowning man from a boat, standing up in court, and, rather mysteriously, laying hands on a man sitting peacefully in front of a stove. They did, apparently, restore 7,300 lost children in a nine-year period. This nevertheless failed to endear them to their charges in the poorer areas. A writer of the 1880s observed a representative scene:

> One Fourth of July morning, a few years ago, the writer of these pages was coming up Third avenue on a street car. Looking down East 35th street a singular sight presented itself. A platoon of police formed across the street was slowly retreating backward, with revolvers drawn and pointed, while two of their number held on to a rough looking prisoner, whom they carried along with them. Following them was a mob of several hundred ruffians, yelling, cursing, and occasionally throwing stones. Wishing to see the result, I

sprang from the car and hurried to a livery stable just oppo-
site the Police station in 35th street, and about a hundred
yards from Third avenue, from which I could see the whole
affair. The police retreated slowly across Third avenue, and to
the station house, into which they quickly disappeared with
their prisoner. A cheer went up from the mob, and the ruffians
thronged about the station as if intending to attack it. Im-
mediately the doors were thrown open and the entire force on
duty at the station dashed into the street, armed with their
long night clubs and headed by their Captain. "Give them
the locusts, men," came in sharp, ringing tones from the
Captain, and without a word the force dashed at the mob,
striking heads, arms, and shoulders, and in less time than
it takes me to relate it, the ruffians were fleeing down the
street and dispersing in all directions. Not all escaped, how-
ever, for each officer returned to the station with an ugly look-
ing prisoner in his grasp.[2]

Indiscriminate use of the nightstick remained a police hallmark. Cornelius Willemse, who became a cop at the turn of the century after
having worked as a bouncer and lunch man in Bowery saloons (he
was originally refused entry to the force by then Commissioner Theodore Roosevelt on the grounds that "No one connected in the faintest
way with the liquor traffic will ever be a policeman"), relates in his
memoirs that he and his fellow recruits were lectured by a police
instructor, Michael Smith:

"Men, when you get your nightsticks, they're intended to
be used on thieves and crooks, but don't use them on inoffen-
sive citizens. By no means strike a man on the head. The
insane asylums are filled with men whose condition has been
caused by a skull injury. Strike them over the arms and legs,
unless you're dealing with real bad crooks. Then it doesn't

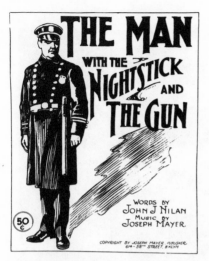

A song from the teens,
its popularity at the
time unknown

Studio portrait circa
1919

An inner courtyard of the Tombs, showing the Female
Department

Convicts breaking rocks on Blackwells Island.
Photograph by Jacob Riis

Loading coffins into the common trench, Potter's Field,
Randalls Island. Photograph by Jacob Riis

make any difference whether they go to the insane asylum or to
jail. They're enemies of society and our common foe.

"Protect the good people and treat the crooks rough.
Thereby you'll have the respect of your superiors and the citi-
zens of New York. If there's danger, take a chance. The po-
lice of New York have a reputation you've got to uphold.
Policemen make mistakes. They're human beings like every-
body else, but we have no use for a coward. When you're in
battle, and you'll be in plenty, go to work with your night-
stick, but be sure to keep your back against a wall so they
can't jump you from behind.

"You'll meet a lot of drunks who are poor, hard-working
men. Don't lock them up. If they show fight, there are cer-
tain parts of the body where you won't break any bones.
Don't lose your head when one of these fellows calls you
names and you can make a great many friends on your post
by giving them a square deal. Make a good friend of every
business man and a bitter enemy of every crook, and you'll
be a success on your post. If every policeman would do that,
there'd be very little crime."[3]

These pious sentiments were immediately contradicted by a desk sergeant, who reprimanded Willemse for bringing in suspects without
working them over with his stick, but gave him a chance to square
things by taking the culprits down to the station-house cellar. "There's
more religion in the end of a nightstick," the sergeant told him, "than
in any sermon preached to the likes of them." The victims of these
tactics retaliated in various ways. Youth gangs in San Juan Hill at the
turn of the century had a trick of extinguishing the gas lamps on a
block, opening the coal chutes and sewer covers, and then yelling for
the police, who would rush in and fall into the traps, resulting in
injuries that were sometimes quite serious. The same stunt might be
tried with a rope or wire stretched across the dark street, and there

was the ever-popular option of pelting the cops with bottles and bricks from the rooftops.

The brutally long stretches of duty and reserve continued. Until 1902, when a three-platoon roster was inaugurated in the precincts, cops on reserve were confined to the station houses, where they could rest on cots in a dormitory. A typical such room held forty beds, placed eighteen inches apart, with scant ventilation and no shower facilities. The major perquisite was beer, sent up in cans from a saloon below by means of a clothesline. The station force was a social unit having much in common with a gang or a fraternity. Rookies, called "Goo Goos," were mercilessly hazed. The cops in the latter half of the nineteenth and for much of the early twentieth century were almost exclusively Irish. Germans, who were called "Dutch," and Anglo-Saxons, called "Narrow-backs," had a very hard time breaking into the ranks, and it was virtually impossible for members of other ethnic groups.

When cops made an arrest, the persons they had booked would be taken into holding pens in the station houses, these cells generally being adjacent to the homeless shelters (until Roosevelt eliminated the latter) in basements or annexes. The city's major prison, to which they would be removed in a closed wagon called a Black Maria, was the Tombs, situated on the block bounded by Centre and Elm (later Lafayette), Franklin and Leonard Streets, on the site of the island within the Collect Pond which had been used to stage whippings and hangings. The prison's official name was the Halls of Justice, but it had been modeled after an Egyptian mausoleum illustrated in the book of *Travels* published by John L. Stevens of Hoboken. It was built between 1835 and 1838, with subsequent additions over the years, and the whole thing was eventually condemned in 1938, though its last vestiges were not torn down until 1974. It was designed to hold some 350 prisoners, but the number constantly increased, until it held several thousands toward the end. It had an inner building and an outer building, separated by a yard in which executions were held and linked by a Bridge of Sighs, so called because it constituted the last walk for condemned prisoners. The executioner was always masked and anonymous; the longest-term holder of the office in the nineteenth century was known only to have once been a butcher's apprentice, and he was called Monsieur New York, or, more simply, George. Only officials and political patrons were invited to witness the hangings, but the public crowded onto the top floor of a neighboring building and craned their necks to look over the wall. The Tombs complex also included a women's prison, a boys' prison, a police court (one of several in the city), and a court of special sessions. There were minimum-security cells and infirmary cells, and a capacious vagrant and drunk tank on the Franklin Street side, known as Bummers' Hall. Prisoners were allowed to bring in their own furniture and carpets, presuming, of course, that they could afford to do so; in the front of the building were six cells reserved for the very rich. The main part of the Tombs was reserved for serious criminals (persons convicted of murder, armed robbery, felonious assault, and the like). It was the site of many successful escapes over the years, via windows, delivery wagons, forged passes, and disguises.

The city's federal prison was the Ludlow Street Jail, in which parties bound on federal charges were held in transit, including soldiers and National Guardsmen accused of crimes, but the place was most commonly used by creditors, who would have debtors locked up there on the pretext that they appeared ready to skip town. By the 1920s it was familiarly referred to as Alimony Jail. Petty criminals of all other sorts— petty thieves, drug addicts, morals offenders—were sent to Blackwell's Island. This long, narrow, 120-acre strip of land in the East River was bought by the city from the Blackwell family in 1829. A complex of social-welfare institutions was built there in addition to the prison, including an almshouse, a workhouse, pavilions for the insane, and a set of hospitals. It was renamed Welfare Island in 1929, and more recently Roosevelt Island when it was turned over to private developers, a transaction which left only two hospitals, as well as the ruins of some of the other buildings. The Blackwell's Island prison, sheltered from public view, was a grim and unsanitary place, always overcrowded, and noted for its various tortures, prominent among which were the "cooler" cells, the dousings by means of 120-pound-pressure fire hoses, and the "water drop cure." It was frequently the site of riots. Among famous prisoners incarcerated there at various times were Boss Tweed, Mme Restell, Emma Goldman, the birth-control advocate Ethel Byrne, and Mae West, jailed for staging her play *Sex* in 1929.

Corruption was always a fact of police life, and it rose to extraordinary heights in the last three decades of the nineteenth century. Under the Tweed Ring, the police force was an amalgam of fiefdoms, each precinct at the mercy of its captain, who, more often than not, ran it as an extortion ring for his personal benefit. Individual policemen were cut off from profits and ceased to care. The *Evening Telegram* assessed the situation in 1875:

> *The rank and file of President [Commissioner] Matsell's
> "best police in the world" are rapidly drifting into a state of
> utter demoralization, if we are to judge by the alarming in-
> crease in the number of burglaries, highway robberies, and
> petty thefts, as well as the reports of outrages perpetrated by
> these model guardians of the public peace in various pre-
> cincts of the city . . . Burglars now roam the city at will,
> enter residences, stores and offices and pillage them under the
> very eye of the police; river thieves boldly board vessels at the
> piers within sight of a uniformed officer's post, commit pira-
> cies and when resistance is offered use the knife and slung
> shot upon their victims and escape; highwaymen's friends
> will inveigle an officer into a corner grocery and while he is
> there canvassing with his boon companions the respective
> merits of Morrissey and Fox, Disbecker and Smith [John
> Morrissey and the other three Police Commissioners], the
> partner of his entertainers is at his post committing highway
> robbery or picking pockets . . .*[4]

Despite the hysterical language and rather antiquated imagery, the picture presented in this account is not far from the truth. According to another account, the year 1868 saw 5,423 criminal cases, booked at station houses, vanish before reaching court. The breakup of the Tweed Ring and the resulting investigation of 1875 instilled a temporary fever of rectitude. Inspector Thomas Byrnes, who became chief of the Detective Bureau in 1880, was a genuinely tough cop, who did not appear corrupt, although, on the other hand, he had little respect for the constitutional rights of suspects and was more than inclined toward dividing the human race into "criminal" and "respectable" classes. His achievements include the establishment of the Rogues' Gallery and the broadcast of photographs and information on criminals nationwide, as well as the establishment of the Dead Line, an invisible barrier that bounded the area between Fulton and Greenwich Streets, the Battery, and the East River. Any known crook found within this zone, which included the financial district, was subject to immediate arrest.

The same period saw the rise of Patrolman Alexander S. Williams, who was seemingly of the same mold as Byrnes. Assigned to clean up the gangs in the vicinity of Broadway and Houston Street in the late 1860s, he began his offensive by hunting down the two toughest specimens and hurling them through the window of the Florence Saloon. In 1871 he was made captain of the 21st Precinct, which oversaw the Gas House District, and there he broke up the first incarnation of the Gas House Gang. He also first gave shape to the motto rephrased by Patrolman Willemse's mentor: "There is more law in the end of a policeman's nightstick than in a decision of the Supreme Court." After this, he acquired the sobriquet "Clubber," was named Inspector, and was presented with the Tenderloin on a plate. There he prospered, and the extent of his success was only suggested by the investigations of the 1894 Lexow Committee and the 1897 Mazet Committee. Captain Max Schmittberger, who later became a Chief Inspector, testified that he had collected tribute from gamblers and pimps and paid it personally to Williams. One madame, who owned a chain of brothels, testified that she paid Williams $30,000 annually for protection, while other madames with smaller operations said that they had paid initial fees of $500 apiece when they opened their houses and a retainer varying between $25 and $50 per house thereafter. Streetwalkers came forward and told how they paid for permission to practice their trade, while thieves submitted that they had paid him a percentage of their takings. More than six hundred policy shops paid Williams $15 a month each, while pool rooms contributed as much as $300, and the higher-class gambling joints even more. Williams also had an interest in a brand of whiskey, which he forced saloonkeepers to sell. It was revealed that Williams owned an estate in Cos Cob, Connecticut, whose dock alone was valued at $39,000, as well as a town house in the city and a yacht. His explanation to the investigators was that he had made his fortune through speculating on real estate in Japan. Lexow and Mazet ultimately took no action against him. He resigned, however, and went into the insurance business, dying a multimillionaire in 1910. During the investigation he coined his second most famous line. When asked why he had made no effort to close down the whorehouses in his district, he replied, "Because they were kind of fashionable at the time."

The Lexow investigation also proved the end of Byrnes, a man who, it was noted, did not bother to investigate robberies if the victims failed to offer a substantial reward. Although he had never earned a salary greater than $5,000 a year, he somehow had amassed $350,000 in real estate and a fortune, held in his wife's name, of $292,000. When asked about this, he said that they were the result of "gratuities" paid him by Wall Street businessmen.

William S. "Big Bill" Devery was a more straightforward case. Known for his personal motto, "Hear, see, and say nothin', eat, drink, and pay nothin'," and for beginning many of his sentences with the phrase "Touchin' on and appertainin' to," Devery was a classic East Side clubhouse man, with connections that reached deep into the Democratic Party. It was well known that he was corrupt; he in fact admitted as much quite readily. In common with some reformers of his day, he believed in the establishment of vice districts, where fees could be regulated by the police; he blamed widespread corruption on the dispersal of the old East Side brothel concentration. His payoff routine was ingenious: his bagman was a tailor, and anyone who owed Devery or wished for a favor from him would go to the tailor and order a suit, leaving a deposit of, say, $1,000. He was also intimately involved in police hiring and promotion. In 1892 the *Mail and Express* reported that it cost $300 to become a patrolman, $1,400 to advance to sergeant, and $14,000 to be made captain, although a certain Captain Creedon testified before Lexow that his rank had in fact cost him $15,000, while Captain Schmittberger complained that the prices were inflated, since at the precinct level the Tenderloin was only worth $200 a month in graft. Devery was dismissed from the force in 1894 and indicted for extortion, but was acquitted two years later, and his badge was restored by the Supreme Court. The Police Commission attempted to try him again but was restrained by an order from the high court. He was appointed Inspector in 1898, and six months later was made Chief of Police, a title he tainted so thoroughly that it was abolished after his resignation in 1901.

The less exalted Lieutenant Charles H. Becker of the Gambling Squad, who was eventually executed for ordering the murder of the gambler Herman "Beansy" Rosenthal, may have been called the "crookedest cop who ever stood behind a shield," but in light of his predecessors, such a superlative must be viewed relatively. He made his mark, however, by combining corruption with unrelieved brutality, a distinction he seems to have shared only with Williams among his illustrious forerunners. No doubt, many cops on the beat level pursued this combination of activities, but for the most part, cops of the period who were not ambitious enough to hoist themselves into the upper ranks of profit were simply attempting to get by, and so sought modest graft. In the small time, graft came in two classes, clean and dirty. The "dirty" label applied to shakedowns of gamblers, pimps, and whores, and petty extortions of liquor dealers and saloonkeepers. Clean graft, which was much more common, was essentially a victimless crime and took in the general category of donations from business-men—for overlooking construction and vehicle violations, for example; for recovering lost and stolen property; and for finding open doors in lofts and stores and locking them. Clean graft also covered the moon-lighting practice of cops who spent their days off standing guard in front of the better gambling houses. Cops spent even more time cadging free meals and drinks in restaurants and saloons, engaging in what were referred to as "joke thefts" (mostly of food), and cooping, which even today is police parlance for sneaking off somewhere to take a nap. "Did you ever see policemen semaphore to each other?" asks Willemse. "Two arms extended means you did not see him, one arm pointed means you have seen him and he is going in the direction his hand points. Arms akimbo, means he's in a coop and won't be out or has sent word everything is all right."[5]

The time-honored image of the rotund Clancy picking his apple from the groceryman's crate, allowing himself to be pacified by stew and ale at the corner saloon, gently arresting prostitutes to make his quota and then letting them go out a side door on a technicality, too dreamy and dopey and benevolent to notice the crooks hauling entire sets of furniture out of the showroom, perhaps even watching their cart horse for them while they are thus occupied, is one of those clichés that have endured because they are based on fact. The ordinary foot-soldier cop of the time was very often cut from the mold of the civil-service loafer, a sinner more by omission and complacency than by active intention. Nevertheless, this same character was capable of being casually brutal to non-criminals who did not speak English—for ex-ample, to blacks, to street peddlers and hoboes—and, as has been illustrated, found it most convenient to ask questions with his stick. The overwhelming impression is that cops were simply not much good to anyone who did not have the wherewithal to hire them as private day laborers or night watchmen.

3 · *The* TIGER

IT MAY SEEM ARBITRARY TO RELE-
GATE POLITICS TO ITS OWN CHAP-
TER, SINCE POLITICS LIES BEHIND
EVERY TOPIC COVERED SO FAR IN
this text, from transportation to housing and
from faro to prostitution. The distinction that
should be observed, however, is between politics as the science of power (a category broad
enough to take in everything from the divine
right of kings to anarcho-syndicalism, with
concerns ranging from mineral rights to the
taxation of root crops) and politics as it has
classically been practiced in New York City,
which is to say a form of vice midway between
gambling and whoring, a game for the strong,
an affliction upon the weak, and a joke to those
fortunate enough to regard it from a distance.
Every locality breeds its own brand of politics, and New York is hardly the only American city to have harbored the municipal

equivalent of a floating crap game in its executive chambers (Chicago, for example, comes to mind, as does New Orleans, not to mention such lesser burgs as Atlantic City and Jersey City and Covington, Kentucky), but in New York this game is distinguished by its extraordinary longevity. For the better part of two centuries the enterprise was dominated by a single entity, Tammany Hall, and its name comes readily to the fore whenever machine politics are considered, even in the present day, when an unhappy recent history of splinterings, realignments, and sundry incarcerations has left it dormant.

Tammany Hall, officially the Society of St. Tammany, or the Columbian Order, has misty origins as an anti-British secret society during the Revolution. It derived its name from Tammany, or Tamanend, a semi-legendary chief of the Leni–Lenape tribe about whom little is known beyond the hazy fact that he gave the British particular trouble. Its emblem is that of an Indian brave, though later it came to be identified with the image of a tiger, introduced by Boss Tweed from its old function as symbol of the Americus Club. It stuck, possibly because its workings reminded people of the similarly manipulated game of faro, which was also identified with the image of a tiger. The society was revived as a politico-fraternal order in 1789 by William Mooney. In spite of this gentleman's obviously Hibernian provenance, the order was initially anti-immigrant, which at the time was virtually synonymous with anti-Irish. Its original constitution specified that none but native-born Americans could ascend to the position of sachem, or leader.[1] The order met at a tavern owned by Brom Martling at Chatham and Spruce Streets that was dilapidated enough to be called the Pig Pen by the Federalists, until $28,000 was raised and a new Wigwam (as all Tammany headquarters were called) was built in 1811 at Chatham and Frankfort, a conveniently short hop from the Five Points. Tammany was changing its tune on the Irish question, realizing that the Democratic Party, which it represented locally, needed immigrant votes, and that it held a logical advantage in attracting them by being the party of Jefferson, the champions of the poor. It solicited the allegiance of immigrants almost surreptitiously until the 1840s, by which time it controlled the vote in the slums of the Fourth and Sixth Wards, the so-called Whiskey Wards.

This period was one of major turmoil in downtown politics. The gangs were becoming major forces, and vying for their favor were a number of factions that included the Van Burenite section of Tammany, the Equal Rights Party (whose members were known as Locofocos), the radical Democrats led by Mike Walsh, and various right-wing organizations. The most prominent of the latter was the American Party, founded in 1842 by anti-Irish Democrats who had split from Tammany, along with members of secret proto-fascist societies. When asked questions by outsiders, members of the American Party professed ignorance on all topics, hence their more common appellation, the Know-Nothings. They declared they stood for "Anti-Romanism, Anti-Bedinism, Anti-Papistalism, Anti-Nunneryism, Anti-Winking Virginism, Anti-Jesuitism."[2] A spate of rival groups came up late in that decade and in the 1850s, including the Order of United Americans (of whose Charter Oak chapter on the Bowery P. T. Barnum was briefly a member), the Order of the Star-Spangled Banner, the American Protestant Association, the Order of United American Mechanics, and the Order of Free and Accepted Americans, known as the Wide Awakes (from their peculiarly shaped white felt "wide-awake" hats) and as the Order of the American Star (their badge was a star emblazoned with the number 67, which stood for George Washington's age at the time of his death). These groups were mostly noted for holding noisy parades on holidays sacred to them, principally the Fourth of July, Washington's Birthday, and the anniversary of the Battle of Bunker Hill, although the Wide Awakes would deploy themselves as an honor guard to escort anti-Catholic speakers into Catholic neighborhoods. Anti-Catholic crusaders of the solo variety were everywhere. One of them, John S. Orr, known as the Angel Gabriel, would hold forth on Sundays from the steps of City Hall, accompanied by his sidekick accordion player, Moses.

At the other end of the political spectrum was Mike Walsh, unquestionably the most radical figure to emerge from New York before the Civil War. Walsh was born in County Cork, Ireland, in 1810, and emigrated to the United States as a child. He was a Protestant, and always considered himself "a true American," although he came to champion the rights of Irish Catholic immigrants. He began as a newspaperman, writing for the New York *Aurora* (then edited by Walt Whitman), and started two papers of his own, the relatively short-lived *Knickerbocker* and then the *Subterranean*, which he proclaimed "the voice of subterranean democracy." In 1840 he began the Spartan Association, a group that, like Tammany, partook equally of the political club, the fraternal order, and the gang, although it had even more of a deliberately proletarian cast to it. He was a rabble-rouser, whose supporters were called "plug uglies" (although this could be said of nearly every other political operator in the Fourth and Sixth Wards); as a journalist he was equally provocative, and in his own journals would denounce enemies with such epithets as "rat-faced swindler," "cowardly, hang-dog, state's evidence ruffian," "sneaking, pimping, red haired little scamp," "imbecile lump of mere organized animal matter." His followers, the proverbial "soap-locks, butt-enders, and subterraneans," would mob Tammany rallies and shout "Go it, Mike!" after which he would take the stage to rail against the Democratic Party leadership. He broke with Tammany in 1841 to run for Congress (unsuccessfully) on the Carroll Hall ticket set up by Catholic Bishop John Hughes, returning to the Democrats the following year as an independent, distinct from both Tammany and the would-be radical Jacksonians. In 1842 the Spartans briefly took over the Tammany nominating process and established its own list of candidates, including Walsh; although Tammany eventually put through its own list and got them elected, Walsh managed to get 3,000 out of the 20,000 votes cast.

That same year, Walsh's political arena began to widen in scope. Assisted by twenty Spartans, he helped the Dorr Rebellion that sparked in Providence, R.I., nearly capturing the arsenal; when the rebellion's failure led to repression, he threatened to lead five hundred b'hoys in sacking Providence. Walsh was earning the respect even of his enemies

by this time, for his unassailable integrity and articulation. He began
to develop an interest in land reform, visited Brook Farm in 1844, and
got the support of various Fourierists and Owenites in New England.
He denounced the "slavery of wages," and allowed himself to be called
a leveler. Of reformers and temperance activists he said, after calling
them "a fanatical, hypocritical set of imbecile humbugs": "They regard
God as a cruel and capricious tyrant. How is it possible for such servile
slaves to be republicans at heart?" Capital he called

> *that all-grasping power which has been wrung, by fraud,*
> *avarice, and malice from the labor of this and all ages past*
> *[.]—It is the great—the icy-hearted despot of civilization,*
> *whose swords, spears, and battle-axes are shin-plasters, sil-*
> *ver dollars, and doubloons . . . Demagogues tell you that you*
> *are freemen. They lie—you are slaves, and none are better*
> *aware of this fact than the heathenish dogs who call you*
> *freemen. No man devoid of other means of support but that*
> *which his labor affords him can be a freeman, under the*
> *present state of society. He must be a humble slave of capi-*
> *tal, created by the labor of the poor men who have toiled,*
> *suffered, and died before him.*[3]

In 1846 Tammany nominated him for the State Assembly, and he won,
with 20,000 votes. In public office he cultivated an image as a raffish,
brawling, proletarian dandy who used slang "like any tramp who had
graduated from the gutter," and combined ragged clothes with diamond rings and a silver-knobbed cane. He was strong on issues of
monopolies, the allocation of building contracts, and labor questions.
It began to seem as though he could spearhead a strong, genuinely
radical movement in the city. As Walt Whitman was to write to a friend
some years later:

> *I have been at Washington and know none of the great men,*
> *but I know the people. I know well (for I am practically in*

*New York) the real heart of this mighty city—the tens of
thousands of young men, the mechanics, the writers, &c.,
&c. In all of them burns, almost with a fierceness, the divine fire which more or less, during all ages, has only
waited a chance to leap forth and confound the calculations
of tyrants, hunkers, and all their tribe. At this moment,
New York is the most radical city in America.*[4]

But Walsh was becoming too ensnared in Democratic Party machinations. Indeed, he had become a "hunker"; that is to say, one of the
pro-slavery faction (as opposed to the "barnburners"). In the North
in this period the slavery question was seen by many working-class
activists as an obfuscatory issue that made a mockery of their fight
against wage slavery. Walsh allied himself with supporters of John C.
Calhoun and, after he had been elected to Congress in 1852, began
devoting most of his energies to the Southern cause, arguing against
the Kansas–Nebraska Bill of 1854. He not only had chosen a questionable side but had been seduced away from the interests of his own
constituency. He was not reelected. He had always been a drinker, but
alcohol took him over after his defeat. In 1859 he was found after a
binge, lying dead on Eighth Avenue with his pockets emptied.

The 1840s were a period of chaos and deepening corruption in city
politics. In 1842, for example, a contract for street cleaning was sold
to a firm that quoted a rate of $64,500 per year for five years, while
competing firms had demanded only $25,000 a year. Convicts were
allowed to escape from Blackwell's Island on condition that they voted
for the right candidate, while others, up for release, were kept in stir
until election day so that their votes could be monitored. The genteel
politics of the post-Revolution period were clearly at an end, and family
connections and social origins no longer mattered. Andrew Mickle,
who was elected mayor in 1846, was born in a Sixth Ward shanty where
pigs were kept in the attic; he died a millionaire.

The first man to organize the slums into a voting bloc in any thor-
oughgoing way was Isaiah Rynders, who had been a Mississippi gam-

bler and knife fighter, and had been chased from Vicksburg in 1835 by the Vigilantes. He arrived in New York shortly thereafter and lost little time establishing himself. He soon owned six groceries on Paradise Square and set himself up at Sweeney's House of Refreshment on Ann Street, where he held court to his retinue, eventually organizing the Empire Club, headquartered in the Arena on Park Row. His supporters were a motley passel of b'hoys, boxers, saloon rats, and thugs, including such names as Yankee Sullivan, Dirty Face Jack, Country McCleester (or McCluskey), Hen Chanfrau, Dutch Charlie, and Edward "Ned Buntline" Judson. The primary function of Rynders and his cohort was to meet immigrants on the dock, put them up, find them work, and pledge them to vote for Tammany. Rynders was a fixer, and although he was named a U.S. Marshal, his political aspirations of a more conventional sort came to naught, as he was stymied in his sole attempt to stand for the State Assembly. (He did get a street named after him, however, the former Collect Street, renamed Centre Street once warm memory of him grew cold.) Rynders was a friend to the Irish, and was a light of Tammany for more than twenty-five years, but for a few years in the 1850s he allowed himself to be swayed by the Native Americans, changing the name of his club to Americus and enlisting as his helpers the prominent Nativist enforcers Tom Hyer and Bill the Butcher Poole.

Hyer was a boxer; Poole was a former Bowery Boy who now had his own gang, a semi-political alliance of forces that included the Washington Market Gang, the "Red Rover" Engine Company Number 34, the boxers Smut Ackerman and Tommy Culkin, and the future "wickedest man" The. Allen, at that time a small-time gambler and polling-place manipulator. Poole's opposite number on the Tammany side was the boxer and gambler John Morrissey, who could call on the services of such toughs as Blacksmith Dan Edgar, Lew Baker, Paudeen McLaughlin, Bill Mike Murray, and Awful (Orville) Gardner.[5] Morrissey had tried and failed to wreck the Americus Club, but Rynders had been impressed enough to offer him a job. Morrissey refused it and instead went to work for Tammany power John A.

Kennedy, his initial task being to surround the polls with Dead Rabbits and their ilk at a dollar a head, to prevent Poole's men from playing havoc, a tactic that succeeded admirably.

Before long, however, the factions were embroiled in a dispute of a more personal nature. The bad blood between them was in any case hardly a matter of ideology, being instead indefinably composed of ethnic pride, peer pressure, territorial competition, pure cussedness, and professional rankles spilling over from the boxing ring. In 1854 Tom Hyer beat Yankee Sullivan, at first off the record, in an oyster saloon on Park Place, and then officially in a pugilistic contest. The following January, Sullivan's friends Jim Turner and Lew Baker ran into Hyer at a saloon in the basement of Wallack's Theater on Broadway. Turner hooked Hyer's drinking arm and made him spill his hot rum, whereupon everybody pulled out guns. Turner fired a bullet that hit Hyer in the neck, Hyer retaliated by making Baker drop his gun, and the melee became general. A cop came in and Hyer demanded the arrest of Baker and Turner, but the flatfoot declined. The fight progressed out in the street until Turner fled. A few days later, Butcher Poole beat up Baker in a saloon on Canal Street, but the fight was broken up by cops. Thereafter, Baker went out heavily armed and accompanied by Turner and Paudeen McLaughlin (who had lost a nose some time previously in a Five Points altercation). A few weeks after that, Poole ran into Morrissey, who bet him that he could not name a place where Morrissey would refuse to meet him in a fight. Poole cited the Christopher Street pier, which happened to be the heart of his own turf, and Morrissey paid up and asked for another. When Poole named the Amos Street (now West Tenth Street) dock, Morrissey accepted, and a time was set, seven the following morning. On that occasion Morrissey arrived with a dozen men, to find Poole missing and a delegation of two hundred bruisers there in his stead who beat them until a delegation of Tammany politicians came to their rescue.

The two met again some days later in a bar on Broadway and Prince. Morrissey, who had been playing cards in the back room with Mark

Maguire, "King of the Newsboys," fired at Poole, but the gun mal-
functioned. He asked Poole, who by then had drawn his own gun,
"You wouldn't shoot an unarmed man, would you?" The chivalrous
Poole threw down his gun and offered a duel with knives. Morrissey,
knowing well that Poole was, after all, a butcher, declined, and just
then cops came in and arrested them both. Poole later returned to the
same bar and was met by another group of Tammany sluggers, including Turner, Baker, and McLaughlin. Poole put five dollars in gold
on the bar, betting on his victory in a fight. Turner pulled out a Colt
revolver and shot himself in the arm, and then hit Poole in the leg.
Baker then pulled a gun, shooting Poole in the heart and in the abdomen. The indestructible Poole yet managed to get to his feet, bran-
dishing a carving knife, and threw the knife at the fleeing Tammanyites
as he fell to the floor, the blade sticking in the doorjamb. All surren-
dered but Baker, who took off for the Canary Islands, but a rich Nativist
lent his boat to the police, who caught up with Baker's vessel two
hours off the coast of Tenerife. Baker, Turner, Morrissey, McLaughlin,
and a few minor accessories went to trial, but the case resulted in a
series of hung juries and eventually charges were dropped.

Poole lived for fourteen days after being shot, ultimately expiring
in the midst of his political allies, his last words allegedly being "Good-
bye, boys, I die a true American." He was given a funeral of major
proportions, with thousands of mourners forming a cortege that wound
down from the end of Christopher Street to the Battery, where a ferry
took the remains to Green-Wood Cemetery. The. Allen, who in the
same series of incidents had had both eyes gouged by Tammanyites
so that they hung down his cheeks (they were put back in their sockets,
but his vision was never the same), years later recalled that so many
people crowded onto the roof of the house across the street from Poole's
at the funeral that the whole house collapsed, resulting in four deaths
and numerous injuries.[6] Morrissey had, meanwhile, mustered an array
of Five Points thugs, including the "Original Hounds" Engine Number
36 and a gang called the Short Boys, and these threw rocks and bricks
at the mourners, killing at least one. The Seventh Regiment eventually

had to intervene. Later that night the Nativists destroyed the Original Hounds' engine house. The rancor from that series of events was to linger in the New York political scene for decades afterward.

Such low-level rowdyism might seem to be of only tangential political importance, but in an era when elections were decided by repeat voters and poll-box smashers, by the intimidation and beating of citizens before they could cast their votes, gangland vendettas were more integral to the electoral process than any set of laws or principles. The equation between gangsters and aldermen could not have been more open: throughout the 1850s the members of the city's Common Council were generally referred to as the Forty Thieves. Reform elements might therefore place their faith in an outsider, someone independent of the intricate system of alliances and debts that overlaid the city's entire structure. Such a man was Fernando Wood, a Philadelphia Quaker (born 1812) who had begun as a cigarmaker and grocer and had served one undistinguished but not disgraceful term in Congress. He had been accused of fraud in 1839, a matter of some $8,000, but that could be overlooked, since he had never been convicted. When he was elected to his first term as mayor, in 1844, he received four hundred more votes than there were voters in the Sixth Ward, but even that could be dismissed as a bureaucratic error. In fact, when he assumed office, he appeared to be the man to reform New York. As the Tammany historian Gustavus Myers noted, he "closed saloons on Sundays, suppressed brothels, gambling houses and rowdyism, had the streets cleaned, and opened a complaint book."[7] A biography of Wood written by Daniel McLeod (Xavier Donald) as promotional literature for his second-term campaign in 1856 depicts the chaos Wood faced upon assuming office, and phrases it in the past tense, as if he had cleaned it up:

> *When Wood was first elected mayor, New York was a wild metropolis, wherein we were disappointed if we had not two or three murders or a spicy riot or two for breakfast entertainment.*

People rollicked in the muddy streets; the press was filled with complaints of official corruption, useless expenditures of public moneys, overtaxation and improper contracting. The streets were filthy to an abominable degree, and the health of the city exceedingly endangered; paupers in myriads were emptied from polluted ships upon our shores, to become the prey of immigrant runners, or a burden upon the charity of the city.

He [Wood] found the streets of this great metropolis ill-paved, broken by carts and omnibuses into ruts and perilous gullies, obstructed by boxes and sign-boards, impassable by reason of thronging vehicles, and filled with filth and garbage, which was left where it had been thrown, to rot and send out its pestiferous fumes breathing fever, cholera and a host of diseases all over the city. He found hacks, carts and omnibuses choking the throughfares, the Jehu drivers dashing through the crowds furiously, reckless of life; women and children knocked down, trampled on, and the ruffians driving on uncaught. Hackmen overcharged and were insolent to their passengers, baggage smashers haunted the docks, tearing one's baggage apart, stealing it sometimes, and demanding from timid women and strange men unnumbered fees for doing mischief or for doing nothing at all; emigrant runners, half bulldog and half leech, burst in crowds upon the docks of arriving ships, carried off the poor foreign people, fleeced them, and set them adrift upon the town; rowdyism seemed to rule the city; it was at the risk of your life that you walked the streets late at night; the club, the knife, the slungshot and revolver were in constant activity; the Sunday low dramshop polluted the Sabbath air, disturbed the sacred stillness, and in the afternoon and night sent forth its crowds of wretches infuriate with bad liquor to howl and blaspheme, to fight or lie prone on the sidewalk or in the gutters.

> *Prostitution, grown bold with immunity, polluted the*
> *public highways, brazenly insolent to modesty and common*
> *decency; and idle policemen, undistinguished from other cit-*
> *izens, lounged about, gaped, gossiped, drank and smoked,*
> *insolently useless upon street corners and in saloons.*[8]

This model campaign biography, its picture of the damage inflicted by prior incumbents continuing to find echoes in political propaganda down to the present day, nevertheless neglected to mention that Wood, after an initial surge of rectitude, took the plunge headlong into corruption. He extorted bribes from the police; and those cops who failed to contribute were assigned twenty-four-hour watches. He sold the office of Commissioner to Charles Devlin for $50,000 in cash. To immigrants, his workers gave out three thousand to four thousand cards addressed to the Court of Common Pleas, requesting that the bearer be naturalized on demand, so long as the bearer promised to vote for Wood.

In the 1856 election Wood garnered the support of saloonkeepers by promising not to enforce the Sunday closing law he had been instrumental in passing the year before. The election of 1856 saw riots break out in the First, Sixth, and Seventeenth Wards, with Wood supporters led by the Dead Rabbits battling the pro-Nativist Bowery Boys and both parties smashing ballot boxes and scaring off voters of the opposite camp. Wood had prepared for this eventuality by sending nearly the entire police force on furlough the night before election day. He won, to some degree because the forces of Paradise Alley were stronger than those of the Bowery. The final tally was 34,860 votes for Wood over 25,209 for his Native American opponent Isaac O. Barker, and it was said that ten thousand of Wood's votes were fraudulent. The year of his second term, 1857, was marked by both the aforementioned police riots and a financial panic, during which twenty banks and some ten thousand businesses failed. Wood had become so arrogant that he was turned out by Tammany in the preparations for the next election, and even though Wood still had sufficient support in that body that he was named in their nominating process for mayor, the Wigwam supported Daniel Tiemann, who won by fewer than three thousand votes over Wood's Mozart Hall ticket. Wood was elected to a third term in the election after that. He reconciled with Tammany, and Mozart Hall was assumed into the Wigwam. Wood had become a dictator by this term, and actually made a short-lived attempt to secede from the Union before the Civil War, merging Manhattan, Staten, and Long Islands into the city-state of Tri-Insula. The plan was approved by the Common Council in January 1861, but rescinded three months later, after the Fort Sumter incident.

As bad as Wood was, he would find himself eclipsed in corruption by the Tweed Ring. William Marcy Tweed, born on Cherry Street in 1823, began as a runner for Engine Number 12 and rose to be foreman of "Big Six" in 1849. He joined the Americus Club under Rynders and was elected an assistant alderman in 1850, on the Forty Thieves board. He was named last on the Seventh Ward leaders' list in 1857, first on the same list in 1858, and that year he took advantage of Wood's schism to take over Tammany leadership from the aging Isaiah Rynders. Tweed set about ingratiating himself with the Tammany ward leaders, girding for the fight against Wood. Although he was set back by Wood's 1859 victory, he spent the next few years gradually eliminating the latter's power base and at length overcame him. In 1861 he made James Conner Grand Sachem, winning back all straying Irish Catholics, and in 1863 he himself was appointed officially to the position he all but held, chairman of Tammany's General Committee, a body that he filled with his henchmen, including the fading but still useful Rynders, Richard "Slippery Dick" Connolly, and Peter B. Sweeney, who became known as Bismarck or Brains. He raised funds to build the grand Fourteenth Street Wigwam in 1867, an institution that endured for more than fifty years. He brought a Republican named A. Oakey Hall into Tammany and the Democratic Party, and nominated him for mayor in 1868. The city's reform elements held their own convention that year, nominating John Kelly for the post on the Mosaic Hall ticket, but Tweed got to him and persuaded him to take a European vacation for his health. Kelly complied, staying in England for three years, and Hall was elected.

Tweed was then set to remake the city in his own image. He abolished the Board of Aldermen and the State Commissions, drew up his own charter and implemented it in 1870, its statutes placing the bulk of municipal power in the hands of a Board of Special Auditors—made up of Tweed, Hall, and Connolly. The corruption of the Tweed regime extended from top to bottom and penetrated every corner of the city's structure. Small-time crooks suddenly became untouchable, and often found themselves with governmental sinecures. A mayhem artist and gambler named Tim Donovan became deputy clerk at Fulton Market; the comedian "Oofty Goofty" Phillips was made clerk to the Water Register; the crook Jim "Maneater" Cusick became a court clerk. Under Tweed, the city spent $10,000 on $75 worth of pencils, $171,000 for $4,000 in tables and chairs, and squandered some $12 million on the infamous courthouse behind City Hall, including $1,826,000 for a $50,000 plastering job, $7 million for furniture and decorations, and roughly $3,500,000 for alleged repairs in the first thirty-one months after the building's completion. Tweed invested in judges, who sold receiverships, court orders, and writs of habeas corpus on the open market and used the Tombs as a private oubliette. One of them, Albert Cardozo, once held two women there incommunicado for seventeen days for reasons that were never disclosed, and in a period of about three years released more than two hundred clients of Howe and Hummel in exchange for financial considerations. Tweed all but bought newspapers as well: the *World* was his organ in the days before its purchase by Joseph Pulitzer; one of the three directors of the *Times* was his business partner; at one point he was paying the *Post* $50,000 a month. Tweed's own profits were not merely intangible: by 1870 his worth was estimated at $12 million, and he was the third largest land-owner in the city. He had his generous side as well. He built and supported a variety of hospitals, orphanages, schools, churches, and old soldiers' homes, created a public works program, and devised a social security program that was widely hailed even if it was not quite legal. In the winter of 1870–71 he gave $1,000 to each alderman for coal for the poor of his district, and $50,000 to the poor of the Fourth Ward. According to the historian Alexander Callow, the state legislature appropriated a bit over $2 million for private charities in the years from 1852 to 1869; under Tweed's influence, the same body gave away $2,225,000 between 1869 and 1871. No wonder that after Tweed's downfall people said, "Well, if Tweed stole, he was at least good to the poor." And if he had built $100,000 worth of stables at his summer home, and if his daughter's wedding had brought in $100,000 worth of gifts, well, then, he had modestly declined to have a statue of himself erected, as proposed by the *Sun* in 1871.

Electoral manipulation had become a joke. There was even a vaudeville routine: "Come off it," said the election official. "You ain't Bishop Doane." "The hell I ain't, you son of a bitch," replied the voter. When black voters tried to mark their ballots in the 1870 election, they found that all their names had already been voted by white repeaters. A wave of reaction was massing just offshore. In 1871 the New York City Council of Political Reform, which included such prominent citizens as Henry Ward Beecher, William Evarts, and William Havemeyer, reported before a meeting at Cooper Union that the city's debt had risen from $36 million in 1868 to $136 million in 1870. In 1871 Sheriff James O'Brien went to press a claim against the city for a mere $350, but Tweed refused to comply. In revenge, O'Brien went to the *Times* with a selection of documents he had copied from Comptroller Connolly's books. A Committee of Seventy was formed, with judicial powers, and they indicted Tweed and Hall. Connolly resigned his post as comptroller in November of 1871 and was arrested five days later. Tweed was arrested the following month, was gotten out on a writ of habeas corpus and then on $50,000 bail. He resigned his post as Commissioner of Public Works and his Tammany position, was tried in January of 1873, fled to California, was retried that November. He was found guilty on ninety out of 120 counts, and sentenced to twelve years in prison and a $12,000 fine. His lawyers got him out of jail in January 1875 on a technicality, but civil suits pressed by Samuel Tilden and others caused him to be rearrested immediately upon his release, and this time he was held on $3 million bail. He escaped that December, working his way from New Jersey to Brooklyn, from there to Florida, to Cuba, and finally to Spain, where he had the extraordinarily bad luck to encounter a Spanish customs official in the post at Vigo who recognized him from Thomas Nast's cartoons. He was brought back to New York in irons, and locked up in the Ludlow Street Jail, where he occupied the warden's parlor for a fee of $75 a week. His health was broken; the end was near. He offered to tell the whole truth in exchange for being allowed to die outside of jail, but the offer was spurned. He expired in April 1878. After it was all over, the sums were toted up: the Ring was estimated to have stolen a total of $200 million between 1865 and 1871, $75 million in the last two years, a great deal of this amount deriving from the sale of fraudulent bonds. Only $876,000 was recovered.

The Ring had eviscerated the city's economy, resulting in the Panic of 1873 and a temporary fad for moral rectitude among politicians. Corruption was deeply ingrained, however, and new vultures merely took over the carcass. Honest John Kelly, who had, fortuitously, been in Europe for three years and thus was free of the taint of the Ring, became Grand Sachem of Tammany in 1872, winning out over John Morrissey. Kelly, born on Hester Street in 1822, had begun as a grate setter and mason, and had gone to Congress in his youth, beating Mike Walsh by eighteen votes. Tammany had failed to make him Police Commissioner in 1863, so he led his Irish bloc over to the Germans and got C. Godfrey Gunther elected mayor. Tammany lured him back by making him sheriff, but in the meantime he somehow had acquired a reputation as an independent, even a reformer. Tammany not surprisingly lost the 1872 elections, but the winner in the mayoral contest, reformer William Havemeyer, made the mistake of attacking Kelly on his lowly origins and vocational training, a tactic which got Havemeyer defeated the next time around, bringing up Tammany man William H. Wickham. Kelly's dictatorship of the Wigwam lasted until his death in 1886 and was marked by relatively discreet graft.

The tiger of the
Americus fire company,
then appropriated by
the Americus Club and
finally by Tammany
Hall

The Tammany tiger at
the height of his
powers, too successful
to care for his dignity

THE SUBTERRANEAN.

MIKE WALSH, Editor.

Independent in every thing—Neutral in nothing.

SATURDAY, JANUARY 24, 1846.

KNAVES AND TYRANTS BEWARE, THIS

IS UPON YOU.

Mike Walsh's *Subterranean*: the voice of underground
democracy

Tammany Hall on East Fourteenth Street, 1904. Note Tony
Pastor's in its left-hand corner, with the Academy of Music
next door

Murder in an unidentified political clubhouse.
NYPD evidence photo

He was succeeded by Richard Croker, who was born in Ireland in 1843 and emigrated with his family three years later, to wind up in a shantytown somewhere in the vicinity of the present Central Park. He was a machinist, a prizefighter, a leader of the Fourth Avenue Tunnel Gang. He was twice elected alderman in the late 1860s, although he supported John Morrissey's breakaway group Young Democracy. His buoyancy was such that Connolly appointed him Superintendent of Market Fees and Rents, and he survived the Ring's fall well enough to be named coroner in 1873. The following year he was involved in a political quarrel on a street corner in the Gas House District during the course of which he shot and killed an innocent bystander. He was indicted by a grand jury, but, with the luck of the Wigwam, his case resulted in a hung jury. He was reelected coroner and subsequently became Fire Commissioner for several terms. More than Tweed, more even than Kelly, Croker was the model of the late-century Tammany boss; he was a rough-and-tumble fighter, a boy of the slums who did not bother to put on airs. He had made his reputation as a slugger rather than as a thinker, and his chores for Tammany included such tasks as shepherding a detachment of several hundred local toughs to commandeer the Philadelphia elections of 1868. He proved himself a wily politician, however, as in the 1886 mayoral elections. The Democrats were split into two camps, Tammany and reform, the latter supporting the nomination of Abram S. Hewitt against the Republican contender, Theodore Roosevelt, and the Socialist Henry George. Croker persuaded Tammany to back Hewitt, who won by a significant margin. Hewitt was branded an ingrate when he refused to be bought off and went on a tear of closing down such places as Harry Hill's, Billy McGlory's, the American Mabille, the Black and Tan, and the Haymarket; but Croker got his own back by dumping Hewitt in the next election, in favor of Tammany tool Hugh J. Grant.

Under Croker's leadership, which lasted until the election of Seth Low in 1902, Tammany essentially swallowed the Democratic Party, turned the local ward heelers' clubs into gangs and the gangs into clubs, so that an organization like the Limburger Roarers or the Bowery

Indians was both a front for criminals and a social-welfare agency, and pursued the management of vice in a businesslike way. The 1897 municipal campaign was indicative of Tammany's barefaced frankness: Asa Bird Gardiner, running for district attorney, took as his slogan "To Hell with Reform"; his supporters hailed him with cries of "Wide open!"; when Robert Van Wyck was elected mayor, crowds in the Tenderloin sang, "Well, well, well, reform has gone to hell."

Even more quintessentially the Tammany operator than Croker was Timothy D. "Big Tim" Sullivan. His first nickname was Dry Dollar, which apparently originated when, as a toddler, he thought the revenue seal on a barrel of beer was currency, and peeled it off and carefully dried it, rushing home to tell his ma he had found a "dry dollar." His career began in his teens, when he became a saloonkeeper and host to the Whyos, pursuing a sideline as controller of the Whyos' votes and as a repeat voter of truly phenomenal talent, as well as a wholesaler of papers to newsboys. His enterprise paid off; he soon had four saloons, one of them across the street from the Tombs Police Court, and was on his way to a political career. Elected to the legislature at a tender age, he first made a name for himself by defying Inspector Thomas Byrnes, whose rebuttal that Sullivan was a mouthpiece for criminals had little adverse effect. In 1892 Croker promoted him to head of the Third Assembly District, and in the fall of that year he carried the district by a margin of 395 to 4. That achieved, he ascended unto the position that was to be his life's work, as chief of the Bowery Assembly District.

Sullivan's organization began with his considerable family. His cousin Florence, called Florrie (who was male, incidentally), helped manage the saloons, of which Big Tim eventually had six, and, as was brought out before the Lexow Committee, helped Big Tim beat up poll watchers. Various jobs were handed out to his brothers Paddy and Dennis, known as Flat-Nose Dinny, his half brother Larry Mulligan, and his cousins Christy and Timothy P., called Little Tim. He was nearly always accompanied by his bodyguard, Photo Dave Altman, who had the honor of putting him in nomination every time he ran for public office, and by Thomas F. Reilly, called Sasparilla, who, when Big Tim was elected to Congress in the late 1890s (he hated it, and served only one term), volunteered to be his valet, since Bowery denizens were under the impression that having a valet was mandatory in Washington (as, in fact, they also tended to believe that the wearing of dress suits was the law in that city).

Big Tim's political style was simplicity itself. Alvin Harlow quotes one of his speeches, given on behalf of "Battery Dan" Finn's run for alderman, as representative of his oratory:

> *"Boys, I'm a Democrat [cheers]. I've been a Democrat all my life [loud cheers]. I have voted the Democratic ticket straight all my life [uproarious cheers]. I never scratched a ticket since I cast my first vote when I was seventeen, and I never will [pandemonium]."*[9]

He explained the principle of repeat voting, insisting that one needed "guys with whiskers":

> *"When they vote with their whiskers on, you take 'em to a barber and scrape off the chin-fringe. Then you vote 'em again with side-lilacs and mustache. Then to the barber again, off comes the sides and you vote 'em a third time with just a mustache. If that ain't enough, and the box can stand a few more ballots, clean off the mustache and vote 'em plain face. That makes every one of 'em good for four votes."*[10]

Big Tim was a genius of the shakedown, which in its most basic form took on the contours of a slightly glorified racket. Local merchants, gamblers, whores, liquor vendors, saloonkeepers, and the like would be required to buy tickets to Big Tim's clambakes, chowder suppers, and summer outings to College Point. For the latter, there would be a parade down to the dock with some retired boxer or other acting as Grand Marshal. The boat would be equipped with an open bar, stuss and poker tables, and private rooms for the more distinguished guests. At the picnic spot there would be a spread of chicken, chowder, clam fritters, coffee, beer, and ice cream, in addition to swimming, footracing, amateur boxing and wrestling tournaments, and baseball games. When the boat docked in the city that night, there would be a torchlight parade back to the Bowery, accompanied by fireworks.

Big Tim had a certain natural generosity that balanced his equally natural chicanery. Even his political enemies conceded that he gave away on the order of $25,000 a year to the poor, and personally went out at dawn with groups of the unemployed to find them jobs on the docks. Such a paragon as William Travers Jerome could say of him: "Tim Sullivan is crooked, if you please, but he lives up to his principles, such as they are, and he is true to his friends. He never had a chance when he was a boy to become anything more than what he is . . . I would rather entertain Tim Sullivan at my table than ———— [naming a more upright Democratic Party official]."[11] When Big Tim went to Europe, in 1909, he personally took charge of repatriating dozens of stranded Americans (and was everywhere hailed as King of the Bowery). On a trip to California, he ran into a party of thirty-seven assorted sports who claimed they knew him, and he brought them all back to New York in a private railroad car. He gave a $3,000 dinner in a hotel ballroom for an elevator operator. After he separated from his wife in 1905 he moved into the Occidental Hotel at Bowery and Grand Street, and there he oversaw a poker game that according to legend ran for five years straight. He would always put a poor onlooker in charge of the kitty and pay him when he folded his hand; one man was rumored to have made $18,000 a year at the job. He was famous for his Christmas dinners for Bowery indigents. The 1909 version, for example, served 5,000 men and saw the consumption of 10,000 pounds of turkey, 500 loaves of bread, 200 gallons of coffee, 5,000 pies, and a hundred kegs of beer. In addition, every man got a pipe, a bag of tobacco, and new shoes and socks.

Big Tim, in the Tammany style, never smoked or drank. His favorite novel was *Les Misérables*; he cared about serious literature, and once declared that "Anybody who reads *Three Weeks* [by Elinor Glyn] ought to get ten days." He was a compulsive gambler and supported his habit by shaking down all forms of gambling, in conjunction with Big Bill Devery and Frank Farrell. He owned a series of racehorses, one of whom made him $100,000, but one called the Bowery was notoriously bad. He was called the "Big Feller" and his associates were known as the "wise ones."

In spite of the inroads into corruption made by the Lexow and Mazet Committees, the late 1890s and early 1900s were the height of Tammany influence, at least in that it was accepted with a minimum of hypocrisy. The government had become a joke. In one of Harrigan and Hart's Mulligan plays, the Board of Aldermen visit Mulligan's house and fall asleep in the dining room. Mrs. Mulligan is concerned: "Whatever will I do? The aldermen are all sound asleep. Will I wake them?" To which Mulligan replies, "Lave them be. While they sleep the city's safe." In 1905 the revue *Fantana* introduced a song called "Tammany," with an endless number of verses, that was long to remain a local standard:

> *Hiawatha was an Indian, so was Navajo,*
> *Paleface organ grinders killed them many moons ago.*
> *But there is a band of Indians, that will never die,*
> *When they're at the Indian club, this is their battle cry:*
> Chorus:
> *Tammany, Tammany, Big chief sits in his tepee,*
> *Cheering braves to victory, Tammany, Tammany,*
> *Swamp 'em, swamp 'em, get the wampum, Tammany.*
>
> *Chris Colombo sailed from Spain, cross the deep blue sea,*
> *Brought long the Dago vote to beat out Tammany.*
> *Tammany found Colombo's crew were living on a boat,*
> *Big Chief said: "They're floaters," and he would not let*
>   *them vote,*
> *Then to the tribe he wrote:*

Chorus:
Tammany, Tammany, get those Dagoes jobs at once,
They can vote in twelve more months.
Tammany, Tammany, make those floaters Tammany voters,
    Tammany.

Fifteen thousand Irishmen from Erin came across,
Tammany put these Irish Indians on the Police force.
I asked one cop, if he wanted three platoons or four,
He said: "Keep your old platoons, I've got a cuspidor,
What would I want with more?"
Chorus:
Tammany, Tammany, your policemen can't be beat,
They can sleep on any street.
Tammany, Tammany, dusk is creeping, they're all sleeping,
Tammany.

Croker, who had become something of a grand seigneur, could no longer stand it when Seth Low, whom Big Bill Devery had dubbed Little Eva, was elected mayor in 1901, and quit as Grand Sachem, to be replaced by Charles Murphy (born in the Gas House District in 1858). Murphy was not a unanimous choice, having in some obscure way made an enemy of Devery. As a result, the forces were split in the 1904 mayoral campaign of Wigwam man George McClellan, but he won nevertheless, and served for six wide-open years, which were marred only slightly by his irrational distaste for motion pictures. Meanwhile, Big Tim went up to the state senate in 1908, took his grand tour of Europe in 1909, and upon his return persuaded Mc-Clellan to fire Police Commissioner Bingham, who had begun an inconvenient cleanup of the dives around Chatham Square. Big Tim's last major official act was a rather uncharacteristic one: his successful introduction of the Sullivan Law, which made it a felony to carry a concealed firearm. He seemed fated to have mental problems. It ran in the family: Florrie and Little Tim (Big Tim's opposite in both appearance and personality) both died lunatics in 1909. The Big Feller began acting strange in 1912, right around the time the Lieutenant Charles Becker case broke open. He was removed to a sanatorium and then parked in a house in Eastchester. Paddy took him to Europe that summer, and then he was bundled off to Eastchester again. That September, he kept his guards up all night playing cards, and one morning, as they slept, he fled. He was missing for two weeks, and manhunts were organized in every corner of the metropolitan area, until it was discovered that a body believed to be that of a tramp, found near some railroad tracks in the Bronx after having been run over by a New Haven train, was actually that of Big Tim. He was given an elaborate funeral at Old St. Patrick's, for which occasion the streets in the vicinity were scrubbed clean. Eight priests officiated, carloads of flowers arrived, and 25,000 people followed the body to Calvary Cemetery.[12] His estate turned out to be worth a little over $1 million, with an estimated $700,000 in unpaid loans and notes. His political organization soon fell apart as a result of quarrels among his heirs.

A less outstanding figure of the time was George Washington Plunkitt, who, in spite of seeming less colorful, was perhaps more representative of the average Tammany operative. He was the leader of the Fifteenth Assembly District on the West Side, served as a Sachem and as chairman of the Wigwam's Elections Committee, and held posts as state senator, assemblyman, police magistrate, county supervisor, and alderman. In one year he simultaneously manned four different public offices and collected salaries from three of them. Overall, he held office for some forty years. He introduced bills to establish parks in the outer boroughs, the Harlem River Speedway (later Drive), the Washington Bridge over the Harlem River, the 155th Street viaduct, the grading of Eighth Avenue north of Fifty-seventh Street (Central Park West), and additions to the Museum of Natural History. He was a close friend of and adviser to Charles Murphy. He might nevertheless not be remembered at all today were it not for the fact that a reporter named William L. Riordon spent a great deal of time listening to him, took down his perorations verbatim as they were issued from Plunkitt's rostrum on the bootblack stand of the County Courthouse at a period when he found himself out of office, and published them as a book in 1905. The result, *Plunkitt of Tammany Hall*, is a document of inestimable value, as an articulation of Tammany philosophy, as a textbook on practical graft, and as a record of the day-to-day workings of the machine. Plunkitt is plain-spoken throughout, making no attempt to disguise anything in high-flown rhetoric, and yet in his words graft comes out sounding thoroughly sensible, even altruistic, even a bit socialistic.

Plunkitt distinguishes between "honest graft" and "dishonest graft," the latter being the shaking down of gamblers, saloonkeepers, and whores. Of the former, he says, "I seen my opportunities and I took 'em," giving as an example his practice of informing himself well in advance of public works projects, and then going in and buying land at low rates in the area, saving it to sell high when the time came. He is dismissive of the value of education as a political tool: "A young man who has gone through the college course is handicapped at the outset. He may succeed in politics, but the odds are a hundred to one against him." He points out that Tammany leaders have never been speechmakers: Murphy, Croker, Kelly, hardly a speech out of any of them:

> *"Did I offer my services to the district leader as a stump-speaker? Not much. The woods are always full of speakers. Did I get up a book on municipal government and show it to the leader? I wasn't such a fool. What I did was to get some marketable goods before goin' to the leaders. What do I mean by marketable goods? Let me tell you: I had a cousin, a young man who didn't take any particular interest in politics. I went to him and said: 'Tommy, I'm goin' to be a politician, and I want to get a followin'; can I count on you?' He said, 'Sure, George.' That's how I started in business. I got a marketable commodity—one vote. Then I went to the district leader and told him I could command two*

votes on election day, Tommy's and my own. He smiled and told me to go ahead. If I had offered him a speech or a book-ful of learnin' he would have said, 'Oh, forget it!' "13

Eventually he collected sixty men and formed the George Washington Plunkitt Association. He got men jobs:

"This civil service is the biggest fraud of the age. It is the curse of the nation . . . I know more than one young man in past years who worked for the ticket and was just overflowin' with patriotism, but when he was knocked out by the civil service humbug he got to hate his country and became an Anarchist."14

He tells an anecdote of a local boy, a former Tammany worker ("He was the most patriotic American boy on the West Side. He couldn't see a flag without yellin' himself hoarse"), who, forced to take a civil-service exam, becomes so disillusioned he ships out for Cuba and enlists on the Spanish side, falling at San Juan Hill. Politics, says Plunkitt, is a regular business just like any other, and reformers are not real politicians.

"I've seen more than a hundred 'Democracies' rise and fall in New York City in the last quarter of a century. At least half a dozen so-called Democratic organizations are formed every year. All of them go in to down Tammany and take its place, but they seldom last more than a year or two, while Tammany's life is like the ever-lastin' rocks, the eternal hills, and the blockades on the 'L' road—it goes on forever."15

He recruits youth, via glee clubs, ball games, dances, by showing up at fires where there's sure to be a crowd. His theory of patronage is a matter of reciprocity, one hand washing the other, and he states that

the greatest political crime is ingratitude. His vision of graft, interestingly, is as a slightly bent version of "from each according to his
abilities to each according to his needs." Votes, in the end, ensure
jobs, and jobs ensure votes.

Of Tammany leaders, he states categorically that they are not book-
worms, that they never wear dress suits, and, above all: "The successful
politician does not drink . . . Look at the greatest leaders of Tammany
Hall! No regular drinkers among them. Richard Croker's strongest
drink was vichy. Charles Murphy takes a glass of wine at dinner sometimes, but he don't go beyond that." The only drinkers on the precincts
of Tammany Hall are there as powerless ornaments. He is nevertheless
against the Raines law, and the excise laws, insisting that the excise
laws promote bucket shops and therefore death.

He gives an example of his daily routine: at 2 a.m. he goes to bail
out a bartender who has been booked on violation of the excise laws.
At 6 a.m. he hears fire engines and goes out to collect the fire's victims
and put them up in hotel rooms and get them food and clothing. At
8:30 a.m. he goes to Police Court to bail out drunks. At 9 a.m. he is
in Municipal District Court to pay the rents of those about to be evicted
from their apartments. At 11 a.m. he is busy setting up jobs for his
constituents. At 3 p.m. he has, in quick succession, an Italian funeral,
a Jewish funeral, and a bar mitzvah. At 7 p.m. he attends a meeting
of election district captains and hears reports on voter turnout. At
8 p.m. he is at a church fair, kissing babies. At 9 p.m. he has bought
church-outing and church-bell subscription tickets and tickets to the
district baseball game, and is listening to the complaints of persecuted
pushcart peddlers. At 10:30 p.m. he is at a Jewish wedding. At midnight
he is in bed. "Is it any wonder," asks Riordon, "that scandals do not
permanently disable Tammany and that it speedily recovers from what
seems to be crushing defeat?"

Before one is tempted to enshrine George Washington Plunkitt as
a latter-day Robin Hood, however, it should be recalled that he was
pursuing profits, not ideals, unless the principle of natural selection
inherent in laissez-faire capitalism can be dignified as an ideal. Never-

theless, what helped Tammany succeed over so many years was that its operators did not stand on ceremony, did not make class distinctions with anyone willing to play the game, and, above all, had a realistic understanding of weakness and vice. Plunkitt's views on the excise laws are well taken; temperance is a fine notion, but its enforcement is another matter. Tammany in its many guises was a confidence game, an often foolish embezzlement ring, an oligarchy of wise guys, and it cost the city incalculable millions in various boondoggles, swindles, and white elephants, but it provided the people of the slums with bread and with circuses, and with no lectures to spoil enjoyment of the latter.

4 · SAINTHOOD

IT WAS INEVITABLE THAT A CITY SO
RICH IN EVERY VARIETY OF SIN
SHOULD AS A COUNTERMEASURE
BRING FORTH SAINTS, AND NOT THE
humble and pacific saints of meadow and
mountain but avenging saints, stern wielders
of holy wrath whose task it would be to topple
the various idols, painted calves, and pleasure palaces that ornamented the city's mire.
As so often happens, however, the saints of
New York City were flawed, their major flaw
being that, in their innocence from sin, they
were also innocent of it; that is, while they
might see sin behind every bush, they had
little imagination for the forms it might take.
Anything foreign might be wrong, any error
might be deliberate, anything fleshly was undoubtedly bad, but at the same time they
honestly couldn't tell you what went on
in waterfront whorehouses, they were per-

suaded that murder and robbery gave sensual satisfaction rather than that they proceeded from fear and want, they thought that poverty itself was indicative of corruption on the part of its victims. The saints were seldom poor, nor had they ever been so, and therefore they were prepared to be immaterial, to take literally the biblical conceit that the Word would be sustenance enough. Sainthood meant a renunciation of the body, a harder trick in the alleys of the city than in the arcadias where earlier saints had melded with nature and lived as both more and less than themselves. There were, in fact, saints who fed and clothed and housed others, who protected the very young and the very old from the city and its ravages, who themselves went down into the streets unprotected and lived what they believed, but these did not often make the newspapers. The famous saints were heroes of an unreality set forth in books; they gave their time to a crusade of making life conform to fabulous dictates of a heaven of law. They were true idealists, naïfs in fact, while those they inspired in a succeeding generation were martinets and disciplinarians and specialists in punishment. One sort of purity led to another sort of corruption.

The reformist impulse seems to have come fairly late to the city, at least as far as any prominent and publicized movements were concerned. It is not until the middle of the nineteenth century, for example, that such manifestations arise as the Washington Total Abstinence Society (an all-male temperance society that, unlike its later counterparts, based its philosophy not on religious or moral precepts but on the strictures of "pure reason") and the New York Association for the Suppression of Gambling. But these crusades were among the many pantomimes through which the city tried to act out its dawning role as a center of power in the world. The newspapers were less likely to take notice of individual toilers in the fields, and less notice in proportion to their dedication and selflessness. A case in point was that of the Reverend Lewis Morris Pease, noted in an earlier chapter. Pease and his wife had been sent as missionaries to the Five Points in 1850 by the Ladies' Home Missionary Society of the Methodist Episcopal Church. Once Pease was established on Cross Street, however, his aims and that of his parent body began to diverge. The Methodists saw the ills of the neighborhood as owing mostly to Romish influence, and they wanted converts. Pease recognized the material wants of the slum dwellers and sought economic and educational reforms. The Ladies' Home Missionary Society fired him finally, because on the day of their official visit to his base he was out bringing bolts of cloth to neighborhood workrooms. The Society's book *The Old Brewery* (1854) failed to mention Pease by name but alluded vaguely to "our first missionary." The book was published on the occasion of the construction of the Society's Missionary House at a cost of $36,000 on the site of the building reputed to be the city's worst hellhole, a symbolic act that accrued wide publicity—so wide that even today the brewery remains fixed in city lore as a slum beyond all measure, even though there is little evidence beyond the publicity of the Methodist Church that it was indeed any worse than innumerable rookeries of the period. Pease, for his part, remained in the quarter and went quietly about his work, in 1856 establishing the Five Points House of Industry, a workhouse that at least kept its charges fed and clothed. In 1864 a permanent House was built on the site of Cow Bay.

Reform next entered the spotlight in 1868, in the waterfront comedy that saw the Reverend A. C. Arnold of the Howard Mission and several other divines claiming that they had achieved the conversion of several of the most disreputable dive-keepers on Cherry and Water Streets. The reader will recall that the *Times* exposed the farce a few months later: John Allen had been renting his house to the ministers for $350 a month, Kit Burns let them invade his Rat Pit for one hour a week at a rate of $150 a month, and another former Dead Rabbit, the crimp Tommy Hedden, was using the scheme to avoid an indictment on charges of shanghaiing. The actual congregants at the saloon services were almost uniformly businessmen from other parts of town, and even these were less than steadfast in their attendance, being driven out of Kit Burns's, at least, by the overpowering stench of rat and dog carcasses buried under the bleachers.

The 1870s began the glory days of public reform movements. For any number of reasons, the time was ripe: the sobriety in the wake of the Civil War, the boom-and-crash economic cycle of the period, the rise of New York's first families to the point where they could forget they had been oystermongers and ragpickers less than a century before. Dwight Moody and Ira Sankey, famous nationally, held their first revival in 1873, the year of the panic, when paper fortunes made during the war collapsed. A year or two later, Reverend T. DeWitt Talmadge of the Brooklyn Tabernacle began his crusade against the "modern Gomorrah" across the river. Talmadge, with his colleague Henry Ward Beecher (who soon had to abstain from the practice, owing to scandals of a fleshly sort besmirching his own person), would make expeditions in mufti to the Manhattan fleshpots to gather material for sermons. Talmadge's sermons were, indeed, said to be rather lurid. The anonymous author of *Snares of New York* (1879) thought they made the best possible advertisement for the Tenderloin.

During the same period, genuine attempts were also made at improving the lot of slum dwellers, without resort to purple oratory. In 1872 Jerry McAuley opened his first mission on Water Street. McAuley had been a waterfront boozer who had come under the influence of ex-Morrissey follower Orville "Awful" Gardner, founder of the Fourth Ward Temperance Coffee House and the anti-liquor society, the Dashaways. McAuley was less interested in piety than in curing alcoholism, and, by all accounts, his meetings bore a striking resemblance to sessions of Alcoholics Anonymous today. Mostly, attendees would get up and testify to the hell of their past lives, and a combination of faith, example, and peer pressure would inspire newcomers. McAuley did not lack wit, either. In 1882 he opened a mission on West Thirty-second Street, next door to the Cremorne Dance Hall, and hung out a sign of his own that said "Cremorne." Neophytes would wander in, thinking they were entering the den of vice, and before they knew where they were, McAuley had locked the doors. His missions thrived for decades, swelling up with converts especially in the 1910s, as the Bowery entered its long hangover, and in fact the institution survives today, now located on Centre and White Streets. There were others

like McAuley who cared more for substance than for churchly de-
meanor. Tom Noonan, known as the Bishop of Chinatown and founder
of the Doyers Street Mission on the site of the bloodstained old Chinese
Theater, was one of these. When he died in 1922, the speakers were
all old scalawags who retained their swagger in spite of (or perhaps
really because of) having found sobriety, so that the roster reads like
the committee list of an 1899 racket: Black Jubal Burr, Bismarck,
Baron Mike Keefe, Blonde Katie Welsh, Armenian Mary, Snow Peters,
Mother Clark, and somebody known only as Honey.

Quite the opposite in every way was Anthony Comstock (1844–1915),
who incarnated the New York Society for the Suppression of Vice.
Comstock was, in the name of moral reform and the advancement of
purity, a punitive monster who boasted that he had hounded sixteen
people to their death by suicide and misadventure. His absolutism and
terrier-like fixation with rooting out anything remotely objectionable
eventually earned him a word, "comstockery," use of which is only
now dying out. Comstock grew up in Connecticut and began his career
at eighteen, by opening the spigots of kegs in a New Canaan liquor
store, and went on to enter the employ of the YMCA. He began the
Society for the Suppression of Vice in 1873, got it recognized as a quasi-
official body during Republican and reform administrations, and under
its aegis arrested at least three thousand persons for obscenity and
destroyed some 160 tons of literature under various pretexts. He was
best known for his entanglements with famous people of his day. Some
credit him with having pressured the Department of the Interior to
fire Walt Whitman; he brought legal proceedings against George Bernard Shaw for *Mrs. Warren's Profession* (it was Shaw who subsequently
coined "comstockery") and against Paul Chabas for his painting *September Morn*, a sentimental, hardly salacious tableau that is perhaps
the most famous barroom nude of all time; he got the city to ban
Margaret Sanger's works on family planning. He held up a 1909 issue
of Emma Goldman's *Mother Earth* because of an article on the white-
slave traffic. When the censor could find nothing objectionable in it,
Comstock denied that it had ever happened and claimed the whole

The breadline at Big Tim Sullivan's on the Bowery near
Rivington Street. Photograph by Brown Brothers

A politician handing out bed tickets on the Bowery.
Photograph by Brown Brothers

The mysterious streets of Chinatown, where Westerners could let their imaginations run rampant. Photograph by Jacob Riis

Inside the Bowery Mission, a diverse collection of types. Photograph by Brown Brothers

thing to have been a publicity stunt on Goldman's part. His last battle occurred in San Francisco, where he was attending the International Purity Congress as the official American delegate. As a sideline he initiated prosecution of department-store window dressers for garbing nude mannequins in full view of the public, but he lost, and for once did not recover from the attendant ridicule.

The king of reform in New York was a more substantial and complex person, the Reverend Charles H. Parkhurst, pastor of the Madison Square Presbyterian Church. He began his campaign, and the public phase of his career, with a thunderous sermon delivered on Valentine's Day, 1892, in which he railed at

> *the polluted harpies that, under the pretense of governing*
> *this city, are feeding day and night on its quivering vitals*
> *. . . a lying, perjured, rum-soaked and libidinous lot . . .*
> *Every effort to make men respectable, honorable, temperate,*
> *and sexually clean is a direct blow between the eyes of the*
> *Mayor and his whole gang of drunken and lecherous subor-*
> *dinates, in this sense that while we fight iniquity they shield*
> *or patronize it; while we try to convert criminals, they man-*
> *ufacture them; and they have one hundred dollars invested*
> *in the manufacturing machinery to our one invested in the*
> *conversion machinery . . .*[1]

Parkhurst was already over fifty at the time, but had been in the city only a little over a decade. He had just been appointed president of the New York Society for the Prevention of Crime. He seems to have been utterly sincere in his crusade, but partisan political underpinnings cannot entirely be ruled out: in his Madison Square congregation was the Republican boss Thomas Collier Platt, who had recently fallen out with Tammany boss Richard Croker. Parkhurst's sermon did not shy from alluding directly to the city's political forces; he called Tammany "a form under which the Devil disguises himself." The sermon was picked up by all the newspapers and became the day's major topic. It was not, however, well received. Charles A. Dana's pro-Tammany *Sun* called Parkhurst a follower of "Saint Billingsgate," and even W. E. Carson's *World*, now owned by Joseph Pulitzer, and the major anti-Tammany organ in the city, took an ambiguous position, giving the story major play without characterization on the front page, but editorializing against it within. Tammany retaliated by summoning Parkhurst before a grand jury presided over by its own District Attorney, DeLancey Nicholl. Parkhurst could not offer proof of his charges and was officially reprimanded for making unsupported statements. A week later he returned to Nicholl, having in the meantime amassed evidence of Sunday closing-law violations by nine East Side saloons, but the D.A. refused to act. This affair finally garnered Parkhurst press support, from the *Times*, the *Evening Post*, the *Mail and Express*, and eventually the *World*.

At this point Parkhurst decided to go undercover in the manner of Talmadge and investigate matters for himself. He hired a private detective, Charles W. Gardner, at a rate of six dollars a night. This was either luck or intelligence on Parkhurst's part: Gardner had long experience in the Bowery and Tenderloin, was nobody's fool, and took an ironic view of the whole escapade. He made an excellent tour guide. Parkhurst arrived per appointment at Gardner's rooms, accompanied by a pious young congregant, John Langdon Erving, apparently known as Sunbeam. As Gardner told the story in his book *The Doctor and the Devil* (1894), the reverend and Erving were dressed like Christians and could not be taken anywhere without arousing suspicion. So Gardner made them over: he decked out Parkhurst in a dirty shirt, loud black-and-white-checked trousers, and a dude's double-breasted reefer jacket; he tore a sleeve from an old red flannel shirt and wrapped it around his neck as a tie; he smeared his long curls with a bar of laundry soap and stuck a shapeless slouch hat on top. Upon reflection, he decided he would not have to shave off the doctor's luxuriant side-whiskers: "It would not be necessary to harvest your lilacs at present." Evidently, in his new guise, Parkhurst could pass for an aged lecher from the hinterlands. Sunbeam was young enough that his accoutrement mattered less: he was merely assigned a red tie and a pair of rubber boots.

Thus bedecked, the trio went off in search of sin. Their first stop was the Cherry Street saloon of the fence Tom Summers, where they had to take a drink or two for verisimilitude, whereupon, as Gardner later put it, Parkhurst acted as though "he had swallowed a whole political parade, torchlights and all." They moved on to a saloon on Third Avenue, where Parkhurst, to his great discomfort, ran into an old Amherst classmate; some nudging and winking saved him from exposure. The drinking, gambling, and cussing at these joints was all authentic enough, but Parkhurst became suspicious, beginning to believe that he was being shown a polite version of iniquity; he demanded he be shown the depths. Gardner accordingly led him through the underworld. They visited several "tight houses," so called because they were completely staffed by young women wearing tights. They went to an opium den, or at least a fake opium den, whose inmates included an eight-year-old boy. They called at the Golden Rule Pleasure Club on West Fourth Street, owned by one Scotch Ann. As Gardner described it, it was a basement divided into small cubicles. "In each room sat a youth whose face was painted, eyebrows blackened, and whose airs were those of a young girl. Each person talked in a high falsetto voice and called the others by women's names." Parkhurst was totally dumbfounded by this spectacle, and Gardner had to take him aside and explain it to him, whereupon the reverend blanched.

At Marie Andrea's, also on West Fourth, they witnessed a "French Circus," an orgy of some sort undescribed by Gardner, who professed himself "sickened" by the sight, while, he noted, Parkhurst "blandly smiled." At Hattie Adams's West Twenty-seventh Street whorehouse, they observed five young women dancing the cancan in the nude, and then they played leapfrog, using Gardner as the frog. Hattie Adams had her doubts about Parkhurst—something about the wide-eyed, bewhiskered, stern-faced civilian did not accord with her usual client profile, but Gardner reassured her, explaining that Parkhurst was "a gay boy from the West." After their tour Parkhurst, Sunbeam, and

Gardner all swore out affidavits, and then Gardner hired a squad of detectives to check up on saloons, and they came up with a list of 254 that ignored the Sunday closing laws. In his second topical sermon, on March 13, Parkhurst touched on all these matters, without going into the scandalous details of what he had seen, but citing specifics of location—he listed thirty whorehouses within the precinct of the church.

Reaction was immediate. Hattie Adams and Marie Andrea were indicted for keeping disorderly houses. Inspector Byrnes ordered enforcement of the widely ignored Sunday closing laws, albeit a temporary and cosmetic measure. The police raided a brothel on West Thirty-first Street and forced the whores out into the snow without letting them get their coats. They were operating, they claimed, on orders from Parkhurst himself. The prostitutes thereupon marched straight to the Madison Square vicarage and crowded into the parlor. As it turned out, Parkhurst was able to convince them of his innocence, and his wife served tea and cookies. The press was split along the usual lines on the matter, while the atheist Robert Ingersoll condemned Parkhurst for his "skulking methods and decoy tricks."

The trials of Adams and Andrea made a great hit with the public, who reveled in the unseemly details. Everywhere people sang:

> *Doctor Parkhurst on the floor*
> *Playing leapfrog with a whore*
> *Tarara Boomde-ay*
> *Tarara Boomde-ay*

It was clearly a show trial. As a matter of course, madams went up before the Court of General Sessions, pleaded guilty, and paid a $50 fine, but Byrnes, it was generally believed, thought a public trial would discredit Parkhurst, since evidence of what he had witnessed would make him, to the popular mind, an accomplice. Adams was represented by the inevitable William Howe, while Parkhurst was advised on his testimony by Jacob Riis and Lincoln Steffens. When asked about Parkhurst by a *World* reporter, Adams said, "I thought he was a pickpocket. He sat there solemn and his eyes were rolling everywhere as if he had some scheme." In the trial itself, Howe declared of the reverend doctor: "In the words of M. Thiers, I cannot elevate him to the level of my contempt. Speak as you will of her, Hattie Adams is worth a thousand of his kind." And Parkhurst later sized up Howe and Hummel: "They are truly the devil's advocates. But they never unsettled me." The two shysters were described as alternately giggling and looking shocked as the divine recounted his adventures. Both madams were found guilty and sentenced to six months in jail. It is not recorded what became of Scotch Ann.

Parkhurst had established himself as a figure of considerable importance, and as time went by, he defined his role increasingly as political rather than moral. He took particular pains to distance himself from Comstock, insisting that he was not out to censor anything but merely to point out the links between the police, Tammany, and the underworld. He played a major role in advising the investigators of the Lexow Committee in 1894, and went on providing counsel to reformers and quotes for the newspapers until his death in 1933, at the age of ninety-one, when he fell off the porch roof at his summer house while walking in his sleep. His associate Gardner was not so fortunate. In 1892 he was arrested for promoting the prostitution of his ex-wife—an unquestionable frame-up by Tammany hands. At his trial he was defended by Lexow heavyweights John Goff, Frank Moss, and William Travers Jerome, but he was nevertheless found guilty and sentenced to two years in jail. The conviction was subsequently reversed by the State Supreme Court and he was released from the Tombs after a year, but he was penniless and broken. He wrote *The Doctor and the Devils*, which had a certain success, and then he moved to the West.

After Parkhurst's case, one reform attempt succeeded another: the Committee of Fourteen, immediately followed by the Committee of Fifteen, tried to root out prostitution; the Lexow and Mazet investigations focused on police corruption; William Travers Jerome dedicated himself to the suppression of gambling, and he succeeded in putting Howe and Hummel out of business (but not until 1907, after Howe's death). All these currents swelled, crested, and broke like waves, having a certain temporary effect and putting small players out on the street or into jail, but leaving the superstructure essentially untouched. The police-politicians-underworld troika changed colors and configurations through minor ebbings and flowings of fortune, and to some degree benefited from reform campaigns, since public outrage tended to result in the failure of independent operators and guided the further concentration of power into a few, politically safe-guarded hands. Prohibition did little but exaggerate this condition, as was demonstrated in the 1930s by the Seabury Committee, the largest probe yet, which brought down Mayor Jimmy Walker's administration and found criminal ties in the police department to be, if anything, deeper than in the 1890s.

Meanwhile, reform of another sort was being effected more by eco-nomics than by morals, as in the prewar decline that saw the Bowery change from a street of saloons and dime museums to a street of missions and flophouses: by 1914 the Salvation Army, the Bowery Mission, Hadley Hall, the Holy Name Society, the All-Night Mission, and the YMCA were crowded into a veritable salvation alley on that avenue, elements of which still exist today. This drive for redemption was, of course, shortly to be succeeded by the excesses of Prohibition, during which men and women drank as a matter of course in ordinary life about as much as the marginals of two decades previous had imbibed in full-time occupation in the dives of Chatham Square. The moral of the story, if any, is that in New York City abstemiousness and license, the wide-open town and the broom of reform succeed each other primarily as fashions. Novelty is ever the greatest agent of persuasion.

5 · RUBBERNECKERS

BEFORE REFORM MOVEMENTS HAD
COME TO VISIT THE CITY WITH THE
REGULARITY OF LOCUST SWARMS,
BEFORE THE POLICE DEPARTMENT
had been organized at anything above the
gentleman-amateur level, before tenement-
house construction began in earnest, before
the membership of gangs was well known to
the readers of sensational newspapers, New
York had already become known as a sort of
theme park of squalor. Since the Revolution,
foreign tourists had been coming to the
United States to observe the social experiment in a manner not very different from that
of the critics and curiosity-seekers touring the
Soviet Union in the 1920s. They took in ports
and plantations, noted the curious local accents, observed industry, learning, and op-
timism if they were favorably disposed,
barbarism, rusticity, and ignorance if they

were not. Among the latter camp especially, it became the fashion to visit New York's lower depths, which usually meant a rapid escorted stroll on the Bowery, to be followed by diary jottings of the appalling mix of races and the lack of fastidiousness in dress to be found there.

The ground-breaking work in this direction was done by Frances Milton Trollope, the mother of the novelist Anthony Trollope. In 1829 Mrs. Trollope accompanied her ever-impecunious husband to America with the intention of opening a shop in Cincinnati. The business failed very quickly, but in the course of her three years' stay in the United States she observed a great deal. Upon returning to England in 1832, she published the results as *Domestic Manners of the Americans*. The book was a popular success both there and in the United States. As noted in an earlier chapter, her views of the Bowery b'hoys did not take very long to get back to the b'hoys themselves. The centerpiece of her account of New York City was, in fact, her record of an evening spent at the Bowery Theater:

> *I observed in the front row of a dress-box a lady performing the most maternal office possible, several gentlemen without their coats, and a general air of contempt for the decencies of life, certainly more than usually revolting . . . We saw many "yet unrazored lips" polluted with the grim tinge of the hateful tobacco, and heard, without ceasing, the spitting, which of course is its consequence. If their theatres had the orchestras of the Feydeau, and a choir of angels to boot, I could find but little pleasure, so long as they were followed by this running accompaniment of* thorough base.[1]

Mrs. Trollope's observations drew some of their vinegar, of course, from her feeling that she had been thrust against her will into a mode of life far beneath her station. Although her views of the Bowery Republic added fat to the fire of anti-English sentiment in the Irish-American slums, it should be noted that about the rest of America she is remarkably unsnobbish, and her book was something of an advertisement for the young country. She set apart only lower Manhattan.

Other foreign visitors in the early part of the century noticed something that has not yet ended—the resentment in which New York was held by people from other parts of the country. New York was the seat of arrogance, of cosmopolitanism, of luxury, of vice. It stood as an affront to the God-fearing pioneers, to the farmers who were attempting to turn the wilderness into tame landscape for the benefit of Christians. The frontiersman Davy Crockett was a prime example of the Western ideal, a man who had come up from the land, unlettered and unrefined, and by dint of courage and stubborn independence had eventually risen to the status of congressman from Tennessee, even though he was something of a rogue and a fabulist and perhaps only partially effective as an advertisement for rustic piety. Several autobiographical accounts came out under his name, although they were presumably ghost-written, since their prose has a professional veneer (albeit with countrified mannerisms and artful misspellings) unlike anything found in his letters. In one of these, *An Account of Colonel Crockett's Tour to the North and Down East*, published in 1835, the year before he died defending the Alamo, he recounted his first visit to New York. His guides thought it would be instructive for him to see the slums:

> . . . *in the midst of that great city we came to a place where five streets all come together; and from this it takes the name of "Five-points." The buildings are little, old, frame houses, and looked like some little country village. The houses all had cellars; and as that day was fashionable to moove, they were moooving too. The streets looked like a* clearing, *in my part of the world, as they were emptying and burning the straw out of their beds. It appeared as if the cellars was jam full of people; and such fiddling and dancing nobody ever saw before in this world. I thought they were the true "heaven-borns." Black and white, white and black, all hug-em-smug together, happy as lords and ladies, sitting sometimes round in a ring, with a jug of liquor between them:*

and I do think I saw more drunk folks, men and women,
that day, than I ever saw before. This is part of what is
called by the Regency the "glorious sixth ward"—the regular
Van Buren ground-floor. I thought I would rather risque
myself in an Indian fight than venture among these creatures
after night. I said to the colonel, "God deliver me from such
constituents, or from a party supported by such. In my coun-
try, when you meet an Irishman, you find a first-rate gentle-
man; but these are worse than savages; they are too mean to
swab hell's kitchen."[2]

The partisan political slant is rather obvious; Crockett was, after all,
a Whig. Even so, the image of the hardened Westerner, veteran of
blizzards, floods, gun battles in the woods, the intimate of the heathen
redskin, being appalled by what he sees in one of America's first cities
has proved endlessly renewable over a century and a half, and its
essence can today be found in all sorts of places, from the sermons of
evangelists to episodes of television cop shows.

A few years later Charles Dickens, known among other things as the
chronicler of the London slums, was given his own tour of the Five
Points, and he was suitably shocked, as he recorded in *American Notes
for General Circulation* (1842):

What place is this, to which the squalid street conducts us?
A kind of square of leprous houses, some of which are at-
tainable only by crazy wooden stairs without. What lies be-
hind this tottering flight of steps? . . . Let us go on again,
and plunge into the Five Points. This is the place; these
narrow ways diverging to the right and left, and reeking
everywhere with dirt and filth. Such lives as are led here,
bear the same fruit here as elsewhere. The coarse and bloated
faces at the doors have counterparts at home and all the
whole world over. Debauchery has made the very houses pre-
maturely old. See how the rotten beams are tumbling down,

and how the patched and broken windows seem to scowl dimly, like eyes that have been hurt in drunken frays. Many of these pigs live here. Do they ever wonder why their masters walk upright instead of going on all-fours, and why they talk instead of grunting?

Open the door of one of these cramped hutches full of sleeping Negroes. Pah! They have a charcoal fire within; there is a smell of singeing clothes, or flesh, so close they gather round the brazier; and vapours issue forth that blind and suffocate. From every corner, as you glance about you in these dark retreats, some figure crawls half-awakened, as if the judgment-hour were near at hand, and every obscure grave were giving up its dead. Where dogs would howl to lie, women, and men, and boys slink off to sleep, forcing the dislodged rats to move away in quest of better lodgings. Here, too, are lanes and alleys paved with mud knee-deep; underground chambers where they dance and game; the walls bedecked with rough designs of ships, of forts, and flags, and American Eagles out of number; ruined houses, open to the street, whence through wide gaps in the walls other ruins loom upon the eye, as though the world of vice and misery had nothing else to show; hideous tenements which take their names from robbery and murder; all that is loathsome, drooping and decayed is here.[3]

He also gave an account of a Five Points dance:

Heyday! the land lady of Almack's thrives! A buxom fat mulatto woman, with sparkling eyes, whose head is daintily ornamented with a handkerchief of many colors. Nor is the landlord much behind her in his finery. How glad he is to see us! What will we please to call for? A dance? It shall be done directly, sir. "A regular breakdown." . . . The dance commences. Every gentleman sets as long as he likes to the

opposite lady, and the opposite lady to him, and all are so
long about it that the sport begins to languish, when sud-
denly the lively hero dashes in to the rescue. Instead the fid-
dler grins, and goes at it tooth and nail; there is new energy
in the tambourine; new laughter in the dancers. Single shuf-
fle, double shuffle, cut and cross-cut; snapping his fingers,
rolling his eyes, turning in his knees, presenting the backs of
his legs in front, spinning about on his toes and heels like
nothing but the man's fingers on the tambourine; dancing
with two left legs, two right legs, two wooden legs, two wire
legs, two spring legs—all sorts of legs and no legs—what is
this to him? and in what walk of life, or dance of life, does
man ever get such stimulating applause as thunders about
him, when, having danced his partner off her feet, and him-
self too, he finishes by leaping gloriously on the bar-counter,
and calling for something to drink, with the chuckle of a
million of counterfeit Jim Crows, in one inimitable sound.[4]

In spite of his occasional exclamations and rhetorical questions, Dickens was less hysterical about the experience than were most of his
counterparts. After all, he had conducted similar tours of Seven Dials
and other London slums with police escort, as recounted in the pages
of *Everybody's*. It is certainly difficult to find any comparable writing
about slum culture, such as the dance scene Dickens renders with
obvious relish and even admiration, in the works of his stateside contemporaries, who were usually given to describing such performances
in terms reserved for grand-mal seizures. It is also significant that he
managed to be less overtly racist in his account than were most American writers of the period.

The race mixing in New York slums of the period tended to fascinate
European witnesses, while the Americans found it unutterably loathsome and avoided going into too many details. It is striking how seldom
black people are ever mentioned in journalistic accounts of New York
in the nineteenth century, unless they had the misfortune to get them-

selves publicly lynched, as happened during the Draft Riots of 1863
and again in the race riots that disfigured the West Side several times
around the turn of the century. Europeans found American blacks
colorful and exotic, but white Americans would not even accord them
that. The taste for domestic exotica had to wait for the arrival of the
Chinese, who were not treated with much more respect, but dazzled
whites with their apparent incomprehensibility.

Guided tours of Chinatown became a popular fad in the 1890s,
when any number of East Side hucksters set themselves up as experts
and would lead adventurous bourgeois through the narrow streets,
regaling them with fanciful lies, and then take them off to the Western-
ized restaurant called the Chinese Delmonico's for a meal of something
as inauthentic as chop suey, which they nevertheless usually professed
to find unpalatably strange. Chuck Connors was the past master of
this trade, but he had considerable competition in the lesser ranks.
Steve Brodie once escorted General William Booth of the Salvation
Army on such a tour, insisting beforehand that the general had to don
a pair of false side-whiskers, for no apparent reason except to add to
the glamorous intrigue. The expedition included the usual visits to
the Joss House and its attendant restaurant, and a price-gouging round
at Callahan's (apparently every slummer's first stop, and a pickpockets'
paradise). It was cut short when a cop tried to arrest the general for
wearing obviously false whiskers, and a rapid explanation by Brodie
was needed to clear matters up.

The fascination with Chinatown was summed up by the policeman
Cornelius Willemse in his memoirs:

> *It's an old story to the police. Visitors are more or less of a
> nuisance in Chinatown and a good many times they're dis-
> appointed. For they've built up such fantastic ideas of what
> goes on down there that if they don't see a few Chinamen
> disappearing down traps in the pavement pursued by some-
> body with a hatchet or a long curved knife, they haven't had
> any fun and they go home disappointed. As a matter of fact*

*Chinatown is a peaceful neighborhood most of the time and
there isn't much for the casual visitor to see. So to make it
interesting for out-of-town visitors sometimes we used to copy
the sight-seeing guides and arrange a set-up so as not to
disappoint them.*[5]

The practice of seeing the city's squalidly poor or exotically foreign
quarters as a playground of the imagination followed a distinct curve
over the decades. At first such things, if they were accidentally perceived
by the middle or upper classes, were met with a shudder and hurried
by. Then they were thought to be somehow morally instructive, so
that parties of church trustees might take in a quick swath of Cherry
Hill in order to go home and, after the fashion of the biblical Pharisee,
address their thanks to the Deity that they had not been created so
base. After that, Americans became more cosmopolitan, at least in a
surface way, so that in the nineties the intelligentsia might go ponder
the decay of Mulberry Bend and persuade themselves that they were
looking upon as picturesque a hubbub as could be found anywhere
short of Mediterranean port cities, while their country cousins would
pay confidence men to take them to Chinatown and intoxicate them
with visions of unmentionable vice, a sort of pornography of race. After
this, there came the logical successor to the Chinatown phenomenon
in the form of the Harlem slumming tours of the 1920s, which permitted white suburbanites to go out and actually live their fantasies,
complete with actual sex, drugs, and crime.

The other issue of this increasing fascination with urban low life
was a phenomenon that is distinctly of the twentieth century and
throughout the century has crested and waned in fashion in counterpoint to the waves of the reformist impulse. This tendency, alien to
the last century, is the wish to enter the slums and actually settle there,
via a complicated concatenation of motives that include the old allure
of exotica and frisson, the wish to cleanse oneself, the pioneer spirit,
the search for the mythical simple life, rebellion against the established
order, and, of course, the search for a bargain. The 1980s have supplied

a word for this curious phenomenon: gentrification. It is an admirable word that conveys quite efficiently the fact that middle-class newcomers to the slums are apt to change their surroundings, usually to the detriment of those who preceded them there out of necessity, in spite of their professed desire to submit themselves to a way of life foreign to their backgrounds. The word may be new, but the idea itself is not at all. The first place in New York to undergo the changes wrought by this trend was Greenwich Village; its change took place before World War I. Brooks Atkinson, who lived in the Village for economic reasons before he went on to fame and modest fortune as a drama critic, described the impact on his Bank Street neighborhood in a memoir published some years after the fact:

> Bank Street . . . where I eventually settled down, was in-
> fected with progress, resulting in a bizarre mixture of in-
> habitants and customs. The Bank Street culture was
> definitely slum. Across the street family tenements stood firm
> while the gentry were edging in. Hoodlums played gangster
> games in the streets, shot crap as soon as they were home
> from church on Sunday, built bonfires of barrels and pack-
> ing boxes in the gutters, smashed milk bottles as a form of
> self-expression, and once they playfully shot a bullet through
> one of our windows at a political poster that violated neigh-
> borhood loyalties . . . We on the bourgeois side of the street
> had little of which to complain. We were accepted as inevi-
> table. We came and went as we pleased. Top hats—those
> towers of gloom—promenaded the block unmolested. White
> flannels, rakish Panama hats, malacca canes apparently of-
> fered no offense and provided little temptation. In fact, it was
> only a question of time before the gentry would crowd out the
> hoodlums and reclaim Bank Street for astringent living with
> style. Already the real estate speculators were introducing a
> program of uniform American refinement as the logical way
> to increase taxes, rentals, and profits. The bootblack, who

had his stand at the corner of Bank and Bleecker, and who
was incidentally the janitor to the Italian bank, was looking
for a new location. The ice, wood, and wine merchant sold
the remnants of his trade to his countryman in the adjoining
block and retired to the country for his health. Bank Street,
where once sea captains had lived, was infected with progress. Nothing could stop Bank Street! While they were waiting, the real estate men dozed over their morning papers in
the windows.

As usual, they were right. What transformations the real
estate men, who knew the vanities of the public, could ac-
complish were magical and humorous. Under artful auspices, cold-water tenements became artists' studios within
ninety days; rooms once rented at $15 a month rented for
$100 before the plumbers had finished. Dingy houses that
seemed to be on their last legs suddenly became "apartments
of distinction" as soon as the plasterers had patted the new
entrance into shape and the carpenters had hung a new door
with strap hinges. Backyards became terraces; clothes closets
became kitchens; servants' quarters became drawing rooms;
rough garrets were highly prized as shrines to the current
Muses. Whatever a man believed was the truth for him. The
old residents—the "neighbors" as they called themselves—
might snicker derisively up their sleeves, but little good that
did them. For the landlords collected their rent in advance.
The tenants entered Paradise. After arranging their candle-
sticks carelessly on the chimney shelf, after putting up their
bizarre wall-hangings and crowding a few new books together and buying plain parchment lamp shades, they were
the gentry. They were cultured. They could tipple until three
in the morning. Whatever you could say, it was certainly
more fun than moving into a sixteen-story pill box. You
could get into the street without having to be civil to a
flunky.[6]

Very little about this account would need to be changed to make it apply to the present day, some three-quarters of a century later. Perhaps the principal difference between eras is that the "dingy houses" of Bank Street were and are much more durable structures than their Lower East Side equivalents, which were built as quick-profit slap-up housing and have outlived their expected dates of expiration by half a century or more. In any case, beyond all the dubious motivations, the *nostalgie de la boue*, the hunt for the picturesque, the steps that lead to gentrification are also pointed by a desire for community, a commodity that becomes less available with every decade, every swelling of the population, every milestone in large-scale construction, every yard of distance between neighbors imposed by technological advancement. From this perspective, the enforced contact between people in the straitness of tenements can seem positively arcadian. Unfortunately, it is impossible to concentrate on that one ideal while disregarding the misfortunes that accompany it, especially if one has known more accommodating circumstances. The result is discomfort or worse for everyone concerned: displacement for some, cramped and unstable dwelling places for others, and the only party to benefit will be the inevitable real estate speculator, whose only task is to wait. When the tide of fashion turns again, the bulldozers can be called in, and the cycle can start anew.

PART 4.

[· *The Invisible City* ·]

THE MAP OF THE CITY HAS NOT GREATLY CHANGED IN THE PAST CENTURY AND A HALF. A FEW STREETS HAVE BEEN CUT THROUGH AND OTHERS HAVE BEEN ELIMINATED, BUT IN GENERAL THE PLAN HAS BEEN CONTINUous. At least, so much is true for the objective map. Subjective maps are subject to constant change; the city at any given time is composed of wildly varying superimposed grids. One person's main drag is another's back alley. A Jewish resident of Chrystie Street in 1903 would carry around a very different internal plan than would an Italian resident of Elizabeth Street in the same year, even though the centers of their lives were only two blocks apart. Even so, their views would be anchored to some recognizable features on the objective map: a market, a square, a streetcar line.

Then there were—and are—those citizens of New York City for whom invisibility was a way of life. Abandoned children, the outcasts, the mendicants, the insane were ignored when they needed to be seen and noticeable only to their own cost, only when they were needed for blame, for reform, for institutionalization. Thus, they developed maps completely at variance with the objective plan, versions of the city that shed recognizable features and wrapped around hiding places and clandestine access to the necessities. Bohemia grew as a self-conscious refusal of ordinary existence. Bohemians wanted not just to produce poetry but to realize it in their surroundings every day. Their city was an imaginary landscape willed into concrete existence, with mixed results. It intersected with the city of politics and newspapers and money at oblique angles, at least until landlords figured out its boundaries.

Riot and parade, feast and uprising: these were occasions on which a mass of people, propelled by some collective jolt, would set about to reconfigure their streets by occupying them in new and explosive ways, festooning them with blood or bunting. The carnival transforms the map, turns spatial and social relationships inside out. The effect is cathartic but temporary. In other places such upheavals may have changed life in lasting ways, but in New York they merely led to the cleanup the day after, sometimes preceded by fire. Night is the permanent revolution, that of the globe. Every sundown the streets change, becoming sinister or libidinous, or, for that matter, longer or narrower or unexpectedly twisted. The familiar rebels against those who presume to know it. The map is altered and time is telescoped. Daylight restores things to their normal condition, or is that really their normal condition? The map of the city wrinkles and unfolds, wrinkles and unfolds.

1 · ORPHANS

THEY WERE NOT ALL LITERALLY ORPHANS. THEY WERE OFTEN CAST OUT, OR THEY RAN OUT THEM- SELVES, FROM FAMILIES TOO BIG OR too small to support them. In the prevailing conditions of extreme poverty, children might be carried along by the family only through the nursing stage, and then they would be expected to provide their own sustenance. Frequently enough, there was not even room for them in the corner oc- cupied by the family in the space shared with as many as four or five others, so that they willy-nilly had to find other accommoda- tions, often at an age when children in our time are not yet allowed to cross the street. Historians have noted that childhood was not recognized as a particular state until recent times, and point to paintings of the sixteenth or seventeenth centuries, in which children are depicted as miniature adults, their proportions grotesquely mature. In New York this idea was still operative among large sections of the poor in the nineteenth century, and it in fact can still be said to exist today here and there (as witness those tabloid accounts of infants being maimed or killed by their parents for failing to respond properly to verbal challenges they could not possibly understand). Children in the nineteenth-century slums were not only accorded all the responsibilities and attendant hardships of adulthood without the advantages of strength and experience; they were expected to cope with the single item of particular status conferred upon them: invisibility.

Until the reformers of the 1890s began making public the plight of New York's poor children in sweatshops and on the street, such children simply went unnoticed. This had its advantages and its disadvantages. It made theft, for example, more convenient. It also means that today we can get only the most rudimentary and indeterminate idea of the numbers involved. In 1849 it was estimated there were 40,000 homeless children in Manhattan; in the 1860s, between 10,000 and 30,000; in 1871 the estimate was 28,610; in 1872 the figure was put at 15,000; in 1876 it was said to be between 20,000 and 30,000. Children on their own were of necessity members of the criminal and mendicant classes; if they were employed, they were de facto enslaved. They slept on the docks, in cellars and basements, in alleys and doorways. Sleeping outdoors was already known then as "carrying the banner." A "country visitor" quoted by the reformer and missionary Charles Loring Brace in 1876 wrote that "two little newsboys slept one winter in the iron tube of the bridge at Harlem; two others made their bed in a burned-out safe in Wall Street. Sometimes they ensconced themselves in the cabin of a ferry-boat, and thus spent the night. Old boilers, barges, steps, and, above all, steam-gratings, were their favorite beds."[1] They burrowed into the empty and derelict spaces, not that there were many in a city where adults fought for sheltered hallways and cellar corners. Being small and beneath notice gave them the mobility as well as the status of rats.

The boys on the street divided into two classes: street arabs and

guttersnipes. Although these two terms have come to seem interchangeable, they had distinct meanings then: street arabs were older
and tougher, got jobs and stole significant objects, and they controlled
and ordered around the younger, weaker guttersnipes, who lived on
crumbs and leavings and waste. Kids tapped barrels and sacks on the
docks and in markets, cutting holes in the containers and draining as
much of the contents as they could carry away. They raided the stands
and crates outside grocery stores. Their thievery was generally restricted to open-air locations, since they would not be allowed into
shops. They made themselves available to hold horses for people running errands, and after the introduction of the automobile, this task
was translated into watching parked cars. They begged, whether
straightforwardly, or with the theatrical addition of a crying or fainting
routine, or with a perfunctory mercantile cover, such as the hawking
of pins or matches. They had, as has been noted earlier, their peddling
specialties: flowers, songs, newspapers, toothpicks, cigars for girls, and
neckties and pocketbook straps for boys. Flower girls at various periods
were ubiquitous, and their ostensible trade could be cover for any
number of pursuits, from setting up for pickpockets to child prostitution. Children invariably accompanied organ-grinders, collecting the
pennies, and although these were generally the grinder's own children,
a childless grinder found it necessary to hire children to work up the
necessary sympathy in his audience. Children, particularly Italian children, also worked as street musicians themselves, playing harps and
violins in pairs or trios.[2]

Sweatshop work for kids was usually available, but these jobs were
so grinding, regimented, and the hours so excessively long that the
children who worked at them were generally consigned to them by
their families; few kids who had the liberty to choose would prefer
them to the risky options on the streets. In light manufacturing, kids
were employed at repetitive tasks that were best carried out by small,
delicate fingers: cutting feathers from cocks' tails, stripping feathers,
stripping tobacco, making twine, making paper collars, making envelopes (which in the 1890s paid three and a half cents per thousand),

making paper boxes, making gold leaf, making artificial flowers, bur-
nishing china, sewing buttons. As might be suspected, more girls than
boys held down these kinds of jobs. Boys more often held the bottom
rank of menial occupations, such as cleaning pigstys or shoveling coal.
They also worked as bootblacks, and, of course, as newsboys.

As a rule, very young boys sold papers and graduated to the more
stable and secure profession of bootblacking around the age of ten.
Newsboys sold only the evening papers and extras, the morning editions being, by some unwritten rule, reserved for the kiosk vendors.
Competition among the boys was fierce. Merely obtaining stocks of the
paper was a competitive activity, especially in the case of extra or special
editions, and there was competition for turf, which was fought over,
paid for, subcontracted, bequeathed. A good corner was a major necessity, a subway entrance or El station stairs or a ferry landing were
prime. Newspapers were thin in those days, seldom running more than
sixteen pages, so that a fair number of them could be carried even by
a small boy; a newsboy's stock would, however, be determined by his
ability to pay for the papers at the point of distribution. Profits were
negligible: in the 1870s they averaged thirty cents a day, and two
decades later the numbers had not improved substantially. Profits were
furthermore reduced by overhead costs, which could include paying
for the use of selling space, for representation of a particular newspaper,
or for protection or tribute to an older boy who might collect weekly
or at longer intervals, his fees literally extortionate, as much as a dollar
a week, or half the boys' total profits.

The great majority of newsboys were homeless. After the Civil War,
institutions were founded to lodge independent and vagrant children:
first the Children's Aid Society (funded by Charles Loring Brace), and
then the Girls' Lodging House on St. Mark's Place and the Five Points
Mission for girls on Catherine Street, and, for boys, the Newsboys'
Lodging House on Park Place (later between Duane and Chambers
Streets). If we consider that such institutions would receive only a
fraction of the city's wandering children, the numbers are impressive:
in one two-year period the Newsboys' House admitted 8,835 different

A bunch of East Side kids hoisting an effigy. Photograph by Brown Brothers

Street arabs, 1896. The caption claims they lead ''a careless, happy existence, looking for sport and mischief everywhere,'' but their eyes tell a different story

boys—82,519 in seventeen years. At least, we have the administrators' word for it that there were no repeaters in this tally; those of the boys who did not run away were kept a month or two, depending on their need for rehabilitation, and then were shipped off to farm labor in the West, effectively a form of indenture. In the aforementioned two years, the House's inmates contributed $3,349 toward expenses; they were charged six cents for a layer of a bunk bed and ten cents for a private cubicle. Contemporary journalistic accounts of this institution are numerous, and nearly identical. Their genre was Good Little Devils, the well from which the Bowery Boys series was to draw much later. We would be shown the boys being piously sentimental, indulging in tearful memories of Mother, and then being cutely raucous, expressing themselves in the apostrophe-heavy cipher that polite journalism substituted for popular speech. Space would be devoted to their colorful nicknames: Mickety, Round Hearts, Horace Greeley, Wandering Jew, Fat Jack, Pickle Nose, Cranky Jim, Dodge-Me John, Tickle-Me-Foot, Know-Nothing Mike, O'Neill the Great.

The Reverend Lewis Morris Pease, when he opened his Five Points House of Industry in 1850, was among the first to notice the extent of the youthful underworld. Just as the street gangs had female auxiliaries, they also had farm leagues for boys. In the Five Points there were the Forty Little Thieves, the Little Dead Rabbits, and the Little Plug Uglies, and on the waterfront the Little Daybreak Boys. Considering that the "adult" gang members were often in their early teens themselves, we may speculate on just how young these trainees might be. Their major value to the gangs was their size. They all worked as lookouts and decoys; among the river gangs, they were important for their ability to crawl through portholes. Pease's efforts to arouse the finer instincts among these waifs did produce one apparent success. He boasted of having converted Wild Maggie Carson, who was the leader of the Forty Little Thieves. He claimed to have overseen her first bath, at the age of nine, and subsequently to have gotten her sewing buttons. Eventually he married her off, to the scion of a pious family.

The details of the kid underworld are not significantly different from what Dickens observed of its London counterpart. There were Fagin schools, and even if we are tempted to think that nineteenth-century journalists saw them everywhere as a consequence of having read *Oliver Twist*, a striking number of criminals in later years attributed their own professional training to such institutions. Children as young as five or six were enrolled to learn pocket picking, purse snatching, and cart robbery, tasks at which they might outdo their seniors. One of the most prominent was run by Jack Mahaney, known as American Jack Sheppard, who had run away from a good home at the age of ten, and then from the House of Refuge after the cops picked him up shortly upon his arrival in town. In association with a character named Italian Dave, he operated from a house on Paradise Square in the Five Points, teaching thirty boys at a time, ages nine to fifteen, by a careful method that involved the use of dummies at first, and then went on to live models and eventually to field trips. In the 1890s the major Fagin was Monk Eastman's sidekick Crazy Butch, who had also begun his own career very young. He proved his pedagogic ability by first teaching his dog, Rabbi, to snatch purses, and then went on to coach pre-adolescents. He also formed his charges into an Eastman auxiliary, the improbably named Squab Wheelmen. They were most noted for one trick: a member would hit a pedestrian, preferably an old woman, with his bicycle, and then dismount and begin screaming at the victim. As an interested crowd gathered, the other members would pick their pockets.

All the while, there were numerous children's gangs independent of older leaders or advisers. They often hired themselves out as touts or spies or lookouts in brothels and houses of assignation, or as errand runners and pullers-in for maverick prostitutes. By and large, kid gangs engaged in reduced-scale versions of the activities of older gangs. Irish Catholic gangs robbed Protestant churches and institutions, and although the reverse phenomenon has been less well documented, it undoubtedly was nearly as common. Some children's gangs appear to have successfully managed to create their own domains and social structures away from the adult world. The Fourth Avenue Tunnel Gang, best remembered for having been led by future Tammany boss Richard Croker, lived in niches in the train tunnels leading out of Grand Central, a warren used today by homeless adults. The Baxter Street Dudes, as has been noted, fared reasonably well, and accrued a large amount of publicity, by running their own theater specializing in blood-and-thunder melodrama.

There was very little that adult gangsters practiced or enjoyed that child gangsters did not contrive to reproduce on their own scale. There were boys' saloons, with three-cent whiskies and little girls in the back rooms, and there were children's gambling houses, in which tots could bilk other tots at the usual menu of faro, policy, and dice games. About the only significant activity from which children were barred was election-poll repeating, although they could prepare for their eventual participation by working as runners for the ward heelers. Elections were nevertheless of great significance to children, criminal or not, because it was their task to build and maintain the ritual bonfires on the streets that marked these events. The rivalry that developed between groups of kids over these fires forms an interesting parallel to their elders' rivalries over putting out blazes. They would have full-scale pitched battles over the relative sizes of the fires, raid each other's supplies of wood, fight it out with knives and bricks, using wash-boiler covers as shields. These contests were always territorial, and never had anything to do with politics, which stands to reason, since in the slums everybody always voted Democrat anyway.

If it seems that these children must have very early used up the entire stock of adult pleasures—sex, drink, gambling, extortion, racketeering, fraud, intimidation, unfair competition, price-fixing, terrorism—it should be remembered that the life expectancy for kids growing up under those conditions could not have been very high. The whole adult order of high and low sensations had to be experienced in fifteen or twenty years at best before they succumbed to disease, malnutrition, exposure, stab wounds, or gunfire. In an era during which New York produced three or four adolescent crooks called Billy the Kid, all of whom disappeared in some fashion before they were old enough to vote, and all of whom were reported incorrectly to have gone West and become *that* Billy the Kid, it is remarkable that any young person from the slums survived to adulthood at all. Those who did can be assumed to have been the most pious, the most enterprising, or the most murderous—in any case, the least childlike of children.

2 · *The* DRIFT

THE LUCKLESS, THE UNCONNECTED,
THE NEWLY ARRIVED WHO HAD NO
RELATIVES AND NO COMMAND OF
THE LANGUAGE, THE DESTITUTE,
those afflicted with illness, those made pariahs
by sores or other disfigurements, the insane,
those made insane by war or prison or more
personal horrors, alcoholics of varying se-
verity, misdiagnosed epileptics, the retarded,
the brain-damaged, victims of all sorts of im-
aginable or unimaginable circumstances, the
anchorites, the refusers, the resisters, the
outcasts: they, too, dwelled in a separate
sphere in the last century, and partook of an
invisibility to the general public. They lived
in a silence that broached the supernatural,
and might be seen as omens, as memento
mori, as demons, as damned souls, as spec-
ters and walking reproaches. Charity toward

them by individuals had a medieval flavor about it that suggested acts of appeasement.

In the early part of the nineteenth century the city could allow for them. Drifters were allowed to sleep in the common grounds, in City Hall Park and Battery Park. They had allotted trades as street vendors and street musicians. From stands, carts, and spread newspapers they would sell watches and jewelry, or cigars, or sweets, or domestic animals, or used books, or ice. Organ-grinders were usually Italian and rented their instruments by the day, since they were too poor to buy them; at first these were portable barrel organs, but later in the century piano organs, mounted on wheels, predominated. Old women played cylindrical hand organs; Irishmen played uillean pipes. There were street singers, as well as yard singers, who would go into apartment-house courtyards or the open centers of blocks, and collect donations flung from windows; they were a fixture, in some areas, well into the present century.[1]

In the late nineteenth century, however, much of the goodwill or at least benign neglect evinced toward the city's nomads began to be eroded, perhaps as a result of the increase in their numbers, swelled both by immigration and by the presence of injured war veterans. The Tweed Ring passed laws prohibiting sleeping in the parks, and their cops duly enforced them by rapping sleepers across the legs or groin with their nightsticks. The homeless were henceforth relegated to the usual blind corners and waste areas: doorways, alleys, steam vents. Most favored were the hay barges on the river, in season. Otherwise, police-station lodgings were available, if despised by all, until Theodore Roosevelt took Jacob Riis's well-meaning advice and shut them down in 1896. There were the bed houses and flophouses and stale-beer dives and ordinary dives that allowed patrons into their back rooms after closing time. There were public charities and missions which extracted a toll from their beneficiaries in the form of long hours spent attending to sermons and in other ways simulating piety. And then there were the various attempts on the part of the city government to house the homeless: the workhouse and almshouse on Blackwell's

Island, and the Municipal Lodging House, which opened in the 1890s as a floating barge attached to a pier at the foot of East Twenty-sixth Street. The almshouse existed primarily for the relief of those made indigent by disability—the blind, the terminally ill, the paralyzed. The workhouse was that essentially Victorian institution, the prison for the poor, who were incarcerated until they were found work at their level elsewhere. The Municipal Lodging House was, at least in theory, more open to the discretionary needs of vagrants, but it was overcrowded, noisy, anything but restful, and its guests were gotten up before dawn to put in the five hours of labor that paid for their meal and lodging.

Begging was an increasingly crowded field through the century, the competition so great that mendicants began to develop specialties. Men known as "crumb throwers" would plant a hunk of bread in the gutter; when the right kind of crowd came by, they would precipitate them-selves upon it and devour it. Mock epileptics were in the business of "chucking dummy fits." Mock cripples devised all sorts of ingenious accoutrements: fake harnesses and prostheses, elaborate swaths of bandages. There were, in fact, Fagin-style begging schools called "crip-ple factories" that would supply the equipment and teach its use, in return for a percentage of the returns, and these had annexes in the form of saloons, where the "lame" and "halt" could walk normally, the "blind" see, and the "deaf and dumb" converse, all of them spend-ing their receipts at the company bar, safe from the eyes of their benefactors. Beggars were always in demand around election time, when they were used as repeat voters and made a reasonable wage at it; if they were sharp, they could also collect any number of free meals, drinks, and cigars by following around campaigning politicians.

Tramps as a phenomenon first appeared in the 1870s. Many of them were probably war veterans who hadn't been able to adjust. They were little noticed in the city at first, for one thing because trampdom was generally rural and was thought of as a menace only in farm and range country; for another, because tramps themselves were generally of rural origin and conducted themselves accordingly, remaining mobile and discreet. In the years when Central Park was new, tramps would hide out there, living in its sylvan recesses. They attracted notice as a public nuisance by their penchant for lying prone on the pavement and draining the lees from empty beer kegs set out in front of saloons. For some years, toward the end of the century, a tramp shelter operated quietly in a former hotel at Prince and Marion (Lafayette) Streets. Vagrants were given bed and board, and in return they chopped logs for the firewood business that financed the institution.

After the turn of the century, tramps and hoboes began showing up in the city in greater numbers: adventurers drifting back eastward from the settled West, rag ends of Coxey's Army, men put out of work from suburban factories as a result of the Panic of 1897. New York was a minor way station for tramps and hoboes, and they were only perceived in significant numbers in the city between circa 1901 and 1917. Most of the railroad vagrants shunned the city for its expense, its gangs of hoodlums and lush-rollers, its uncertain police force, and also because of its underground rail platforms, which made it difficult to hop trains from anywhere but the stations of the West Side river line. Other cities, such as Chicago, Denver, and San Francisco, became major vagrant hubs, but New York was both unfriendly and ill situated. But the first decade and a half of the twentieth century was an era of extremes of rootlessness. There were so many people without fixed abode in the city that flops of all sorts sprang up; the Western tramps must have heard of New York as a storehouse of cheap beds. When they got to the city, though, they found a great deal of competition. In 1909 it was estimated there were 25,000 people on the bum on the Bowery and Park Row alone, in hotels, lodging houses, flophouses, missions, sleeping on chairs, in barrels, on saloon floors, in doorways, in stairwells, on fire escapes.

Tramps and hoboes provided a good deal more fodder for Sunday-supplement human-interest stories than the more typical city vagrants, however. They were usually native English speakers, for one thing, and they were independent, more or less eccentric and colorful, more or less non-violent and healthy. They bore monikers like Denver Pete, Boston Slim, Ike the Rustler, Champ the Bed, Calamity Burke, Short-

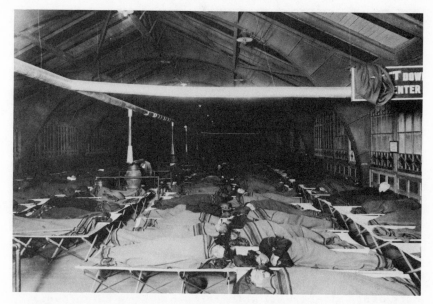

A scene in the first Municipal Lodging House, aboard a barge docked at the foot of East Twenty-sixth Street. Photograph by Brown Brothers

Tramps riding the tops of boxcars down the North River line, in view of Riverside Drive. Photograph by Brown Brothers

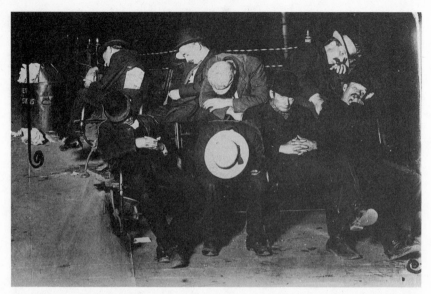

Park-bench sleepers (slightly retouched for a rotogravure section). Photograph by Brown Brothers

An actor being advised on his movements for a scene in Herbert Brenon's film *The Street of Forgotten Men* (1925), set in a Bowery cripple factory

Tail Kelly, Gulper Mooney, Angel Face, some of these the kinds of tags that might have been worn by Irish thugs of the Five Points gangs that by this time rested in convenient memory, in contrast to the newer breed of more foreign-sounding gangsters. Among the tramps and bums were enigmatic sorts and instant legends. There were said to be Oxford graduates, and men with dueling scars from German universities. There were remittance men from old families whose month would follow a rigorously determined cycle: funds would arrive, followed by new clothes and feasting and carousing, then the money would be gone, the clothes would be pawned, and there would follow a week or two of utter destitution, each stage accompanied by a corresponding shift of lodging. One Bowery character, known only as J. Black, would ceremoniously extract a dark suit from hock for a few days each month and disappear to read in the public library. There were the usual legendary rich bums, the authenticity of whose fortunes remains as questionable as in the rumors of our own day. A man named William Smith, who died in 1913 at the age of eighty after some three decades as a vagrant, was said posthumously to have been playing the stock market all along and to have left some $200,000 in cash and securities. Another man was rumored to have bequeathed $35,000 to two road companions. The punch line of such stories usually turns out to be that such people amass fortunes from handouts; if there is any truth in them at all, it is that there are extremes of parsimony.

There were also legends of altruistic bums: Jew Dave Kelly, for example, who spent all his money feeding stray cats; and Chinatown Gertie, once employed in a fake opium den, who had dedicated her twilight years to the relief of the poor, and likewise a reformed drunk called the Captain. A prostitute called Gold Tooth Fanny would come around on winter mornings and distribute food to the men of the Bowery. The great model of the responsible vagrant was James Eads How, the "hobo millionaire," who had devoted his life and the whole of his inherited fortune to improving conditions for hoboes and tramps, establishing shelters, medical facilities, and hobo colleges at key spots throughout the country; in New York he opened a lodging house for the homeless of all sorts on Fourth Street. Among his followers was Jeff Davis, one of many claimants to the title of King of the Tramps, who settled in New York for a few years in the teens. His great project was the Itinerant Workers Union, a largely unsuccessful attempt to establish collective bargaining on behalf of migrant and seasonal laborers. His other enterprises were marked by similar imagination and initiative. In the harsh winter of 1914 he persuaded the owners of an empty building at Worth and Centre Streets to rent it to him for a dollar a year and opened it as an enlightened, sanitary, and comfortable flophouse he called the Hotel de Gink. Earlier, in 1910, Davis had organized an Outcasts' Festival at Pacific Hall on East Broadway in conjunction with his Chicago counterpart, Dr. Ben Reitman. The event combined the hobo college mission of educating tramps with Reitman's determination to have hoboes speak for themselves into the ears of the press and therefore the public. It made for an unlikely and extraordinary gathering of tribes: Emma Goldman spoke; the writer Hutchins Hapgood read a letter from the imprisoned Alexander Berkman; the quintessential radical bohemian Hippolyte Havel gave a talk on the vagrancy of Adam and Eve and of Jesus Christ; Sadakichi Hartmann read his play *Mohammed*; and a number of vagrants held forth, including Pittsburgh Joe, Mickey the Farmer, and Chuck Connors himself, speaking in favor of the dissolute life.

The Bowery's term as a magnet for tramps was finally ended by the approach of World War I, especially by the 1917 "Work or Fight" order that conscripted into the armed forces anyone not demonstrably employed, a law that cut a great swath through the area's population and finally killed the street as an entertainment district for anyone but the pathetic smoke drinkers who remained through Prohibition. It provided a handy excuse for the police to make sweeps of the rootless and unprotected in other areas as well, such as Hell's Kitchen and Harlem. The numbers were of course to return little more than a decade later, when the Depression struck and shantytowns went up in the parks and Hoovervilles along the waterfront.

The history of the homeless and uprooted and drifting in New York must perforce remain skeletal, its particulars being located literally on the margins of life. To its floating population, New York was a parallel construction, a map of hiding places and safety zones unknown to the general mass of people. To the drifters, the great squares and avenues might scarcely exist, their central place in the city's scheme taken up by back courts and alleys and vacant lots and wharves and the terra incognita in the north of the island before it was urbanized. Their history generally consists of what was seen of them by institutions, charities, police, and journalists; their own lore remained secret or became useless as soon as anybody else learned it. Knowledge of the city's hiding places remains dormant for decades at a time, until it is learned all over again by those who have need of it. Today we can see the destitute finding the niches in railroad tunnels, the abandoned cuttings, the caves in Inwood, and the alcoves under bridge supports that were left for them by previous occupants.

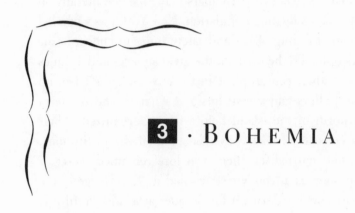

3 · BOHEMIA

IN ITS GENERAL OUTLINES, THE HIS-
TORY OF BOHEMIAN NEW YORK IS
ENDLESSLY FAMILIAR: A SUCCESSION
OF OVERLAPPING CYCLES CHARTING
a course from obscurity, poverty, ambition,
recklessness, eccentricity, idealism, to fame
for some, early death for others, bitterness
and disillusionment for the rest, along the
way the furniture of bars, magazines, feuds,
landlords, pronouncements, publicity, and
the alchemical transformation of original
ideas into meaningless trademarks, and be-
havioral tics into popular fashions. This routine, which has never gone away but only
mutated over the generations, is more or less
a creation of the early nineteenth century, its
basic terms being found in Henri Murger's
La Bohème and in the real-life activities of
the "Jeunes France" of the 1830s (Nerval
walking a lobster on a leash, Petrus Borel

drinking wine from a skull, various dramatic suicides) and, in America, in the visionary work and desperately unhappy life of Edgar Allan Poe.

Before Poe, the artistic life in New York was genteel and respectably settled into the social order. Washington Irving was the city's first great literary figure, and the rustic Fenimore Cooper was established in a house on St. Mark's Place. No one today can identify Fitz-Greene Halleck, let alone read him, but for a century or more he was officially recognized as the city's bard, and his bust stands in Central Park. Halleck and his even more forgotten colleague Joseph Rodman Drake were the versifiers of the last era of semi-rural downtown bourgeoisie, and their poesy was sufficiently mediocre to appeal in later decades to reactionaries of several generations.[1] Poe, on the other hand, was treated mostly with contempt during his lifetime, and only intermittently recognized. Plagued by alcoholism, depression, and disease, he wandered from one temporary residence to the next among the Middle Atlantic states—in New York City alone, he lived on Waverly Place, on Carmine Street, on Greenwich Street, on Amity (West Third) Street, on Broadway, on Bond Street, on Eighty-fourth Street, and up in the Bronx. He finally died in Baltimore in 1849, possibly from the effects of a bender and brawls along its course, although the cause of death has never been firmly established.

After Poe's death, everything seemed to refer back to him and to have been prefigured by him. His spirit was most nearly palpable at Pfaff's, the city's first bona-fide bohemian hangout, opened in a cellar on the west side of Broadway just above Bleecker Street sometime in the early 1850s. Pfaff's was a tavern and restaurant presided over by a jovial German who by all accounts did not have much of a talent for cooking but who kept a decent bar and did not mind his clients sitting around all day nursing the minimum purchase. The bohemians collected there gradually and invisibly, until it came to be noticed that they had annexed as their permanent spot a vaulted alcove at the far end of the room. After a while, curiosity-seekers came to stare, drawn principally by the self-serving accounts printed in the circle's own house organ, *The Saturday Press*, published by Henry Clapp, the King of Bohemia.

Clapp, who was born on Nantucket in 1814, was a wit and a non-conformist, with genuine talent as an impresario. In 1864 the *New York Leader* summed him up:

> *He is a queer fellow—a character. He is a born Yankee;*
> *speaks French like a native; plays poker like a Western man;*
> *drinks like a fish; smokes like a Dutchman; is as full of*
> *dainty conceits as a Spanish or Italian poet; is as rough in*
> *his manners as a Russian or a Russian bear. His writings*
> *are as original as original sin.*[2]

The description is archetypal, instantly fitting any hundred bohoes of any subsequent generation. Clapp's writings have not, however, stood the test of time, and he seems to have reserved his best lines for table talk. He called Wall Street "Caterwaul Street" and suggested that its motto was "In Gold We Trust." He called Cuba "the land of the flea and the home of the slave." He called Horace Greeley a self-made man who worshiped his creator. "As there appear to be no lady contributors to the *Nation*," he once wrote, "it has been suggested that for this and other reasons its name be changed to the *Stag-Nation*." He was a socialist and a sometime follower of Fourier. His friends called him the Oldest Man because he always looked the part, at whatever age. He died of the effects of drinking in 1875. His *Saturday Press* was rather pretentious and self-dramatizing—its columnists all had decorative pseudonyms: Clapp was Figaro, Ned Wilkins was Personne, the future naturalist John Burroughs was All Souls—but it was also among the first periodicals to recognize Whitman's stature, it published Mark Twain's first great work, "Jim Smiley and His Jumping Frog," in 1865, and was in fact the first Eastern publication to feature his writing.

If Clapp was King, the Queen of Bohemia was the young phenomenon Ada Clare. She was born Jane McElheny in the South in 1836

and published her first poem in the literary weekly the *New York Atlas*
when she was only nineteen. It astonished everyone and made her an
instant star, although it is a bit difficult now to see what all the fuss was
about:

> *Oh sleep my darling, sweetly sleep,*
> *No sound shall break thy deepest rest;*
> *Oh! let thy dreamings faintly rise*
> *From the sweet dreamland of my breast;*
> *Oh! sleep, my darling, sleep!*[3]

Perhaps its success lay in its coy sublimation of sexuality; in any event,
Clare's genius was clearly a matter of her mode of living, which was
the essence of bohemianism. She defined the role herself in 1860:

> *The Bohemian is by nature, if not by habit, a cosmopolite,*
> *with a general sympathy for the fine arts, and for all things*
> *above and beyond convention. The Bohemian is not, like the*
> *creature of society, a victim of rules and customs; he steps*
> *over them with an easy, graceful, joyous unconsciousness,*
> *guided by the principles of good taste and feeling. Above all*
> *others, the Bohemian must not be narrow-minded; if he be,*
> *he is degraded back to the position of mere worldling.*[4]

She was always ready to defend the bohemians against the ridicule of
the popular press; bohemians did not strive to be poor, she tirelessly
explained to various editors. She had numerous lovers; John Burroughs
described her beauty as "singular, unique" (in her picture she looks
a bit square-jawed; also, oddly, a bit like Rimbaud). She had an
illegitimate son, Aubrey, whose father was believed to be the composer
and pianist Louis Moreau Gottschalk; one and all were shocked that
Aubrey called his mother by her first name. She certainly was not shy
about her genius—writing, under the name Alastor, articles in praise
of herself.[5]

The first mentions of the "great American novel" come with this crowd, and Clare was one of those who made a stab at it: *A Woman's Heart*, which got very bad reviews. Eventually she became dissatisfied with the meager rewards of the literary life and aspired to the stage. She made her New York debut as Julia in *The Hunchback of Notre Dame*, by all accounts a crashing failure, and in 1864 departed for California, where she was to meet the dashing Adah Isaacs Menken, from whom she hoped to learn the secrets of theatrical success. She instantly hated California, although she was apparently well received there. In 1866, by now serious enough in her ambition to take on a new pseudonym, the stage name Agnes Stanfield, she went on a theatrical tour of the South. She married one of her fellow actors two years later and spent the rest of her life hanging around trying to get parts in New York productions. While so engaged at an agency on Amity Street in 1874, she was bitten through the cartilage of her nose by the resident dog. The wound was cauterized but she died of rabies two months later. William Dean Howells, no friend to bohemians, who wrote that that generation "never said nor did anything worthy of their awful appearance," nevertheless eulogized Ada Clare, calling her fate "pathetic at all times, out-tragedies almost any other in the history of letters."

Among those in the circle who deserved better than Howells's contempt was Fitz-James O'Brien, an Irish soldier of fortune and brawler who was nicknamed Fist and Gammon O'Bouncer. He had started writing for Dickens's *Household Words* while living in Ireland, but Poe was his exemplar, and his example drew O'Brien across the sea. In America he established himself in the decade after his arrival in 1852 as a flamboyant romantic who would not divulge the names of his lovers, who shook hands with his opponent after even the worst fights, who would borrow huge sums to host banquets at Delmonico's but always paid the money back, and who would give money away when he had any of his own. He also made a name for himself as a writer of short stories, in fact rather Poe-like but with a certain charm quite their own; "The Diamond Lens" is the best-remembered. He, too, was at work on a great American novel, and it might actually have laid some claim to the title, but he enlisted in the Civil War and in 1862 died of lockjaw from an infected wound after a skirmish. H. L. Mencken later remembered him as the only significant artist to have perished in the Civil War.

The Pfaff's crowd was death-haunted, and eight of them died of other than natural causes: Clapp; Clare; O'Brien; Ned Wilkins, a playwright and the theater critic for the *Herald*, who died of pneumonia literally as a result of living in a leaky garret; the poet and songwriter Fitz-Hugh Ludlow, who died of "lungs and nerves shattered by hashish and opium," according to the historian of bohemia Albert Parry; the journalist and novelist William North and the outdoorsman and writer Henry Herbert, aka Frank Forester, who were both suicides; and the wit and gadabout George Arnold, who died of "paralysis ascribed to dissipation." Arnold was to some extent responsible for the breakup of the scene at Pfaff's. He was always a contrarian and delighted in starting arguments by defending the memory of Benedict Arnold (who was no relation). In 1862 Arnold, who was staunchly pro-Union, nevertheless could not stand the single-minded patriotic conformity of the Civil War climate and one day proposed a toast to the South. Greatly offended by this was Walt Whitman, Pfaff's greatest asset. After the ensuing fight, he shunned the place and took a great deal of the scene's remaining glamour with him, not returning until its reputation was winding down altogether, in new quarters on Twenty-fourth Street.

In its heyday Pfaff's was a crowded place, full of talk and argument, full of promising young writers hoping to get published (among them William Dean Howells, whose cool reception there perhaps accounted for his later attitude toward the bohemians), full of exiles (Clemenceau was one, for a while), and full of Whitman. The critic William Winter, a notable enemy of Walt's, wrote in later years of his "eccentric garb of rough blue and gray fabric—his hair and beard grizzled, his keen, steel-blue eyes gazing, with bland tolerance, on the frolicksome lads around him."[6] He also kept his hat on, and unbuttoned his shirt to display his hairy chest. Whitman set the tone for the others, and his enemies became the enemies of all bohemia: Thomas Bailey Aldrich, E. C. Stedman, R. H. Stoddard, Bayard Taylor, all powerful critics in their day, and known only to historians now. Whitman was more interested in expanding the boundaries of bohemia, and invited to Pfaff's his beloved stage drivers, and young doctors from New York Hospital. By that time, in the decade before the Civil War, bohemia was becoming more than a state of mind; it was an actual place, as artists, writers, actors, and pretenders moved into Bleecker, Bond, and Spring Streets, then murky and rather dangerous thoroughfares. Journalists were soon describing the area as being full of long-haired artists in garrets, semi-amateur prostitutes, and (a term that had acquired a derisive sense) "ballet dancers." The *Times* was moved to define a bohemian as "an artist or an author whose special aversion is to work."

This certainly could not be said of the sisters Victoria Woodhull and Tennessee Claflin, who were the preeminent bohemians of the 1870s, even if they were never so called at the time. Woodhull and Claflin, who appeared in New York around 1870, were ahead of their time in an extraordinary number of ways. They were somehow taken up as protegées by Commodore Vanderbilt, and set themselves up as brokers on Broad Street, decked out in what was then considered masculine attire (short hair, jackets and ties, ankle-length skirts), earning, so it was said, $500,000 at this trade within a few months. Meanwhile, both were hugely interested in the supernatural: Woodhull was a spiritualist, while Claflin described herself as a "magnetic healer"; she was alleged to have obtained stock-market tips from Vanderbilt in exchange for "healing" him. The two also published *Woodhull and Claflin's Weekly*, whose motto was "Progress, Free Thought, Untrammeled Lives." In that spirit, Woodhull announced her candidacy for President in the 1872 race, blithely disregarding the fact that women's suffrage did not exist and was not to be entered into the Constitution until nearly half a century later. Her platform was founded on women's rights, primarily, and she stood for free love and medical inspection of prostitutes. In 1870 she had presented a memorandum to Congress arguing for women's suffrage, and in early 1871, in conjunction with the convention of the National Women's Suffrage Association, addressed the House Judiciary Committee. Subsequently, she traveled the lecture circuit with Susan B. Anthony, Elizabeth Cady Stanton, and Lucretia Mott. Her 1872 race was on the Equal Rights ticket, and her Vice Presidential candidate was Frederick Douglass.

While all this was going on, the sisters were being constantly attacked and ridiculed in the press, and every skeleton was dragged out of their closet in an effort to discredit them. It was divulged, for example, that the three other sisters with whom they lived were all divorced, and various unsubstantiated rumors about their pasts were aired—some kind of blackmail, an alleged house of assignation in Cincinnati, a putative manslaughter case outstanding in Illinois. The papers also made sport of their house's two other occupants: Victoria's husband, Dr. Woodhull, a drunken ex-practitioner kept chiefly as a pet, and the ancient anarchist Stephen Pearl Andrews, responsible for the first American translation of the *Communist Manifesto*, which was duly published in the *Weekly*. The most fierce attacks appeared in the editorial pages of papers controlled by the Reverend Henry Ward Beecher (and at least one of these squibs was the work of his sister, Harriet Beecher Stowe). The sisters promptly retaliated by publishing details of Beecher's adulterous liaison with Elizabeth Tilton. Reliably, Anthony Comstock then came forward to press for their conviction on obscenity charges. The United States District Attorney, who happened to be a member of Beecher's Plymouth Church, had them jailed for three months. Beecher was roundly ridiculed and condemned, but he had the last word, maintaining his authority through it all, while the sisters faded from the public eye after their imprisonment. Their whirlwind careers had taken up a densely packed three years.

One of Woodhull and Claflin's allies was George Francis Train, himself no slouch in the convention-busting department. A Midwesterner by birth, the Champion Crank, as he called himself, pursued a knot of careers that spanned the globe and most of the century. He was variously a banker, a stock manipulator, a railroad speculator, an intimate of the Queen of Spain (who may have bankrolled his efforts to

build streetcar lines in London and in Liverpool), a hotelkeeper, a
grubstaker in the California gold rush, a friend of Marx's and Baku-
nin's, an author of popular books on foreign lands for boys, a pauper,
a vagabond, a semi-lunatic. He was arrested at some point in the 1870s
for his outspoken advocacy of free love, and William Howe's defense
of him before the court was that there were no obscenities in Train's
speeches or writings, and that if there were, he was not guilty by reason
of insanity. The court preferred the latter half of this argument, and
offered to release Train if he would plead insanity, but Train refused.
He stated that he would rather die in jail than be a hypocrite, and
cried, "Take me back to the Bastille! Away with me to the donjon!"
He stayed in the Tombs for a year, amusing himself by writing poetry
for Woodhull and Claflin's paper and, to his extreme delight, being
elected to the coveted presidency of the Murderers' Club. Every once
in a while the charade would be reenacted: Train would be taken
before the court, the court would ask him to plead insanity, and he
would shout, "Back to durance vile!" Eventually, he was put into
solitary confinement, and after a certain amount of this he caved in.
Upon his release he complained, "My lawyers did not understand me.
They are like all lawyers. They think it better to lie your way to freedom
than to suffer for the truth." He died several decades later in the Mills
#1 Shelter on Bleecker Street.

New York bohemia in the 1880s and nineties was rather lax. Artists
and writers, mostly forgotten now, succeeded each other in the boardinghouses of Washington Square and the studios of Tenth Street, in
the Italian restaurants on Sullivan and MacDougal Streets and the
French restaurants on Greene Street and University Place. The great
artist of the period was Albert Pinkham Ryder, although hardly anybody
knew it. He had been a founder of the Society of American Artists,
but by then, although he was doing his strongest work, he existed in
obscurity in a garbage-filled back room on the third floor of a tenement.
Across town, meanwhile, the successful artists of the Tile Club passed
themselves off as bohemians, and although the talents of Augustus Saint-
Gaudens, Stanford White, Edwin Austin Abbey, William Merritt Chase

et al. were considerable, their poses as a group were little more than ritualistic. Perhaps more representative of the period was a young writer named Henry Harland, who worked all day as a clerk in the Surrogate's office, and all night wrote chronicles of the Jewish ghetto on the Lower East Side, keeping himself awake with black coffee and with wet towels wrapped around his head. Almost as soon as these novels (which he published under the name Sidney Luska) began to garner favorable notices, he went to England to become the editor of *The Yellow Book*, that standard of fin-de-siècle decadence, so that the two halves of his career appear to belong to two different people.

By the middle nineties, bohemia had come to mean a constellation of widely disparate milieux, most of them oblivious to all the others. Some of these were defined entirely by their favorite resorts, and so appear less as collections of particular people than as atmospheres through which a stream of juxtaposed personalities came and went. James Ford, who published a running tally of these scenes in various newspapers over several decades under the rubric "Bohemia Invaded," could categorize them no better than by nationality, which might refer to the nationality of the restaurant in which bohemians coincided, or the nationality of the bohemians themselves. The German bohemia, for example, was essentially culinary; it prevailed at Allaire's, or Scheffel Hall, on Third Avenue and Seventeenth Street, a place best known for the occasional presence of O. Henry, a colorless former embezzler from Texas who divided his time between drinking in saloons and churning out vast numbers of short stories, dissipating his considerable talents not so much in drink as in overproduction. French bohemia was scintillated by the atmosphere in various boîtes south of Washington Square. Italian bohemia consisted of two restaurants: Buchignani's on Third Avenue, favored by performers from the Academy of Music, and Maria's, on MacDougal Street, where a whole generation of artistic types learned to eat spaghetti while simultaneously listening to a singer who called himself Mickey Finn; prominent among the noodle-twirlers were various future Ash Can School painters. The Russian, Polish, and Yiddish bohemias of the Lower East Side were

a different matter. In cafés on East Broadway and Canal, Grand, and
Rivington Streets, beginning in the late 1880s, poets, journalists, actors,
musicians, socialists, and anarchists held forth, many of them recently
transplanted from the café life of Russian and Central European cities.
A representative figure of that era was the Hebrew poet Naphtali Herz
Imber, author of the Zionist anthem "Hatikvah" and editor of the
journal *Uriel*, who had arrived in New York after pursuing an itinerary
that took him from Galicia to Vienna to Constantinople to Egypt to
Palestine to London. The Jewish and Slavic bohemias were distinctly
more heated and argumentative than their Western counterparts; in
an early hybrid coining, the locals of the former set became known as
"kibbitzarias."

The bohemian circle that attracted the most attention at the time
was centered on the aesthetes James Gibbons Huneker and Vance
Thompson and their review *Mlle. New York*. The cover of the first
issue epitomizes the scene: languid types of both sexes, wearing straw
hats, are dimly perceiving a singer on a remote stage through a haze
of cigar smoke and a barrage of empty beer steins. Today their pos-
turing appears rather empty and spoiled: they all had money and
shunned the traditional bohemian settings in favor of ostentatious
gastronomic venues—Lüchow's and Lienau's on Fourteenth Street,
Mouquin's on Sixth Avenue near Twenty-eighth, Mould's on University
Place—and they devoted as much energy and passion to the study of
tournedos and Liebfraumilch as they did to the arts and letters. Huneker, principally known as a music critic, had returned to America
after many years in Europe and was convinced of the inferiority of the
United States, a position that did not endear him to the majority of
his contemporaries, but which did in some fashion set the tone for
the Lost Generation. Like the Europeans, but unlike most of the American writers of his time, Huneker staged his work in public, doing
most of his writing at prominent tables in cafés, saloons, and restaurants. His work alternates between the mannered and the vigorous,
often within the same paragraph. He favored the European model, but
it was the American strain in him that was the strongest. He was a

disciple of the individualist anarchist Max Stirner and rather improbably spent time with Johann Most and the other New York anarchists at Justus Schwab's saloon on First Street.[7] The depictions of bohemian life in his novel *Painted Veils* and in the chronicles of *The New Cosmopolis* seem impossibly remote; it is difficult to imagine, for example, a time when furious bar brawls were waged over the relative merits of Brahms. *Mlle. New York*, for all its preening, was responsible for introducing to American readers the work of Ibsen, Strindberg, Verlaine, Verhaeren, Maeterlinck, and Hamsun. Of its domestic contributors, the best-remembered is Lafcadio Hearn, who continued to write for it from his self-imposed exile in Japan. More typical, perhaps, was Edgar Saltus, known as the Pocket Apollo; when asked what books had influenced him the most, he answered, "My own," and when he was asked to name his favorite character in fiction, he replied, "God."

Bohemia became a widespread popular fashion in the middle nineties, as a direct result of the 1894 *Harper's* serialization of George du Maurier's *Trilby*. This gaudy and melodramatic vision of life in Paris's Latin Quarter had nearly as decisive an influence on the stereotypical notion of bohemia as did Murger's stories. Its evil genius, Svengali, survives in the language as a common noun. The novel's impact at the time was formidable: it was published in book form almost immediately, and demand was such that the Mercantile Library kept one hundred copies in circulation; soon it was turned into a play with music. In spite of the fact that bohemians like Huneker denounced it as fake, and that divines fulminated against its moral failings from the pulpit, it affected the habits of American youth, particularly young women, who derived from it the courage to call themselves artists and "bachelor girls," to smoke cigarettes and drink Chianti. In what must be one of the very earliest examples of subsidiary marketing, there soon appeared Trilby ice cream, Trilby shoes, Trilby sausages, Trilby cigars and cigarettes, Trilby cocktails, and the town of Trilby, Florida, which featured as its centerpiece Svengali Square. The Trilby hat lives on today, and the 1931 movie version of the story, filmed as *Svengali*, with John Barrymore in the title role, appears from time to time on television as a relic of pre-cinematic sensibility that modern audiences may find altogether baffling.

While all this was going on, there existed also a bohemia far from the public eye, from fashionable restaurants and cafés. At the base of all the bohemian legends lay a core of deep poverty, of starvation, consumption, winters spent without heat and days at a time without food. One reason why cafés played such a central part in so many artistic movements was that the undiscovered struggling types could go to them to cadge meals and drinks from their more established fellows under the pretext of exchanging ideas. But it was the superficial color of bohemian deprivation that sold newspapers, not its essence, so no attention was paid to groups such as the one with which Stephen Crane lived on East Twenty-third Street at the very beginning of his career, whose members pawned everything they owned to buy paper and canvas, and who broke up the furniture for firewood. Crane made a very minimal living by selling the occasional newspaper sketch, but for three years he mostly went hungry, and walked around the city to stay warm in the winters. During this time he wrote *Maggie: A Girl of the Streets, The Red Badge of Courage, George's Mother*, a considerable number of short stories, and at least part of *Flowers of Asphalt*, his lost novel about a boy prostitute. He spent rather little time arguing aesthetics in cafés, although it is interesting to note that after his rise to fame, feature writers began inventing a more conventionally anecdotal bohemian past for him, alleging, for example, that he had been a tenant in Madame Katherine Blanchard's "House of Genius" on Washington Square South, a rooming house that may or may not have lodged Willa Cather, Theodore Dreiser, O. Henry, Frank Norris, and Adelina Patti. Crane was the very antithesis of a snob, and his interest in and involvement with all sorts of people made him further susceptible to rumor. He was said to be a drunk who had gravitated to the Bowery and scratched out his stories between binges; this tale was probably the result of a distorted reading and retelling of his sketch of Bowery life, "An Experiment in Misery," in which he wrote that "the root of Bowery life is a sort of cowardice." His defense of a prostitute from an attempted shakedown by the notorious Lieutenant Charles Becker of the vice squad brought him no end of troubles, including a protracted court case and gossip that he was a pimp. What probably most galled those with an interest in the society and market appeal of bohemia was Crane's unavailability; instead of appearing at salons and dinner parties and theatrical evenings, he was traveling in the West, or covering the war in Cuba, or collapsed from tuberculosis, which killed him at the age of twenty-eight.

The next stage in the history of New York bohemia was affected by the rise of the automobile, which around 1910 made available the converted stables in Washington Mews and MacDougal Alley as dwellings, once the horses had been moved out to the country. The general vicinity of Washington Square had long been a bohemian nexus, of course, perfect for, among other things, its coincidence of elements of gentility and genteel poverty. There was Club A at 3 Fifth Avenue, for example, a top-drawer salon whose visitors included Mark Twain, Jack London, Upton Sinclair, and Maxim Gorky, all of them very successful radicals. Meanwhile, just a few blocks away at Greenwich Avenue and Christopher Street stood the Working Girls' Home, a saloon so called "simply because it was not," where John Masefield worked for some years as porter and general handyman. A little farther down, at Fourth Street and Sixth Avenue, was the Golden Swan, more familiarly known as the Bucket of Blood, or the Hell Hole, a locale popular with the Hudson Dusters, where the waste-disposal system consisted of a pig kept in the cellar. The area's new bohemian arrivals discovered the place and, inaugurating a pattern that would continue through the century, lost no time in gentrifying it. Soon the Hudson Dusters were relegated to the most distant of the saloon's back rooms. It was said they were depressed by their failure to impress the young bohemian women, who included Dorothy Day, then writing *The Eleventh Virgin* and drinking prodigiously. By the end of the decade, it was the bohemian pioneers of the Village who were being pushed back by a new, slicker crowd, whom they called the "half-villagers" and by whom they were in turn dubbed the "former people."

The middle teens saw Greenwich Village become dense with sub-bohemias. There was a radical milieu, several groupings of theater people, a bohemia consisting of forward-looking landlords, and the rather twee and pretentious bohemia of the tearooms. The first two of these have been amply documented: the Liberal Club, Polly's Restaurant, *The Masses* on the one hand; the Cherry Lane and Provincetown Playhouses on the other. These were the big noises that came out of the Village then and made it glamorous, a magnet for all the local geniuses of the hinterlands and the repressed artistic souls of the suburbs. When pilgrims arrived in the Village, however, it was the other two manifestations of bohemia that they actually confronted. The tearoom craze began gradually enough around 1916 with the Mad Hatter, the Purple Pup, Romany Marie's (run by a former member of Emma Goldman's circle who decided to make hay from her gypsy background; her place featured tea-leaf and palm reading). There was the Pirates' Den, with the employees decked out in bandannas and eye patches, cutlasses dangling from their belts. A gang of Irish street kids tried to engage the waiters in a fight, thinking they were the genuine article; when the owner called the cops, he was instead arrested on a Sullivan Law violation for having a brace of cutlasses hanging on the wall. The Mad Hatter was reincarnated as Down the Rabbit Hole, or, properly speaking, eloH tibbaR eht nwoD, where local youths did their part to improve the atmosphere by throwing dead cats in through the open door. After 1919, whimsy became epidemic, as places with names like the Mouse-Trap and the Vermilion Hound, the Will o' the Wisp and Ye Pollywogge opened one after another. There was a tearoom called La Bohème and another called Trilby's Waffle Shop. The Village had become a theme park of bohemia.

Even before this, however, the Village had become an object of scorn and a target for profit. Sinclair Lewis called it "Hobohemia," and Irvin S. Cobb dubbed it "Hallroomania," noted for its "table d'hôttentots." An entrepreneur named Guido Bruno, who claimed at various times to be Italian, Serbian, and Austrian, rented a vast garret on Washington Square and promoted it as an artistic mecca, roping in such aging

figures as Frank Harris and Sadakichi Hartmann, whose claim to notoriety was by then reduced to his tale of an afternoon spent frying
eggs with Walt Whitman. Bruno issued a series of one-shot little magazines with funds he squeezed from Thomas Edison's forlorn son
Charles, and set up the Thimble Theater, his attempt to compete with
the Provincetown Players, hiring to manage it the self-promoting tramp
poet Harry Kemp. Bruno may not in fact have made a great deal of
money at these pursuits; he vanished from the scene in the mid-1920s.
He was succeeded by professionals who had a much better grasp of
the profits to be made. Most prominent was Vincent Pepe, the largest
landlord in the neighborhood and the renovation king of his time, who
quickly got a lock on the housing market and pushed rents up continually, and served as a model and an inspiration for several generations of future bohemian slumlords.

Before World War I, the air downtown was laden with the certainty
of approaching utopia. For all the varying levels of seriousness, social
consciousness, levity, ambition, and mental stability that were present
in Greenwich Village, nearly all the events, publications, meetings,
and performances were informed by a desire to remake the world. The
loosing of chains of convention and the reinvention of life underlay
everything from the saturnalia of the magazine balls to the demonstrations in favor of Colorado miners and Paterson millworkers to the
varyingly daring poetry of everyone from Edna St. Vincent Millay to
Harry Kemp. Two events of 1913 appear as exemplary in this regard.
They were both slight, almost unnoticed blips, but despite their eva-
nescence—possibly to a certain extent because of it—they contain the
humor and retrospectively visible pathos of the time, the sense of might-
have-been that wreathes our image of the freewheeling prewar bohemia.
First Ellis O. Jones, an associate editor of *Life* (the pre-Luce humor
magazine) and a member of the editorial staff of *The Masses*, sent out a
press release proclaiming the establishment of the Republic of Washington Square. The notice was generally treated as a gag, and Don
Marquis and Franklin P. Adams took note of the upcoming ceremony
in their columns with a requisite deadpan. The police, who had also

been invited, failed to chuckle. The revolution was set for eleven o'clock on a Monday morning at, oddly enough, the Central Park Mall, a setting far from Greenwich Village that was both inconvenient and indicative of a certain seriousness on Jones's part. When the appointed hour came, a slight drizzle started; only Jones and a handful of his friends had shown up. The police, however, arrived in massed ranks, with machine guns, ambulances, and black marias, and carted Jones away in one of the latter. He later blamed the rain for the failure of his coup.

A few months later, the Free Republic of Greenwich Village was proclaimed with even less fanfare by Gertrude Drick, a transplanted Texan and a pupil of John Sloan's. Drick was known to one and all as "Woe" and she passed out black-bordered cards bearing this single word; when asked why, she always replied, "Because woe is me." She discovered a neglected but accessible staircase (now sealed) that led to the top of the Washington Square arch, and on a fall evening led Sloan, Marcel Duchamp, and three actors, Betty Turner, Forrest Mann, and Charles Ellis, up there. They carried Chinese lanterns, red balloons, hot-water bags for sitting on, and supplies of food and wine. Woe read a Greenwich Village declaration of independence, proclaimed the existence of the republic, and everyone fired cap pistols and released the red balloons. The party went on until dawn. In the morning, passersby noticed clusters of red balloons in the neighborhood trees.

What is notable about these invisible secessions—the one slightly crazed, the other somewhat ironic—is that they actually named the thing that all the inhabitants of the Greenwich Village bohemia of that time were aiming for, a revolution in more than just a legislative sense, a free territory untrammeled by convention. Greenwich Village was then very distant from the rest of the country, in manners and mores, in sense of justice, in sense of humor, in sexuality and egalitarianism, a distance that was far greater than anything comparable in the present media-dominated era. Josephine Herbst characterized the time as the "incomparably freewheeling years before the first World War, when modernism had not lost its connection with revolutionary thinking in all social and ethical fields." Soon, however, came the war, anti-German hysteria, the Red Scare, Prohibition, factional feuds, career-ism, money-grubbing, and disillusionment.

After the figures of the prewar bohemia had drifted off to obscurity or teaching jobs or suburban marriages or fame, the only one left carrying the banner for the old ways was the pathetic Maxwell Bod-enheim. This martyr to poetry experienced a few flirtations with suc-cess, mostly as a result of his now-forgotten novels, but he never managed to establish himself. Some combination of obstinacy, chronic drunkenness, and hard-core unconventionality kept him a failure and also kept him trying. Over the years he became a joke and a bum, selling his poems on the street to buy drinks, while still persuaded of his stature as a laureate, haunting several further generations of bo-hemians with the vision both of how they were about to sell out and how they could easily decline. Bodenheim, dragging his tales of past glory behind him, was the Marley's ghost of bohemia. In 1954 he was murdered with his wife in a Third Avenue flophouse by a lunatic fellow barfly.

If the condition of orphans and drifters was invisible, that of bo-hemians was imaginary. Their mode of life was not a material assign-ment but a psychic choice, or perhaps a psychic necessity, like a religious vocation. Thus, it may seem that they do not belong in this section at all, that their lot is rather optional and casual, that they could have stuck with the comfortable patterns of their forebears, who probably were not forced to live in a corner or a sewer. However, it should be noted that bohemians—many of whom did in fact come out of broken families and failed farms, not to mention various kinds of European misery, including the pogroms of Russia—were also im-migrants, even if they reversed the trend and came from the interior of the country. Is it really less of a burden to sacrifice material certainty for the possibility of free thought than to sacrifice ethnic continuity for the sake of someday owning a store? That the bohemians lived in an imaginary city did not mean that they did not also have to live in the actual one, with all its hardships and terrors. Their choice made them have to use two maps at once. The ambition, always potential, to align the plan or the real city with that of the model in their heads was heroic, even if it was usually invisible.

4 · CARNIVAL

THE UNTHINKING USE OF THE TERM
"MELTING POT" BEGS A SIGNIFI-
CANT QUESTION. IF THE PROCESS IN-
VOLVED IS ONE OF TAKING A VARIED
assortment of people of very different national
backgrounds, mostly paupers and peons
from semi-feudal societies with an admixture
of victims of prejudice and persecution, and
dropping them into a kettle where they will
be subjected to brand-new indignities and
discomforts, but with the alleviating promise
that such treatment will eventually stop and
that they will emerge from this stewpot as
equally functioning standard-issue Americans, does the cooking not require an awe-
some heat, a fire of such volatility that it could
easily erupt and blow the kitchen to smith-
ereens? The poor sections of Manhattan in
the nineteenth century were in fact tinderboxes, literally as well as figuratively, since

fire was an everyday occurrence among those shacks and rookeries sloppily made of wood and insulated with newspapers and rags, so that haphazard or unattended cooking fires could strike sparks that would engulf the house, and often its neighbors as well, within minutes. The population mix and disposition were similarly poised for conflagration, and it was set off many times. Possibly the only thing that kept New York City from being destroyed completely during various riots was the absence for the rioters of both a coherent leadership and a single, rallying goal.

The popular insurrections in Europe of the same era possess a clarity of purpose—at least in retrospect—that makes them appear as historical stages, spasmodic passages in a gradual social evolution. The riots of New York City that chronologically paralleled the revolutions of 1830, or the widespread uprisings of 1848, or the Commune of 1871, can claim no such distinction. They simply appear as rampages, headless and tailless and flailing about. One reason for this is that while Europe possessed theorists and an exchange of ideas, and an informed and often enlightened proletariat who had a very good idea of how they were being abused and what to do about it, New York's lumpenproletariat was prey to a variety of opportunists and demagogues who could sway them over any trivial issue of territory or obscure vendetta with the sole aim of increasing their own personal power. It was a matter of setting a match to the powder keg. The similarities between such riots and the style of celebration that marked holidays and other popular festivals suggest that in some way they were one and the same, that they were carnivals where the collected miseries of the population were acted out with torches and clubs and rocks. They represented a groping toward a new form of society, conceived as a vast dance in streets reconfigured by bodies and by the destruction of the buildings not available to those bodies. Unable to imagine social stability as anything but repression, because that was the only form in which they had ever experienced it, the rioters sought a state of permanent riot.

The history of popular outbreaks in New York City is long and tangled. There were riots long before the island could even be called a city. Racial antagonisms surfaced as early as 1712, and erupted in 1741, in the so-called Slave Plot, when black men tried to take over Manhattan—or so it was alleged—but were defeated and publicly executed on an island in the middle of the Collect Pond. The Doctors' Riot of 1788 was a bizarre incident that was sparked when citizens got wind of the fact that medical students were robbing graves in search of bodies for experimental dissection. Nearly all the city's physicians were driven from the island, which was in a state of turmoil for days.

For years, New Year's Eve, the Fourth of July, and later Halloween were occasions for disorders of varying size, harmless enough for the most part, principally distinguished by a lot of drinking, crowds that ranged up and down streets, loud singing, and the stealing of shop signs. As the city became more populated, the tone shifted, and the crowds started becoming mobs. On New Year's Eve, 1829, a crowd gathered on the Bowery in the early evening, carrying on in the usual way, making noise with pots and pans, drums and rattles, horns and whistles. The horseplay got a little more expansive as people threw missiles filled with flour and lime at the red front of a grog shop, bleaching it, and then they seized a cart and hurtled with it down Hester Street. The city watch arrived and collared and hit some of the merrymakers, but the crowd asserted itself, beat up the watchmen, and rescued their friends. The body then surged in a zigzag down Chatham Street, then down Pearl, across on Cortlandt, and finally down Broadway, adding numbers as they went, breaking up boxes and barrels left in the street. They arrived at South Ferry at around one o'clock, by now having swelled to four thousand. They tried unsuccessfully to tear up the iron fence at the Battery, and roamed around the neighborhood, overturning carts and breaking windows. They started back up Broadway and stopped in front of the City Hotel, where a loud party was in progress. The watchmen reappeared, perhaps fearing a raid on the festivities inside, but members of the crowd took a long wagon rope hanging nearby and cut it into three-foot lengths, with which weapons the revelers once again sent the watchmen running. For some reason, the crowd then continued back up Broadway, breaking up in the Five Points around dawn.

It took only a few years for such carryings-on to lead to serious consequences. Most of the city's poor, especially the Irish, were loyal to the Democratic Party, and incited by such local politicians as the interesting but misguided Mike Walsh, they were opposed to the abolition of slavery, the local reasoning being that freeing black slaves in the South could only have a damaging effect on the lot of white wage slaves in the North. In 1833, when a prominent local Abolitionist named Lewis Tappan read the Constitution of the Anti-Slavery Society in public on the Fourth of July, he was shouted down by members of the crowd, who then followed him home and broke windows in his house, as well as in the houses of other patrician Abolitionists who lived in the then fashionably residential Rose Street. By the following summer, things were even worse. On the night of July 7, 1834, a black congregation was gathered at the Chatham Chapel, on Chatham Street, to hear a sermon by a visiting black minister. In the middle of the service a group of whites appeared, representing themselves as members of the New York Sacred Music Society, and asserting that they had rights to the use of the chapel on that night. What happened next is unclear, but somehow a brawl occurred, with chairs and lamps being hurled around, and kids (race not specified in the available reports) throwing pews down from the balcony. On the parquet the pews were broken up and the shards were wielded by the fighters. The cops showed up and cleared the building, but the brawl continued in the street, by now reinforced on the white side by the usual available b'hoys. Once again, Lewis Tappan was recognized by the mob, who followed him and pelted his house with stones and bricks.

On the following night, July 8, a crowd of whites forced their way into the chapel and held an impromptu meeting, with speeches attacking abolition. That the focus of the mob's anger was not specifically limited to race can be seen by the way it responded to agitators waiting outside who struck a completely different chord. The current manager of the Bowery Theater was a man named Farren, who happened to be an English subject. A week or so earlier, he had fired an actor named McKinney, who had been giving him a great deal of trouble. McKinney seized the occasion to address the house from the balcony, claiming that Farren had insulted the flag. He made an appeal to the b'hoys, who were ignorant of the fact that Farren had actually been born in Ireland. Soon handbills appeared on the streets, alleging that Farren had cursed all Yankees and vowed to dupe them on any pretext. The idea was to rally both the Irish and the Nativists against the unfortunate Farren. On the night of July 8, the agitators succeeded in turning the mob's vengeance away from abolition and toward Farren. The mob broke into the theater and stopped the performance, completely disregarding the fact that the benefit production of *Metamora* on stage was headed by the b'hoy favorite Ned Forrest, and tore up the place looking for Farren, who had escaped. Soon the mayor, the Police Justice, a few aldermen, and one hundred of the watch came in, threw out the invaders, and restored order. Outside, the mob switched gears once again and headed back down to Rose Street, to Tappan's house, where they smashed the doors and whatever windows remained intact, destroyed the interior, hauled the furniture out on the street, piled it up, doused it with oil, and set it on fire. As the contents of the house were being handed down, one of the rioters noticed among the effects a portrait of George Washington. According to contemporary accounts that quickly became legend, he seized the painting and cried, "For God's sake, don't burn Washington!" and the cry was taken up by the entire mob. By this time, the firemen had arrived and the crowd soon dissolved.

Five days of rioting ensued. On July 10, mobs attacked residences and stores on Spring, Catherine, Thompson, and Reade Streets, and rampaged in their own territory, on Paradise Square. It was reported afterward that the mobs had appeared suspiciously well organized, with runners passing bulletins between different groups, and posted scouts who warned of approaches by the cops. On both the tenth and the eleventh, property held by blacks was destroyed, including, on the first night, churches on Centre and Leonard Streets, a school on Orange (Baxter) Street, and tenements on Mulberry Street and in the Five Points. Dozens of white-owned buildings were looted and burned as well, and five brothels were invaded and the whores taken out and gang-raped. A passerby was discovered to be English; his eyes were gouged out and his ears cut off. It was rumored that all houses in the Five Points would be destroyed save those that had a candle burning in the window. Instantly, every house in the area featured candles in every available window. A detachment of troops eventually appeared, at around one o'clock, and dispersed the mob. The following night was marked by more of the same, including the destruction of a black church on Spring Street and the erection of barricades across Chatham Square, but again the 27th Infantry arrived, though a bit late in the game, and dispersed the mob. The authorities could not let things get too heated, but at the same time they do not appear to have been overly energetic in their efforts to calm the troubles.

The following year, the whole city was distracted from its controversies by the great fire of December 16 and 17, 1835. On a night when the thermometer plunged to seventeen below zero, thirteen acres of buildings in the city's central commercial and financial district were destroyed, a field of ruin that, beginning on Beaver Street (then Merchant Street), stretched north to Wall Street, east to the river, south to Coenties Slip, and west nearly to Broad Street. During the course of the fire, crowds came down from the Five Points to loot and assist in the spread of the conflagration. One man caught in the act of setting fire to a building was set upon by a group of respectable local citizens, who lynched him. The following week, "much valuable property was recovered . . . in the hovels of the Bowery and the Five Points." The upshot of the disaster was that banks suspended operations, insurance companies were unable to pay off claims, businesses were unable to rebuild, and great numbers of people were thrown out of work. Prices rose, and, by the following autumn, flour had risen first to seven dollars a barrel, then to twelve, and bread had become scarce. The mix of scarcity, inflation, and unemployment worsened, until by 1837 it had

grown into a full-fledged panic. On February 2, a crowd heard demagogues in City Hall Park assert that flour was being hoarded by
plutocrats upstate, and it surged forth to attack a wheat-and-flour
warehouse on Washington Street between Dey and Cortlandt. Rather
than looting its contents, however, they threw barrels and sacks of the
stuff out of windows, shattering the barrels; the sacks, which landed
unharmed, were torn open by the mob and the contents strewn all
over the street. Altogether five hundred barrels of flour and a thousand
bushels of wheat were thus squandered. At length the police arrived,
but the crowd merely headed east and repeated the assault at another
storehouse on Coenties Slip, there ravaging thirty barrels of flour and
a hundred bushels of wheat. The next day the price of flour rose by
a dollar a barrel.

The following decade was devoid of major riots but marked by nearly
constant gang wars, street fights, bar brawls that escalated. In 1845,
for example, on one of the occasions when the Bowery Theater caught
fire, the Municipal Police arrived on the scene wearing uniforms for
the very first time. As they went about their usual business of clearing
a path through the crowd for the firemen to pass through, the Bowery
crowd refused to budge, laughing and calling them lackeys. Then
somebody shouted that the cops had adopted uniforms in order to
imitate London bobbies. This proved a reliable trigger; the b'hoys
attacked the cops, and a minor riot ensued.

Anti-English sentiment was most successfully exploited in the Astor
Opera House Riot of 1849. Whatever the actual sources of this uprising,
in Ned Forrest's jealousy or Macready's arrogance, there is little question that the red rag used to incite the mob was simply Macready's
nationality, a convenient tool for uniting the various Bowery factions,
and that the crowd's ire was further aroused simply by that visible
analogue of the class system—the Bowery theater (at whose flagship
Ned Forrest was then playing *Macbeth*) vs. the uptown theater. The
Astor Place Opera House was just two years old when the celebrated
English actor George Macready was engaged to play, coincidentally,
Macbeth. Its patrons were the city's leaders and substantial citizens,

none of whom, by that time, would venture into any of the playhouses on the Bowery, the upper portion of which lay a mere two blocks from the Opera House. At Macready's first appearance, on May 7, when he was driven from the stage by "groans, jeers, hisses, cat-calls, and cock-crowing," and a shower of rotten apples, lemons, eggs, potatoes, pieces of wood, and finally a bottle of asafetida that broke at his feet, the hecklers shouted not only "Down with the English hog!" and "Three groans for codfish aristocracy!" but also a bizarre slogan meant to bring race into the picture, "Macready and Nigger Douglass!" oddly connecting the Britannic tragedian with Frederick Douglass.

The leaders and substantial citizens of the city pleaded with Macready not to give in to the mob and to go on with his next scheduled performance, on the tenth. The petition with which he was presented to this end was signed by, among a host of others, Washington Irving, John Jacob Astor, and the obscure Herman Melville. The house was equally restive on this night, however, and in the fourth scene of the first act Macready broke character to point out the ringleaders to police waiting in the wings, who locked them in the theater's cellar, where they started a small fire which was not discovered until much later but which did not do too much damage. Outside, a huge crowd lined the front of the theater. An agitator among them (Alvin Harlow believes it was Edward Judson, aka Ned Buntline) shrewdly exploited the event's class undertone by shouting, "You can't go in there without kid gloves on! I paid for a ticket, and they wouldn't let me in because I didn't have kid gloves and a white vest, damn 'em!" The rioters meanwhile tore up the iron railings around a house on the nearby corner of Lafayette Place and used them as clubs, and raided a marble yard across the street for chips, which they hurled at the theater, breaking windows and eventually hitting a chandelier, shattering some of its pendants, and showering the audience, who retreated under the balcony and other projections along the side walls. It may again have been Judson who then exclaimed, "I luxuriate in the scene!" Incredibly, the play was still going on inside. As the audience loudly cheered the duel between Macbeth and Macduff, presumably for a mixture of reasons, the Seventh Regiment came up the Bowery. The mob began stoning them, and their division commander gave the order to fire over the heads of the crowd. Another agitator yelled that the soldiers wouldn't dare fire anything but blanks, and then the commander give the order to shoot to kill, resulting in a toll that was reported as twenty-two dead and more than fifty wounded. The next few days saw sporadic rioting. Macready had been spirited out of the theater by the front door, to New Rochelle, then to Boston and back to England, but people kept reporting sightings of him around town, and fighting predictably ensued. While the Opera House was guarded by troops with cannon, mobs clashed with the police at Waverly Place and Broadway, and set up barricades on Ninth Street just east of the Bowery, where they pelted the cops with marble chips for an hour. Later Isaiah Rynders admitted to having bought and distributed fifty or sixty tickets to the play, and his lieutenant Judson, who had been arrested at the scene, was sent to Blackwell's Island for a short term. The Opera House was closed for six months while repairs were made, but its reputation never really recovered; it was for a long time popularly known as the Massacre Opera House, or the Upper-Row House on Disaster Place.

In the 1850s, riot followed riot, but these were mostly gangland affairs that generally did not result in wholesale destruction of real estate or the killing or maiming of uninvolved parties. Of course, the fact that the better part of the able-bodied white males of the Bowery and the Five Points and scattered outlying areas were in some way connected with the gangs means that these riots were brought home to every New Yorker, especially anyone living south of Fourteenth Street. Even the feud between Tammany and Nativist elements that resulted in the killing of Bill the Butcher Poole was capped by a funeral parade that itself spun off a riot and was really another vast popular carnival, as the cortege wound its way through the downtown streets less as a ritual of mourning than as an occasion for seizing the streets. The Dead Rabbit and Police Riots of 1857 suspended ordinary rules, and allowed for looting, armed robbery, and assorted other violence. The year was a particularly explosive one for the city—even more so than was the norm during the administration of Fernando Wood—as municipal instability led to bank failures and factory closings, and late autumn saw mobs agitating for relief and employment and threatening the arsenals.

The situation was patched up, but only temporarily. The next insurrection was to be the city's most volcanic, the closest it has ever come to actual revolution. In the summer of 1863, Robert E. Lee at the head of a large Confederate force was moving north toward Pennsylvania. When reports of this movement came through to the Union lines, all available troops in New York City were mobilized and sent to points south and west, leaving the city's military strength reduced to about a thousand National Guardsmen, two hundred members of the Invalid Corps, and some seven hundred assorted soldiers, sailors, and marines from the crews of ships docked in the Hudson River. The previous April, Lincoln had called for a draft of 300,000 men, which order was set to be carried out in New York on Saturday, July 11. The draft was tremendously unpopular in the slums, not only because their denizens harbored widespread anti-Republican and anti-Union sentiments but because, under the system that obtained then, a man could be exempt from the draft upon paying a fee of $300, an option that was not available to the residents of the Five Points and the Bowery. Agitation in opposition to the draft was mainly instigated, it was said at the time, by a shadowy organization called the Knights of the Golden Circle, but such agitation was mostly rumor; nothing terribly definite was known about the existence of organized opposition. So it was with some apprehension but without alarm that officers of the Provost Marshal began to draw names from the wheel in the Ninth District draft office at Third Avenue and Forty-sixth Street. A crowd, ominous but quiet, stood outside in the street as the first 1,236 names were drawn, and then the draft board decided to knock off until Monday, when they would pick the remaining 264.

Sunday passed without incident, although rumors spread that gangsters downtown were stockpiling rocks, bricks, and clubs for use as weapons. That night the slums were lit up by large bonfires in the streets. Monday morning, just after dawn, a crowd was observed moving north and west, and then up Eighth and Ninth Avenues, gathering strength as it went, with detachments sent into factories along the way to recruit the workers. Around eight o'clock the large crowd had convened in a lot just east of Central Park and was being addressed by agitators. Then it moved again, streaming in two columns down Fifth and Sixth Avenues, joining together at Forty-seventh Street, turning east to Third Avenue, and then down to Forty-sixth Street. Estimates of its size vary from five thousand to fifteen thousand. Asbury cites a witness who timed the column and found that it took between twenty and twenty-five minutes to pass a given spot. Meanwhile another crowd had gathered in front of the other draft office, at Broadway and Twenty-ninth Street. Police reinforcements were rapidly dispatched to both spots and telegrams were sent around the city and to Brooklyn, calling out all reserves. At ten o'clock the members of the "Black Joke" Volunteer Fire Company Number 33 arrived, having evidently just learned that their ordinary dispensations from military conscription had been suspended under wartime rules, and, so it was said, that their leader had been picked in the first round. An agitator fired into the air, and the crowd reacted predictably. The firemen rushed the door, broke in, and destroyed the wheel. More rioters poured into the building, destroyed everything in it (except, apparently, the draft records, which were saved by an employee), and set fire to it. As other fire companies arrived to put out the blaze, they were in turn attacked by the crowd.

The rest of the day was marked by pitched, running battles in all parts of town. After fierce fighting, the fifty-two policemen who were guarding the State Armory at Twenty-first Street and Second Avenue acknowledged defeat and fled through a tiny hole eighteen feet above the ground in the rear of the building, going back to the 18th Precinct station house a few blocks away, which was soon burned to the ground. Rioters seized the armory and worked their way up to the gun room, the door of which they barricaded to prevent a raid. More police had come meanwhile and blocked the entrance to the building, and the mob responded by setting the place on fire. The armory was wood and burned quickly; the rioters in the gun room at first were unaware, and then couldn't get the door open quickly enough. By the time they had unblocked it, the floor had collapsed, killing scores.

There were mobs throughout the city (their numbers were estimated as between fifty thousand and seventy thousand; the estimate of the criminal population was put at between seventy thousand and eighty thousand, presumably including anyone who had ever been arrested). The mobs varied their targets, looting shops, wrecking and burning police station houses and the homes of government and police officials, and attacking blacks. Three blacks were lynched the first day of rioting, blacks' homes were attacked and burned downtown, and restaurants were invaded with the object of beating the black waiters. An assault was also mounted on the home of Horace Greeley, New York's most prominent Republican, and on the office of his newspaper, the *Tribune*. Greeley fled the latter building and was hidden under a tablecloth by a waiter in a nearby restaurant. His newspaper office was seized, and then retaken by police, but the fight there continued; the *Tribune* was attacked four times in three days. That night, a torrential downpour put out most of the fires throughout the city. It was speculated that the better part of the city might have burned to the ground were it not for this bit of meteorological luck, since most of the city's fire companies (which were still manned by volunteers at the time) had joined the mob.

Wednesday began with the killing of two black men downtown and with the erection of barricades across First and Ninth Avenues, for which telegraph poles were chopped down, and which were built up with lampposts, carts, crates, and assorted furniture. A mob captured the Union Steam Works on Twenty-second Street amid heavy fighting, but it was to be their last victory, although sporadic fighting continued through the week. According to one of the Volunteer Specials, a group of private citizens who had been sworn in as deputies for the occasion, a corpse among the proletarian dead was found to possess "aristocratic features, well-cared-for hands, and a fair white skin." Under overalls he was wearing cashmere trousers, an embroidered vest, and a linen shirt. He was never identified, and his body was carried off and probably buried with other dead rioters, under buildings in the Five Points. This story gave credence to the rumors that the mob was being secretly led by Confederate agents, which was certainly not impossible, but at the same time suggests the inability of the city's opinion-makers to believe that the Five Pointers could lead themselves. The accounts of the time, as well as Herbert Asbury, echoing them more than sixty years later, repeatedly cite the mob's "cowardice," and pass over its temporary victories as lucky hits. While it is true that the mob was cowardly in attacking the defenseless, and that they would in any case appear cowardly in contrast to the police, who fought while vastly outnumbered at all times, it is nevertheless a huge assumption to make. What is uniformly striking about all accounts of these riots is that none of the rioters is ever identified by name.[1] The participants are designated solely by size, as "giants," when this characterization will handily color the story of the policeman who killed such a character with one blow.

That the mob was racist is unquestionable: eighteen blacks were lynched and five were forced into the river to drown, while seventy more vanished without trace, and dozens, perhaps hundreds, were forced from their homes, which were burned or otherwise rendered uninhabitable. The Colored Orphan Asylum on Fifth Avenue was also looted and burned, and a little girl was killed; the rest of the children were spirited out the back way and taken to safety on Blackwell's Island. Whether race, or even the draft, was the primary motive of the riot is another matter. The rage present was scattershot, directed variously at the government, the police, the powerful, the rich, as well as at the blacks—people as powerless as the rioters, but whom the mob may have thought were better-favored. The Draft Riots were an outbreak of strong emotion but deep ignorance. There is every indication that the insurgence was spontaneous and essentially led by no one. Such agitators as there were (and the commentators are uniformly silent about the actual content of their speeches) probably did not do more than urge the crowd to attack the draft offices. It is not impossible that there might have been astute demagogues lurking in the wings; such a man was Isaiah Rynders (although by the time of the Draft Riots he was old and had declined in power), who in his day might have attempted a seizure of civil power had he possessed the appropriate mixture of sophistication and gall. Some of the events following the riots support the idea of a conspiracy, whether of Confederate or other origin.

In May 1864 two newspapers published a proclamation by Lincoln asking for a draft of an additional 400,000 men. A riot had nearly begun before the text was proven to be a hoax, the two newspapers were suppressed, and a scapegoat was found and thrown in jail. In November of that year, small fires were discovered in thirteen hotels, as well as in ships in port, in lumberyards, factories, stores, and in Tammany Hall. All were found to have been set by the same method: in each location was found a black bag containing paper, rosin, turpentine, and a solution of phosphorous in water. The inclusion of Tammany Hall in the list sounds distinctly odd, although, if there is merit to the Confederate plot angle, it might actually be bolstered by the targeting of that club, whose leader then was Boss Tweed, as pro-war as he was pro-Irish, and whose ability to straddle both sides in the quarrel had allowed him to restore some peace after the riots. The following July, Barnum's Museum, which had been damaged when the hotel next door had been set on fire in November, was totally destroyed, along with the whole rest of its block. As the fire raged, looters took advantage of it to raid the area, and were noticed standing in front of empty stores, hawking their former contents.

The Draft Riots are not claimed by New York as one of the great events in its history. They are considered an embarrassment, and a large percentage of the city's population have no idea that an insurrection on a vast scale ever took place in their municipality. There are no plaques to mark the sites of battles, no museum exhibits devoted to artifacts, and no perennial feature stories in newspapers on the anniversary of the occasion. Alvin F. Harlow, the Bowery's historian, devotes all of four sentences to the riots in his record of the street:

The Astor Place Opera House riot of 1849, as depicted by
Currier and Ives

The firemen's procession passing the Washington monument
in Union Square, September 1, 1858. From *Valentine's*
Manual for 1861

The Draft Riots, 1863: the scene on Broadway. From a
contemporary feature in the *New York Illustrated News*

The Communist rally in Tompkins Square Park. From the
Daily Graphic, July 27, 1877

"This chronicle has little to do with the Draft Riots, as there was no serious disorder on the Bowery, and few Bowery residents had anything to do with the trouble"—notwithstanding the fact that the core of the participants unquestionably came from the Five Points, a block away.

Nevertheless, their impact is hard to overlook. The numbers alone are eloquent: killed were possibly two thousand rioters, about a hundred black people, three policemen, and around fifty soldiers and guardsmen; the wounded included a minimum of eight thousand rioters, three hundred of the military, and virtually every cop in the city. More than one hundred buildings were burned down, and scores in addition were severely damaged. The property loss was set at $5 million, not counting the much greater loss in business. The police and military seized 11,000 firearms; they also raided the slums and appropriated anything that looked as if did not belong there. As a newspaper account put it:

> Mahogany and rosewood chairs with brocade upholstering, marble-top tables and stands, costly paintings and hundreds of delicate and valuable mantel ornaments are daily found in low hovels. Every person in whose possession these articles are found disclaims all knowledge of the same, except that they found them in the street, and took them in to prevent their being burned. The entire city will be searched, and it is expected that the greatest portion of the property taken from the buildings sacked by the mob will be recovered.[2]

This conjures up the image of desperate rioters, dodging grape and canister shot, running through the burning streets with their pockets stuffed with mantel ornaments. The passage also underlines a fixation of the propertied and educated classes of the time, which turns up again and again in contemporary accounts of the lives of the poor: that the wretches were foreign to beauty, that they dwelled among unrelieved hideousness. The lettering in their signs is invariably described as "crude," their attempts at decoration "pathetic" or "low." Perhaps the Draft Riots were, among other things, a critique of aesthetic standards in architecture and ornamentation.

As the city grew after the Civil War, the outbreaks of class violence were more efficiently contained by the police to within the districts of the poor, and they could, thus, be more successfully ignored by the rest of the population. Such troubles as made the front pages and survived in the lore tend to concern issues that could seem parochial to the uninvolved. The fighting that broke out in 1875 between Orangemen and Irish Catholics in the course of a parade on the West Side is much more often cited by general histories and memoirs than is the Tompkins Square Park riot of 1874. At that time, when the city was estimated to have 10,000 homeless people in its streets and 110,000 unemployed, the result of post-Civil War scarcity, activists arranged for a demonstration permit to hold a march of the afflicted that would wind up in the park. The permit was granted, but abruptly revoked the night before the scheduled march. The marchers could not be notified in time and, as they arrived in the park, were charged by mounted police.

1877 was known nationally as the "year of the riots," as it saw the first instances of organized revolt by the work force in factories and on railroads, with the biggest outbreaks occurring in Pittsburgh, Cleveland, and Baltimore. New York was not an industrial city in quite the same way and may be thought peripheral to the struggle, but it was an intellectual center of radicalism. The city was full of exiled revolutionists, the German Forty-eighters having lately been joined by French Communards. It was at Justus Schwab's saloon on First Street, where such types forgathered, that in early July of that year a police spy overheard plans for a rally. He construed the plans as being for an insurrection that would lead to a New York Commune, and before long, rumor had it that Communists were plotting to take over Manhattan, Brooklyn, and Jersey City. The rally was set for July 24, in Tompkins Square Park. The night before, the park was staked out by the police, and telegraph connections were established linking them with their headquarters and with four National Guard armories in which three regiments were camped. Meanwhile, Schwab had been warned and was prudent enough to meet with the police to try to forestall violence; he was advised that if a single shot was fired, the leaders of the rally would not get out of the park alive. As it happened, the meeting passed without incident, as its crowd of five thousand or ten thousand listened to speeches delivered from three rostrums, for French, German, and English speakers. It was only when the rally was breaking up that a flare-up occurred. Attendees leaving by way of Avenue A looked too much like a marching column to the cops, who charged. Many injuries resulted, although no official statistics were ever produced.[3]

In the pictures and descriptions that have come down to us, the street fights and demonstrations, angry gatherings and spontaneous outbreaks are often difficult to distinguish from the celebratory parades and rallies. The torchlight processions that took place every election night, and on nearly every conceivable pretext—the laying of the Atlantic Cable, the victory at Guantánamo Bay, the Feast of Our Lady of Mount Carmel, E. A. Beach's proposal for a municipal subway—look nearly as frightening as preparations for a riot. The line between a crowd and a mob is thinly drawn, and in the unruly and badly lit night of the nineteenth century it is hardly visible at all. Mass turnouts were often tinged with violence, and violent events had a bit of a holiday air about them. It is not surprising that fights often resulted from the collision of parades, as between two kinds of Irish or two rival fire companies, or that in the hands of a political faction the torchlight procession conveyed as much a threat as an expression of triumph.

New York, a city stingy with plazas and low on boulevards, built in piecemeal clumps rather than around a core, almost seems to have been designed to erase the distinction between spectator and spectacle, the only real separation being between the fixed and the mobile. Parades, riots, revelry, and fever, all in their turn seized the streets and declared themselves the traveling city, a force more powerful than mere buildings. It was not the objective of the marchers to be watched or even feared, so much as to adhere to a giant human snake that would be superior to the tenements and let them take in the usual sights from a new and privileged vantage point. The next logical step was for the snake to squash the buildings altogether. It was not long before the buildings triumphed, however, and doused the power of the torches, replacing it with a flutter of ticker tape.

5 · NIGHT

AT NIGHT SOMETIMES IN CERTAIN
PARTS OF THE CITY, USUALLY IN
THOSE REMAINING STREETS THAT
ARE LEFT DESERTED, USUALLY IN
winter, but sometimes in other seasons if the
streets are sufficiently forsaken, the past can be
seen as if through a smeared window. Sometimes this effect occurs only for an instant:
when you're walking back from someplace
with a head crammed with company and music and sensations, to a point where all new
sensations dissipate, on some dead street in
the middle West Side lined with jobbers and
import showrooms and loading docks and
shuttered luncheonettes, or on a street on the
Lower East Side where the intersections have
no stoplights and everything is nailed down
and dark and the only people to be seen dart
by as furtively as wraiths. There will be no
traffic, and the streetlights will seem to shrink

back into their globes, drawing their skirts of illumination into tight circles, and the rutted streets reveal the cobbles under a thin membrane of asphalt, and the buildings all around are masses of unpointed blackened brick or cacophonies of terra-cotta bric-a-brac or yawning cast-iron gravestones six or eight stories tall. This is the sepulcher of New York, the city as a living ruin.

It is also the bridge to the past, the past that shares the same night as the present, even if it inhabits a different day. The night is the corridor of history, not the history of famous people or great events, but that of the marginal, the ignored, the suppressed, the unacknowledged; the history of vice, of error, of confusion, of fear, of want; the history of intoxication, of vainglory, of delusion, of dissipation, of delirium. It strips off the city's veneer of progress and modernity and civilization and reveals the wilderness. In New York City it is an acculturated wilderness that contains all the accumulated crime of past nights stretching back at least as far as the hangings after the Slaves' Plot of 1741. Every night in New York possesses history this way, as a Walpurgis Night of all nights, and it is not an illusion. It is the daytime that is a chimera, that pretends New York is anyplace, maybe with bigger buildings, but just as workaday, with a population that goes about its business and then goes to sleep, a great machine humming away for the benefit of the world. Night reveals this to be a pantomime. In the streets at night, everything kept hidden comes forth, everyone is subject to the rules of chance, everyone is potentially both murderer and victim, everyone is afraid, just as anyone who sets his or her mind to it can inspire fear in others. At night, everyone is naked.

On any given night, any window can be in 1840, with a woman waiting to dump a bucket of ashes on the passerby's head, so that people can come out from the shadows and pick the writhing body clean of money, jewelry, boots, coat, hat, and maybe slit its throat. Any corner can be in 1860, with the walker hit in the back of the head with a sash weight and taken to a cellar to be stripped, to wake up hours later as a laborer on a ship headed for points east or south. Any passage can be in 1880, with men listening for the rustle of a skirt to leap out and chloroform the pedestrian, who will come to in an obscure mining town as the inmate of a brothel miles from anywhere. Any street where the lights have gone out can be in 1900, with the policeman who rushes in to answer a cry for help falling into an open manhole or taking a stretched wire in the windpipe. Any unfamiliar bar can be in 1920, with the customer smilingly served four ounces of ethyl alcohol laced with chloral hydrate. And any spot can find the subject possessed of nothing at all in the world but a cudgel, or a stevedore's hook, or a brickbat, or a garrote, or a bung-starter, and in desperate need of money.

Night has its own hierarchy, composed of those who hide or go unnoticed in the daytime. During the day, they sleep or recede into the masonry or are invisible to optimistic and responsible parties or pose as something they are not. The maimed and disfigured are visible to the rest of the population only after nightfall; then the eye can't stray off in another direction. Prostitutes sleep during the day, as do pimps and footpads and moll-buzzers and horse poisoners and mayhem artists. Swindlers during the day look like bank clerks, and fences like shopkeepers. These can be seen at night, not working, but spending their take in saloons and disorderly houses. The saloons have their populations of clients who come in at noon and stay all night, or who in fact sleep under tables in the back room and never leave the premises at all except to find money, but night fills the houses with even more voracious drinkers and infects the whole company with the devil. Fights break out over nothing, and beer steins get heaved through mirrors, chairs get broken, paintings get slashed, bottles are snapped at the neck and ground into faces, or a gun goes off and everybody has to slip out the back window.

Other people watch all this from a great distance, though they may be sitting against the nearest wall, glazed with poisons ingested slowly over a long period. Drunks come in all classes. Cornelius Willemse catalogued the leading types circa 1905: kidney or lurching drunks, singing drunks, crying drunks, running drunks, fighting drunks, charitable drunks, talking drunks, important drunks, sneaky drunks, amorous drunks, mischievous drunks, sleepy drunks, animal-loving drunks, something he called taxi drunks, dead drunks. And for every sort of drunk there is a particular locale, from the lobster palaces of Broadway where rich drunks can fall expensively into the arms of retainers, to corner saloons where Dad can repair between supper and bed, to sporting establishments where men who know boxers or men who know men who do can stare at photographs of deltoids and triceps, to political clubs with taprooms, to cripple factories, to joints that look like every other but inside everyone is a Malay or a homosexual or an old woman and none of them can go anywhere else, to saloons run by children for children, to blind pigs in the back rooms of laundries, to grottoes underground where it is assumed the customer will not be leaving any time after finishing his bowl of needled dregs.

Anyway, drunks walk the streets at their peril. There are specialists who wait for them, listening with tuned ears for the stagger step. Women walk the streets not so much at their peril as beyond it. It is understood that any woman walking around at night is a prostitute, and in fact one who is near the end of her career. If a customer takes it into his head to maim her as part of the price, there is very little she can do about it, and cops will make themselves scarce, since she cannot afford to pay them a protection fee. If some more important person is in danger, the cops will summon each other by clubbing the pavement, and the stones carry this tom-tom signal for blocks. The streets are mostly silent, just yelling and cats in heat and breaking glass. The Bowery, however, is alive.

The waiters who double as bouncers at McGurk's Suicide Hall line up in their aprons and harmonize to "The Curse of an Aching Heart." On Chatham Square the policy runners and contract killers are weeping together in a café as an adenoidal kid tries to reach the high notes in "The Picture That Is Turned Toward the Wall." Outside, under the El tracks, an old man in a long coat accompanies himself on a pump organ as he wails "Mother Machree." At Billy McGlory's around the corner on Hester Street, there is a bare-knuckle fight in the middle of the floor, and after blood is drawn, the platform is cleared and a trio ascends—cornet, violin, and piano—and plays a polonaise while the hostesses do a cancan. A *New York Herald* reporter observed in the Grand Street El station of the Third Avenue line in 1882:

> . . . *There is a show of activity in the station. Doubtless there is a certain animation imparted to it by the sounds of life, loud enough and sufficiently varied for the broadest kind of day, that float up to it without ceasing from the Bowery beneath. There is nothing in this glare of light, nothing in this swarming pavement, to indicate that midnight has passed. The windows gleam, the saloons are all aglare, a half-score of pianos and violins send as many airs floating into the night to blend into an instrumental discord that attunes itself fitly to the roysterer's song, the brawler's oath, and the hundred strange voices of the night.*[1]

The Bowery is the capital of night. On its sidewalks, people are crashing through saloon doors, shouldering through crowds looking for a fight, looking for lost fathers or husbands, hooking out-of-towners to try to sell them worthless junk at wild prices, raising money for a bed, picking cigar butts out of the gutter, flashing rolls of bills to impress newly met acquaintances, preaching the gospel to nobody at all, selling stolen watches from under their coats, selling newspapers, selling favors, selling themselves.

Night is when crowds of sailors come breasting down the avenue and shops and saloons lock their doors until they've gone. Night is when gangs whose only discernible difference is that one crowd comes from Norfolk Street and the other from Suffolk Street square off on neutral ground and try to kill each other. Night is when political victories are celebrated with torchlight parades and bonfires that suggest a lynching rather than an enthronement. Night is when people who have lost their life savings playing stuss discover that there is no way at all of getting it back and go drown themselves in the river. Night is when people overcome by despair set their houses on fire and the flames lick through whole blocks of tenements. Night is when people get in trouble, get the horrors, get religion.

Night is the repository of unfinished business in New York City. It is the text of its secret history, the monument to its victims and failures, its predators and police. It is the time of inversion and misrule, the province of vice and intemperance, of misery and blight. New York's clock is directed by a moral spring, and it binds pleasure and harm inextricably together in the night. Night is forgotten and endlessly repeated; it is glorious and it sits next door to death.

A tenement in Little Italy, awakened by murder, circa 1915.
NYPD evidence photo

The mountains of the moon: a vacant lot at night.
NYPD evidence photo

When researching this book, what I was looking for was flavor and incident, anecdote and eyewitness. This grocery list naturally made my search subject to chance, rather more so, in fact, than I had expected. I did not at first suspect, for example, that nineteenth-century journalism could be so wanting in concrete details of time, place, circumstance, and visual appearance—the vagueness of much newspaper writing, especially in the police-blotter category, makes the average gazette of the last century read like a succession of blind items. I was, however, committed to the journey to those parts of the city's past most obliterated in official memory but most alive in the streets themselves, and so I set a serendipitous course, open to every possible wind. Such wandering proved fruitful—I found sources through offhand references in other works, in obvious places I had insufficiently noticed, by contiguity on library shelves, scattered among the furniture at church sales in the country. The process was endlessly self-renewing, and could have gone on forever. I was not, after all, seeking the answer to a particular question. I was traveling.

My guidebooks and charts make up an odd lot. My first encounter with the subject came through Herbert Asbury's *The Gangs of New York* (1927), which ten or fifteen years ago was a cult item among people I knew, a few tattered copies of the 1930s Garden City Press reprint circulating from hand to hand. It is a compelling if somewhat ragtag book, cobbled from legend, memory, police records, the self-aggrandizements of aging crooks, popular journalism, and solid historical research. Tracing some of Asbury's wilder assertions became a subtheme to my research, and indeed I was able to take a number of them back several stages before reaching a dead end. Many derive from the glorious *Police Gazette*, particularly its pink-paged incarnation under the guidance of Richard K. Fox in the last quarter of the nineteenth century and the first decade of the twentieth, when it may not have printed the literal truth every time, but always the poetic truth. (Since issues are rare and ill preserved, interested readers are advised to look up Edward Van Every's *Sins of New York*, 1930, a diverting and reasonably well-informed history and anthology of the journal.) Other stories come from that great clearinghouse of miscellaneous class slander, Frank Moss's *The American Metropolis* (three volumes, 1897). Moss, man-about-town and counsel to the Lexow Committee, uses a casual tour-guide pretext to unroll his after-dinner bonanza of piety, levity, pedantry, and racism. Here one finds, among such items as a record of every attendee of a particular Max Hochstim Association dinner and a six-page list of sundry and undated Italian-American knife fights, the sources for anecdotes of river pirates being eaten alive by rats and the popularity of turpentine derivatives in Bowery saloons, attributed, if at all, to that favorite informant of nineteenth-century chroniclers, "an old resident."

Asbury wrote many other books, a number of which were useful to the present study: his random anecdote collection, *All Around the Town* (1934), the self-explanatory *Ye Old Fire Laddies* (1930) and *Carry Nation* (1929), his study of Prohibition, *The Great Illusion* (1950), and last but not least his monumental history of gambling in America, *Sucker's Progress* (1938), a book that, to the best of my knowledge, remains unique of its kind. Other works of popular history were helpful in varying degrees. Lloyd Morris's *Incredible New York* (1951) is much better than its title would suggest, a swiftly moving overview of the city's history, high and low, from 1850 to 1950. It neither condescends nor grotesquely simplifies, and its author had a knack for finding illuminating oddball details. Alvin F. Harlow's *Old Bowery Days* (1931), to which I owe a large debt, is an extraordinary tome. Sometimes impossibly antique in attitude, as if it were the parish history of a sedate group of old families, it has a thoroughness that is both taxing and impressive; Harlow can bore the reader with many pages on the lives of the heirs of obscure landholders, but his honesty compels him to be just as precise about the less savory aspects of his subject.

Albert Parry's *Garrets and Pretenders* (1933) remains the best book ever written on the early history of bohemianism in America, and its pages contain stories of behavior in the hinterlands that are far stranger than anything that happened in New York. Allen Churchill's *The Improper Bohemians* (1959) more narrowly concentrates on the Greenwich Village scene of the teens and twenties, and does a good if standard job of it; his *Park Row* (1958) treats the early-twentieth-century newspaper world with a certain amount of color. No one today writes anything like the way Thomas Beer did; his *The Mauve Decade* (1926) is a vertiginous aerial survey of the 1890s and possibly the next best thing to being there. He makes no attempt to explain his allusions, and his book is *all* allusion. One is not reading about the period but bathing in it. Dennis T. Lynch's prose is annoyingly smug and his ideas hardly less so, but both *The Wild Seventies* (1941) and *"Boss" Tweed* (1927) have their value as information. Abel Green and Joe Laurie, Jr., contrived a potential pop classic: *Show Biz from Vaude to Video* (1951) is a history of prewar American popular culture derived from the files of *Variety* and narrated in that paper's side-of-the-mouth style. It is a treasure trove of anecdotal details that illustrate the paradox that, just as the past is another country, so is there nothing new under the sun. Frederick L. Collins's *Money Town* (1946) and Richard O'Connor's *Hell's Kitchen* (1958) were also intermittently helpful.

Perhaps the only rule I made for myself at the outset of this project was that I would avoid all recent works of "hard" history. This was to be, among other things, an exercise in naïve and personal history and I did not want to be shanghaied by anyone else's methodology. I managed to break even this rule, however, and referred to two admirable recent works for help in difficult territory: Anthony Jackson's *A Place Called Home* (1976) was invaluable as a comprehensive history of the New York tenement; Sean Wilentz's *Chants Democratic* (1984) guided me through the wilderness of the city's early-nineteenth-century popular democracy. I certainly could not have written this book without assistance from that monument among historical studies of New York City: the late John A. Kouwenhoven's *Columbia Historical Portrait of New York* (1953). Also useful in some particular areas were Edwin K. Spann's *The New Metropolis, 1840–1857* (1981), Stephen Longstreet's *City on Two Rivers* (1975), Seymour Mandelbaum's *Boss Tweed's New York* (1965), and Abraham Callow's *The Tweed Ring* (1965).

Old guidebooks are for me an unending source of fascination. I spent weeks and months browsing through them: they are the nearest thing to walking down the avenues of the past, even if this meant very specifically the avenues, with no excursions permitted down alleys or back streets. Moses King's *Handbook of New York* (1892) and all his subsequent *Views* and *Portraits* are well made, boosterish, thorough, largely irrelevant, and unwittingly revealing of a great deal about the assumptions of their time. Robert Macoy's *Centennial Guide to New York* (1876), Ernest Ingersoll's *A Week in New York* (1892), and, somewhat later, Fremont Rider's *New York* (1923) are more explicitly intended for the tourist trade, and their lists of commonplaces are valuable, not least for cleansing the mind of anachronistic commonplaces. In this regard, almanacs are also significant, and I made considerable use of many numbers of the *New York World* and *Brooklyn*

Eagle series. R. M. De Leeuw's *Both Sides of Broadway* (1910) is literally that: its photographs depict every building in every block from Bowling Green to Columbus Circle, a staggering achievement and an excellent source of accidental and peripheral data. The nonpareil guidebook to the city remains, of course, the Federal Writers' Project's *New York City Guide* (1939), an important resource even if it dates from two decades after the terminus of this book. In a not dissimilar way, Jack Lait and Lee Mortimer's leering *New York: Confidential* (1948) functioned as a sort of milestone between the book's domain and our own time, in this case by keeping me abreast of the march of voyeurism and predatory sexual behavior over the decades. This amazing document, which provides such services for its readers as a list of the telephone numbers of wardrobe mistresses at Broadway theaters, makes for a nice counterpoint to the *New York Press*'s *Vices of a Big City* (1890), which lists every blind tiger and bagnio, ostensibly so its readers will know how to avoid them.

Among nineteenth-century genres fallen into desuetude, the hybrid of guidebook and front-line report looms large. They come in two orders: the first is a host of leaflets, frequently both anonymous and undated, bearing such titles as *New York in Slices*, *New York by Gas-Light*, *New York Naked*, *Snares of New York*, and *Man-Traps of New York*. The others are fat volumes, with a similarity that extends to their titles: James M. Dabney's *Secrets of the Great City* (1863), Edward W. Martin's *Secrets of the Great City* (1868), Junius Henry Browne's *The Great Metropolis* (1868), James D. McCabe's *Lights and Shadows of the Great City* (1872), and his *New York by Sunlight and Gaslight* (1882). The first group tend to dwell on danger and vice and remain obstinately vague (incidents occurring to "a man from Philadelphia," at a time "not long ago," somewhere "in a dark street of the east-side"); the latter are more respectable in their concerns, focusing on the "sunlight and shadow" contrasts that became emblematic of the city. The books are generally ill written, haphazardly organized, given to both vacuous sermonizing and genuflections to persons of power, and yet they articulate a sense of the entire city, or at least the latter grouping does, even if inadvertently by, say, having a chapter on the curse of drink followed by one on female seminaries and then one on old-clothes peddlers. McCabe, who nearly prefigures modern journalism, was even better than that, paying attention to scandalous housing conditions and the lack of public hygiene, at a time when genuine reformers were few.

Religious tracts and reformist propaganda have their own merits, often to be found between the lines. It is extraordinary how little substance there is on the surface of a work such as *The Old Brewery and the New Mission House at the Five*

Points (1854), by the Ladies of the Five Points Mission; its real text consists of what it doesn't say. Charles Loring Brace's *The Dangerous Classes of New York* (1872) and Mrs. Helen Campbell's *Darkness and Daylight in New York* (1892) are cannier, deploying concrete examples and approaching actual social concern amid their attitudinizing. Such tracts as *Dave Ranney, or Thirty Years on the Bowery* (1910) and Philip I. Roberts's *The Dry-Dock of a Thousand Wrecks* (1912) describe the process of salvation, but as timid as they can be when discussing vice, they are positively evanescent when trying to tackle virtue. The whole genre is given a hilarious spin in Howe and Hummell's shameless anti-tract *In Danger* (1888). Jacob Riis could also be considered as falling within this category, even if his ends were more practical. As excellent as his accomplishments (and his photographs) generally were, the evangelist within him is responsible for the indigestible prose, palatable only when the journalist within him wakes up and provides cold fact, in *How the Other Half Lives* (1890), *A Ten Years' War* (1900), *The Making of an American* (1901), *The Battle with the Slum* (1902), and *The Peril and the Preservation of the Home* (1903).

Another sort of propaganda could be termed the service panegyric: Augustus Costello's huge and daunting *Our Police Protectors* (1885) and his *Our Firemen* (1887), and John J. Hickley's update, *Our Police Guardians* (1925). These must be read with care for the bits of information they contain between swaths of testimony to the memories of men who stopped runaway horses at great peril to themselves, with no discussion whatever of scandals, feuds, graft, or internal or external investigations. A useful corrective, at least in attitude, is to be found in Cornelius Willemse's superbly honest memoirs, *Behind the Green Lights* (1931) and *A Cop Remembers* (1933). By and large, however, in this period the dry-eyed and ironic gaze tends to be reserved for political ax-grinding. Gustavus Myers's ostensibly neutral *History of Tammany Hall* (1901) draws blood in subtle ways, while broadside attacks such as John D. Townsend's *New York in Bondage* (1901) spare nothing in the way of rhetoric, an assault that becomes well-nigh hysterical in William Thomas Stead's *Satan's Invisible World Displayed* (1897). Somehow, though, corruption, and in particular Tammany corruption, always seemed to have the capacity to arouse humor in its foes. In Charles W. Gardner's *The Doctor and the Devil* (1894), the laughs are evenly distributed and fully intentional; Gardner is suavely tongue-in-cheek, much of the vice is pretty risible, and even Reverend Charles H. Parkhurst, the doctor of the title, is self-aware enough to see the humor in the situation—even if not much of it appears in his own *My Forty Years in New York, and Our Fight with Tammany* (1923), which, it should be noted, is a far from stupid book. That Tammany itself did not lack humor is wonderfully evident in the book-length monologue *Plunkitt of Tammany Hall* (1905), by William L. Riordon, a virtuoso piece of American idiom that belongs on the shelf next to Mark Twain. Finally, the comedy of graft was eloquently revived by Richard Rovere in his wise and entertaining *Howe and Hummel* (1947).

Journalism, as has been noted, was erratic through much of the period covered in this book. The dispassionate reporting we take for granted today scarcely existed until the 1890s, when it appeared in various guises: in Riis's crusades, in Stephen Crane's moral explanations and dazzling Fauve prose (his journalism is well represented in the Library of America collection of his *Prose and Poetry*, 1984, and its context is brilliantly supplied by John Berryman in *Stephen Crane*, 1950), in James L. Ford's flânerie (collected in *Bohemia Invaded*, 1895, and then remembered in *Forty-Odd Years in the Literary Shop*, 1921), in Hutchins Hapgood's sketches (most pertinently, for the purposes of this study, in *Types from City Streets*, 1910), in the dabbling of Rupert Hughes (*The Real New York*, 1904) and James Gibbons Huneker (*The New Cosmopolis*, 1915). The more popular sort of journalism could be useful, too: Louis J. Beck made an honest stab at comprehending the values of a mythically obscured foreign culture in *New York's Chinatown* (1898), and Alfred Henry Lewis married the penny dreadful with bonafide crime reporting in *The Apaches of New York* (1912) and *Nation-Famous New York Murders* (1914).

For a sense of the city as it passed through time, I made use, at least atmospherically, of a great deal of later work, the actual material of which was sometimes pertinent, sometimes not. Particularly impressive or useful were the evocative *New York Nights* (1927) by the expatriate Englishman Stephen Graham, Morris Markey's *That's New York* (1927, with John Bull) and *Manhattan Reporter* (1935), Charles E. Still's police-blotter collection *Styles in Crime* (1938), Simeon Strunsky's *No Mean City* (1944), Stanley Walker's simultaneously insouciant and densely textured *The Night Club Era* (1933) and *City Editor* (1934), and Edmund Wilson's sketches of bohemia and low theaters, collected in *The Shores of Light* (1952) and *The American Earthquake* (1958). Most indelible of all was the work of three masters of the middle of this century: A. J. Liebling (especially in *Back Where I Came From*, 1938), Meyer Berger (*The Eight Million*, 1942, and *Meyer Berger's New York*, 1960), and the great Joseph Mitchell (*My Ears Are Bent*, 1938; *McSorley's Wonderful Saloon*, 1943; *Old Mr. Flood*, 1948; *The Bottom of the Harbor*, 1959; and *Joe Gould's Secret*, 1965; all of which are, astonishingly and inexcusably, out of print).

The antiquarians of the old tradition, with their cobwebbed visions of departed graciousness, were useless for my purposes, much as were the diaries of those two staunch nineteenth-century diarists Philip Hone and George Templeton Strong, who tended to apprehend most of the collective matter of this book as a low, indecipherable rumble emanating from somewhere downtown. Among antiquarians, though, homage must be paid to that indefatigable collector of trivia Henry Collins Brown, for his *Book of Old New York* (1913) and for his often surprising *Valentine's Manual of Old New York* (1916–28). I did make use of many memoirs, diaries, and travel journals, most significantly Mrs. Frances Trollope's *Domestic Manners of the Americans* (1832), Davy Crockett's *Autobiography* (1835), Charles Dickens's *American Notes for General Circulation* (1842), P. T. Barnum's *Struggles and Triumphs* (1869), Charles Stelzle's *A Son of the Bowery* (1926), Art Young's *On My Way* (1928), Emma Goldman's *Living My Life* (1931), (Justin) Brooks Atkinson's *East of the Hudson* (1931), Frank Weitenkampf's *Manhattan Kaleidoscope* (1947), Maxwell Bodenheim's *My Life and Loves in Greenwich Village* (1954), and Raoul Walsh's *Every Man in His Time* (1974).

I read many bad novels and a few good ones, the most noteworthy and pertinent being William Dean Howells's *A Hazard of New Fortunes* (1890), Stephen Crane's *Maggie: A Girl of the Streets* (1893), and Edward Townsend's *Chimmie Fadden* and *A Daughter of the Tenements* (both 1895), as well as the stories in Fitz-James O'Brien's *Fantastic Tales* (1859) and O. Henry's *The Four Million* (1909). The great poems of New York are, of course, those by Walt Whitman, including the ones written in prose in *Specimen Days* and *November Boughs*, and they are joined by Theodore Dreiser's somber and elegiac poem in the form of essays, *The Color of a Great City* (1923). I am also indebted to Esther Morgan McCullough's enormous anthology of literary New Yorkiana, *As I Pass, O Manhattan* (1956). A word, too, is owed Arthur Bartlett Maurice's curious little *New York in Fiction* (1901), a self-defeating exercise in hunting down the real models for fictional locations, but distinguished by suggestively murky photographs. Finally, B. A. Botkin's *New York City Folklore* (1956), a weird but illuminating assortment of rumors, graffiti, jokes, fables, and nostalgia, helped clarify the early direction of this book.

Various works played important roles in very specific ways. Kenneth Holcombe Dunshee's *As You Pass By* (1952), half a tribute to the city's firemen and half a reconstruction of colonial Manhattan, aided in mapping the progress of the city's infrastructure, as did Robert Daly's *The World Beneath the City* (1959), a doughty study of the island's innards. James Weldon Johnson's *Black Manhattan* (1930), David Levering Lewis's *When Harlem Was in Vogue* (1981), and Jervis Anderson's *This Was Harlem* (1982) all mostly deal with a period after the close of my own time frame, but were crucial to my quest for a picture of black life in New York in the nineteenth century. James B. Walker's *Fifty Years of Rapid Transit* (1918), for all the mercantile obviousness of its purpose, presented a clear view of the early climate of mass transportation in the city. T. Allston Brown's dense three-volume *History of the New York Stage* (1903) contained much valuable information on theater riots and the geographical evolution of the entertainment district. *The Great Rascal* (1952), by Jay Monaghan, is the only attempt at a biography of the elusive Edward Z. C. "Ned Buntline" Judson. Sigmund Spaeth's jolly *Read 'Em and Weep* (1926) told me a great deal about saloon music. Dean Latimer and Jeff Goldberg's *Flowers in the Blood* (1981) filled me in on the early history of drug use in America. Alexander Johnson's *Ten—and Out!* (1927) is an entertaining history of boxing, including, despite its title, much on the bare-knuckle era.

The work of the linguist and criminal-milieu expert David Maurer cannot be praised too highly. Someone should reissue his extraordinary *The Big Con* (1940); *Whiz Mob* (1955), a study of pickpockets, is more technically difficult but still essential. His *Language of the Underworld* (1981), in tandem with H. L. Mencken's *The American Language* (in its many editions), guided me through the ever-changing undergrowth of slang. Prostitution was not much written about during the period I covered, but I found it useful to read William W. Sanger's *History of Prostitution* (1876) and Maude Emma Miner's exposé *Slavery of Prostitution* (1916). Inspector Thomas Byrnes's *Professional Criminals of America* (1881), the prototypical rogues' gallery, was fascinating as an exhibit of physiognomies, nicknames, and identifying scars. Roger A. Bruns's biography of Dr. Ben Reitman, *The Damndest Radical* (1987), filled important gaps relative to the condition of tramps in the city at the beginning of the century, and the subject was further amplified in more atmospheric ways by Josiah Flynt's *Tramping with Tramps* (1899) and *My Life* (1908), Jack London's *The Road* (1907), Nels Anderson's *The Hobo* (1923), and Jack Black's *You Can't Win* (1926). Joel T. Headley's *The Great Riots of New York* (1873) was indispensable for its approach to the city's eruptive tradition; it also provided the most serious near-contemporary view of the Draft Riots, a view furthered by William Stoddard's memoir, *The Volcano Under the City, by a Volunteer Special* (1887).

Finally, I want to mention a couple of picture books that strongly underlay my decision to embark on this project: Nathan Silver's *Lost New York* (1967), the now-classic work that spurred the urgent effort of historical preservation in the city; and Roger Whitehouse's *New York: Sunlight and Shadow* (1974), a superb collection of nineteenth-century photographs and an impressive document of growth and waste, expansion and misery. I cannot possibly acknowledge the pileup of ephemera, clippings, postcards, chance remarks, marginal references, accidents of lighting, and artful trash that also played a part in this book, but I must cite those great and wretched palimpsests, my original inspiration, the tenements of the Lower East Side.

N O T E S

PART 1.

1. THE BODY

1   *Redburn*, p. 164, in *Novels*, vol. 2, 1983.

2   Quoted in *As I Pass, O Manhattan*, p. 915.

3   *The Dangerous Classes of New York*, p. 151.

4   Quoted in Kouwenhoven, *The Columbia Historical Portrait of New York*, p. 207.

5   Another theory holds that Broadway was intended to encircle Union Square, which had already been planned in its present location, but the surveyors noticed rather belatedly that the course Broadway was taking would miss the square by a block.

6   The "dollar" was undoubtedly the Western influence; the "shilling," the Eastern. For much of the nineteenth century, the two denominations were nearly interchangeable. Restaurant bills of fare, for example, might list prices in S. and D., the "D." meaning pence.

7   *Glimpses of New York* (Charleston, 1852), quoted in Kouwenhoven, op. cit., p. 207.

8   McCabe, *Lights and Shadows of New York Life*, p. 192.

9   "A Bird of Baghdad."

10   Still standing, but now a synagogue.

11   In an alternative version of the tale, Williams spotted the criminal lawyer Abe Hummel at Delmonico's and chided him, "You'd better behave yourself, Mr. Hummel, or you won't be coming in here for any more of them juicy beef steaks you're always eating."

"Speaking of that, Inspector," Hummel replied, "that's a pretty juicy tenderloin they just handed you."

12   Nineteenth-century usage applied the term "hell's kitchen" to any dismal area or bad situation. The extensively interviewed gangster and fall guy Georgie Appo, for example, indicated his relief at quitting a factory where he was abused by saying, "I was glad to get out of that hell's kitchen."

13   Rupert Hughes, *The Real New York*, p. 241.

2. HOME

1   It has since been established that nearly all these tales are wild exaggerations having their origins in church propaganda.

2   But "a portion of the Old Brewery still remains standing on the west side of [Baxter] Street, south of Worth Street," noted Frank Moss in 1897 (*The American Metropolis*, vol. 3, p. 58).

3   Brace, *Dangerous Classes*, p. 150.

4   Many of these began their careers as housing for workers in the nearby soap, candle, and button factories and brass and iron foundries.

5   Quoted by Asbury, *Gangs of New York*, p. 12.

6   Both were improvements on the overall tenement death rate in 1872, which was 96.7 per thousand. In the same year, the death rate for the whole city was 32.6; that of London was 21.4; and that of San Francisco was 17.2.

7   Some enterprising immigrants managed to do fairly well as sub-landlords. An Italian organ-grinder in 1871 paid $14 a month for two rooms at 38 Baxter Street. He hosted eight lodgers, of whom six paid 75¢ a week for straw shakedowns, and the other two a dollar apiece for real beds. Thus, the organ-grinder could net a profit of $12 a month, once he had paid off the furniture.

8   Their population during the quarter-century prior to their closing varied annually between 100,000 and 250,000 overall.

9   Such flops may have originated with the "tramp rooms" that sprang up in the straitened financial conditions after the Civil War. These were cellar spaces generally measuring ten by fifteen feet and seven feet high, containing no furniture but a stove. Lodgings were a nickel a night, and a pint of stale beer cost two cents.

10   *A Hazard of New Fortunes*, 1983 ed., p. 160.

11   *A Daughter of the Tenements*, p. 60.

12   *The New Cosmopolis*, p. 5.

13   Stelzle, *A Son of the Bowery*, p. 25.

14   *The Color of a Great City*, p. 64.

15   *The Bottom of the Harbor*, p. 56.

3. STREETS

1   Quoted in *As I Pass, O Manhattan*, p. 919.

2   *Specimen Days*, pp. 702–3, in *Poetry and Prose*, 1982 ed.

3   *A Hazard of New Fortunes*, p. 66.

4   Ibid., pp. 158–59.

5   Weitenkampf, *Manhattan Kaleidoscope*, p. 31.

6   In 1838, a hot-corn girl was murdered by her procurer, Edward Coleman, who became the first person to be hanged in the court-yard of the Tombs.

7   Quoted in *As I Pass, O Manhattan*, p. 919.

8   According to legend, a pie first baked by George Washington's nurse.

9   Bernard Botkin, in *New York City Folklore*, quotes a typical spiel, recorded at Bayard and Elizabeth Streets in 1921: "Here. Today's special. A la chic de Paree. A two-piece, no vest, but like a rock. A pair of pants like an ox. Fresh. No charge for looking. Yes, indeedy. Cheap, cheap, cheap. C'mon, don't waste your time. It's a Saks Fifth Avenue. Take it. Quick come, quick go. It's new, new, newy. Slip off your coat and try it on." The broad outlines of the spieler's routine were translated to the vaudeville stage, and a comic sketch of this sort has been preserved in Eddie Cantor's number in the Florenz Ziegfeld cinematic extravaganza *Glorifying the American Girl* (1929).

10   Brace, op. cit., pp. 152–53.

11   Ragpickers had their own slums-within-slums, known as Bone Alleys, the last of which stood on East Thirteenth Street, between B and C, until the turn of the century.

12   Dreiser, op. cit., pp. 260–1.

PART 2.

1. THE LIGHTS

1   Unfortunately, it no longer exists, but it is pictured in Kouwenhoven, *Columbia Historical Portrait*, p. 194.

2   Whitman, *November Boughs*, p. 1189.

3   "Lady Washington" was simply Martha, ennobled by popular sentiment; the English aristocratic ideal died hard in the young United States.

4   *History of the New York Stage*, p. 284.

5   He passed the baton to B. F. Keith, who devised the winning formula of combining established stars with novelties and sideshow routines, and went on to found the first successful vaudeville syndicate, the Keith and Albee chain.

6   Tommaso Salvini was the Italian actor best known for playing Othello to Booth's Iago.

7   The native reaction to such developments is perhaps suggested by that of the sanctimonious Frank Moss: "The Windsor Theater, where 'Johnny Thompson On Hand' and 'Hands Across the Sea' delighted old-fashioned Bowery audiences, now sadly yields to strange Oriental crowds, who talk desperately about Salome and other characters unknown to us" (*The American Metropolis*, vol. 2, p. 399).

8   Ragtime was then already in decline among black audiences.

9   They profited, at least temporarily, from Prohibition. In 1919, for example, Huber's Museum took over the site of Murray's Roman Garden. Cheap entertainments commandeered the ground-floor spaces as speakeasies moved upstairs or to the basements.

2. SALOON CULTURE

1   It then moved several times, the franchise finally disintegrating in the 1890s in a drab location at Third Avenue and Twenty-fourth Street.

2   The trick was taken up later in the century by a "dead house" on Eighteenth Street that so dispensed rotgut, to devastating effect.

3   Some notable crimp houses included, on Water Street, Peersall's, Fox's, Tom Norton's, Mother McBride's, the Saranac, and the

Pipe; on James Street, the Flag of Our Union; on Peck Slip, the Band Box; on Catherine Slip, the Glass House; and on Cherry Street, Tommy Hedden's, Dan Kerrigan's, and Mrs. Tighe's.

4   James Ford writes: "He adorned the walls of his dance hall with a fine set of Hogarth engravings to be gazed at by the nightly assembly of rakes and harlots" (*Forty-Odd Years in the Literary Shop*, p. 197). Ford also notes that Hill's was the site of the first Salvation Army meeting in the United States, the proprietor having consented for its curiosity value.

5   "Some New York streets have mayors, but they are not elected. A man lives on a street until the mayoralty grows over him, like a patina" (A. J. Liebling, *Back Where I Came From*, p. 21).

6   Joints with a bit more class kept what was known as a "velvet room" in the rear, where favored customers were permitted to retire with a bowl of alcohol and the promise they would not be disturbed until morning.

7   Unfortunately, the legend of his jump inspired a number of imitators who were unwise enough actually to go through with the stunt, with fatal results. Nevertheless, the *Daily News* of August 19, 1990, reported that one Brian Lockhart, thirty-one, survived the plunge, effected for unknown reasons, which made him putatively the twenty-second such survivor in 107 years.

8   Lavelle first bounced at the James Street crimp house the Flag of Our Union, then at a denatured-alcohol joint on Baxter Street.

9   *Bowery Life*, pages unnumbered.

10   A variation on the standard Connors legend asserts that Chinatown Nellie, Nellie Noonan, and the wife who made Chuck literate were all the same person.

11   Both Brodie and Connors remained household names for decades after their deaths. For many years, a jump of any kind was referred to in slang as "doing a brodie"; Brodie appears as a character not only in *The Bowery* but also in Samuel Fuller's *Park Row* (1951), made a full half century after his death. Their names were further perpetuated by being assumed by two B-movie and television actors: Steve Brodie (born John Stevens in 1919) and Chuck Connors (born Kevin Joseph Connors in 1921).

12   Mitchell, *McSorley's Wonderful Saloon*, pp. 124–45.

13   Hughes, op. cit., pp. 355–56.

14   *The Great Illusion*, p. 211.

15   There were, nevertheless, saloons around town that never actually closed at all or stopped serving their usual fare, thanks to the *bienveillance* of the police department. The champion in this category was McSorley's Old House at Home, on Seventh Street, still going strong after 136 years.

3. HOP

1   The facts remain obscure. Louis J. Beck, in *New York's Chinatown* (1898), claims that female and child slaves were trafficked by families in China and bought by Chinese New Yorkers in Mexico, at a rate of $38 to $45 in gold apiece.

2   "Opium's Varied Dreams," p. 853, in *Prose and Poetry*, 1984 ed.

3   In the nineteenth century, "dope" tended to mean any heavy, viscous solution, and in this connection may have derived from the Dutch *doop*, meaning sauce. How it came to signify "information" and "fool" as well has not been adequately charted.

4   Crane, op. cit.

5   This version cited by Sigmund Spaeth in *Read 'Em and Weep*, pp. 117–19.

6   Hashish was periodically a vogue drug among aesthetes for nearly a century before this.

4. CHANCE

1   Although Mencken himself, in *The American Language*, insists the evolution took place the other way around, with bunco or banco deriving from buncombe, Asbury, in *Sucker's Progress*, makes a case for bunco being the corruption of a term ultimately derived from "bank," which certainly makes more intuitive sense. It has also been speculated that buncombe owes its origin to a particularly windy congressman from the North Carolina county bearing this name. It may simply be that two distinct etymologies happily merged.

2   The essential principle of this con was later refined for more sophisticated schemes, a common one involving the sale of useless

swampland in Florida to a sucker convinced of its lucrative resale value.

3   Rupert Holmes cites a silent match, with no bells, held at a saloon in the Dry Dock, at Seventh Street and the East River. The saloon bore a shingle reading "Young Men's Reform Club," the event scheduled was called an "election," and customers were charged a "poll tax," a prohibitive $10 a head.

5. THE LOST SISTERHOOD

1   In the 1860s the prominent uptown hostess Mrs. Pierre Lorillard Ronalds caused a sensation when she appeared at a costume ball, in the guise of "Music," decked out in just such a costume.

2   Small wonder the drink was popularly called "wealthy water."

3   It is perhaps coincidental that street pimps were called "Bowery statues," in reference to cigar-store Indians.

4   *In Danger*, pages unnumbered.

5   Not that nineteenth-century homosexuals were as hidden or timid as might be supposed. Cornelius Willemse, recalling his days as a bartender on Cooper Square, notes that his joint was across the way from the notorious Paresis Hall, which "caused me plenty of trouble. Don't think for one moment that some of those fags can't put up a battle. I certainly miscalculated on some of them and one, especially, gave me more than I handed him. Just listen to this. Two of them came in one day and ordered milk punches with eggs. The bartender yelled, 'Nothing doing, get out of here!' When they got to the door, one of them turned and said acidly, 'We may be fags but we're no common bartenders anyway.' A barrage of lumps of ice was the answer from the bar" (*A Cop Remembers*, p. 53).

6   New York Press, *Vices of a Big City*, pages unnumbered.

PART 3.

1. GANGLAND

1   Smaller black gangs of the time included the Geneva Club and the Free Masons.

2   The same Edward Coleman who was hanged for the murder of his hot-corn girl.

3 Mencken, in *The American Language*, quotes Poe, who in his *Marginalia* in turn cites an 1806 newspaper account of "banditti . . . calling themselves *high-binders*." He goes on to say that in a subsequent issue of the same journal "the association are called *hidebinders*."

4 *The New York Times*, July 6, 1857.

5 The Swamp Angels were conveniently headquartered in a Cherry Street rookery called Gotham Court, which provided indoor access to the great sewer running under the street that led to the river in one direction and to caves used for hideouts and storage in the other. However long the Swamp Angels lasted, this location served river pirates of some variety until its condemnation by the Board of Health in 1871.

6 Or, per Charles Loring Brace: "Though the crime and pauperism of New York are not so deeply stamped in the blood of the population [as in London or Paris] they are even more dangerous. The intensity of the American temperament is felt in every fibre of these children of poverty and vice. Their crimes have the unrestrained and sanguinary character of a race accustomed to overcome all obstacles. They rifle a bank, where English thieves pick a pocket; they murder, where English prolétaires cudgel or fight with fists; in a riot, they begin what seems about to be the sacking of a city, where English rioters would merely batter policemen or smash lamps" (op. cit., pp. 26–27). In other words, here in America we even grow bigger crooks.

7 *Forty-Odd Years in the Literary Shop*, p. 47.

8 Howe and Hummell, op. cit., pages unnumbered.

9 Compare this for enduring verity with the words engraved on a brass plaque that until very recently hung on a building on East Third Street, across from the Hell's Angels headquarters and attributed to a deceased member of that organization, Big Vinnie: "When in doubt, knock 'em out."

In general, however, the lingo of crooks in the 1870s certainly was peculiar, if we are to believe the detective's manual glossary quoted by James McCabe, which includes such brain-twisters as "bill of sale" to signify widows' weeds, "brother of the bolus" to mean a medical practitioner, "blue-billy" to signify "a strange handkerchief," and, topping them all, "bowsprit in parenthesis" as meaning "a pulled nose."

10   The con pretends to find a wallet on the street within view of his pigeon, and discovering that the wallet is stuffed with bills (counterfeit, of course), proposes to the mark that a large reward is surely offered for its recovery. He is in a hurry, however, and will gladly trade said reward for a modest cash settlement, counting on the fact that the mark will be mentally adding up the wallet's contents, intending to keep it all for himself.

11   Quoted by Asbury, op. cit., p. 259.

12   He later gave his name to a pigtailed duck in George Herriman's *Krazy Kat*.

13   By a bizarre coincidence, a second hoodlum who called himself Kid Twist, who came up with the bootlegging gangs of the 1920s, was also murdered in Coney Island, in 1941.

14   The 1870s and eighties record a few Minetta Lane knife fighters: No-Toe Charley, Bloodthirsty, Black Cat, Jube Taylor. Apart from this, there is a striking lack of data on black crime in the nineteenth century.

2. COPPERS

1   The term has no etymological connection with "copperhead," the name given to northern Democrats around the time of the Civil War.

2   McCabe, *New York by Sunlight and Gaslight*, pp. 282–83.

3   Willemse, *Behind the Green Lights*, pp. 30–31.

4   *Evening Telegram*, November 10, 1875, quoted by Townsend in *New York in Bondage* (1901).

5   Willemse, op. cit., pp. 122–23.

3. THE TIGER

1   The fanciful titles within the order also included Sagamore, Wiskinski, and Father of the Council.

2   The meaning of Anti-Bedinism remains obscure. As for the extrasyllabic Anti-Papistalism, it seems to fit with the early-nineteenth-century phenomenon noted by Mencken in which American speakers, especially those of rustic origin, asserted their claim on the

language by adding extra parts to words and making free with prefixes and suffixes—which resulted in such coinages as blustiferous, to exflunctify, and to obflisticate.

3   Quoted by Wilentz in *Chants Democratic*, p. 332.

4   *Correspondence*, 1961 ed., quoted by Wilentz, p. 389.

5   Gardner was later to reform, founding both the Fourth Ward Temperance Coffee House and an anti-saloon group he attempted to glamorize by dubbing it the Dashaways.

6   The. Allen, omnipresent in the chronicles of nineteenth-century shenanigans, was not only a dive-keeper, policy dealer, and ballot-box stuffer, a "Jack of all evil," according to the press, a man fond of poking lit cigars in people's eyes. He was also, at least in his younger days, a constant presence on the political scene, running the "Workingmen's Reform Club" from a room over a bar at Prince and Mercer, and later managing branches of the Labor Reform and Greenback Parties from headquarters at 615 Broadway. He effectively milked the publicity angle of his wickedness for half a century, finally surrendering at the very end of the nineties to William Travers Jerome by flinging the keys to his last establishment on the District Attorney's desk.

7   *History of Tammany Hall*, p. 103.

8   Quoted by Townsend, op. cit.

9   Quoted by Harlow, *Old Bowery Days*, pp. 504–5.

10   Ibid.

11   Ibid., p. 511.

12   Among the surviving monuments to Big Tim are a column surmounted by a globe that stands on the traffic island at the head of Delancey Street, and, directly opposite, Kenmare Street, cut through in 1904 and named after the Big Feller's native village in Ireland.

13   Riordon, *Plunkitt of Tammany Hall*, pp. 14–15.

14   Ibid., p. 20.

15   Ibid., p. 106.

4. SAINTHOOD

1   *The New York World*, February 15, 1892.

5. RUBBERNECKERS

1   Mrs. Trollope, 1949 ed., p. 340.
2   *The Autobiography of David Crockett*, 1923 ed., pp. 158–59.
3   *American Notes for General Circulation*, 1892 ed., pp. 127–28.
4   Ibid., pp. 129–31.
5   *A Cop Remembers*, p. 309.
6   *East of the Hudson*, pp. 18–21.

PART 4.

1. ORPHANS

1   Brace, op. cit., p. 97.
2   Children also harvested nuts and gathered wood in the last undeveloped areas of the city, which by the late nineteenth century were reduced to a few patches uptown along the East and Harlem Rivers.

2. THE DRIFT

1   They survived long enough for a witness in Yorkville to hear them sing "Come, Josephine, in My Flying Machine."

3. BOHEMIA

1   Although Ezra Pound found something in it; he called Halleck "the American Byron."
2   Quoted by Parry, *Garrets and Pretenders*, p. 46.
3   Ibid., p. 16.
4   Ibid., p. 26.
5   Walt Whitman later did the same thing, but more craftily and less transparently, publishing enthusiastic reviews of his own work under various pseudonyms in various periodicals.
6   Quoted by Parry, op. cit., p. 39.
7   Other regulars at this bar, which boasted a clientele of international radical refugees, included Ambrose Bierce and Sadakichi Hartmann, and eventually Emma Goldman, who had a troubled relationship with Schwab's friend Johann Most. The bar's political direction evolved from Communist to anarchist over its three decades of existence.

4. CARNIVAL

1   Some of the newspaper accounts refer vaguely to an agitator who spoke at one of the rallies on the first day, naming him "Mr. Anderson of Virginia." No more information was given; he may have been a journalistic invention.

2   Quoted by Asbury, op. cit., p. 169.

3   Schwab's went on to become a permanent police scapegoat. "The police felt called upon to arrest somebody around Tompkins Square about once a month. Anarchist Outrages was the usual newspaper head-line" (Huneker, op. cit., p. 6).

5. NIGHT

1   Quoted by McCabe, op. cit., p. 191.

INDEX

PHOTO CREDITS

Following page xiii: (bottom) Museum of Modern Art Film Stills Archive.

Following page 7: (first page, bottom) Museum of the City of New York.

Following page 16: (first page, top) Brown Brothers; (second page) Brown Brothers.

Following page 30: (first page, top) Museum of the City of New York; (first page, bottom) New-York Historical Society; (second page, bottom) Brown Brothers.

Following page 40: (first page, top) Brown Brothers; (first page, bottom) Museum of the City of New York; (second page) Museum of the City of New York.

Following page 52: (first page, top) Museum of the City of New York; (second page) Museum of the City of New York.

Following page 75: (first page, top) Museum of the City of New York; (first page, bottom) New-York Historical Society; (second page) Museum of the City of New York.

Following page 102: (first page, top) Brown Brothers; (first page, bottom) Museum of the City of New York; (second page) Museum of Modern Art Film Stills Archive.

Following page 124: (first page) Brown Brothers; (second page) Municipal Archives, Department of Records and Information Services, City of New York.

Following page 146: (first page, top) Brown Brothers; (first page, bottom) New-York Historical Society.

Following page 174: (first page, top) Museum of the City of New York; (first page, bottom) New-York Historical Society; (second page) Museum of the City of New York.

Following page 207: (first page, top) Museum of Modern Art Film Stills Archive; (first page, bottom) Municipal Archives, Department of Records and Information Services, City of New York; (second page, top) Museum of the City of New York; (second page, bottom) Municipal Archives, Department of Records and Information Services, City of New York.

Following page 242: (first page, top left) New-York Historical Society; (second page) Museum of the City of New York.

Following page 266: (first page, bottom) New-York Historical Society; (second page, top) New-York Historical Society; (second page, bottom) Municipal Archives, Department of Records and Information Services, City of New York.

Following page 282: (first page) Brown Brothers; (second page, top) Museum of the City of New York; (second page, bottom) Brown Brothers.

Following page 308: (top) Brown Brothers.

Following page 315: (first page) Brown Brothers; (second page, top) Brown Brothers; (second page, bottom) American Museum of the Moving Image.

Following page 352: (first page, top) Museum of the City of New York; (second page, top) Museum of the City of New York; (second page, bottom) New-York Historical Society.

Following page 362: Municipal Archives, Department of Records and Information Services, City of New York.

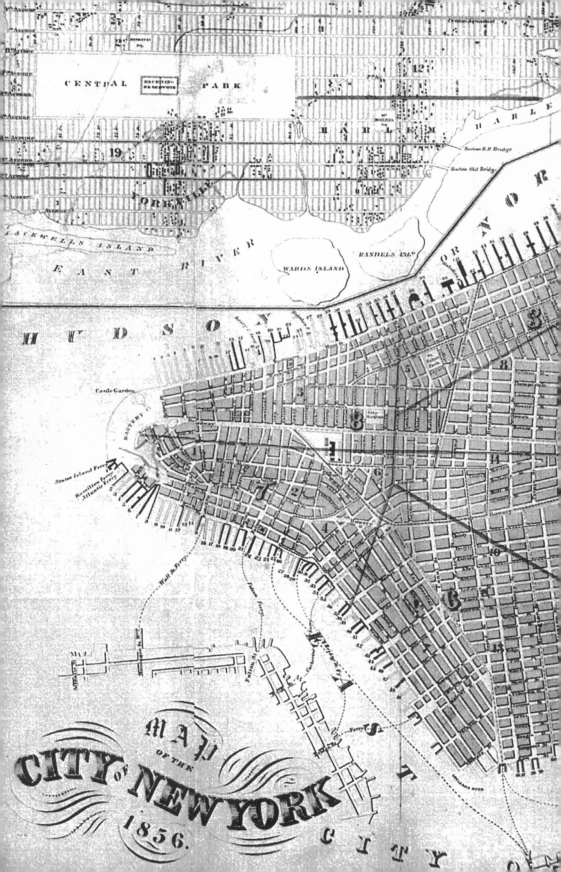